Managing PUBLIC RELATIONS

Methods and Tools for Achieving Solid Results

Peter M. Smudde, Ph.D., APR

Illinois State University

New York   Oxford
OXFORD UNIVERSITY PRESS

Oxford University Press is a department of the University of Oxford.
It furthers the University's objective of excellence in research,
scholarship, and education by publishing worldwide.

Oxford   New York
Auckland   Cape Town   Dar es Salaam   Hong Kong   Karachi
Kuala Lumpur   Madrid   Melbourne   Mexico City   Nairobi
New Delhi   Shanghai   Taipei   Toronto

With offices in
Argentina   Austria   Brazil   Chile   Czech Republic   France   Greece
Guatemala   Hungary   Italy   Japan   Poland   Portugal   Singapore
South Korea   Switzerland   Thailand   Turkey   Ukraine   Vietnam

For titles covered by Section 112 of the US Higher Education
Opportunity Act, please visit www.oup.com/us/he for the
latest information about pricing and alternate formats.

Published by Oxford University Press
198 Madison Avenue, New York, New York 10016
http://www.oup.com

Library of Congress Cataloging-in-Publication Data
Smudde, Peter M.
   Managing public relations : methods & tools for achieving solid results /
Peter M. Smudde, Ph.D., APR.
     pages cm
   ISBN 978-0-19-998517-3
  1. Public relations. I. Title.
   HD59.S5367 2015
   659.2--dc23
                                                          2014016041

Printing number: 9 8 7 6 5 4 3 2 1

Printed in the United States of America
on acid-free paper

Table of Contents

Preface

"Public relations graduates do not know enough about business." This is a frequent lament of hiring managers across the country. Well beyond that lament about new-hires in the profession, organizational executives have long complained that public relations professionals generally do not know enough about business operations and strategy. Both confessions have been well documented, from reports about education from the Public Relations Society of America to scholarly research and pragmatic book-length analyses of what it takes to get PR "at the table" with organizational executives. As a recent report from the Arthur W. Page Society (2007) also argues, public relations people must understand, embrace, and apply business/management concepts and methods more effectively, systematically, and, most of all, strategically.

Public relations programs at colleges and universities typically require their students to cap off their major with a course on campaign design and development. The substance of such a course is, indeed, valuable because it brings together lessons learned about the what, how, and why of public relations in a systematic approach to public communication. To think that campaign design and development is precisely or even sufficiently analogous to understanding what a manager or an executive in charge of a whole public relations operation—an agency or a corporate department (including nonprofit, nongovernmental, and governmental organizations)—must do is shortsighted at best.

Indeed, with today's and the foreseeable future's economic and business environments, a campaigns course is woefully insufficient as the capstone to a PR major: It lacks a kind of business focus that organizational leaders need their employees to possess. *Not only must public relations professionals be expert communicators for any purpose and in any medium, they also must be competent business people.* And that business competence must at least begin at the advanced-undergraduate level. Yes, public relations graduates must know how to develop and lead campaigns, but, more important, they must understand the day-to-day matters of what it takes to run a public relations operation. After all, students' graduating with an acute awareness of how they will be managed *and* how their work fits into a larger strategic picture, even down to the profit-and-loss statements and resource allocations, will make them far more valuable and valued than being just bright technicians.

Although double majoring in public relations and business or even majoring in PR and minoring in business (or vice versa) may be alternative solutions to educating public relations students about business dimensions of public relations, for many students these alternatives are not possible or are out of reach. Many students come to public relations after trying business programs, which means they have divorced themselves from that arena to join one that is assumed related and (perhaps) easier or more suited to them. Many other students never consider business because they are more interested in the technical and (I daresay) the "sexy" matters of public relations that include events, celebrities, interviews, and other things. Other students integrate public relations with another field, such as theater, biology, or athletics, because they sense a synergy between the two fields that would serve them well as a communicator, for example, in a fine arts organization, a biotechnology company, or a sports team or equipment manufacturer.

What is missing in all of these approaches is a sharp focus on the fundamentals of business, management, leadership, and other operational areas that precisely matter to the effective running of a public relations group on a daily basis. The solution, then, for public relations programs in higher-education institutions is a new, nontraditional course focused on public relations management, and this textbook targets this deficiency. No longer is it necessary or appropriate to save fundamental concepts about business operations and leadership until someone begins a graduate program in business, PR, or other related field.

Although this book could not begin to replace the formal study of business and management, it can and does place business, management, leadership, and basic operations squarely in the public relations field for new professionals. Accordingly, this book's purpose is to introduce to undergraduates of PR programs (and early-career PR pros) selected, key concepts and practices involved in the running of a PR operation in any organization. In this way this book will be of great value to those embarking on their public relations careers because they will have a sensitivity to and sensibility about essential management matters in the successful running of a PR operation. In other words, readers will know how they will be managed so they can perform better than they would without this foreknowledge, and readers will be better positioned to grow in their careers as they obtain opportunities for advancement in their careers. The pressures for excellence in all facets and all phases of one's career, beginning at an entry level, require at least a basic understanding at the undergraduate level of business matters that enable specific PR operations to do what they do and do it successfully—adding value to an organization.

Why This Book

Managing Public Relations: Methods and Tools for Achieving Solid Results is a direct outgrowth from these observations about public relations education and my unique combination of industry and academic experiences gained over 26 years. I held an executive-level position in charge of public relations, worked in corporations, worked in an agency, was a consultant, and am a university professor with a strong record of effective teaching and research publication. This book combines scholarship and best practices for students and professors.

With the help of a few peers acting as sounding boards, I designed and implemented a course in public relations management in 2004, and since then I have led one or two sections of it almost each semester. Students are asked to assume to the best of their abilities the mindset of a public relations executive, and the substance of the course is to help them achieve that mindset more and more every day. The biggest challenge is in getting students to quit thinking like students and think like their future bosses and colleagues think, most of whom were trained and experienced in traditional business. It is essential that public relations professionals understand the business needs and expectations of their colleagues, yet academic programs in public relations spend little or no time formally training students in business thinking.

No textbook has been available to cover the combination of topics needed for this nontraditional course. Yet there is a range of books available that address matters of public relations management. I am familiar with many of them and have used them selectively in my course preparation. To me the extant books cluster in three groups: (1) highly academic books, (2) practice-area–focused textbooks, and (3) big-picture management books.

The highly academic books rely on theory so heavily that PR professionals are scarcely familiar with the literature cited; more important, they are too heavily academic in their content to be usable, useful, and used by practitioners. I know of one book in particular that inordinately addresses traditional matters of research methods that do not seem to fit; these sections could be removed and the reader would not necessarily miss them.

The practice-area–focused textbooks break down public relations into the staid categories of media relations, consumer relations, investor relations, etc. but do not connect these things to the larger business picture and strategy. They reflect a kind of silo approach to public relations practice. Moreover, these textbooks are more focused on campaign management than the overall successful management of a whole public relations operation on a daily basis.

The big-picture management books are the closest to this book because they are the only ones that address many of the day-to-day matters of running a public relations operation. But they are either too old or are too focused on either just corporate or just agency operations or just one process approach—more the corporate-agency split than the others. The choice to address public relations mostly in noncorporate, agency organizations seems based on the prominence (i.e., "sex appeal") of PR firms and consultants, even though corporate PR operations are dominant in the field. None of these books address matters of overall business strategy and, especially, the measurement of business performance against the strategy that management requires today.

All three groups of books miss the mark for what today's (and tomorrow's) public relations students must understand about how successful PR operations work in both corporate and agency organizations. The first two groups of textbooks treat the subject of PR management by focusing on the more popular, "sexy stuff" of public relations (especially the stuff that appeals to academics) at the expense of connecting the dots among the daily, sublime business matters that must be addressed to keep the public relations function a valuable and valued part of any organization.

Managing Public Relations uniquely addresses the day-to-day management matters for public relations executives in both corporate (broadly conceived and inclusive of for-profit, nonprofit, institutional, nongovernmental, and governmental organizations) and agency PR operations while it, at the same time, connects the dots between practice and theory. In other words, this book is about leading and managing public relations operations. In addition, this book addresses how to use strategies to manage public relations resources and tactics for proactive and reactive situations with a variety of stakeholders.

Where and When This Book Would Best Work

Managing Public Relations is meant to spark a new, nontraditional approach to the capstone course in public relations that is more focused on the day-to-day matters of running a PR operation than individual communication campaigns. The point of the book is that public relations functions in a much bigger business picture than what is covered in any other course, and PR students/graduates must be introduced to that and apply tools for PR business so they can add the greatest value to their employers or clients.

Managing Public Relations breaks into a fragmented market for advanced public relations textbooks that can appeal to academic audiences. The book is most useful for upper-division college/university courses in public relations, where students are completing their undergraduate work in PR, are required to take a course in the management of public relations, and are seeking their first jobs in the field after graduation. This book could also be used in a traditional campaigns course to particularly ensure that matters of daily business operations frame how it is that campaigns can be developed at all, making that traditional course richer and more valuable. Graduate students, too, would find this book useful for its revelations about the business and operations of public relations.

Students would obtain the knowledge they need to begin their careers on a better footing than those without education in the management practices of public relations. Professors who teach, research, and serve in public relations education would have a textbook that enables them to address the most salient matters for the effective management of a public relations function in any organization. Additionally, the book also would serve well as a ready resource for practitioners wanting guidance about fundamental matters of running PR operations. Overall, then, *Managing Public Relations* insightfully and uniquely bridges theory with practice for its target readers, and it does so purposefully, leaning toward the pragmatic matters of operations management.

What Is in This Book and Its Supporting Material

Managing Public Relations touches on matters about the field that emanate from its theory and research foundation and does so to springboard into the salient matters about running a public relations operation. This book does not cover the full range of theories about public relations because students would have covered them in previous, prerequisite courses. Instead, this book focuses on those theories and practices that function most effectively in enabling someone to understand the what, how, and why of the daily business of PR.

The book's content is based directly on my experience leading public relations programs and projects in corporations, in an agency, and as a consultant and my familiarity with published material on management issues and the management of public relations functions. Indeed, the latter led me to realize a real niche could be carved out for a book focused on managing public relations in ways that are more in sync with current and future business needs and public relations practices that are not addressed in extant books. Portions of this text have appeared in my other publications, and I have repurposed them where they apply best.

The unique features and strengths of this textbook include:

- First textbook to address the leadership and management of a public relations function that balances agency and corporate/nonagency worlds simultaneously, which demonstrates the greater degree of similarity than difference among the places and ways PR is employed organizationally.

- Specific features for the benefit of readers:
  - Initial outlines of chapters' contents, so readers see how they will progress.
  - Graphics that illuminate key topics, so readers obtain additional insight into matters addressed in the text.
  - Lists of key words and concepts, so readers can focus on and use ideas more effectively during and after reading. Key words are italicized in the text so they can be found and understood in context.
  - A number of problem-based opportunities to apply chapters' contents, so readers can explore the real-world implications of what matters to PR leaders.
  - Lists of recommended readings at the end of each chapter, so readers may continue their learning and, if desired, build their libraries about important matters to managing public relations.
- Direct application of current, foundational research from the public relations field and business concepts and approaches common to leaders of public relations functions. This application gives readers the most contemporary understanding of the theory, demands, and methods for effective management of public relations operations.
- Concise recapitulations of selected foundational concepts and principles of public relations that should be familiar, remembered, and, most important, applied anew within the bigger context of top management's demands for successful PR in any organization.
- "Day-to-day" connections between an organization's overall strategic plan and how public relations, like all other organizational functions, must devise and enact its own plan to help the overall organization achieve success, which demonstrate the specific things executives and their departments must do as contributors to the overall business.
- Up-to-date explanations and examples of management practices and technologies not addressed in other and older texts, which would bring to bear an ample range of scenarios on readers' need to "see" how they work. The chapters' content and design allows individual instructors to (a) apply their own knowledge and experiences to build upon that content (plus an instructor's manual) and (b) take the class in directions that fulfill students learning interests.
- First-person testimonials from actual PR executives representing corporate and agency worlds—"Executive Viewpoints"—about key concepts in the chapters make principles, methods, and tools all the more "real" to readers as they realize how they work and why.

Supplemental material also makes the textbook more valuable. Instructors will find useful, instructor-focused material in an instructor's manual, which provides guidance and ideas for class discussions, assignments, and a course syllabus. Other instructor-focused material includes a dedicated website for this book hosted by Oxford University Press.

Readers will find that social media are addressed in this book; however, social media (or any individual medium or selected media) will not be addressed in tactical ways because they are already covered in PR writing texts and courses. In this book social media and other forms of PR discourse are matters of any tactics that could be chosen in light of a thorough strategic planning process (see Chapter 4). In particular, social media and all tactics are resources that require meticulous management (see Chapter 6). Focusing too much on social media, which make up only one tool for PR, would require similar focus on press releases, events, annual reports, and all the rest, and that approach is antithetical to this book's purpose and thesis. In this way the context of running the business of PR operations is kept in sharp focus, even addressing matters about the future direction of the PR field and PR practice and management.

Who Deserves Thanks

A handful of people deserve special recognition for their help at various times with this textbook. First is John Luecke, who gave me great support and counsel for initially designing the course in 2004 while I worked at the University of Wisconsin–Whitewater, and it is a course I have led ever since. Additionally, while at UWW, Kris Maag Kranenberg and Kim Hixson also gave me helpful input about content matters for the course in its earliest form.

Next is Jeff Courtright, who has been a joy to collaborate with over the years on our scholarly and academic projects in public relations. His counsel about content in the course (and, consequently, this book) has been highly valuable and greatly appreciated. Lance Lippert's review and comments about the first chapter were especially helpful to ensure consistency with the leadership literature. Also, Maria Moore reviewed and commented on the third chapter, and her feedback was most valuable in making sure the content accurately reflects the knowledge base. Wilfred Tremblay provided me with the basic design for Figure 3-4 in Chapter 3. Additionally, Chad Woolard was my part-time research assistant in the fall semester of 2012, and his help was most timely and valuable. Especially important were students in my fall 2013 and spring 2014 *Public Relations Management* classes, who "test-drove" drafts of the manuscript and gave me valuable feedback so that future students and readers may benefit from improvements they suggested be made to this book.

I am deeply grateful for the public relations leaders whose insights and counsel are given in each of this book's 11 chapters. Their contributions make the concepts and, most important, the day-to-day business of leading and managing public relations come alive in vivid ways.

At Oxford University Press, Mark T. Haynes, editor for communication and journalism, has been enthusiastic about this project from the start and most helpful with guidance about making this book the best it can be. Also, Olivia Geraci and Bev Kraus made sure this project rolled along, John Beletsky gathered and sorted out feedback from reviewers, and Diane Lange was copy editor.

The reviewers of this project also deserve recognition and many thanks for their feedback on my project proposal and, most especially, the manuscript for this textbook. Their comments and questions, combined with Mark Haynes's recommendations and insights, have resulted in a much better product than it would have been without their help.

Finally and most gratifyingly, my family deserves kudos for their constant love and support for me and my work. Patty, Matthew, and Jeffrey, I love you and appreciate you more than words can ever express.

Reference

Arthur W. Page Society (2007). *The authentic enterprise: Relationships, values and the evolution of corporate communications*. New York: Author. Available online at http://www.awpagesociety.com/images/uploads/2007AuthenticEnterprise.pdf.

Reviewers

Alisa Agozzino—Ohio Northern University

Tracie Babb—Rowan University

Bob Batchelor—Kent State University

Suzanne Berman—Hostra University

Jeffrey Brand—University of Northern Iowa

Brigitta R. Brunner—Auburn University

Cassy Burleson—Baylor University

Jennie Donohue—Marist College

Sandra Duhé—Southern Methodist University

Gregg Feistman—Temple University

Cliff Fortenberry—Mississippi College

Amiso George—Texas Christian University

Kay Green—West Virginia University/New York University

Laura Hammel—Ursuline College

Timothy Howard—California State University

Dean Kazoleas—California State University at Fullerton

Jennifer Keller—Western Washington University

Sun Young Lee—Texas Tech University

Julie Lellis—Emerson College

Lan Ni—University of Houston

Katrina Olson—University of Illinois at Urbana-Champaign

Michael Palenchar—University of Tennessee

Bob Pritchard—University of Oklahoma

Gemma Puglisi—American University

John Wirtz—Texas Tech University

Brenda J. Wrigley—Syracuse University

Chapter 1

LEADERSHIP AND MANAGEMENT IN PUBLIC RELATIONS:
Two Sides of the Same Coin

How great is public relations? Very! In fact, public relations is a valuable and valued organizational function, especially among top organizational leaders. According to the Generally Accepted Practices (GAP) VIII report from the University of Southern California's Annenberg School for Journalism and Communication

(2014), "About 40% [of the senior-level communication professionals surveyed] report that PR/Com actively participates in corporate strategic planning, while over 45% view this as grey area" (p. 17), and nearly 60% of survey respondents said C-Suite executives take public relations recommendations seriously and almost 32% also see it as a gray area (p. 18). Additionally, public relations is seen in the C-Suite as a valuable contributor to financial success (p. 19).

This great value that public relations has garnered, as the GAP VIII study shows, has not been easy over the years. Since the first public relations positions were officially created more than a century ago, professionals have had a long uphill battle to gain respect and, most important, make links to organizational performance beyond the number of news stories produced in a given period of time. It is, therefore, incumbent on public relations as a field and public relations professionals individually to continuously improve PR's perceived and real value to organizations and society. This chapter takes the first step into the arena of managing public relations operations as a valued and valuable part of any organization. The key here is that public relations management is dependent on effective leadership that, in turn, informs management practices. To this end, this chapter presents a historical view of public relations, how it is defined, and what operational areas it includes. This historical context relates and builds up to perspectives of leadership, management, and followership that are crucial in the work environment. Important components of the discussion are models of public relations that guide the practice, the current state of leadership in public relations, and lessons to be learned from job postings asking for public relations leaders.

History's Revelations

We know much about the historical evolution of the practice of public relations over the past century and beyond (see for example Cheney & Vibbert, 1987; Cutlip, 1994, 1995, 1997; Cutlip, Center, & Broom, 1994; Ewen, 1996). The formal practice of "public relations" does not emerge until 1889, when Westinghouse competed with Edison General Electric over the establishment of alternating electrical current over direct current and Westinghouse created the first formal public relations position (Cutlip, 1995, p. 202; Cutlip et al., 1994, p. 98). Until this point, the responsibilities that eventually came to be associated with public relations were referred to under terms like "publicity," "promotional activity," and "press agent," all of which were closely associated with coverage of corporate activity in the press. The term and function of "public relations" then was still fairly new but not without a heavy load of semantic baggage, as it "became institutionalized in the large public agencies that arose to meet several environmental challenges [of social order (labor unions), political order (Roosevelt's New Deal), economic order (the Great Depression), and technological order (radio and 'mass culture')]" (Cheney and Vibbert, 1987, p. 169).

Public relations and those who have practiced it are seen through a negative lens that seems based on negative first impressions. As Grunig and Hunt (1984) put it, "in its early development, public relations was equated with persuasion and/or propaganda [i.e., a secular approach to "propagating the faith" about an organization]. Most people still have that concept of public relations today, explaining the common suspicion, mistrust, and even fear of it" (p. 21). For example, growing out from the labor movements in the early 1900s, primarily in the steel, oil, meat-packing, and railroad industries, and fertilized by muckraking journalistic practices about what was going on, both business and government alike adopted aggressive practices of public communication and defense (Cutlip, 1997, p. 23). So in the eyes of business and government leaders, public relations was seen as an essential means to combat hostility and court public favor, but in the eyes of the public it was seen as a way to manipulate people's thinking about issues. Contemporary social critics continue to claim that the ideal of "free and robust debate" that is at the heart of our culture is in grave danger of being "seriously imbalanced by the large, money-stuffed war chests and armies of skilled communicators that the powerful special interests can put into the field of debate" (Cutlip, 1995, pp. 280–281).

From William Henry Vanderbilt's 1882 statement, "'the public be damned'" (Cutlip, 1995, p. 188), to today's sense and reference from terms like "spin" and "spinmeisters," negative views of public relations have long guided people's thinking about the profession and public relations professionals. To stem the tide of negativity against public relations, the Global Alliance for Public Relations (GAPR) launched a program in 2010, called *The Stockholm Accords*, for promoting public relations anywhere in the world over a two-year period (Skoogh, McCormick, & Falconi, 2010). In 2012 the GAPR launched *The Melbourne Mandate* to build upon the efforts of the first program. At worst, public relations suffers from a poor image—an unscrupulous endeavor of wordsmithing or shameless image-mongering. Cases like the staged FEMA (Federal Emergency Management Agency) news conferences about its response to California wildfires in 2007 support such negative views. But cases like the Johnson & Johnson's superb management of the Tylenol tampering, Northern Illinois University's outstanding management of an on-campus shooting in 2008, and numerous excellent product launches and other campaigns show (e.g., annual PRSA Silver Anvil winners and IABC's Gold Quill winners) that there are far more positive and ethical examples of public relations.

Defining the Field

Remember, too, that other professional fields, like accounting, law, engineering, and medicine, have had their share of troubling and triumphant examples of unethical and stellar professionalism and performance. Even in the face of these troubles and triumphs, people have been able to understand these other fields better than public relations. Indeed, throughout public relations' history it has not been as well defined and easily understood as those other fields. The principal reason seems to be that public relations' importance over the preceding 100 years has grown and grown in so many different ways with innovative means of communication that it looked as if it was one thing *and* many things at once. So, depending on one's view (not necessarily those definitions expressed in scholarship and textbooks), public relations was simply a matter of press coverage or media relations. Another definition could express public relations as a matter of orchestrating beneficial relationships with publics. Still other definitions would focus on functional matters of informing people, cultivating attitudes, or inspiring particular behaviors. The multiplicity of definitions about PR has made it more difficult to understand than other fields that are comparatively easier to define and more widely or intuitively understood because of their reliance on mathematics, science, and, especially, centuries of tradition.

Various efforts to define public relations have been made, most frequently within the scholarship about the field. Recognizing this difficulty of identity for the profession, the Public Relations Society of America (PRSA) in 2011 embarked on a focused effort to define public relations. Although the PRSA had had its own definition since 1982, the organization sought to build consensus about a definition through a process of co-creation (i.e., "crowdsourcing" over the Internet) among professionals rather than a process of argumentation to advocate for adherence to one preexisting definition, no matter its source. And the scope of the definition includes all practice areas of public relations. The result of the PRSA's work was this definition: "Public relations is a strategic communication process that builds mutually beneficial relationships between organizations and their publics" (2012, ¶2).

Purview of Operations

As the profession evolved, so too did its purview of operations. In this way public relations came to subsume much more than any single category of communication, like media relations. Public relations came to be the central authority on matters about the ethical use of language and symbols to inspire cooperation between organizations and their publics. Practice areas that may have once belonged to one functional unit, like employee communications can to human resources or investor relations can to finance and accounting, were placed under the public relations umbrella. Communication expertise was the key and operational efficiencies were the benefit.

Public relations, then, includes multiple areas, many known well and some not known much at all: media relations, employee relations, retiree relations, government relations, investor relations, dealer/retailer relations, analyst relations, and others, including event planning, Internet sites, and social media. It seems funny that any audience that could be identified and joined with the word "relations" qualifies as a practice area. But that is okay because public relations is fundamentally a matter of inspiring cooperation between organizations and their various audiences as much as practicable, depending on an organization and its purposes. Table 1-1

Table 1-1. CORE RESPONSIBILITIES BASED ON PR'S CONTROL OVER BUDGET.

ACTIVITY	% CONTROL
Media relations	92.8
Corporate communication/reputation (other than advertising)	85.0
Crisis management	83.0
Social media participation	81.3
Social media monitoring	79.0
Executive communication	76.4
Measurement and evaluation of communication effectiveness	73.2
Social media measurement	72.0
Corporate external website	71.5
Employee/internal communications	70.0
Corporate image (logo usage, etc.)	67.1
Issues management	66.0
Community relations	65.4
Marketing PR/product PR	64.8
Public affairs	59.4
Advertising-corporate image, issues	58.8
Multimedia production	53.6

shows PR's "core budgetary responsibilities," which means that PR has more than 50% of the control over the budget for any listed activity, as found through the GAP VIII report (Annenberg School, 2014, p. 57). Notice that this list presents, on the one hand, a kind of prioritization of essential public relations work (also called "practice areas") for virtually any organization of any kind and, on the other hand, a revelation about how much PR can be tied to other organizational functions, like marketing and human resources.

The general approaches taken in any practice area and the overall operations of public relations can be understood in terms of Grunig and Hunt's (1984) models of public relations, which are shown in Table 1-2. Indeed, their models of PR are

Table 1-2. **PUBLIC RELATIONS MODELS AND THEIR USABILITY.**

MODEL	PURPOSE	RESEARCH	COMMUNICATION FLOW	PREFERENCE	PRACTICED
Publicity/ press agentry	*Propaganda; truth not essential*	*None or little*	*Linear (source to receiver)*	*3rd*	*1st*
Public information	*Information dissemination; truth important*	*Little; focused on secondary audience studies*	*Linear (source to receiver)*	*4th*	*2nd*
Two-way asymmetrical	*Scientific persuasion; truth essential*	*Formative and primary studies to evaluate reactions and attitudes prior to official release*	*Single-cycle recursive, unbalanced effects (source to receiver to source [feedback])*	*1st*	*4th*
Two-way symmetrical	*Mutual understanding; truth essential*	*Formative and summative primary studies to evaluate understanding*	*Continuously recursive, balanced effects (source to receiver to source and back again [dialogic])*	*2nd*	*3rd*

SOURCES: *Hunt & Grunig (1994); Grunig & Grunig (1992)*

especially helpful in capturing salient matters of management, especially resource allocations. Based on both the history and contemporary practice of public relations, these models provide us with a good starting point to dig into the soil of managing PR.

As Table 1-2 shows, public relations models progress from simple, one-way, organization-focused communication to complex, two-way, all-party–focused communication. Indeed, from a management perspective, these models explain why certain communication choices are made. The linear models are the simplest compared to the two-way models. The linear models can be conducted with minimal resources an organization has available to get the word out and not interact with any members of target audiences. The publicity/press agentry model, for example, allows for "hosing out" as much information as possible without regard to audience reception, and the public information model only applies already-known audience concerns during development. The recursive models, however, require more resources because of the interaction between an organization and its publics. The two-way asymmetrical (2WA) model favors an organization and is less resource-intensive than the two-way symmetrical (2WS) model, which favors all publics equally. All models could and should employ methods to measure effectiveness and value for the investment after a communication effort is completed; we will touch on this topic in Chapter 5.

One way to think of the 2WA model is that it is the public information model on the steroids of primary research for audience feedback. The reason 2WA is more complex than the public information model but less complex than 2WS is that the 2WA model only requires one research cycle between an organization and representatives of its target audiences, thus favoring the organization in the process using a single-cycle recursive process to obtain feedback. That single cycle of interaction between an organization and audience representatives is enough to obtain sufficient and authoritative feedback about messages, symbols, media, and other facets of a planned communication effort before it is formally rolled out to all audience members. The continuously recursive 2WS model requires dynamic, ongoing, and built-in dialogic channels in an entire communication effort. Those channels both (1) facilitate dialog between an organization and its publics and (2) measure communication effectiveness and value for the investment. Such symmetry necessarily requires thorough and expensive arrays of time, human, technological, facilities, and other resources to make it work 24/7 for anyone who wants to use it.

Most important for all four models, these resource-allocation matters reveal why in the two righthand columns of Table 1-2 there is such a pronounced difference between what public relations professionals prefer to use and what they actually practice. Simply put, PR professionals greatly value the ideal of dialogic communication and would easily want to engage in it every time, but the daily press of business and the constraints on resources make dialogic communication something best reserved for projects when the luxury of time, people, material, and money are better available. The usual practice, then, for public relations professionals is not dialogic but, rather, monologic, as the typical small staffs of corporate communication groups make do with the limited resources they have and communicate *to* audiences more than *with* them.

There is a fifth model—the *contingency* model—that allows for combinations of the other models of public relations to be employed in ways that best suit communication needs and resource availability, especially within the context of campaigns. For example, the contingency model works as an organizing framework for an entire public relations operation; whereas, such an operation can work solely as one model and then shift to another model as business needs dictate. On a more complex level, the contingency model can explain how a company launching a product may design a two-phase PR campaign. The first phase could be publicity to pique people's interests in a new product and do so in ways that evoke mystery and curiosity along with major benefits of ownership. The second phase could involve a two-way asymmetrical model as the company engages in primary research to test messages, symbols, media, and other facets of the remainder of the campaign on one or more representative samples of target audiences so that the final communication effort is as effective as possible when all its components are ultimately rolled out.

Another example of the contingency model would be the handling of emergency situations (i.e., organizational crisis, intentional crisis, unintentional crisis, issue, or incident). Remember that not everything is a "crisis." An emergency may feel like a crisis because of heightened internal attention and resources given to it, and there may be some public visibility; however, the key to whatever the emergency is depends on its characteristics. These kinds of emergencies require allocation of resources in ways that are commensurate with the situations they involve (Smudde, 2001). An *organizational crisis* is "a specific, unexpected, and nonroutine event or series of events that create high levels of uncertainty and simultaneously present an organization with both opportunities and threats to its high-priority goals" (Ulmer, Seeger, & Sellnow, 2011, p. 7). These emergencies are likely the result of mistakes, oversights, or system deficiencies. *Intentional crises* are events "that are initiated by intentional acts designed to harm an organization" (Ulmer, Seeger, & Sellnow, 2011, p. 9). Examples of intentional crises are terrorism, sabotage, workplace violence, poor employee relationships, poor risk management, hostile takeovers, and unethical leadership. *Unintentional crises* are "unforeseeable or unavoidable" (Ulmer, Seeger, & Sellnow, 2011, p. 11) events that harm an organization. Examples are natural disasters, disease outbreaks, technical interactions, product failure, and economic downturns. An *issue* is a matter that arises unexpectedly from someone or some group that argues for its importance and demands something be done (Crable & Vibbert, 1985; Smudde, 2001, 2011). Issues develop methodically over time through public argumentation between an organization and those who brought the issue to public importance plus interested stakeholders until it is resolved. *Incidents* are particularly isolated matters of importance that arise fairly commonly in organizations and are resolved within the operational area in which they occurred (perhaps with the assistance of one or more other areas or an external service specialist, like a plumber, electrician, or someone from the same or another department) within a very short time span (often within the same day). Examples of incidents would include computer crashes, copier breakdowns, absent employees, assembly line tooling malfunction, transportation problems, customer complaints, and water leaks (see Coombs, 2012).

Among these five types of emergency situations, the incident is the simplest and also the most common, which means contingency plans and resource allocations are easier to muster and manage. In contrast, for the remaining four types, what begins as one emergency can beget another and still another. For example, Hurricane Katrina in 2005 devastated the Gulf Coast region encompassing Louisiana, Mississippi, and Alabama. Katrina obviously was a disaster when it happened. But before Katrina hit, it technically was an issue of public safety because civic leaders knew the limitations of the levee system and escape routes and knew that they were not ready for a hurricane of Katrina's magnitude. After Katrina, organizational crises arose for the FEMA, New Orleans and other effected cities, and the states in that region.

In terms of Grunig and Hunt's public relations models and resource management, the kind of emergency situation can dictate the type of PR model that applies (if at all) and, subsequently, resource allocations. Indeed, as Figure 1-1 shows, effective contingency planning efforts, which examine risk to an organization in terms of (1) the probability of any emergency with (2) its degree of impact on an organization (Fink, 1986; Ulmer, Seeger, & Sellnow, 2011), must to the best of their ability articulate how certain resources must be allocated, including the most effective and efficient model for communicating with publics. The most dominant communication during emergencies likely would be one way, which is either press agentry and/ or public information. There is little time to incorporate two-way communication until such time that a dominant model of dialogic communication makes sense. In the case of issues, because the time span from inception to resolution is typically much longer than it is for crises of any sort, a dialogic model may be in effect from the beginning.

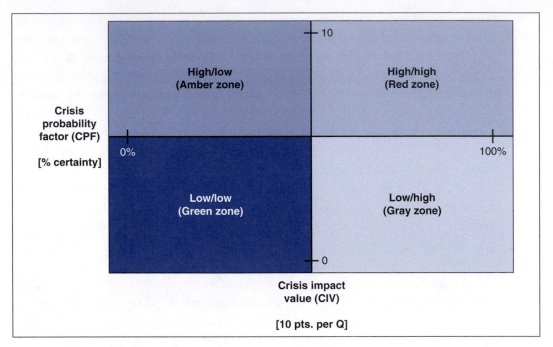

Figure 1-1. EMERGENCY RISK-PLANNING GRID.
SOURCE: Fink (1985, p. 45)

Key to the effective application of any model of and all available resources for public relations is leadership. Two concepts directly related to leadership are management and followership, and all three concepts are our next stop.

Similarities and Differences Between Leadership and Management

When we think of leadership, we think of what it takes to ensure that people work well together on something in which they all have a stake. Leaders without followers are alone, and followers without leaders are lost. Leadership, then, necessarily involves followers and is an enabler of group success or failure, balancing task and relationship matters along the way. More specifically defined, "leadership is human (symbolic) communication which modifies the attitudes and behaviors of others in order to meet shared group goals and needs" (Hackman & Johnson, 2009, p. 11). The literature about leaders and leadership is vast, and this small section on the subject is only meant to be a usable and useful introduction to selected concepts that would prove valuable in the running of a public relations function. Important, too, is the relationship between leadership and management. Both skill sets are essential for effectiveness in public relations, although it is rare that any one person may be truly "excellent" in both. The balance of this chapter explores the interrelationship between leadership and management, including interactions with followers.

Leadership definition and approaches

Someone's performance as a leader is founded on several dimensions. First is personal character, which concerns one's ethos—who someone is, what someone stands for, how someone presents one's self verbally and nonverbally, how other people think about and respond to someone, and the personality someone exudes. Second is situations, which are occasions someone handles well or not and can define that person as a good or bad leader. Third is the nature of the task, which dictates the kinds of expertise needed to handle it and reveals the level of competence someone has with it. Finally is relationships among group members, which should be nurtured in ways that inspire attitudes and behaviors that result in desired outcomes. Interestingly, a leader's unique role in a group allows for some behaviors that differ from those of all other members if and only if those behaviors provide direction and uphold group norms. Figure 1-2 lists the kinds of expectations people have of leaders.

Leadership can also be examined in finer levels of detail, all of which are helpful to understanding what it takes to lead a public relations function. Two categories of detail are *styles* and *types* of leaders. Leadership styles, Hackman and Johnson (2009) explain, concern five categories of attitude and behavior patterns.

- Trust. Respect. Honesty. Realism.
- Stand up for the group. Recognize exemplary results. Give credit where/when due.
- Effective/Best all-around communicator
- Define & track expectations (buy-in at individual & group levels)
- Openness to alternative, better ways
- Organizational change
- Treat people individually – identification; create & maintain a good work environment within corporate culture
- Manage conflict well
- Delegate assignments effectively
- Look out for individuals' interests, including new challenges & jobs to excel in

Figure 1-2. LEADERSHIP EXPECTATIONS.

Authoritarian leaders are those who want complete control ("my way or the high-way"). They are leaders who selfishly dictate that something will be done according to their own wishes and no other way. In contrast to this negative, malevolent kind of authoritarian leader, there is a positive, benevolent form. A benevolent authoritarian leader engages in reasoned explanation about why things must be done in the manner she or he demands so that others understand. *Democratic* leaders are those who seek consensus ("everyone must have a say"). These leaders actively pursue people's views and feedback, then consensually weigh the pros and cons of alternatives to reach a mutually agreed-upon decision. *Laissez-faire* leaders are those who keep a distance ("leave them alone"). These leaders take two forms: a positive form and a negative form. The positive form of laissez-faire leader functions as a sage guide who is available to group members for direction and advice while also giving them the freedom and authority to explore and solve problems. The negative form of laissez-faire leader functions as a disinterested party, abdicating responsibility to the group and letting it struggle with interpretations, procedures, direction, and all other matters until final products of the group are in.

Two additional styles of leadership are each largely one-dimensional, which can be risky when someone only practices one without some attention to the other. The first is *task-focused* leaders. These leaders are primarily concerned with getting a job done and done on time. They may also be fastidious or even dogmatic about adhering to project specifications. The second is *relationship-focused* leaders. These leaders are primarily concerned with people working well together. To these leaders group chemistry and team spirit are vital to success. Both of these styles imply the other, because to get a job done well, on time, and on spec means people must get along to some positive degree. And having people who enjoy working together means they should have complementary backgrounds and produce successful results. But task-focused leaders often can be too task focused, which means group morale suffers from too much work and not enough personal recognition, support, or "play." And relationship-focused leaders often can be too relationship focused, which means group productivity suffers as group members see they are expected to play more than to work. Leadership across all five styles, then, means there must be a favorable balance between task and relationship needs when times demand more attention to work than relationships and vice versa.

Types or "views" of leaders is the second level of detail about leadership, and leadership types concern characteristics of leaders that cluster in eight categories. The *traits* view concerns how well leaders exhibit effective interpersonal behaviors, cognitive/intellectual abilities, personality, motivation to perform, and experience/knowledge in areas required of them in their positions. *Situational* leaders are adaptive to group, individual, and environmental demands, which means they have a kind of intelligence to size up and respond well to what is going on in context. *Functional* leaders are those who, like we saw in the leadership styles, play particular roles when needed, such as task, relationship, or individual focus to reestablish a better balance within the group so it can reach its goals. *Relational* leaders are those who rely on a combination of hierarchical and social positions between themselves and others to move people to action and meet group goals. *Transactional* leaders are the traditional form of leadership that uses formal authority to procure resources and inspire followers' involvement, commitment, and productivity. In relation to Maslow's (1954/1997) hierarchy of needs (see Figure 1-3), transactional leaders enable group members' lower-order needs, beginning with physiological needs, then safety and security, then love and belonging. Transactional leaders, then, may be thought of as stereotypical managers. In contrast, *transformational* leaders are those who are visionary, address and go beyond transactional leadership, and enable people to become more than they are by appealing to self-esteem and self-actualization needs especially through empowerment strategies. As Figure 1-3 shows, transformational leaders also must be transactional leaders (i.e., good managers), but transactional leaders do not necessarily

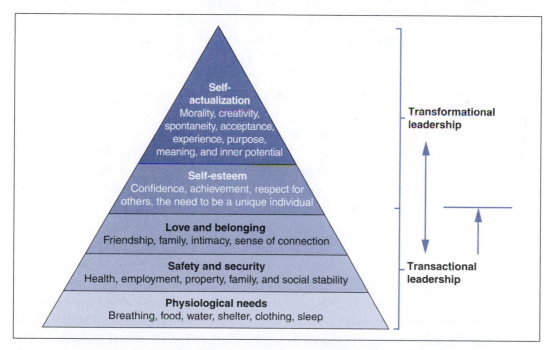

Figure 1-3. MASLOW'S HIERARCHY OF NEEDS SHOWING TRANSACTIONAL AND TRANSFORMATIONAL LEADERS.

SOURCE: http://www.costaricantimes.com/the-broken-road-maslows-hierarchy-of-needs/23122

have to be transformational leaders. *Servant* leaders are those who focus on others' needs first and, thereby, see themselves as stewards of both the organization and its people, including customers. Servant leaders see followers as partners and distribute rewards fairly, which fosters an equitable and just environment in which to work. *Charismatic* leaders are seen as especially gifted leaders who possess and exude self-confidence and competence; they tend to be extraordinary orators, linking symbolic myths and group goals effectively. Charismatic leaders usually arise at just the right time when a group is facing dire consequences and needs a highly inspirational, visionary, influential, and enthusiastic leader. Both servant and charismatic leaders are, in a sense, more advanced transformational leaders.

Management definition and approaches

On the other side of the coin from leadership is management. Indeed, someone may be both a leader and a manager. But the two terms cause some confusion. One word that is often thought of as synonymous with leadership is "management." The verb forms of these two words, "to lead" and "to manage," contribute to this thinking but need clarification. One useful way to compare leadership and management is this: *Managers are people who do things right and leaders are people who do the right thing* (Bennis & Nanus, 2003, p. 20). On the one hand, leaders seek and produce change by engaging in processes that (1) create an agenda through establishing direction with vision for the future and strategies for producing change, (2) develop a network of people to achieve the agenda through their own example (align words and deeds), and (3) obtain results according to the agenda through helping people to channel their energies to overcome obstacles, realize the vision, and satisfy personal and professional needs. On the other hand, managers seek and produce predictability and order by engaging in processes that (1) create agenda through planning and budgeting, (2) develop a network of people to achieve the agenda through organizing and staffing, and (3) obtain results according to the agenda through monitoring and controlling operations and problem solving (Hackman & Johnson, 2009, pp. 12–13). Managing, simply put, involves systematic and ethical ways of directing people, allocating resources, and getting things done according to defined strategic objectives, including ingenuity and innovations along the way that can make processes, outputs, and customer experiences better than expected. The literature about managing and management is enormous, and this section, like the one on leadership, has a decidedly sharp focus. Indeed, this short section introduces you to the basic concepts of management that will continue to be developed throughout the rest of this book as it bears on the running of a public relations function.

Peter Drucker, the celebrated and acknowledged guru of the management field, explained that being an effective manager is learnable and has three equally important tasks that must be performed to be successful: (1) "[establishing] the specific purpose and mission of the institution, whether business, enterprise, hospital, or university;" (2) "making work productive and the worker achieving;" and (3) "managing social impacts and social responsibilities" (1973/1993, p. 40). Drucker is responsible for articulating a highly recognized concept: "management by objectives" (MBO). The key in MBO is for a manager *and* each follower (also called a "subordinate") to work together and define particular objectives that are in tune with the strategic plan, can be achieved within a definitive span of time, and add value to the operation (Drucker, 1954/2006, 1973/1993). Once the objectives are defined, the manager and employee structure a system to monitor and measure an employee's progress toward meeting those objectives. That system ensures the employee's performance is on track and feedback is given and, if performance is not on track, corrective action can be made sooner than later. We will cover performance management in more detail in Chapter 5 and other management matters for public relations throughout this book.

In the grand scheme of things, as Drucker (1967/2006) observes, "Effectiveness is what executives are being paid for, whether they work as managers who are responsible for the performance of others as well as their own, or as individual professional contributors responsible for their own performance only" (pp. ix–x). For Drucker, the substance of an effective executive is found in eight practices he defined in 2004 (rendered in Table 1-3), after a 65-plus year consulting career.

Notice how the eight rules cluster into three categories of benefits for the executive and, thereby, subordinates and the organization. The benefits proceed from the foundational practices that enable learning as much as practicable, to taking action on that knowledge, and then to making sure everyone is committed to and involved with achieving desired results. To these eight practices Drucker (1967/2006) adds one that he considers so vital that he called it a rule: "Listen first, speak last" (p. 63). His point is that all these practices can be undermined by people who allow their "personalities, strengths, weaknesses, values, and beliefs" to get in the way of anything individuals and the group need and want to accomplish.

Discipline is absolutely essential, Drucker argues, and these eight practices and the overarching rule to listen make up a solid recipe for enacting that requisite discipline and realizing management and organizational success. Discipline guides managerial decision-making, which concerns (1) identifying a situation as generic or an exception, (2) defining the parameters of possible solutions, (3) describing the ideal solution no matter what the constraints or concessions that must be made,

Table 1-3. DRUCKER'S EIGHT PRACTICES OF EFFECTIVE EXECUTIVES.

PRACTICES	BENEFITS
Asked, "What needs to be done?"	*Obtain needed knowledge*
Asked, "What is right for the enterprise?"	
Developed action plans	*Convert knowledge into action*
Took responsibility for decisions	
Took responsibility for communicating	
Focused on opportunities rather than problems	
Ran productive meetings	*Foster organizational responsibility and accountability*
Thought and said "we" rather than "I"	

(4) devising an action plan to carry out the chosen solution, and (5) measuring the validity and effectiveness of the decision in the real-world context (Drucker, 2001, pp. 242–243). In many ways, the practices of management apply exceptionally well to the most effective types and styles of leadership. No leader or manager can exist without followers. The key is how well effective leaders and managers work *with* followers/subordinates and vice versa.

Follower types

A leader without followers is alone, and followers without a leader are lost. The literature about followers and followership is broad, so generally speaking, as Hackman and Johnson (2009) explain, there are three categories of followers. The first is "best" because these followers think for themselves and take initiative. The second category is "worst" because these followers must be told what to do, how, and when and need constant supervision. The third and final category of followers is "typical" because they take direction well and complete work according to stated expectations.

Five specific types of followers can be easily placed within these three categories. Leaders have the special challenge to determine effective ways to involve each type of follower and enable critical-analytical thinking to achieve success. *Alienated* followers are highly independent, disillusioned, and interested in fighting rather than serving. These followers can provide healthy skepticism, if invited. *Conformist* followers are committed to group goals, rarely express their own ideas out of fear, and agree with a leader's view ("yes people"). These followers can offer valuable alternative viewpoints when invited or challenged to do so. *Pragmatist* followers are moderately independent and engaged people who cope well with uncertainty but are unlikely to be promoted to jobs with greater responsibility and authority. These followers can contribute well when asked to assess pros and cons, risks and benefits. *Passive* followers project little original thought or commitment, rely heavily on supervision, meet minimal expectations, and may possess a small skill set or suffer from repeated defeats from authoritarian leaders. These followers can be engaged by giving specific invitations to do so in ways that play to their strengths or areas of expertise. *Exemplary* followers are critical thinkers and active participants who contribute innovative ideas and go above and beyond expectations. These followers are always willing and responsive to engagement challenges. According to Kelley (1992), these followers add value to an organization, weave effective webs of relationships, and cultivate courageous conscience.

One type of exemplary follower is *servant* followers, which is the complement to servant leaders. Servant followers are people who want to remain followers instead of becoming leaders, which reduces destructive competition and conflict and keeps focus on organizational goals. Servant followers assume leaders seek the best for the organization and work to assist the leader with his or her work, which helps the team as well. Another type of exemplary follower is *courageous* followers, who place the organization, its purpose, and its values as supremely important, not a leader. In this way, then, courageous followers accept higher levels of risk than other followers. Courageous followers take responsibility for themselves and the organization, and these followers reflect well on themselves and how they can personally improve in any way that helps the organization. Courageous followers will take initiative to change the organizational culture through challenges to its rules, assumptions, and procedures (Hackman & Johnson, 2009, pp. 359–360).

Leaders should carefully observe followers' characteristics so that the leaders have a sound sensibility about each person's motivations, attitudes, knowledge/expertise, skills, work ethic, and so on that can help or hinder individual *and* group performance. Followers (and other organizational leaders), too, should carefully observe leaders' characteristics so that the followers (and other leaders) can accurately assess and effectively work with each other. An effective leader looks after her or his followers, and effective followers look after each other and their leader. In sum, hallmarks of effective leader–follower dynamics parallel Lonergans's (1990) "transcendental imperatives" for human relationships: attentiveness (i.e., being alert to what is going on and listening carefully to others), intelligence (i.e., reading one's attention, recognizing patterns, and making good sense of things), reasonableness, (i.e., weighing the products of one's understanding and arriving at good judgment), responsibility (i.e., owning up to one's thoughts, attitudes, and actions then apply or improve them in practical ways), and charity (i.e., love what you do, do what you love, and do what you do out of love). With this background about the nature of leaders, managers, and followers, the next step is to examine the practices for effective leadership in public relations.

Characteristics of Effective Public Relations Leaders

Among the many topics addressed in the literature about public relations, leadership historically has not been well covered. In recent years, however, more investigations about the nature and practice of leadership in public relations have been conducted and published. Indeed, the single most-comprehensive study of leadership in public relations was completed and results released in October 2012. The study, Cross-Cultural Study of Leadership in Public Relations and Communication Management, led by Bruce Berger at the University of Alabama, addresses multiple dimensions of leadership and is truly global in scope (Berger et al., 2012). The Cross-Cultural Study also identified the ten most pressing issues for public relations leaders (Figure 1-4). Because of the study's great importance for and prominence in the field, this section briefly summarizes its findings and implications, including supporting research published separately. The study stands as the source of the latest and greatest insights about leadership for the profession. The study also fits our focus well for the leading of public relations functions.

---

1. Dealing with the speed and volume of information flow
2. Being prepared to effectively deal with crises that may arise
3. Managing the digital revolution and rise of social media
4. Improving exployee engagement and commitment
5. Improving the measurement of communication effectiveness
6. Dealing with growing demands for transparency
7. Finding, developing, and retaining top talent
8. Meeting demands for corporate social responsibility
9. Meeting communication needs in diverse cultures
10. Improving the image of the profession

Figure 1-4. THE TEN BIG ISSUES FOR PUBLIC RELATIONS LEADERS.

SOURCE: Berger et al. (2012, p. 9)

The work of Meng, Berger, Gower, and Heyman (2012), which was instrumental in the Cross-Cultural Study, specifically investigated "excellent" (i.e., "ideal") leadership in public relations. Guiding their study was this definition:

> Excellent leadership in public relations is a dynamic process that encompasses a complex mix of individual skills and personal attributes, values, and behaviors that consistently produces ethical and effective communication practice. Such practice fuels and guides successful communication teams, helps organizations achieve their goals, and legitimizes organizations in society. (Meng et al., 2012, p. 24)

This definition reflects the topics we covered in this chapter about leadership and followership. Based on this definition, the researchers identified a number of components of excellent leadership and tested them. Indeed, the study's findings "are consistent with those in traditional managerial leadership research" (Meng et al., 2012, p. 32). A usable and potent model of excellent leadership in public relations is shown in Figure 1-5.

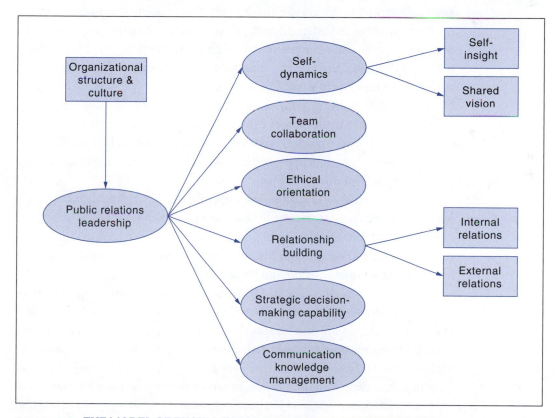

Figure 1-5. THE MODEL OF EXCELLENT LEADERSHIP IN PUBLIC RELATIONS.

SOURCES: Meng & Berger (2013); Berger (2012)

In this model, originally articulated by Meng (2012) and tested as part of the Cross-Cultural Study, there are six components to excellent leadership in public relations, shown in the six ovals stacked in the center. A seventh component is the rectangle in the upper left, which reflects the effect individual organizations have on how people perform their public relations functions. The components complement one another and make up a cohesive and balanced structure for understanding excellence in PR leadership. The Cross-Cultural Study showed that this model is valid for public relations practiced in other nations and the United States (Berger et al., 2012, p. 49; see especially Meng & Berger, 2013). The components of the model are defined as follows:

- *Self-dynamics*—Concerns the degree to which a leader lives up to expected characteristics of successful leaders (see Figure 1-2). This component relies on leaders understanding themselves (e.g., strengths, weaknesses, etc.) and "present[ing] traits such as high self-confidence, emotional maturity, initiative, and stress tolerance" (Meng, 2012, p. 337).
- *Team collaboration*—Concerns the intensity of collaboration and, thereby, cohesiveness that is fostered among those on the PR team. The PR leader's role here is to "create a climate of trust and flexibility within the team, facilitate positive interdependence among team members, and between team members and leaders" (Meng, 2012, p. 337).
- *Ethical orientation*—Concerns the degree to which PR leaders believe in, uphold, and enact principles of ethical conduct in their work. Involved in this component of the model is adherence to values and standards of professionalism while contributing to organizational goals for strong performance plus doing good for others.
- *Relationship building*—Concerns the capabilities and successfulness of PR leaders in building networks of beneficial relationships for both the organization and its stakeholders, which affects its influence and performance. Relationship building through "interaction, information exchange, and linkage between an organization and its publics" (Meng, 2012, p. 337) is key to resource acquisition and allocation, and it fosters success in communication.
- *Strategic decision-making capability*—Concerns how well PR leaders understand and balance an organization's external and internal environments such that the knowledge about these can be applied to strategic decision-making plus all facets of the organization's communication needs. Particularly important are leaders' abilities "to stimulate new ideas, persuasively sell new ideas to higher-ups, and improve responsiveness in a rapidly changing, complex environment and information market" (Meng, 2012, p. 337).

- *Communication knowledge management capability*—Concerns "the process of gaining, applying and converting public relation [*sic*] and communication knowledge and expertise into effective tactics and strategies" (Meng, 2012, p. 337). This component of PR leadership focuses on educating people about public relations' importance, value, and contributions to organizational effectiveness.
- *Organizational structure and culture*—Concerns "the extent to which PR leaders could be excellent" (Berger, 2012, p. 15). More particularly, "leadership style in an organization is not only determined by the organization's legitimating principles and values but also largely moderated by the social structure and cultural norms within the society it operates" (Meng, 2012, p. 338).

Earlier studies of leadership in public relations made important findings about not only the types of leaders of PR operations, but also the more effective type that seems to be most successful. In her survey of public relations leaders, Jin (2010) found that four leadership types occur among them: transactional, transformational, democratic, and situational. Of those four, transformational was determined to be characteristic of the best for successful leaders. As she says, "The findings reflect the trend of participative management and the balance between task and relationship skills of public relations managers. . . . Stronger transformational leadership is more likely to emerge among more empathetic leaders . . . [and] bring more confidence among employees" (p. 174). This conclusion supports Werder and Holtzhausen's (2009) study about public relations leaders, where "inclusive leadership style was a significant predictor of transformational leadership style, which supports the importance of collaboration, shared decision making, and participative practices in effecting change in public relations environments" (p. 424). MBO, then, can be all the more successful in a PR operation, strengthening the team's overall performance and ensuring individual team members' success.

Leaders must be competent in other ways beyond those covered so far. The dimension of emotional competence has emerged as an important and especially telling characteristic of public relations (and other) leaders. Jin's (2010) study explored this characteristic in detail. Indeed, her study revealed five important features of emotionally competent PR leaders:

1. PR leaders must be empathetic, a core trait that drives PR leaders' accurate assessment of employees' emotions and helps PR leaders to address those emotions with sensitivity and understanding.
2. PR leaders should be flexible in decision-making power sharing and be strategic in the power-sharing negotiation process at the same time.

3. PR leaders should be very experienced in motivating and maintaining optimism at the workplace by creating experience of enthusiasm and excitement among employees.

4. PR leaders should know how to take accommodative actions and express their accommodation when confronted by disagreeing employees if resolving the disagreement will lead to task efficiency.

5. PR leaders should enhance their skills of negotiation and influence-gaining when communicating their disagreements with top management in decision-making conflicts.

This last point about leaders' abilities to negotiate with and influence others is especially pronounced for leaders. In fact, one's emotional competence must be exercised ethically for one's self and others. That is, emotional competence must be used for good and not evil—not use emotions and emotional appeals for manipulative purposes (Kilduff, Chiabaru, & Menges, 2010; also see Alexander, 2011; Grant, 2014). At this point, persuasion is a vital tool in a leader's toolbox. Effectiveness in persuasion is more about establishing common ground than getting one's way. Ethically, persuasion also must avoid deception, while one must also be on guard to identify deception. As we have already seen, leaders must balance matters of tasks and relationships, but they also must do so with an acute sense of the larger context surrounding a situation and those involved. That larger context is defined by the organization's strategic plan plus its overall history of operations, participation in a particular industry, and adherence to legal, community, and other expectations. Public relations leaders work among other leaders, all of whom need and want to achieve certain things on their respective agendas—presumably in tune with the organization's strategic plan.

Because of the natural *boundary-spanning* business of public relations, PR leaders may be among the most adept at building relationships and working well with those in an organization's "dominant coalition" (Grunig, 1992), which "is that inner circle of organizational members, often executives, who hold the greatest power. They make strategic choices, allocate resources, influence organizational values, and shape organizational ideologies" (Berger, 2007, p. 223). Public relations leaders, as we saw at the beginning of this chapter, are increasingly becoming part of organizations' dominant coalitions, which means PR leaders are increasingly involved in strategy development, resource allocations, values shaping, and ideology. In many ways today and beyond, public relations leaders (and the PR professionals that work with them) perform a highly valuable function of conscience *plus* communication expertise *plus* business savvy that is vital to organizational success at every level.

Managing Across Generations

Employee engagement in public relations necessarily spans multiple generations, each with much to offer the other. The matter of managing not only younger generations of workers but also mixed generations of workers has risen to prominence, with good reason: people work later in life as more and more new workers join the ranks, especially in professional fields like public relations.

Generational differences on a broad, social scale have been a popular topic of analysis at least since baby boomers noticed significant differences in the ways they grew up compared to their next cohort, "generation X." More recently, analyses have expanded to address the subsequent generation under their referent of "generation Y" (aka "millennials" or the "net generation"). The generation after this is (what else) "generation Z" (aka the "new silent generation").

At a basic level, the generational differences in the workplace revolve around values. Generational analyses about workers' values provide insights about not so much differences in kind but in degree. These analyses confirm that values about work, leisure, professionalism, reward, and punishment matter to everyone. The key seems to be expectations for living up to these values as all generations of workers negotiate them with each other, starting with employee handbooks and branching out to workplace interpersonal interactions. Most particularly, as Deal (2012) demonstrates, all generations share common ground, but the challenge is establishing it in the best ways that work for people (i.e., know your audience).

In public relations, many budding professionals come from colleges and universities as interns and recent graduates. They collaborate and, most of all, learn from seasoned professionals in all stages in their careers. Therefore, having both sensitivity to and sensibilities about generational differences is important to successful leadership, followership, and operational success. The essentials to effective leadership in PR, as given in this chapter and especially in the previous section, are necessary to effectively manage public relations.

The managing of public relations operations relies on the competence, work ethic, and character of leaders *and* followers. Never in the profession's history has this statement not been true. In those vastly abundant times of successful and ethical communication, public relations professionals show well that they are expert and moral beings that use language and symbols to inspire cooperation between organizations and their publics. In the next chapter we will look at the similarities and differences between public relations practiced in corporate settings (i.e., for-profit, nonprofit/institutional, nongovernmental organizations) and in agency settings (i.e., businesses specifically focused on providing PR expertise for corporate clients).

EXECUTIVE VIEWPOINT

Public Relations Is an Organization's Skin

Mark Phillips, Chief Marketing Officer and Associate Director for Membership, Marketing and Events at FONZ (Friends of the National Zoo)

Through two decades of practice, I've come to see organizations as living organisms, with public relations serving as the organization's skin. I think most people, even those who have not studied or practiced PR, would agree. After all, skin is what's visible to the world. It provides the first impression. It is the visible look and feel, encompassing all public-facing elements, from logos and packaging to key messages and communications activity across all channels. PR provides the external representation of the organization, just as it does the organism. However, while PR provides this relatively superficial surface appearance, the benefits it provides go much deeper than that.

Effective PR leadership shapes the organization's culture, how it presents itself to its publics, its culture and how it behaves, and the experiences its publics have as a result. Because these experiences communicate in perhaps the most powerful way what an organization values and who it really is, this is incredibly important. Interestingly, how an organization behaves is dependent on how it senses and reacts to its environment. And that's where PR delivers its most important value to the organization and its publics.

Both organisms and organizations survive and thrive based on how well attuned they are to their environments, and how well they can adapt to changes; effective PR helps the organization be attuned to its environment. Our skin allows us to sense changes in touch, temperature, movement, and other environmental elements. As the organization's skin, PR is a sensory organ that can provide vital information about how well the organization is getting along with its publics and whether there is friction or conflict. If I touch a hot stove, I pull my hand away almost instantly, because the nerves in my hand are hardwired into my central nervous system, primed for a quick response to pain. This rapid response helps ensure survival.

Public relations can provide a similarly valuable function by enabling an organization to be aware of and quickly react to changes in its environment, particularly with its publics. We see this happen daily, such as when companies announce price increases, cuts in benefits, layoffs, and other decisions that affect their publics. We see it also with organizational crises that involve betrayals of public trust. In each case there is a rapid and powerful response from the organization's publics. Organizations exist in a social environment and PR gives the ability to detect environmental changes, make meaning of these changes, and respond in ways that enhance the organization's ability to react appropriately.

Effective PR leaders ensure the organization has the ability to pay attention to, and even predict, public reactions. They do this by following a two-way communication model that includes listening to their publics. Publics voice their concerns, expectations, and values in many ways, including feedback to customer service; online comments, postings, and reviews; voting with their wallets and feet; and in many other ways that are observable and measureable. This ability to detect and respond quickly to inputs from publics is important; more importantly, however is the ability to predict public reactions before organizational decisions are made. This enables organizations to make informed decisions that minimize conflict with publics and help foster mutually beneficial relationships.

As a PR leader, you can help an organization understand its environment and make decisions that enhance positive relationships and minimize negative relationships with publics. This is based in large part on your ability to empathize with various publics to predict how they will react to organizational decisions. This is done by seeing these decisions through their eyes and understanding how they will think and feel about the decision.

Highly effective PR leaders in excellent organizations serve as part of the dominant coalition (i.e., those who make decisions at the highest levels of the organization). They earn this position of trust through solid performance and on-target counsel. In this position, they use information about publics' attitudes, opinions and behaviors, along with empathy for how these publics will react, to inform decision making.

Another key trait of effective PR leaders is the ability to balance a broad strategic view of the organization and its environment with a more narrow focus on tactics and the technical expertise to execute these tactics. The strategic view focuses on the organization's relationships with its publics, its long-term goals, and asks questions about where the organization is going and why. The tactical view focuses on what must be done to achieve the strategic goals and how these tasks can be done as efficiently and effectively as possible.

In addition to balancing strategy and tactics, strong PR leaders also help their organizations balance risk and opportunity. I've seen this many times in the interplay of counsel provided by the legal and PR departments. Legal counsel frequently is designed to minimize risk from litigation or regulation. To minimize these risks, legal counsel often defines the boundaries of courses of action available to the organization's leaders and advocates for releasing as little information as possible for fear that it could be used against the organization. PR counsel is also concerned with risk, but focuses on risks to key relationships, such as with strategic publics (i.e., those upon whom an organization depends).

To preserve these relationships, PR leaders often advocate for transparency and communications that are as open as possible. This is done with the understanding that crisis presents both threats and opportunities. In many cases, the opportunity is to improve relationships by demonstrating openness, transparency, trust, and so forth. Another way to look at this is that legal counsel often argues for what *can* be done according to the law, while PR counsel argues for what *should* be done in the interest of key relationships. Both of these approaches are valuable; having advocates from legal and PR who can persuasively represent their views helps the organization make informed decisions.

In short, the most effective PR leaders have solid technical communication skills continuously honed throughout their careers, they can consider many perspectives simultaneously, are flexible and adaptable to change, are capable of empathy, behave ethically, are able to tolerate risk, have earned places of trust with organizational leaders, and are able and willing to advocate for their positions.

Public relations is the organization's visible skin, but its true value is far more than skin deep. With effective leadership, PR helps the organization survive and thrive in a changing environment by making informed and ethical decisions that foster mutually beneficial relationships. This is only possible when PR leaders have the technical, emotional, and leadership skills to create this value.

Key Words

Leadership styles

Leadership types

Management

The Stockholm Accords

The Melbourne Mandate

Models of PR

Crises (three types)

Issues

Incidents

Eight practices of managers

Follower types

MBO

Ten issues for PR leaders

Excellent PR leadership model

Emotional competence

Boundary spanning

Dominant coalition

Exploration of Public Relations Leaders and Managers

Collect six to eight or more actual job postings from various organizations for executive-level public relations positions. Use them to explore leadership in public relations along the following lines:

1. Identify and analyze patterns in the job duties, background requirements, compensation, and other factors across all the jobs.
2. Find any evidence about the preferred leadership types that the hiring organizations want in the people they hire.
3. Reveal through your own inference the kind of public relations model(s) that seem to dominate the way the organizations conduct their public relations efforts. What implications are there for the kind of leaders each organization seeks that you found for question 2?
4. Uncover information about how the organizations portray the work environment, especially in terms of leader–follower relationships. Use websites, corporate reports, and brochures to accompany the information from your

job postings. For example, find out what an organization says about how well people work together, how innovative the organization is, and what its corporate culture is like.

References

Alexander, R. (2011, April). The dark side of emotional intelligence. *Management Today*, 46–50.

Annenberg School for Journalism & Communication, Strategic Communication & Public Relations Center (2014). *GAP VIII: Eighth communication and public relations generally accepted practices study (Q4 2013 data)*. Los Angeles: University of Southern California Annenberg Center on Communication Leadership. Available online: http://ascjweb.org/gapstudy/

Bennis, W., & Nanus, B. (2003). *Leaders: The strategies for taking charge* (2nd ed.). New York: Harper Business Books.

Berger, B. (2007). Public relations and organizational power. In E. L. Toth (Ed.), *The future of excellence in public relations and communication management* (pp. 221–234). Mahwah, NJ: Lawrrence Erlbaum Associates.

Berger, B. (2012). *Key themes and findings: The cross-cultural study of leadership in public relations and communication management*. Tuscaloosa, AL: The Plank Center for Leadership in Public Relations. Available online: http://plankcenter.ua.edu/the-summit/.

Berger, B., Zerfass, A., Reber, B., Meng, J., Jin, Y., Petersone, B., Erzikova, E., & Herrera, M. (2012, November 1). *Cross-cultural study of leadership in public relations and communication management*. Presentation made at The Plank Center Leadership Summit in Chicago, IL. Available online: http://plankcenter.ua.edu/the-summit/.

Cheney, G., & Vibbert, S. L. (1987). Corporate discourse: Public relations and issue management. In F. M. Jablin, L. L. Putnam, K. H. Roberts, & L. W. Porter (Eds.), *Handbook of organizational communications: An interdisciplinary perspective* (pp. 165–194). Newbury Park, CA: Sage.

Clampitt, P. G. (2010). *Communicating for managerial effectiveness* (4th ed.). Thousand Oaks, CA: Sage Publications.

Coombs, W. T. (2012). *Ongoing crisis communication: Planning, managing and responding* (3rd ed.). Thousand Oaks, CA: Sage.

Crable, R. E., & Vibbert, S. L. (1985). Managing issues and influencing public policy. *Public Relations Review, 11*, 3–16.

Cutlip, S. M. (1994). *The unseen power: Public relations, a history*. Hillside, NJ: Lawrence Erlbaum.

Cutlip, S. M. (1995). *Public relations history: From the 17th to the 20th century, the antecedents*. Hillside, NJ: Lawrence Erlbaum.

Cutlip, S. M. (1997). The unseen power: A brief history of public relations. In C. L. Caywood (Ed.), *The Handbook of Strategic Public Relations and Integrated Communications* (pp. 15–33). New York: McGraw-Hill.

Cutlip, S. M., Center, A. H., & Broom, G. M. (1994). *Effective public relations* (7th ed.). Upper Saddle River, NJ: Prentice Hall.

Deal, J. J. (2007). *Retiring the generation gap: How employees young and old can find common ground*. San Francisco: Jossey-Bass/John Wiley & Sons.

Drucker, P. F. (1993). *Management: Tasks, responsibilities, practices*. New York: HarperBusiness. (Original work published 1973)

Drucker, P. F. (2001). Effective decisions. In P. F. Drucker, *The essential Drucker: The best of sixty years of Peter Drucker's essential writings on management* (pp. 241–260). New York: HarperCollins.

Drucker, P. F. (2004, June). What makes an effective executive? *Harvard Business Review, 82*(6), 58–63.

Drucker, P. F. (2006). *The effective executive*. New York: HarperCollins. (Original work published 1967)

Drucker, P. F. (2006). *The practice of management*. New York: Harper & Row. (Original work published 1954)

Ewen, S. (1996). *PR! A Social History of Spin*. New York: Basic Books.

Fink, S. (1986). *Crisis management: Planning for the inevitable*. New York: AMACOM.

Global Alliance for Public Relations (2012). *The Melbourne mandate*. New York: Author. Available online: http://melbournemandate.global-alliancepr.org/.

Grant, A. (2014, January 2). The dark side of emotional intelligence. *The Atlantic*. Available online: http://www.theatlantic.com/health/archive/2014/01/the-dark-side-of-emotional-intelligence/282720/.

Grunig, J. (1992). Communication, public relations, and effective organizations. In J. Grunig (Ed.), *Excellence in public relations and communication management* (pp. 1–30). Hillsdale, NJ: Lawrence Erlbaum Associates.

Grunig, J. E., & Grunig, L. A. (1992). Models of public relations and communication. In J. E. Grunig (Ed.), *Excellence in public relations and communication management* (pp. 285–325). Thousand Oaks, CA: Sage.

Grunig, J. E., & Hunt, T. (1984). *Managing public relations*. New York: Holt, Rinehart & Winston.

Hackman, M. Z., & Johnson, C. E. (2009). *Leadership: A communication perspective* (5th ed.). Long Grove, IL: Waveland.

Hunt, T., & Grunig, J. E. (1994). *Public relations techniques*. Fort Worth, TX: Harcourt Brace.

Jin, Y. (2010). Emotional leadership as a key dimension of public relations leadership: A national survey of public relations leaders. *Journal of Public Relations Research, 22*(2), 159–181.

Kelley, R. (1992). *The power of followership: How to create leaders that people want to follow and followers who lead themselves*. New York: Doubleday/Currency.

Kilduff, M., Chiaburu, D. S., & Menges, J. I. (2010). Strategic use of emotional intelligence in orga-

nizational settings: Exploring the dark side. *Research in Organizational Behavior, 30,* 129–152.

Lonergan, B. (1990). *Method in theology* (2nd ed.). Toronto: University of Toronto Press. (Original work published 1973)

Maslow A. M. (1997). *Motivation and personality* (3rd ed.). New York: Pearson. (Original work published 1954)

Meng, J. (2012). Strategic leadership in public relations: An integrated conceptual framework. *Public Relations Review, 38,* 336–338.

Meng, J., & Berger, B. (2013). An integrated model of excellent leadership in public relations: Dimensions, measurement, and validation. *Journal of Public Relations Research, 25*(2), 141–167.

Public Relations Society of America (PRSA) (2012). *What is public relations? PRSA's widely accepted definition.* Retrieved from http://www.prsa.org/aboutprsa/publicrelationsdefined/.

Skoogh, Y., McCormick, G., & Falconi, T. M. (2010). *The Stockholm accords.* Stockholm, Sweden: Global Alliance for Public Relations. Retrieved from http://www.wprf2010.se/draft-of-the-stockholm-accords/.

Smudde, P. M. (2001). Issue or crisis: A rose by any other name. . . . *Public Relations Quarterly, 46*(4), 34–36.

Smudde, P. M. (2011). *Public relations as dramatistic organizing: A case study bridging theory and practice.* Cresskill, NJ: Hampton Press.

Ulmer, R. R., Seeger, M. W., & Sellnow, T. L. (2011). *Effective crisis communication: Moving from crisis to opportunity.* Thousand Oaks, CA: Sage.

Werder, K. P., & Holtzhausen, D. (2009). An analysis of the influence of public relations department leadership style on public relations strategy use and effectiveness. *Journal of Public Relations Research, 21*(4), 404–427.

Recommended Reading

Berger, B. K., & Meng, J. (2014). *Public relations leaders as sensemakers: A global study of leadership in public relations and communication management.* New York: Routledge.

Drucker, P. F. (2001). *The essential Drucker: The best of sixty years of Peter Drucker's essential writings on management.* New York: Collins Business Essentials.

Gregory, A., & Willis, P. (2013). *Strategic public relations leadership.* New York: Routledge.

Kelley, R. (1992). *The power of followership.* New York: Currency.

Kouzes, J. M., & Pozner, B. Z. (2006). *A leader's legacy.* San Francisco: John Wiley & Sons.

Levine, A., & Dean, D. R. (2011). *Generation on a tightrope: Portrait of today's college student.* San Francisco: Jossey-Bass/John Wiley & Sons.

Maxwell, J. C. (1999). *The 21 indispensable qualities of a leader: Becoming the person others will want to follow.* Nashville, TN: Thomas Nelson.

Maxwell, J. C. (2007). *The 21 irrefutable laws of leadership: Follow them and people will follow you,* revised & updated ed. Nashville, TN: Thomas Nelson.

Selden, B. (2008). *What to do when you become the boss: How new managers become successful managers.* Denver, CO: Outskirts Press.

Twenge, J. M. (2006). *Generation me: Why today's young Americans are more confident, assertive, entitled—and more miserable than ever before.* New York: Free Press.

Chapter 2

DISTINCTIONS BETWEEN CORPORATE AND AGENCY OPERATIONS

Public relations is, truly, a growth industry. One of the most interesting and promising facts about the public relations profession is that, according to the U.S. Bureau of Labor Statistics annual report, *Occupational Outlook Handbook*, the job outlook continues to grow by double digits every year. Indeed, the 2012 *Handbook* shows that the job outlook for the period 2010–2020 shows a "faster than average" rate of 21%. Additionally, the Generally Accepted Practices (GAP) VIII report from the University of Southern California's Annenberg School for Journalism and Communication (2014) shows that 64% of the respondents from private companies expect their public relations budgets to increase in 2014 from 2013, 40% of the respondents from public companies expect their PR budgets to increase, and the remainder of the respondents for either group expect no change or a decrease in their PR budgets (p. 49).

So the overall picture for the public relations profession looks very good, and it should. Almost any kind of organization needs or will need to inspire cooperation between itself and its publics through systematic communication efforts. Many organizations have their own public relations operation or someone who handles it (e.g., an attorney, chief executive, or founder), while others do not. In any case, it is very possible that outside firms—public relations agencies—would be invited to "bid" on the PR work an organization needs.

In the public relations industry, there are two basic arenas of practice: corporate and agency. Importantly, public relations practiced in agency and corporate ("nonagency") arenas are more similar than different. This chapter briefly summarizes the salient matters about corporate and agency PR most prominent among PR leaders and new hires. (More detailed treatments are rare, but a very good one to turn to is Wilcox, Cameron, Reber, and Shin's [2013] book, *Think Public Relations*.) This chapter also addresses parallel topics for both corporate and agency public relations so that similarities (they share the same topics) and differences (they approach those topics uniquely) can be explored. Plus, this chapter looks into data about corporate and agency public relations leadership positions through job postings for executives.

Corporate Public Relations Operations

The "corporate" arena of public relations includes a variety of organization types. The reason is simple: they differ significantly from agencies, which are in the business of serving clients, including other agencies. The players in the corporate arena of public relations (also called "nonagency" PR), then, include for-profit companies/corporations, nonprofit/institutional organizations (e.g., public universities, religious organizations, hospitals, organizations complying with the 501[c]3 provision in the U.S. tax code, some professional organizations, many civic/community groups, philanthropic organizations, political action groups complying with the 501[c]4 provision in the U.S. tax code), governments and affiliated bodies (e.g., departments of transportation; health and human services; secretaries of state; etc.), and nongovernmental organizations (e.g., local and national, domestic and international; private educational institutions, Roman Catholic Church, Amnesty International, Doctors Without Borders).

Public relations practiced in the corporate arena is considered "in house." This designation refers to the fact that organizations of these types almost always have a communications department of some sort, and that department or group does the internal and external communication with an organization's publics. That communication can encompass all or most of the core practice areas of public relations, such as media relations, employee relations/internal communications, government

What Are NGOs?

The term "non-governmental organization," or NGO, came into currency in 1945 because of the need for the UN to differentiate in its Charter between participation rights for intergovernmental specialized agencies and those for international private organizations. At the UN, virtually all types of private bodies can be recognized as NGOs. They only have to be independent from government control, not seeking to challenge governments either as a political party or by a narrow focus on human rights, non-profit-making and non-criminal.

The structures of NGOs vary considerably. They can be global hierarchies, with either a relatively strong central authority or a more loose federal arrangement. Alternatively, they may be based in a single country and operate transnationally. With the improvement in communications, more locally based groups, referred to as grass-roots organizations or community based organizations, have become active at the national or even the global level. Increasingly this occurs through the formation of coalitions. There are international umbrella NGOs, providing an institutional structure for different NGOs that do not share a common identity. There are also looser issue-based networks and ad hoc caucuses, lobbying at UN conferences. . . .

At times NGOs are contrasted with social movements. Much as proponents of social movements may wish to see movements as being more progressive and more dynamic than NGOs, this is a false dichotomy. NGOs are components of social movements. Similarly, civil society is the broader concept to cover all social activity by individuals, groups and movements. It remains a matter of contention whether civil society also covers all economic activity. Usually, society is seen as being composed of three sectors: government, the private sector and civil society, excluding businesses.

NGOs are so diverse and so controversial that it is not possible to support, or be opposed to, all NGOs. They may claim to be the voice of the people and to have greater legitimacy than governments, but this can only be a plausible claim under authoritarian governments. However, their role as participants in democratic debate does not depend upon any claim to representative legitimacy.

SOURCE: Willetts (2012; reprinted with permission)

relations, investor relations, community relations, and so on. Additional communication work, including social media, advertising, website content, executive and board of directors communication, and others can also be included, depending on the needs and structure of an organization.

Within the corporate context a public relations department is viewed as an internal resource of experts about communication. It is important, then, to recognize that those working in a corporate PR department are being paid to be the best communicators in and communication counselors for the organization. The various practice areas in public relations, as we touched on above and in Chapter 1, require competent technicians and managers. The many and varied communication needs an organization can have means that the experts in the PR department must be well equipped and well positioned to handle them. (If a communication opportunity is large or diverse enough, an agency may be called in to help; we will address this point later in this chapter.) For corporate contexts, it is useful to think of an organization's various operational groups as internal customers of the PR department. Communication, as Jensen (1995) argues, is "a core competency" (p. 15), which means that public relations (alternatively called "corporate communication" in many organizations; it is also called "public affairs" in governmental organizations) is "an enabler that makes all people skills and competencies effective. It is a *core enabling competence* for any company that wants to implement the plans and strategies it's designed" (p. 17, emphasis added).

Any organization operates according to some plan for how it does its business. Such a plan covers the entire organization and specifies particular objectives the whole organization seeks to achieve. In this way organizational plans are strategic in nature because they define what, how much, when, by whom, and for whom things will get done in the big picture. Each operating unit, like a public relations department, must have its own strategic operating plan to show what of the organizational plan the department will specifically support with defined objectives of its own. We will address strategic plans in more detail in Chapter 4. At this point, though, it is important to recognize how an organization's separate operating units work together for the greater good of the organization. It is equally important to recognize for our purposes that the PR operation supports—enables—the work of other operating units. In this way other operating units in an organization stand as internal clients to the PR department, and the department executive is responsible for ensuring that those clients' needs can be met successfully every time.

For example, if an organization has a research and development department, where great innovations are conceived, designed, and implemented into prototypes, top management and the public relations department may want to call attention to particular innovations. Such "calling attention" could involve developing a campaign that celebrates the specific advances and reflects important values that customers and other publics want and need to know. Another example would be benefits changes. The human resources department would work with the PR department to make the best communication effort possible among employees and, perhaps, retirees, who are usually considered "family" like employees because they worked there, care about, and feel connected with the company and are collecting a pension from the company.

Corporate public relations officials work with their organizations' top management and the management of operational areas, such as research and development, manufacturing, legal staff, human resources, finance and accounting, and marketing. Instrumental in these working relationships are the subject matter experts in operational areas that give credible, technical information and guidance about subjects being addressed in communication efforts. Much technical information, ranging from organizational performance to product specifications and beyond, is required for accurate, complete, and timely information that would be communicated in any manner with any public. For example, when an organization must disclose information about its financial performance, PR officials will involve not only the chief financial officer (CFO) but also others who work for the CFO, such as the treasurer and designated corporate accountants who assembled performance data for the required public reports. Another example would be organizations that are announcing a new product or a new innovation for an existing product. PR officials would work very closely with the lead product engineer and product-line manager plus particular experts on any components or systems as needed. The idea is to obtain the most accurate and complete information that can be communicated in the chosen media that will fulfill strategic objectives.

The reputation of the corporate PR operation and its staff must be impeccable. Competence in communication is primary for all PR professionals. Competence as a leader and manager is essential for the executive in charge of the public relations function. Having a strong reputation among all other operating units and top organizational management is an everyday responsibility for the PR executive and the PR staff. Ample research and profession-specific literature has documented the fundamental skills public relations professionals are expected to have, especially as times and technology change. (Chapter 11 covers these skill sets.) Generally speaking, those skills fall into the categories of writing, interpersonal communication, ethics, knowledge of the business, strategic thinking, project management, meticulous attention to detail while keeping an eye on the big picture, technical command of communication channels (traditional and electronic), measurement and evaluation (analytics), and taking initiative or being proactive. *Internal reputation*, then, is a function of doing good work, being good coworkers, and being good stewards of the organization's image, reputation, objectives, particular market offerings, and overall business.

From an outside perspective, a corporate public relations group can also have a strong reputation. In this way other organizations of any type in any industry would think of a particular company's PR operation as a standout example among all others. This kind of *external reputation* for a corporate PR function can be facilitated through the leader publishing articles, giving speeches or presentations about the profession, serving in professional organizations (e.g., Public Relations Society of America, International Association of Business Communicators, and Arthur W. Page Society), and other outlets. Winning prestigious awards, especially at a national or international level, can also enhance the reputation of a corporate public relations department. For example, State Farm Insurance won a 2011 Silver Anvil Award from the PRSA for a campaign it conceived, designed, and executed with its own public relations staff. The campaign was about safely deep-frying turkeys during Thanksgiving and featured actor William Shatner, who had burned himself a few years earlier while using his deep-fryer for a turkey.

One's successfulness in a corporate PR setting would be the basis for career advancement. Often career advancement for those working in corporate PR at any level typically is done through promotions to positions of higher authority, bigger challenges, and greater responsibility, but finding a better job elsewhere (corporate or agency) works well too. Public relations people tend to be among the most well-connected people in business, so leads about job openings can be shared easily and quickly by word-of-mouth, including text messages, e-mail, and social media. We will look into this area of career advancement in the last chapter of this book.

Agency Public Relations Operations

The "agency" arena of public relations includes only one type of organization: business firms of various sizes that provide any other organization with the specific expertise and resources to solve particular communication problems. The players in the agency arena operate on a full range of dimensions: one or a handful of people to hundreds of employees, local to global offices, and general to specialty foci. Agencies are in the business of serving other organizations, called "clients," so they have an active part of their operation in finding new clients as well as identifying new opportunities with existing clients. In this way organizations in the corporate arena of PR could be clients in the agency arena, and agencies sometimes serve other agencies when projects are large enough to warrant the extra outside help.

Because agencies seek business opportunities from other organizations, they are outside of those organizations and, consequently, are referred to under the terms of "outsourcing" or "out-of-house" or "outside" firms. Agencies can encompass as much or as little of the universe of public relations as they wish, and they may include other areas like advertising, marketing, and technical communication. Essentially all the core practice areas that could be employed in the corporate arena can be handled in the agency arena, and agencies can specialize in any one of them up to all of them. Supporting areas, such as graphic design, Internet and electronic communication, and measurement/evaluation can be included together with the core practice areas or handled individually as an agency's sole business.

Those agencies that focus on individual practice areas are called "boutique" agencies. For example, Reputation Partners Public Relations, located in Chicago, is exclusively focused on "enhancing, protecting and rebuilding corporate reputations" by being expert in subjects that pose much risk and benefit to organizations: corporate reputation management, issue and crisis management, labor communications, employee communications, corporate sustainability, and social media strategy (Reputation Partners, 2013). Other agencies may focus on specific kinds of businesses or industries. For example, Morgan & Myers, a prominent public relations firm near Milwaukee, has served clients primarily (but not exclusively) in the food industry, from farm cooperatives and manufacturers to retailers and industry trade groups.

Viewed as external experts, agencies possess and provide the essential and needed expertise that clients need. Any independent business or organization can be a potential client for an agency. In this way, too, individual consultants, who operate as sole practitioners, can also offer organizations the needed expertise, and consultants will have a network of other specialists, from graphic artists and printers to event planners and video production houses. Consultants can be brought in to help agencies or corporate PR clients, and we will address consultants more in Chapter 9.

The variety of clients an agency may serve requires a lot of flexibility and discipline. Because of the nature of its business, an agency serves many clients. Most important, an agency serves any client as if it is the only one the agency has, even though the client knows otherwise. (We will cover client-centered communication in Chapter 10.) After all, the client hired the agency because it demonstrated an appropriate and definitive track record of success, expertise, and resourcefulness that impressed the client more than other agencies. Any track record of success is testimony to an agency's ability to serve many clients on many projects and programs at once because the staff *knows* the clients' businesses very well—maybe even better than the clients. (How agencies build their businesses will be examined in Chapters 7 and 8.) Agency PR professionals serve multiple clients by working on multiple client teams, so mindful focus and disciplined work on each client's jobs is vital. Flexibility to shift to new demands for any one client at any one time is also vital. The best way to ensure that focus and progress are not lost on any client is to know yourself well and manage your own time and projects meticulously. That focus and work requires much reading, writing, discussions, and other work to provide clients with excellent public relations and excellent service on the accounts.

The starting point for any public relations work is deep knowledge about any client's strategic plan at the organizational level (the big picture for the client) and the operating level (the specific picture for designated parts of a client's business that is involved, beginning with PR). Interestingly, agency personnel are often viewed by their clients' executives as replaceable because, in the corporate realm, client organizations tend to have more loyalty to their in-house experts. Consequently, agency personnel must truly know the client's industry and not rely on the client for education about its industry. Additional deep knowledge about a client itself is also vital to know, such as its history (i.e., from its founding to the present plus its performance record, especially from the last five to ten years), target market(s) and market positioning, reputation and image, community involvement, awards, litigation, regulatory environment, certifications, and other dimensions. Knowledge about a client in these areas provides necessary background to explain how and why a client is the way it is today and what it wants to and can be in the future according to its strategic plan. Again, we will examine strategic plans in more detail in Chapter 4.

This deep client knowledge also is essential for agency professionals to possess and apply when working with clients' management. As we covered in the section about corporate public relations, there are potentially many levels of leaders in a client's organization that may be involved in a PR project or program, from top executives to operational leaders to subject matter experts. You would be working with people at various hierarchical levels with exceptional degrees of experience and knowledge, and interpersonal skillfulness and credibility in your work is essential. It is a matter of both professionalism and relationships. We will focus more on professionalism in the next chapter, client communication in Chapter 10, and social skills in Chapter 11. For now it is important to recognize that being *genuinely* respectful, honest, credible, and forthright with anyone makes up the basis for good client interactions that fuel your good work.

Because agencies live and die by the clients they serve and how well they serve those clients, reputation for good work hangs in the balance. That reputation spreads exclusively externally because of the nature of agency business. People talk about the good, the bad, and the ugly of agencies that have served them and others. Rumors about ineffective agencies can truly harm their businesses just like reputations about stellar agencies truly help build their businesses. Agencies with good reputations tend to attract better and more employees as well as better and more clients. So the quality of work and track record for success for any agency are the

PR Agency Arena's Breadth and Depth

- According to the University of Southern California Strategic Public Relations Center's Generally Accepted Practices (GAP) study:

  - Agency-of-record (AOR) relationships are vanishing. Over the last 10 years, the use by client organizations of a single outside PR agency of record has consistently decreased. In 2002, more than 50 percent of public corporations reported an AOR relationship. This number decreased continuously and has now shrunk to just over 15 percent for public companies. At the same time, the number of agencies used by corporations on an ongoing or project basis continues to increase. This is likely the result of a need for specialized and/or regionally focused agency services.

- According to the 2011 year-end survey of members conducted by the Council of Public Relations Firms, 70 percent of participating firms reported increased revenues in 2011 over the previous year, with nearly 50 percent reporting double-digit growth.

  - The Council projects 10 percent year-over-year industry growth.

  - Over one-third (35.5%) of firms anticipated higher budgets in 2012, up from only 21.8 percent in the Council Q3 2011 member survey, suggesting a recent uptick in client spending.

  - Hiring across PR firms is on the rise. The Council reports that more than 60 percent of participating firms reported increased headcounts at the end of 2011 as compared to 2010 totals.

    - Nine out of 10 firms anticipate increased hiring in 2012, with the most sought-after talent at the account executive to account supervisor levels.

    - One-third of all firms planned to increase the ranks of non-traditional hires coming from outside public relations.

  - Industry growth is expected across a diverse set of sectors:

    - Two-thirds of Council members expect growth in social media.

    - One-third anticipate growth in business-to-business, corporate communications and issues/reputation management.

- According to the 2011 International Communications Consultancy Organisation (ICCO) World Consultancy Report:

  - Public relations agencies reported double-digit revenue growth in 2010.

    - U.S. consultancies posted an average 11-percent increase in overall fee revenue.

    - U.K. consultancies saw a 13-percent increase.

  - The top-five challenges for public relations consultancies are: staffing; client budgets; profitability; pricing; and competition.

- According to mergers-and-acquisitions firm Stevens Gould Pincus, as reported by The Holmes Report:

  - The average monthly agency fee in 2010 was $8,385, down from $9,808 in 2009.

- Firms with revenues between $10 million and $25 million averaged fees of $12,222; firms with revenues more than $25 million averaged fees of $12,811.

- Revenue per professional staff was $205,941 in 2010, up from $197,714 in 2009.

- After sinking to a four-year low in 2009, profitability among U.S. public relations agencies rose to 15.6 percent of revenues in 2010—the same profit margins the industry enjoyed in 2008.

- Firms in excess of $10 million revenues averaged more than $230,000.

- Agency staff turnover for the year averaged 22.9 percent, slightly under the previous year.

- According to the U.S. Bureau of Labor Statistics:

  - To attract and maintain clients, public relations agencies are diversifying their services, offering advertising as well as public relations, sales, marketing and interactive media services.

SOURCE: Public Relations Society of America (2013)

biggest factors in the spreading of reputations. Similar to corporate PR operations, agencies can greatly enhance their reputations externally by their leaders publishing articles, books, or book chapters about matters that are key to their agencies' businesses. Those same leaders can also give important speeches, presentations, or seminars that educate, inspire, and challenge the state of the public relations business. While the agency leaders gain notoriety for themselves, they also bring great recognition to their agencies, which is a strong combination for building agency image and reputation.

As an agency's reputation improves and grows, it gets associated with its employees who have been integral in that success. Career advancement in agencies is typically achieved through promotions within the firm but also by finding opportunities for advancement with other firms. Sometimes clients will be so impressed with a member of an agency's team that it wants to hire that person full time for its public relations department. Note, however, the contractual agreement between an agency and a client may expressly forbid clients from actively seeking to hire ("poaching") agency employees. The reverse of this situation is different. An agency employee working on a client's account, however, may ask a client if it would be interested and willing to hire that agency employee. Overall, the extensive networks that public relations people have are instrumental in their getting leads about job openings. Again, we will look more into career advancement in the last chapter of this book.

What Job Descriptions Tell Us

Although it might not be obvious, job postings for management-level employees are a great place to find what organizations want in their leaders. More specifically, job postings for public relations leaders in the corporate and agency arenas specify particular qualities and professional backgrounds that are sought for executive-level positions. Many online resources are available to find such job postings. Plus there are many companies that specialize in searching for executives in particular industries—they go by terms like "executive search firms" or "headhunters." Remember, too, that word-of-mouth communication about open leadership (and other) positions can be especially valuable because the people passing the word along to you likely have the information before many other people do and may believe you are especially well suited for the job. (We will cover career paths in public relations in Chapter 11.)

Research about the public relations profession has defined two basic roles: technician and manager (Dozier, 1992). Simply put, the *technician* role focuses on the development of public relations material of many types for particular purposes, such as writing and campaign design. Technicians include interns, assistant account executives, account executives, senior account executives, communications coordinators, and supervisory and middle-management employees. The *manager* role, in contrast, focuses on matters including strategic planning, business development, resource allocations, and staff development. Managers are organizational leaders/executives with titles like director, executive director, assistant vice president, vice president, senior vice president, executive vice president, chief communication officer, principal, partner, or president.

It is very important to note that even though the word "executive" formally occurs in a low-level technician position (usually at agencies), it is not an actual executive-level position. Technicians are not necessarily required to possess leadership abilities, but they are expected to be excellent users of language in any medium, observant, creative, and very well organized. In other words, technicians are either traditional or exemplary followers. Notice, too, that the concept of manager subsumes what we have addressed in Chapter 1 about both concepts of leadership and management, and the role of manager assumes someone also is a highly competent technician who can do the job when required. In other words, the most effective managers are transformational leaders who are also emotionally competent, as we saw in Chapter 1. Of the two basic roles in public relations, we are primarily focused in this book on the manager role and leave matters pertaining to the technician role to sources about public relations writing and campaign design. In cursory reviews of a large number of U.S. job postings collected by my students in PR management courses, certain patterns emerged for PR leaders in corporate and agency arenas (Table 2-1).

Table 2-1. **SOME DOMINANT CHARACTERISTICS FOR CORPORATE VS. AGENCY TRUE-EXECUTIVE POSITIONS.**

CORPORATE/NONAGENCY	AGENCY
• *Master's degree preferred (especially MBA) but bachelor's degree acceptable*	• *Bachelor's degree*
• *7–15 years of experience (10 years and over is most common) and proven track record of success, especially in leadership and corporate strategy*	• *7–10 years of experience and proven track record of success, especially in leadership*
• *Superior writing and interpersonal communication skills*	• *Very strong public speaking and writing skills*
• *May ask for agency experience*	• *Focused on and highly skilled at pitching and bringing in new clients*
• *Previous managerial and supervising roles are desired*	• *Varied experiences in both agency and corporate PR desired*
• *Experience in the corporation's industry is needed*	• *Able to handle a high-stress workload*
• *Competent in all areas of public relations techniques, especially social media and measurement/evaluation*	• *Focused on teamwork and team building*
• *Relationships with established networks are essential*	• *Competent in all areas of public relations techniques, especially social media and measurement/evaluation*
• *Promote the organization, especially brand and image*	• *Able to think creatively and come up with sound ideas quickly and efficiently*
• *Experience with planning, budgeting, and human-resources matters*	• *Experience with planning, budgeting, forecasting, and personnel development*
• *Pay range: $80,000–$1,000,000* [1]	• *Pay range: $95,000–$300,000* [2]

[1] *Corporate career path (2007)*   [2] *Agency career path (2007)*

Any review of job openings for any position in public relations reveals a certain consistency across organizations and industries. The reason is that public relations is the common denominator for all job postings, and the variations from one job to the next will be based on how an organization operates, has operated, and plans to

EXECUTIVE VIEWPOINT

The Intersecting Worlds of Corporate and Agency PR

Cheryl I. Procter-Rogers, Senior Consultant, A Step Ahead PR Consulting and Coaching

When asked by public relations and marketing students whether they should pursue opportunities in an agency or a corporation, I respond with, "It depends." The truth is it doesn't matter if you work for a corporation, nonprofit, government office or agency. What does matter is that you find a place where you can hone the essential skills and acquire the management experience you need to be successful in any arena.

Early in my career I thought titles were really important until I began my public relations job search. It was a daunting experience then and it's even more so today. Now, there can be 100 or more titles describing the same function in corporations. Somehow though, the PR agency world has gotten it right and the titles are relatively consistent from agency to agency. My regional director title at HBO could be equivalent to a vice president title elsewhere or manager at yet another corporation. I stick with senior consultant with my consulting practice as it seems to be a title everyone gets. When a PR manager recruits and hires for an in-house department, it is critical to have an understanding of the misconceptions titles sometimes create. It is very important for a supervisor or manager in an agency to have these same insights as they build relationships with their client contacts.

My first PR job was in the public relations department of a national insurance company. There were three of us, a vice president, a secretary and me. What I gained in experience and knowledge in six short months could not be duplicated in a department of 30 or even in an agency.

When you work alone or with a small staff like we had, you do the writing, editing, photography, media pitching, production, social media, designing and the implementation of various programs. You also serve as an advisor to top management, all before lunch! After lunch, you train others on how best to represent the company, manage internal and external events and manage budgets.

When you manage a large staff, you spend more time in planning, managing the team and advising. The most successful managers in a corporation or agency are generalists and have either performed many of the functions they manage or have an intimate knowledge of the various roles. Also, knowing how and when to use research and how to interpret data are essential for both.

When I was excluded from important meetings or sidelined during business discussions at the insurance company, I quietly questioned why. Finally, I asked the president and learned that it was because they were talking about the *business*, which to them, had nothing to do with public relations. I quickly immersed myself in learning to read and understand financial statements and the business of insurance. This new vocabulary and understanding elevated me in the eyes of management and I'm confident, led to many promotions. Having an acumen for business has served me well in all corporate and consulting roles I've been in since then.

While working in both agency and corporate arenas, I found there are certain aspects of the two areas that are very different:

- **Demonstrate Value:** In-house, you are often given a longer time for producing results, which is quite the opposite in the agency world, where the clock is ticking as billable hours mount.

- **Day-to-Day:** In-house, you are part of the management team. You gain an intimate knowledge of the company because you are there to hear the gossip and give advice accordingly. You're there spotting possible PR opportunities and moving fast to head-off trouble. As a consultant, you are strictly in an advisory role and are often called upon for special projects. The agency performs alone or in tandem with in-house staff. The consultant can't duplicate the loyalty, understanding and attention provided by an effective in-house staff person.

- **Resources:** Depending on the size of the department, an outside agency can bring greater depth and experience to solve problems or take advantage of opportunities.

- **Objectivity:** For in-house teams, personal relationships can cloud judgment and make it harder to say no or challenge traditions. It's easy to get stuck. Agency consultants come to the relationship with fewer biases and are often more objective, bringing a fresh perspective.

Here are life lessons I pass on to you:

- Know how to read a balance sheet and income statement; understand the business of your employer or client. It will accelerate your opportunities to be included in important discussions.

- Build your business acumen through self-study or an additional degree.

- Challenge yourself by taking courses or studying topics outside your core area of communications and marketing.

- A different way to build credibility within an organization and expand your network is by working across the organization. Seek out opportunities to meet with executives in different departments. During these discussions, you may find projects where your expertise could be valuable. Here's a chance for you to stand out and step up!!!

- Trust is critical to your success. Having both people and communication skills can impact how quickly you are able to establish trust. Ineffective communications can result in misunderstandings that can lead to missed deadlines, projects that don't match with expectations and other issues. Those with great people and communication skills help influence their credibility as a leader, friend, spouse and parent.

Finally, just like individuals, agencies and corporations have personalities and preferences too. When considering a career opportunity, I encourage you to connect with your passion for our profession and seek environments that support your continued growth and development!

operate over time in its given industry and its target markets therein. For example, a global corporation that produces fiber-optic cable, a domestic company offering post-disaster clean-up services, a communications agency with several offices across the country, and a local faith-based nonprofit organization that helps the elderly would all need public relations leaders who are expert public relations technicians *and*, most important, experienced in matters of business that include (at least) strategy, performance management, budgeting and forecasting, personnel, communication law, and ethics. Individually, however, those same companies need leaders who have specialized knowledge, skills, and experience that suit their respective businesses. Someone with a great deal of local nonprofit PR background may not be suited for a leadership position at a multinational manufacturing company. But someone with much agency PR experience that included serving many clients successfully over the years in particular industries could make a move to a corporate PR department, especially if the person's experiences were in related industries. The opposite of that could be done as well, as a long-term corporate PR leader has a successful track record plus deep knowledge of an industry and its various players in the market.

Every public relations professional must know how public relations fits into the bigger picture of any organization's mix of activities devoted to promoting it and its offerings (e.g., marketing, advertising, direct mail, customer service)—including situations where an organization is using multiple agencies and has multiple programs underway. Such knowledge, based on a solid understanding of the similarities and differences between agency and nonagency PR operations, is valuable in doing ethical and legal work, developing sound strategic plans, managing the many resources needed for successful communications, making solid decisions while leading an engaged PR team, and building that team's reputation and track record. These topics are the next stops in this book, beginning with ethics and law.

Key Words

Corporate PR	In-house
Agency PR	Outsourcing
NGO	External reputation
Nonprofit/Institutional organization	Technician role
Core enabling competence	Manager role
Internal reputation	

Exploration of Public Relations Arenas

1. Using the job descriptions you found for Chapter 1, explore the individual companies behind those job postings. Examine the combination of the jobs and the firms to identify further similarities and differences between the two arenas of public relations practice and management.

2. Look in the online database of PRSA Silver Anvil Winners (http://www .prsa.org/Awards/Search) and find cases that were (a) handled only by corporate organizations and (b) handled by agencies with their clients. Try to discern from across all the cases the roles each party had in the campaigns so that you can get a feel for the work dynamic for a corporation and for client–agency combinations.

3. Summarize a leader/manager viewpoint about public relations as it is practiced in an agency and a nonagency organization. Why are there many more similarities than differences? How does this awareness help as one works in and with PR pros in either arena?

4. Research the areas of reputation and image, community involvement, awards, litigation, regulatory environment, and certifications to discover what they are and how important they can be to an agency or nonagency organization. How specifically could each area be important in a public relations effort for a real organization, and name an example of such an effort?

5. Choose any agency or nonagency organization that interests you, then follow the daily news for the next week or more. Document whether any specific news items could have any degree of impact on your chosen organization, how much of an impact, why that impact matters, and what could be done, if anything to prepare a public response.

References

Agency career path (2007, August 27). *Career guide 2007* (pp. 28–29). New York: PR Week/Haymarket Media.

Annenberg School for Journalism and Communication, Strategic Communication and Public Relations Center (2014). *GAP VIII: Eighth communication and public relations generally accepted practices study (Q4 2013 data)*. Los Angeles: University of Southern California Annenberg Center on Communication Leadership. Available online: http://ascjweb.org/gapstudy/

Bureau of Labor Statistics (2013). Public relations managers and specialists. In *Occupational outlook handbook*. Washington, DC: U.S. Department of Labor. Available online: http://www.bls.gov/ooh/Management/Public-relations-managers-and-specialists.htm.

Corporate career path (2007, August 27). *Career guide 2007* (pp. 30–31). New York: PR Week/Haymarket Media.

Dozier, D. M. (1992). The organizational roles of communications and public relations practitioners. In J. E. Grunig (Ed.), *Excellence in public relations and communication management* (pp. 327–355). Hillsdale, NJ: Lawrence Erlbaum Associates.

Jensen, B. (1995, August). Are we necessary? The case for dismantling corporate communication. *IABC Communication World*, 14–18, 30.

Public Relations Society of America (2013). *Industry facts and figures*. New York: Author. Available online: http://media.prsa.org/prsa+overview/industry+facts+figures/.

Reputation Partners Public Relations (2013). *About us: Trusted business partners*. Chicago: Author. Available online: http://www.reputationpartners.com/about/.

Wilcox, D. L., Cameron, G. T., Reber, B. H., & Shin, J-H. (2013). Today's practice: Departments and firms. In *Think public relations* (pp. 69–87). Boston: Pearson.

Willetts, P. (2012). What is a non-governmental organization? *UNESCO encyclopaedia of life support systems*. London: City University of London. Available online: http://www.staff.city.ac.uk/p.willetts/CS-NTWKS/NGO-ART.HTM.

Recommended Reading

Actis, R. G. (2006). *Management's last frontier: A communications system to focus and sustain a culture of achievement*. Boston: Pearson Custom Publishing.

Beard, M. (2001). *Running a public relations department* (2nd ed.). London: Kogan Page.

Dickinson, D. (2003). *The new account manager*. Chicago: The Copy Shop.

Inside the minds: The art of public relations: Industry visionaries reveal the secrets to successful public relations. (2001). Aspatore Books.

Maister, D. H. (1993). *Managing the professional service firm*. New York: Free Press.

Chapter 3

PROFESSIONALISM, ETHICS, AND LAW:
The Good Person Representing Organizations Well

Public relations has suffered from a "bad rap" for virtually all of its history, as we saw in Chapter 1. That bad rap is based on rather convenient arguments that cite limited and selected examples of unethical or unlawful public relations to say the entire profession is inherently evil. Because of this kind of card-stacking against public relations, misunderstandings about the profession and negative stereotypes prevail. Sadly, then, the unethical or unlawful behavior of one PR pro can adversely affect everyone as people can often find it easier to point out the bad because it is not supposed to happen, and good things are expected and, therefore, not noteworthy. Such a negative orientation is highly skewed and unreasonable. As we will see in this chapter, public relations operates in many of the gray areas of ethics and law, but clarity about ethics and the law with clients and our organizations not only mitigates any problems but also substantiates the overwhelming efficacy of the profession.

Professionalism

Thanks to the hard work of professionals and scholars the world over, public relations' image and reputation as a vital, ethical, and valuable organizational and social function has improved greatly (see Coombs & Holladay, 2007; Edwards & Hodges, 2011; L'Etang, 2004/2012; Taylor, 2010). Key to improving PR's image and reputation is professionalism. Professionalism in public relations is the sum of many components that at least include the following (Keane, 1974; Pieczka & L'Etang, 2001):

- *Body of knowledge and self-assessment*—A field-specific body of knowledge with unique theory presents and systemizes concepts, terminology, principles, and assumptions that, in turn, may be applied in rigorous methodologies to analyze and synthesize whole cases and particular phenomena of public relations so we can know how to evaluate the practice for what works and why, what is trending, and how is the profession evolving.
- *Ethics code and enforcement/integrity*—A definitive set of principles guides practitioners' decision-making and behavior within the field, including provisions for ensuring practitioners know, enact, and enforce the code of ethics so that the profession's integrity is sustained.
- *Specialized training/education*—A general approach to teaching and learning about public relations functions as a framework for a full range of education/ training content in dedicated resources (e.g., vocational reading, higher-education courses, conference seminars, individual workshops) offered through various, credible institutions and organizations focused on public relations.

- *Entry qualifications, performance standards, certification, and independence*—A basic set of expectations (largely documented and proffered by professional organizations) directs people to what is important to break into a public relations career, exercise great discipline in the discharge of their duties at all times, thrive and advance in one's career and the field, demonstrate and maintain competence, and exercise autonomy to apply one's expertise in PR to "do the right thing" without fear of reprisal or the distraction of second-guessing by others, especially management and clients.
- *Occupational interests and organizational support*—A consistent positive attitude toward the PR profession prevails within individual organizations and among other organizations that value public relations' contributions to business and society. That attitude is sparked by organizations dedicated to the advancement of the PR profession, such as the Public Relations Society of America (PRSA) and the International Association for Business Communicators (IABC).
- *Social legitimacy quest and legal recognition*—A strong record of useful and important contributions from the public relations field demonstrates a significant role in the social and civic factors of everyday life, particularly as practitioners work ethically to improve the status quo and adhere to legal and regulatory requirements.
- *Social responsibility*—A sensitivity to and sensibility about what matters in the public interest and the social consequences of particular actions enables practitioners to balance the needs of their organizations with the needs of the public on the full range of issues, from the mundane to the controversial.

Fundamentally, public relations requires a high degree of professionalism among all practitioners at any level, and this professionalism involves doing the right thing in the right way at the right time for the right people for the right reasons. Because of the evolution of the field of public relations, including all its practices, tools, methods, and principles, the profession also has evolved. Nevertheless, the components of professionalism for the public relations field serve as a good foundation on which to build our understanding of two vital matters: ethics and the law.

Ethics

In the public relations field, there are ample resources about ethics. From the PRSA's website and smart-phone application to individual books and journal articles, the knowledge base about public relations ethics is well established. Indeed, ethics is covered in public relations curricula at colleges and universities. So, the objective here is not to chronicle that enormous knowledge base but, rather, to explore ethics generally and make connections with public relations specifically, especially in terms of the management of PR.

Building up to ethics

Ethics derive from morals and values and not the other way around, as shown in Figure 3-1. That is, *values* are the origin of the hierarchy that builds up to ethics, comprising a shared, intersubjectively developed system of beliefs and mores that govern choices about good/bad, virtue/vice, desirable/undesirable, etc. Values make up the basis for judgment and action and can be applied by individuals and through group consensus. Values, then, are the foundation of a society and, thereby, the basis for morals. *Morals* are standards of personal behavior, obligations, or duties that are based on a hierarchy of values (religious and/or secular) of right and wrong. Morals benefit others, perhaps contrary to self-interest, and, in turn, are the locus of the development of ethical principles. *Ethics* are comprised of social rules, usually codified formally for everyone in a community, and govern individual and group character, conduct, and consequences. The relationships among values, morals, and ethics can be traced among them within the context of a culture (see Boehm, 2012). In terms of professionalism, at an elementary level, values, morals, and ethics together concern what a situation is, how it relates to other situations, and what ought to be done and why—all these matters are germane to public relations.

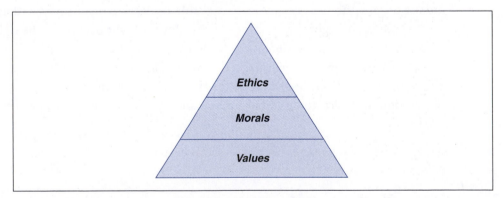

Figure 3-1. HIERARCHY BUILDING TOWARD ETHICS.
SOURCE: Smudde (2011)

Ethics orientations and reasoning

Two great areas of ethics philosophy concern universal and situational ethics, and these two areas often clash in the practice of public relations. The reason for the clash is that people often rely on experience and rules to guide present and future actions, and the orientation about applying experience and rules in matters of judgment and action can differ enough to cause problems in ethical decision-making. For the first ethics area, *universal ethics* involves the study and application of specific ethical principles to all relevant cases equally. The principle of universality is at play here: "if one judges that X is right or good, then one is committed to judging that anything exactly like X, or like X in relevant respects, is right or good" (Frankena, 1973, p. 25). In public relations, for example, a universal principle of ethics is truth-telling, which means the truth must be told every time, including times where there is insufficient information to share.

For the second ethics area, *situational ethics* involves the study and application of ethics principles on a case-by-case basis. This area of ethics is also referred to as *ethical relativism* or *relativism*. Frankena (1973, p. 109) explains three kinds of relativism, one of which is most applicable to public relations:

- *Descriptive relativism* concerns that "the basic ethical beliefs of different people and societies are different and even conflicting."
- *Meta-ethical relativism* concerns that "there is no objectively valid, rational way of justifying one [ethical judgment] against another; consequently, two conflicting basic judgments may be equally valid."
- *Normative relativism* concerns that "what is right or good for one individual or society is not right or good for another, even if the situations involved are similar, meaning not merely that what is thought right or good by one is not thought right or good by another (this is just descriptive relativism over again), but that what is really right or good in the one case is not so in another."

It is important to recognize that, for each of these three kinds of relativism, neither of the other kinds serves as the basis for the other. Of the three kinds, normative relativism is most germane to public relations practice because it can account for professionals' ethical decision-making. For example, the whole truth about an organization's newly launched product would be shared in media relations efforts, but selected truthful matters about the same organization's role in a controversy may be shared through similar media relations to protect corporate interests that may be relevant in a lawsuit to be heard in a court of law. Relativism of any kind, then, is dangerous because it allows for multiple degrees of variation in ethical thinking, calling into question what truly is ethical. If anything in any situation can be rationalized as ethical, ethics is meaningless.

Helping us to make the best ethical decisions are other particular areas of ethics philosophy. Curtin and Boynton (2001) provide us with one of the most usable treatments of ethics philosophy for decision-making in public relations, because they explain "the philosophical principles underlying ethics and relate them to models of public relations practice to demonstrate how form and function mutually inform public relations ethics" (p. 411). Table 3-1 (the first of three tables derived from Curtin and Boynton's work) summarizes specific ethics orientations/ theories, the types of reasoning that are instrumental in each, and the pros and cons to them. In this first table, the fundamental philosophical and intellectual foundations to ethical reasoning in any field are presented in the lefthand column and are essential to the rest of their examination of public relations ethics in the successive, remaining columns. (Note that the orientation of axiology in this table is an addition to Curtin and Boynton's original material, and axiology [i.e., the study or philosophy of values] is included in the subsequent tables to similarly extend Curtain and Boynton's treatment of ethics.)

Ultimately, effective decision-making that results in fair and just action are the concerns for ethics—that public relations leaders (and their staffs) know how to

Table 3-1. **ETHICS ORIENTATIONS AND REASONING.**

ORIENTATION	TYPES OF REASONING	PROBLEMS/CRITICISMS
Teleology — *"emphasizes outcomes; the ends justify the means. Ethical actions are those that result in the greatest good."*	Restricted teleology — *calculates consequences for a particular group or person.*	*Calculations are subjective at best and often unreliable (e.g., value of human life), so such a pseudo-mathematical approach oversimplifies the intellectual rigor necessary to make sound decisions.*
	Utilitarianism — *stresses consequences to society as a whole; seeks the greatest good for the greatest number.*	*Knowing any consequences in advance is inherently difficult (see restricted teleology), and looking at short-term consequences can often be short-sighted.*

Deontology — *"good consequences are not in and of themselves sufficient to guarantee good actions; some acts must be done regardless of their consequences."*	Rule deontology — *follow rules when making ethical decisions (e.g., the Golden Rule, the Ten Commandments, Kant's categorical imperative, professional codes of conduct).*	*Sometimes correct actions have disastrous consequences.*
	Act deontology — *weigh both acts and consequences to determine ethical action; rely on rigorous applications of concepts like duty, justice, rights, etc. (e.g., distributive justice)*	*Inherently difficult to apply and results can often degenerate into ethical relativism, where every situation is approached individually (perhaps to rationalize inappropriate behavior) and no consistent guidelines are applied from case to case.*
Axiology — *values and virtues form the basis for good action.*	Aristotle's Golden Mean — *determine the most appropriate middle ground (i.e., virtue) between two extremes (i.e., vices) within a given context.*	*Can be reduced to mere mathematical "average" between two extremes, which grossly oversimplifies the rigor required.*
	Egoism — *engage in enlightened self-interest so that what one does is good for others as well as good for oneself.*	*The basic motive for action may be purely selfish and masked by a justification for the action's goodness for others.*
	Ethical advocacy — *harness the power of persuasion for ethical ends, provided that the persuasion conforms to criteria for evaluation, priority, sensitivity, confidentiality, veracity, reversibility, validity, visibility, respect, and consent (Gower, 2008).*	*People can still use persuasion intentionally or unintentionally in unethical ways (e.g., logical fallacies or fabricated facts) or for unethical reasons or impure motives.*

make the right choices to do the right things at the right times for the right people and for the right reasons. The series of three tables (Table 3-1 through Table 3-3), then, present a usable way to account for the details of ethical decision-making and action, which you have encountered in your studies of PR.

Table 3-2 summarizes Curtin and Boynton's explanations about the levels, stages, principles, and reasoning in ethical decision-making that mesh with Grunig and Hunt's (1984) models of public relations that we covered in Chapter 1. In this table, we achieve a finer level of detail in ethical decision-making in PR that begins with a kind of attitude about ethics (i.e., "level"; from basic to advanced) and proceeds rather systematically through certain numbered stages of thinking that square with one's level of ethical thinking. Depending on one's stage of ethical thinking, particular principles that rely on a dominant form of reasoning reflect the demands of a specific PR model.

Table 3-3 summarizes Curtin and Boynton's explanations about the biggest picture of ethical decision-making by blending type of (i.e., school of thought about) PR ethics, what it means for PR practice, the kind of reasoning that is involved, the stage of ethical decision making anchored in Table 3-2, and the problems with each orientation shown by row. In this table, which adds the type of "communitarianism" to Curtin and Boynton's work, we can trace in even greater detail how a given school of ethical decision-making applies precisely in public relations as governed by certain kinds of reasoning through certain stages of ethical thinking. Notable, too, in the table is the problematic concerns of the whole scheme to each type/school of ethical decision-making.

A particularly useful tool for ethical decision-making is a code of ethics, which falls into the category of rule deontological ethics. The material in Tables 3-1 through 3-3 is essential to understand because it is the foundation of ethics codes. Ethics codes have their origin in, as Figure 3-1 shows, particular values and, then, make associations with related actions. There are many examples of ethics codes, including international codes (e.g., United Nations Declaration on the Rights of Indigenous Peoples), societal codes (e.g., the Ten Commandments), professional codes (e.g., PRSA's Code of Ethics), organizational codes (e.g., statements of values and ethics in employee handbooks), and personal beliefs every person holds. Like anything, codes of ethics have advantages and disadvantages, and Table 3-4 lays out some of them.

Being mindful of the advantages and disadvantages helps practitioners at all levels understand the benefits and limitations of having a documented set of standards for expected behaviors. Perhaps most important to understanding the importance of ethics codes is the complementary roles they play. As Brinkmann (2002) explains, all ethics codes are values-based, written standards meant to guide

Table 3-2. ETHICAL DECISION-MAKING STAGES AND PR MODELS.

LEVEL	STAGE	PRINCIPLES	REASONING	PR MODEL
Preconventional (focus on self-interest)	*1. Fear of reprisal from superiors*	*Personal goals; situation consequences; emotional reactions*	*Restricted teleological focus on outcomes*	*Propaganda; press agentry*
	2. Exploit situations for personal gain	*Manipulation & deception; short-term rewards sought*		
Conventional (conformity to commonly accepted expectations & standards)	*3. Promote group interests*	*Place goals of & benefits to group above all else*	*• Teleological focus on benefits of actions to group • Axiological focus on values*	*Public information (journalist-in-residence); two-way asymmetrical*
	4. Obey letter of the law	*Reliance on written codes as legitimate authority*	*Rule deontological focus on group-held principles for behavior*	
Postconventional (personal autonomy & critical reflection)	*5. Social concern*	*Societal consequences outweigh client benefits*	*Utilitarianism*	*Two-way symmetrical*
	6. Situational ethics	*Societal benefits based on universal principles of equality, justice, fairness, etc.*	*Act deontology (categorical imperative)*	

Table 3-3. PR ETHICS MODELS AND DECISION-MAKING PARTICULARS.

TYPE	DEFINITION FOR PR PRACTICE	REASONING	STAGE	PROBLEMS
Coorientation	achieve convergence between organization & publics; journalistic standards prevail (media relations)	teleological	3	journalistic norms condemn PR as inherently unethical
Advocacy (social responsibility & persuasion)	advocate position of organizations persuasively; ideas compete in free market of ideas (democratic); guard against deliberate deception, etc.; be organization's conscience	teleological	3, 4	ends not necessarily in best interest of all but of organization; conflicts of ethical interests among person, organization, publics, society; potentially more powerful voice from those who can afford PR
Professionalism	ethics codes, accreditation, licensing; influence of professional associations	• rule deontology • axiology	4	unenforceable & vague codes; accreditation is not necessary & sufficient; cultural differences undermine universality of codes; promotes image of professionalism
Game Theory	decision making calculations of situations' dimensions and probable outcomes; cost-benefit analysis; subjective assigning numerical values; "what if" analyses of all players	teleological	2, 3, 5	Nearly impossible to know outcomes in advance; values are arbitrary; unethical behavior may be allowed; focused on client primarily; possible reduction to gamesmanship
Corporate Responsibility	organization doing good (corporate philanthropy, corporate citizenship) helps bottom line—cost-benefit analysis	restrictive teleology (enlightened self-interest)	3	relies on self-regulation; motivation not always clear; difficult to

Corporate Responsibility (continued)	follow principles that publics are stakeholders & treated as ends in themselves—obligations to rights of internal & external publics plus balance interests between them (issue management)	act deontology (social contract theory)	6	achieve without more organizational power for PR
Structural-Functional Approach	division between technicians (advocates) and PR managers (advisers); strategic goal achievement (systems theory)	rule deontological (RD); teleological (T), if incomplete codes	3, 4	technician = advocate implies organizational loyalty & ethical conflicts (RD→T); managers allowed more autonomy with higher status & ethical leeway/freedom (T→RD)
Accommodation/ Discursive Approach (Habermas)	emphasizes relational aspects (technical, partisan & mutual values); process of communication = place of ethics; ensure possibility of & enactment through collaborative decision-making; unethical clients not like/engage in process	utilitarianism	3, 5	why use rules when persuasive communication solves; systematic approach goes back to S/F approach; ethics is privileged to powerful pros
Contingency Theory	weigh internal & external factors to determine best PR practice; employ four-step framework	act deontology (situational ethics)	6	difficult to apply consistently; danger of reduction to ethical relativism; rationalize inappropriate behavior
Communitarianism	places great emphasis on an organization's responsibilities to society/ communities of operation	utilitarianism (greatest good for the community is good for organization)	5	relies on relativistic thinking; can put an organization into a dilemma when good is contrary or irrelevant to an organization's mission, values, etc.

Table 3-4. ETHICS CODES: PROS AND CONS.

ADVANTAGES	DISADVANTAGES
• *To increase public confidence* • *To avoid increased government regulation (indeed, many codes were developed for this reason)* • *To improve internal operations/ standardize behavior* • *To respond to transgressions*	• *Having a code doesn't necessarily translate into credibility.* • *Codes are written by those who are most likely to follow them.* • *Codes can be written as broadly or as narrowly as members desire.* • *If voluntary, not everyone has to belong to the professional organization.* • *Not all codes are enforceable.* • *Unless meaningful dialogue takes place, the "code" becomes an empty god term.*

SOURCE: Courtright (1996)

practice in a profession or industry. Ethics codes, he argues, are established to mitigate moral conflict, establish professional standards, ensure professional morality, and promote a moral climate in which work is performed. Additionally ethics codes are mostly voluntary while some are involuntary. For example, to be a member of professional organizations, including the PRSA and the IABC, one may be required to sign a pledge to uphold the organization's ethics code, which includes upholding that code in one's own work plus making sure others uphold the code too. In this way a member would behave unethically if she or he did not report another member (or perhaps a member of the profession but not the professional organization's member) who acted in a way that breaks the ethics code or pertinent laws.

All the philosophical and theoretical foundations for ethics are essential for people to both think and act ethically. The ethics principles covered thus far would be fruitless if there were no ways to enact them to make sound ethical decisions.

Resolving ethical dilemmas

Arguably, everything someone does has an ethical dimension. In the field of public relations, anything done to inspire cooperation between an organization and its publics is inherently and unequivocally wrapped in ethics issues. This idea means that ethics is ever-present and, therefore, paramount every step of the way, from the conception of a PR effort through its execution and measurement (e.g., Smudde, 2005). When ethical dilemmas of any magnitude arise, they require appropriate levels of rigor in resolving them. The question is this: What approach can be used to resolve ethical dilemmas, especially in the workplace?

Among the various methods and models for ethical decision-making available, the PRSA prescribes its *Ethical Decision-Making Guide* (Fitzpatrick, n.d.) as a tool for day-to-day application. The process covers six sequential steps:

1. "define the specific ethical issue and/or conflict"
2. "identify internal and external factors that may influence the decision"
3. "identify key values" from the PRSA Code of Ethics (i.e., advocacy, honesty, expertise, independence, loyalty, and fairness)
4. "identify the parties who will be affected by the decision and define the public relations professional's obligation to each"
5. "select ethical principles [from the PRSA Code of Ethics] to guide the decision-making process"
6. "make a decision and justify it"

Important matters to include after this process are monitoring results so you know how well your decision worked and why and retaining information about the whole case so that it may be used at some future point, if necessary. The six steps in the *Ethical Decision-Making Guide* can be visualized in Figure 3-2, which is known as the

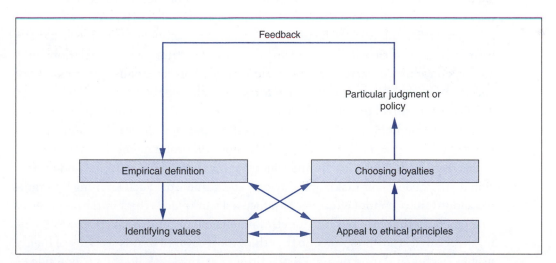

Figure 3-2. THE POTTER BOX.

SOURCE: Christians et al. (2001, p. 6)

"Potter Box," named after Dr. Ralph Potter of Harvard Divinity School, who created it as a model for ethical decision-making. The most notable difference between the two is that the *Guide* adds a step between the boxes about values and ethical princi-ples to identify affected parties and the obligation a PR pro has to each.

At the message level, Baker and Martinson's (2001) TARES test is another useful rule-deontological approach that can help immensely to ensure that any given public relations discourse avoids unethical and unlawful problems. The test, as Gower (2008) presents it, is as follows:

- *Truthfulness of the message.* Does the communication provide the audience with sufficient information to make an informed decision on the issue?
- *Authenticity of the persuader.* What is the communicator's motive? Will some-one other than the communicator benefit from the message?
- *Respect for the persuadee.* Does the message treat the public with respect and as human beings?
- *Equity of the appeal.* Does the communication take advantage of a public's vulnerability?
- *Social responsibility for the common good.* Does the message serve the larger public good?

Because of its particular focus on messages, the TARES test is especially useful during the entire process for developing public relations discourse—from concep-tion to writing to reviews/approvals to editing/revising to final publication. TARES, then, gives practitioners a way to test the very content of their work as they develop it so that it balances ethics issues for both an organization and its publics. Between a code of ethics and the TARES test, there is a strong complementarity because the former helps practitioners account for the bigger picture of public relations as a social good while the latter helps practitioners focus on the smaller pictures of very specific public relations discourse that are part of the big picture.

Ethics is central to public relations. Those who lead and manage a public rela-tions operation hold the key to enabling staff to perform ethically in all respects. More specifically, as Lee and Cheng (2011) show, PR professionals learn best about ethics from leaders who live by and educate their staffs about personal and profes-sional ethical decision-making, behaviors, and standards. Such learning by exam-ple about ethics is more effective than focused workplace ethics initiatives (Lee & Cheng, 2012) that lack rewards for ethical behavior and focus on merely complet-ing structured study programs. So the ethics tools covered in this section are highly usable, useful, and used by any PR practitioner at any level. If ethics is one side of the coin of professionalism, law would be the other side. The two disciplines are essential for practitioners to know and use.

Law

The counterpart of ethics is the law. The two disciplines are interrelated. Successful PR managers are effective decision-makers on ethical and legal issues. Public relations managers are, then, instrumental in making sure ethical and legal matters are systematically and properly addressed throughout the PR function, especially so PR technicians enact those principles well in public relations material. The most successful public relations professionals are those who proactively forge relationships with legal counsel sooner rather than later, during an emergency situation. So before we examine particular matters of the law that pertain to public relations management, we must briefly explore the relationship between law and ethics.

Building a system of laws

Generally speaking, laws "are the principles that structure the relationships between government and the governed and among the people within a society" (Parkinson & Parkinson, 2006, p. 2). Given how societies evolve, and without going into great detail because of space limitations, at some point a system to manage everyone's individual and shared interests will be needed, resulting in a governing structure for a society. That governing structure includes a system for encoding various sanctions on behavior (i.e., laws), resolving disputes that arise among people and groups in a community, and imposing consequences on those who break any law. Because people in a community have come together for a variety of reasons, perhaps most important being matters of mutual interests and benefits to living and working together in one society, the common ground of values and morals evolve into principles of ethics and, ultimately, a system of laws. So extending the scheme and analysis for Figure 3-1, law derives from ethics, which is shown in Figure 3-3.

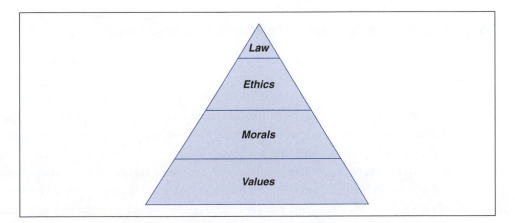

Figure 3-3. HIERARCHY BUILDING TOWARD LAW.

This hierarchy only demonstrates how, similar to the construction of buildings, one element must necessarily be built upon another that is strong and robust enough to support the elements to come thereafter. This construction, then, is why values are the foundation for a community on which to further refine particular principles that guide individual and group actions and decision-making through increasing and necessary levels of complexity. Law is at the top of the hierarchy not because it is best (no element is better than another), but because law is the necessary capstone to the effective functioning of a community that has already encoded and enacted so much of the common ground its people share through supporting structures of ethics, morals, and, most important, values. As elements of the hierarchy may undergo change when communities evolve, the structures above (and perhaps below) them may require commensurate change, similar to the renovation of an old house so that it can be more structurally sound, better to live in, and longer lasting.

With this perspective on the big picture of law, we can begin exploring selected topics that are important for public relations managers as they lead PR operations. Admittedly, the preceding perspective on how laws emerge and sustain communities is simplistic, but it is useful for our purposes. Plus there are ample resources that cover the great depth and breadth of knowledge about the law that cannot be covered in this volume. Indeed, public relations leaders ought to have and use at least one volume that addresses the law and public relations (e.g., Carter, Franklin, & Wright, 1993; Gower, 2008, 2012; Moore, Maye, & Collins, 2008; Parkinson & Parkinson, 2006, 2008). Nevertheless, within the context of managing a public relations operation, this section summarizes the matters of cooperation between PR and legal staffs, the First Amendment to the U.S. Constitution, particular areas of law relevant to public relations practice, and federal regulatory bodies whose jurisdictions affect public relations.

Cooperation between public relations and legal staffs

When they are working together on the same side, lawyers and public relations professionals share the same interest in an organization's well-being and stakeholders' effects. So neither professional wants an organization to be subject to legal scrutiny or have to go to court. Beyond this common ground, there are important differences. Lawyers and public relations professionals can come at a problem from different perspectives, as Table 3-5 shows. Lawyers have as their ultimate venue of concern courts of law, where disputes are contested and decided according to applicable laws. Public relations professionals are ultimately concerned about the court of public opinion, where any matter can be contested at any time by any means and according to any argumentative purpose. Again, PR managers are instrumental in

Table 3-5. LAWYER–PR DIFFERENCES.

	MAIN VENUE	APPROACH
LAWYERS	*Court of law*	*Say, "No comment"*
PR PROS	*Court of public opinion*	*Say something reasonable*

good ethical and legal decision-making, especially with the sound counsel of attorneys and the critical-analytical skills of PR technicians.

Because of the dynamics and demands of each venue, lawyers and PR pros have different approaches to handling incidents publicly. Lawyers are concerned that whatever may be said by company officials could and would be used against them in a court of law. With the proliferation of social media and portable video technology, misstatements can cast a long, dark shadow over an organization in many ways, from a given situation or case to corporate image and reputation. Saying "No comment" is often assumed to be (rightly or wrongly) a sign that something bigger is going on, and it is a matter of time until we all find out. Public relations professionals are sensitive to the need to not say something inappropriate but also are sensitive to publics' need for some kind of statement, even if it is to say that nothing can be said at the time because of certain restrictions (and state them), but more information will be forthcoming as circumstances allow. In this way both legal and ethical matters are upheld for everyone concerned.

At this point it is important to recognize that many lawyers are amenable to public relations pressures and cognizant of the risks of not commenting and of commenting. Indeed, lawyers are naturally very interested in cooperating with public relations and all other operational areas of an organization. Generally speaking, lawyers provide great value to public relations because of their specialized perspective on communication in the corporate and social spheres. In this way the cooperation that lawyers seek with public relations professionals can be built in a few simple and potent ways.

- *Understand the law*—Have a basic knowledge of what lawyers do and, most especially, the kinds of laws and legal matters that are relevant to public relations efforts of any scope. Such knowledge can serve you well while you plan actions, develop material, and share discourse with stakeholders.
- *Critically analyze situations*—Thoroughly examine any situation for both its upside and its downside on the company, primarily, and its stakeholders, secondarily. Such analysis would reveal the range of salient matters about

the impacts of a situation on stakeholders and knowing when to seek counsel from a legal professional.

- *Explain objectives, strategies, and tactics*—Know what precisely you want from a situation on public relations grounds (i.e., affects on awareness, attitude, action), how you are going to do it, and what specific actions you will take. Such an explanation would present the complete picture of what is sought for and from stakeholders through an organized public relations effort of any scope.

Instrumental in this cooperation between lawyers and public relations professionals is dialog about these matters at the outset of any public relations work. So involve lawyers early and throughout any PR effort to make sure an organization follows the law and upholds ethics principles. Lawyers are argumentative by nature and profession, and your ability to present your case matters because you need to reach a decision about what would work best, take action on that decision, and evaluate how well the action fulfilled expectations. In situations that have progressed to the level of legal action in a court of law, a public relations professional's counsel is very important so that stakeholders are informed to the extent that is allowed by legal strategy for defense and, if applicable, restrictions given by the court or stated in an applicable law.

First Amendment

The keystone to public relations practice is the First Amendment of the U.S. Constitution. It presents five specific freedoms (numbered in the text below) that are also general in their individual scopes:

> Congress shall make no law respecting [1] the establishment of religion, or prohibiting the free exercise thereof; or abridging the freedom of [2] speech, or of [3] the press, or [4] the right of the people peaceably to assemble, and [5] to petition the Government for a redress of grievances.

The focus of the first amendment is protecting individuals from government while expressing their opinions publicly (see Zompetti, Moore, Smudde, & Hunt, 2013). Matters about protections for individuals from organizations or protections for organizations from government are contested matters. Indeed, the question about whether and how much organizations have freedom of speech is primary. The answer is yes and no.

Organizations may or may not have protections for free speech, depending on who the target public is, what a message's intent is, and how courts have ruled in related cases. In instances when there is imminent danger to people or property, there must be reason or "just cause" to forbid certain kinds of speech, such as threats and phony calls for help. Very generally, courts have ruled that organizations can speak on their own behalves and be protected under the First Amendment, if and only if the content of their speech can be protected regardless of speaker. So the issue of free speech for organizations is not that they are protected like individual citizens, but rather that as long as what an organization says can be protected under the First Amendment, it must be protected. Indeed, decisions about freedom of speech for organizations are made through the judicial process and are the substance of case law, which includes decisions made in courts of law on individual cases, and we will address this topic shortly. The central factor in such decisions is whether an organization has engaged in political speech or commercial speech, each of which has different levels of protection.

Not all speech is equal, and under the First Amendment, different degrees of protection are afforded to different kinds of speech. Figure 3-4 illustrates the degrees of speech protection. *Political speech* is the most protected because, after all, political speech was instrumental in the founding of the United States of America as the original 13 colonies sought separation from Great Britain and fought a revolution for it. Political speech concerns all matters and manners of commentary about our government and issues of the day in any respect as part of the normal course of democracy. *Artistic speech* concerns the creative expression of ideas using language and symbols for aesthetic purposes, such as creative work done in literature, fine arts, performing arts, and so on, and it can include graffiti and street performances too. *Commercial speech* concerns the use of language and symbols for the purpose of inspiring economic transactions in the marketplace, and examples include advertisements, direct marketing, public relations, online content, and others. In case law, commercial speech is usually considered the least protected form of speech, with clear Supreme Court guidance on justifying governmental regulation and control through the "commercial speech doctrine" from the *Central Hudson Gas* case and the ruling on the *Citizens United* case (see Table 3-6).

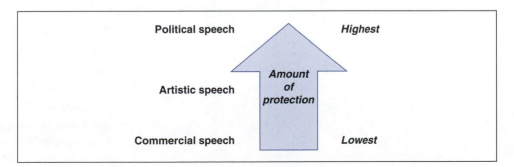

Figure 3-4. DEGREE OF SPEECH PROTECTION UNDER THE FIRST AMENDMENT.

Table 3-6. **SELECTED FREE-SPEECH CASES BEARING ON PUBLIC RELATIONS.**

CASE NAME AND YEAR	CENTRAL ISSUE	DECISION	IMPACT ON PR
Virginia State Board of Pharmacists v. Virginia Consumer Council (1976)	*It was illegal in Virginia for pharmacies to advertise prices for prescription drugs, which was under the purview of the VCC for oversight and enforcement.*	*The court ruled that there cannot be limits on pharmacies' right to provide the public with information about prescriptions, including pricing.*	*Allows for broader range of topics that facilitate marketplace transactions on regulated products, in this case prescription drugs.*
First National Bank of Boston v. Belloti (1978)	*Paid-for, corporate speech affects voting outcome, which FNBB engaged in when it campaigned for a particular ballot measure that was in the company's and its industry's best interests.*	*The court ruled that contributions are permissible for the political process and campaigns in the voters' interests, as long as there is no requirement for employees/members to vote a particular way.*	*Broadens opportunities for organizations, particularly for-profit companies, to assert their positions on ballot measures, candidates, etc.*
Central Hudson Gas & Electric v. Public Service Commission of New York (1980)	*The original law banned electricity utilities' advertising, which CHG&E engaged in when it advertised energy conservation tips.*	*The court ruled that advertising that promotes services for power conservation must not be limited because the issue has greater relevance in the public interest.*	*The decision presents a four-part test for First Amendment violations of government regulations on commercial speech:* *1. Is the expression protected? It must be lawful and not misleading.* *2. Is the asserted government interest substantial?*

			3. *Does the regulation advance the government interest asserted?* 4. *Is the regulation more extensive than necessary to serve government interest?*
Kasky v. Nike (2003)	*There are limits on corporate communication about corporate social responsibility policies, initiatives, and performance, and Nike was accused of false statements about its use of substandard labor practices in the manufacturing of its athletic shoes.*	*The case was settled out of court without a ruling, and Nike agreed to make a $1.5 million contribution to the Fair Labor Association. The U.S. Supreme Court avoided hearing the case on appeal.*	*Without a court decision, the case provides little guidance about commercial speech freedoms, but it does suggest avenues for legal risk organizations should guard against.*
Citizens United v. Federal Elections Commission (2008)	*The case concerned two precedents in campaign finance law and the regulation of paid-for speech by organizations, especially nonprofit, advocacy organizations and labor unions. Citizens United argued that it had the right to air a documentary film about Hillary Rodham Clinton and to air advertisements about the film during the presidential primary season.*	*The Supreme Court ruled in a 5 to 4 decision that Citizens United engaged in political speech that was protected, and there could be no prohibitions or restrictions on organizations' independent expenditures supporting candidates for office.*	*The Supreme Court's ruling gives the strongest First Amendment protection of corporate speech about public issues. Nevertheless, communication professionals, especially those involved in political activities about issues or candidates, must know well federal and state regulations on campaign contributions.*

Of the three kinds of speech, public relations (and advertising and related speech fields) falls largely into the category of commercial speech but can cross over into political speech. Public relations discourse may concern matters of products and services, and it may address matters of social and political issues. Courts have been reluctant to limit corporate political speech; however, limitations have been placed on "buying" candidates (e.g., support and/or votes on certain regulatory matters) and protections of shareholders from "compelled" speech that requires or forces adherence to and advancement of a particular thesis (e.g., to "tow the line" on an organization's stance regardless of one's own view). Historically, courts treated commercial speech as "unprotected" by the First Amendment, although limited protection has been afforded in recent case law. Guidance on free speech protections relies on case law, especially "tests" developed in court rulings. As a result, commercial speech is (at most) a gray area of speech protection because of the varying factors of audience, purpose, and especially decisions in cases tried and decided in courts of law.

Table 3-6 presents a summary of selected cases on political and commercial speech that matter to public relations. It must be noted that there are many cases that concern legal dimensions for public relations, and the cases here represent a small but solid sample of the lot of case law applicable to PR. Any volume on public relations law can serve to add detail to these selected cases and present information about other cases. What is important about the selected cases in Table 3-6 is that they provide a useful overview of the guidance about and "tests" for free speech protection that affect public relations practice. Additionally, matters of commercial speech are regulated by particular agencies of the federal government, most prominently the Federal Trade Commission. Table 3-7 lists federal agencies that have

Table 3-7. PARTICULAR FEDERAL REGULATORY STRUCTURES RELEVANT TO PUBLIC RELATIONS.

AGENCY	SUMMARY
Securities and Exchange Commission (SEC)	• *Established in 1934 to protect investors and ensure that securities markets are fair and honest. Monitors financial affairs of publicly traded companies. Seeks to prohibit fraud, market manipulation, and insider trading.* • *Core principle is that investors should be able to make decisions based on timely and accurate information.* • *Key concepts are* materiality *(i.e., information that would lead a "prudent person" to make an investment decision) and* disclosure *(i.e., material information must be broadly disseminated as soon as it is known).*

	• *Sarbanes-Oxley Act requires tracking and control of internal and external financial reporting accuracy, including compliance among corporate leaders.*
Federal Trade Commission (FTC)	• *Created in 1914 to prevent unfair methods of competition in commerce as part of the battle to "bust the trusts."* • *Especially involved in overseeing/enforcing truth in advertising.* • *Only federal agency with both consumer protection and competition jurisdiction in broad sectors of the economy.*
Federal Communication Commission (FCC)	• *Regulates interstate and international communications by radio, television, wire, satellite, cable, phone, and Internet in all 50 states, the District of Columbia and U.S. territories.* • *Established by the Communications Act of 1934 and operates as an independent U.S. government agency overseen by Congress.* • *Committed to being a responsive, efficient and effective agency capable of facing the technological and economic opportunities of the new millennium.*
Food and Drug Administration (FDA)	• *Purpose is "to protect, promote and enhance the health of the American people."* • *For commercial speech, primary concern is advertisements for food system and pharmaceuticals, including direct-to-consumer ads and video news releases.*
Freedom of Information Act (FOIA)	• *Guarantees individuals access to government records.* • *Media can also make FOIA requests.* • *Ongoing challenge for government public information officers.* • *Can also be a problem for government contractors.*
Foreign Agents Registration Act (FARA)	• *Individuals who represent foreign governments must register and report to the State Department.*
Federal Election Commission (FEC)	• *Federal law prohibits the use of corporate resources to influence the outcome of an election.* • *Political Action Committees (PACs) are used to support candidates and political parties.* • *SuperPACs are groups that support and promote particular social changes.*

jurisdiction over particular areas of law, including industry practices and punishments for illegal actions. The text in this table comes from the respective agencies' websites.

Particular areas of law

Remember that old saying, "Sticks and stones may break my bones, but words will never hurt me"? Under the law, however, words can inflict harm of various kinds and degrees. Plus there is need to protect certain instances of language and symbol use from being misused or usurped without the author's or originator's consent. Six particular areas of the law address matters of harm and ownership that are important in public relations: privacy, defamation of character, copyright, trademark, contracts, and fraud. Table 3-8 summarizes the salient points to these areas.

Privacy

Under the U.S. Constitution, *privacy* is not specifically guaranteed, but it is inferred from the Fourth Amendment's protection from illegal search and seizure and protection for withholding personal information from public view. Privacy is basically the right to be left alone and free from unwanted publicity. The legal basis for privacy has been developed through state laws and decisions in court cases about invasions of privacy. Court cases amount to civil lawsuits of individual versus another individual, or a company versus a company, or an individual versus a company, where the state is the arbitrator. In these civil suits one of five *torts* ("wrongs") would be the focus. The first tort is *intrusion*, which is the improper and intentional

Table 3-8. **LEGAL AREAS PERTAINING TO PUBLIC RELATIONS PRACTICE.**

AREA	DEFINITION/DESCRIPTION	KEY POINTS
Privacy	*The right to be left alone and free from unwanted public scrutiny*	*Four torts ("wrongs") of privacy are intrusion, false light, publication of private facts, and appropriation*
Defamation of character	*Injury to a person's, organization's, product's, or service's reputation*	*Defamation may be defined as libel or slander, depending on particular state law. Individuals or organizations that are defamed must prove defamatory content, publication, identification, damage, and fault. For public figures or officials, the element of fault must rise to a standard of actual malice.*

Copyright	Immediate protection for an originator's expression of ideas, concepts, or principles made in any fixed form	Protection generally lasts the life of the author plus 70 years, expiring on December 31 of the final year. Some copyrights last longer. Formal filing for copyright is not required. Intellectual property falls under this area of law. The doctrine of "fair use" is key, and so is the Digital Millennium Copyright Act.
Trademarks	Protection of a word, phrase, logo, symbol, color, sound, smell, packaging, or other distinguishing characteristic associated with a particular product or service. The use must be specific to a class of goods, distinctive, and avoid confusion in the marketplace.	Three levels of trademark are service mark (SM), trademark (TM), and registered trademark (®). Formal registration is not required for a trademark or service mark, but is strongly recommended. Trademark registration lasts as long as the mark is used in commerce and must be renewed periodically.
Contracts	Legally enforceable promises between two or more parties about something legal and value to all	Parties to contracts can be organizations or persons who are of age (at least 18 years old) and sound mind. Contracts may be written or oral, and the former is strongest to enforce. Sufficient evidence of agreement is essential for enforcement of any contract. Breach of contract occurs when a party does not fulfill its duty under the agreement.
Fraud	Intentionally misrepresenting facts, lying about something, or concealing information for the purpose of personal, financial, or other material gain for one's self or one's organization. The intent of fraud is to induce another person to act upon it and, in turn, suffer legal injury.	Injured parties can be entitled certain remedies based on the nature of the situation (e.g., several times the amount of financial gain the guilty organization sought). Contracts that are based on fraudulent information would be immediately void.

invasion of someone's (including an organization's) physical seclusion or private affairs. Cases of paparazzi using high-powered cameras on public property to take photographs of celebrities in their own homes or property qualify as intrusion.

The second tort is *false light*, which is a distortion, fabrication, or fictionalization of someone's (or an organization's) physical presence/appearance. For example, a dentist who publishes a newsletter for his services with a photo of a patient showing lovely, straight, and white teeth also includes "before" and "after" photos of teeth. While the "after" photo is actually the patient's teeth, the "before" photo that shows grossly uncared-for teeth that are not the patient's teeth. The patient can sue for false light and very probably win because dental records can easily show the difference.

The third tort of privacy is *publication of private facts*, which involves the disclosure of true personal information that may be embarrassing or offensive. Unveiling a list of someone's prescription drugs and any claims about a medical condition without permission on social media would be an example of this tort. For an organization, the publication of a strategy to market a product or service would also be an example because such strategies are confidential to the organization.

The fourth and final privacy tort is *appropriation*, which is the use of someone's (or an organization's) name, voice, or likeness without consent. Organizations are especially vigilant about the use of their brands so that they are not used without permission or misused when permitted to be used. Examples involve brand names that are on clothing on television programs that must be blacked-out because they were not granted permission to be shown. Other examples include celebrities whose likenesses are used to promote a company, product, or service without permission, and those celebrities can seek damages for that illegal use of their likenesses. When any person is portrayed in commercial speech, photo, video, or model releases are essential whether a person is paid or not, as in the case of employees being photographed for company brochures, websites, and annual reports.

Defamation of character

An individual's or an organization's reputation, including the reputation of a brand, product, or service, can be harmed—"defamed"—through *libel* (i.e., written defamation) or *slander* (i.e., spoken defamation). For individuals, defamation of character centers on the concept of "actual malice," which means the perpetrator of defamatory statements intentionally wanted to harm a person's reputation, or "negligence," which involves carelessness with private or privileged matters instead of exercising the care expected of a reasonable person acting prudently. Public officials (i.e., people with a significant level of public responsible for policy making), public figures/celebrities, and ordinary citizens can suffer from defamation of character. For organizations, they may be defamed through libel presented in any medium of communication, written, visual/video, or audio. For organizations to prove defamation through libel, they must establish what the precise content of the defamation is, show how the content was published and possibly republished, show that the organization or any of its assets were clearly identified, demonstrate damage to the organization through false or errant content, and assert the perpetrator is at fault for all the preceding conditions.

Copyright

Intellectual property is protected under copyright law. For an individual or an organization, a work of any kind and content is immediately protected under copyright law from the moment it is put into fixed form in writing, video, photography, audio, drawing, painting, or other medium. Individuals and organizations may file for a formal copyright through the Library of Congress, and forms with instructions are available online. An author or originator of a work may assert copyright protection by saying, "Copyright," and/or © along with the year and the name of the copyright holder (e.g., © 2014 Peter M. Smudde). Copyright protection lasts the life of the author/originator plus 70 years, expiring December 31 of the final year. After a work's copyright expires, the work becomes part of the "public domain." But some copyrights can be extended to legally protect them under the Copyright Term Extension Act.

Under copyright law, only the expression of ideas, concepts, or principles can be protected, not the raw ideas themselves. So, for example, no one can copyright public relations, but anyone may copyright their views of and approaches for public relations. Interestingly, U.S. government documents cannot be copyrighted because they are owned by all U.S. citizens and are provided for their use. Cases of copyright infringement concern whether someone or an organization either misused all or part of a copyrighted work (e.g., plagiarism or violations of "fair use") or caused sufficient confusion in the minds of people so as to make one work appear like the original article (e.g., "knockoffs" of Coach handbags or an advertisement that shows one product in a similar way as that which another manufacturer previously advertised).

The use of copyrighted works is fairly straightforward and requires adherence to several basic points, although the specifics of the law are much more thorough and must be consulted. To use a copyrighted work, an individual or organization must secure the owner's permission. Once permission is secured there may be royalties to pay. However, under the "fair use" doctrine, copyrighted material can be used in limited ways according to the purpose, amount of the work used, any profit that may be gained through the work's use, and whether a parody of the original work is created. In fact, parodies are protected free speech because they are unique works themselves created to be *distorted imitations* of original works to purposefully comment on them. Moreover, creators of parodies are not required to obtain permission from copyright holders. In fair-use cases, however, the original source of a work should be cited, and bibliographic approaches like those from the American Psychological Association (APA) and Modern Languages Association (MLA) offer standards for giving credit to original sources. In the cases for stock photos, for which there may or may not be royalties to pay depending on the provider, sufficient credit may be given by merely stating the source of a photo.

In the digital age the issue of copyright protection is a vital part of the law that public relations professionals must know. The Digital Millennium Copyright Act was passed in 1998 to address the unauthorized copying of software, music, videos, and other content (whether digital or not) into digital form onto other media than their originals. The Act establishes rules for downloading and sharing files, plus it outlaws attempts to circumvent antipiracy measures and outlaws code-breaking devices.

Trademark

Under trademark law, a trademark protects a word, phrase, logo, symbol, color, sound, smell, packaging, or other distinguishing characteristic associated with a specific product or service. A trademark, then, is a name (a "mark") applied to a product to differentiate it from others in a similar class of goods (e.g., the name of one line of shoes, say "FastDash," in a company's full line of all the shoes it offers for sale against all other shoemakers' shoes). Not to be confused with *trade names*, which are the names of organizations that offer products and services, trademarks make goods and services distinctive to avoid confusion in the marketplace. There are three levels of trademark: *trademark* (™), which denotes a physical good or product distinct from all others of its kind or class; *service mark* (℠), which is used to denote the delivery of a service instead of a physical product; and *registered trademark* (®), which denotes a product or service has secured formal protection through trademark registration with the U.S. Patent and Trademark Office or a state's Secretary of State's Office.

The first two kinds of trademarks exist from their first use (i.e., placing the mark on a product or service on a regular basis and not abandoning its use on future goods or services) and do not have to be registered; however, the third kind is the best approach to ensure the strongest legal protection. For example, FastDash athletic shoes would be FastDash™ before registration and FastDash® after registration. The same would be true for a service before and after registration. Registered trademarks must be registered with the U.S. Patent and Trademark Office or a state's Secretary of State's Office to prove ownership and use of the mark, last for as long as the mark is in use, and must be renewed periodically. Before a mark is used as a trademark or service mark, a search for whether the mark is already in use should be conducted to ensure there is no infringement.

Contracts

Contracts are legally enforceable promises (i.e., an offer is extended then, after negotiation, agreement is reached; if no agreement, no contract) between two or more parties about something of value to all of them and something legal to do so. Parties to contracts can be organizations or persons who are of age (at least 18 years old) and sound mind. Contracts may be written or oral, and the former is strongest to enforce. No matter what kind of contract is used, sufficient evidence of agreement is essential for enforcement of any contract. During the course of a contract, the performance of all parties matters so that the terms of the agreement are properly upheld. If the terms are partially upheld by one or more parties, the parties are said to be in *breach of contract* and the other parties may seek remedies, up to and including a lawsuit. Because of the great complexity of contract law, it is best to secure legal counsel when drafting, negotiating, and executing any contract.

Fraud

Fraud is intentionally misrepresenting facts, lying about something, or concealing information for the purpose of personal, financial, or other material gain for one's self or one's organization. In the PR profession, practitioners are in possession of many kinds of information of varying levels of importance to both an organization and its publics. Certain regulations administered by various governmental agencies address what information can be withheld and what cannot. For example, under securities law, organizations must disclose any "material" information that would be important to investors when deciding to buy, sell, or hold shares of stock, bond issues, or other similar financial instruments. If an organization does not disclose material information, or if it discloses erroneous information for the purpose of influencing the capital markets, that organization commits fraud. In contrast, however, organizations do not have to disclose their marketing plans because to do so would compromise the organization's competitive position by making public its business ambitions against its competitors and for its target customers. In another example, if an organization enters into a contract of any kind (e.g., hiring an agency to help its PR efforts) but does not fully disclose or does not provide truthful information that is material to the contract (e.g., the organization has filed for bankruptcy and payment for services may be difficult), that also is fraud.

Fraud invalidates any contracts, and the injured party(s) would be entitled to certain remedies that fit the situation and the financial gain the guilty organization sought. In the end, PR pros always must be on guard against efforts to be anything less than truthful and lawful, and the PRSA Code of Ethics can be most useful in guiding one's conduct. Knowingly providing false or misleading information in any organizational communication is fraud.

Governing Concepts

Public relations professionals have the duty and responsibility to, as Cicero might say, always be "the Good person speaking well" on an organization's behalf for applicable publics. We know there are more good people than bad in the world, and the bad ones are most successful at capturing our attention, especially through mass media, because what they do is not what is expected—what is expected is goodness, not badness. The complexity of the law and ethics, plus how they intertwine with professionalism, must not deter public relations professionals from continually learning about them and applying them. While it may seem to be a lot of work to abide by the many laws of the land, the strict ethics standards for the profession, and the high expectations for everyone in the PR field, two governing concepts could make that work easier: love and discipline.

When we approach our lives, work, and relationships through love—agape love—we make connections with the greater good and truth that each person seeks and shares for one's self and, most important, for others. When we think of love in this sense, it is the "perfect communion between persons" (Burke, 1961/1970, p. 30). Love "is the principle not only of micro-relationships (with friends, family members, or within small groups), but also of macro-relationships (social, economic, and political ones)" (Benedict, 2009, p. 8). Love requires good judgment. It may mean saying no and disappointing someone. It may mean giving harsh truth about something when that truth is not what someone wants to hear. It may also mean celebrating success or mourning loss. Discipline, too, is key as it is instrumental in keeping focus on the myriad things that inundate our senses and sensibilities. Discipline is developed through practical training about public relations and the day-to-day duties, responsibilities, and expectations we have as professional communicators. Discipline also comes from the rules and norms we follow in our daily lives, which all respects both enable and lead us in every experience (Anderson & Englehardt, 2001).

In any situation for public relations professionals, love relies on thoughtfulness, ethics, discipline, and foresight; and love is expressed at least through honesty, tactfulness, courtesy, and sensitivity to others. These aspects are key character traits and hallmarks of professionalism among good public relations counselors, who act justly on the sound basis of knowledge, skills, and abilities. So, in the end, we PR pros truly and always apply values, morals, ethics, and laws to do the right thing in the right way at the right time for the right people for the right reasons.

EXECUTIVE VIEWPOINT

Handling Ethical, Legal, and Professional Pressures

Lewis Pryor, APR, Assistant Vice President of Public Relations for State Farm

professionals. The dilemma among practitioners focuses on what is or is not ethical. This dilemma spans longer than people who believe the myth that the practice of public relations is all about deception, manipulation, and "spin." So it's imperative that practitioners have a clear understanding of and can delineate among ethics and other important issues that practitioners need to consider.

There's a significant difference between ethics and other misused terms, such as morality, legality, lies, and propaganda. These terms are often inappropriately used when attempting to describe ethics. We use morality to describe one's conscience and sense of right and wrong, while legality describes observance and conforming to laws. Lies are intentionally false statements, and propaganda is about the deliberate spread of rumors—true and false.

Ethics is also different from other standards, such as etiquette—doing what's polite—and aesthetics—doing what's tasteful. These definitions are important because sometimes making ethical decisions requires violating etiquette or aesthetics. Understanding these and other differences are key to avoiding pitfalls in the course of representing your company or client. Moreover, acting ethically allows you to wear a badge of honor and competence.

Evaluating ethics within the context of public relations is perplexing and confusing for many reasons. In the quest for black-and-white answers to ethical dilemmas, most professionals are frequently confronted with shades of gray. While professionals are attempting to evaluate whether they're acting ethically, they realize that giving their actions a firm thumbs up or down is—in and of itself—a dilemma.

Applying an ethical lens creates one of the more interesting dilemmas for public relations

Since history is often the best teacher, early and current day examples of ethical dilemmas in public relations provide insight to guide our understanding.

On the heels of the late 1920s Suffragette movement, the American Tobacco Association (ATA) was focused on getting more women smoking despite its associated social taboo. The ATA sought and hired Edward Bernays, known to many as the "Father of Public Relations," to assist. Bernays persuaded a group of women, marching in the 1929 Easter Parade in New York City, to take and light up cigarettes in a campaign dubbed "Torches of Freedom." It was covered extensively by the media and helped to strike down the longstanding taboo on women smoking.

By successfully linking smoking to the equal rights movement, Bernays implied that one could not support universal suffrage without also supporting the right of women to smoke. This strategy also successfully appealed to the large audience of women who wanted to be treated equally and therefore choose to engage in activities such as smoking. This led to a substantial increase of the percentage of smokers for ATA member companies because Bernays' tactics successfully broadened the appeal and practice of smoking to women.

The ethical dilemma of Bernays' tactics can be understood from several perspectives. Many then, and now, have tabbed these tactics as "unethical propaganda." Others argue that the dangers of smoking were not known then as they are today and one cannot act unethically when they have limited information. To others this campaign is immoral and/or violates their ideal of aesthetics.

Fast forward 80 years later to a modern-day example. Burson-Marsteller (B-M), a global public relations and communications firm, found itself in the midst of turmoil and under the national eye when two B-M account executives, one a former reporter and the other a former political columnist, attempted to persuade influential bloggers and mainstream media, including *USA Today*, to report on allegations. These allegations were later learned to be fabricated. The account executives shared allegations that Google violated privacy rules. What wasn't shared was that B-M was representing Facebook, a Google competitor.

The reporter who received the initial pitch asked who was paying for the project, and the Burson executives refused to reveal their client. After uncovering inconsistencies in their allegations, the reporter decided to make B-M the focus of the story—even posting the email exchange with B-M execs online. After Facebook acknowledged being represented by B-M but not commissioning the work, the two execs were required to engage in an ethics course.

This example offers a different set of circumstances to consider. Based on information that's been uncovered, most practitioners agree these B-M employees broke basic rules such as producing known lies, intentionally deceiving and providing facts they knew to be false. Moreover, they violated PRSA code of ethics by refusing to identify their client.

These two examples show the complexity of the ethical dilemmas public relations professionals face every day. Understanding what ethics is—and perhaps more importantly, what it isn't—can guide decisions and actions. Each dilemma will be unique and require careful evaluation. Successfully navigating these situations not only benefits clients, but also ensures public relations remains a highly regarded profession for many years to come.

Key Words

Professionalism	Law
Values	PR–Attorney relationship
Morals	First Amendment
Ethics	Three speech types covered by the First
Relativism	Amendment
Teleology	Case law
Deontology	Six areas of law for PR
Axiology	Love
Resolving ethical dilemmas	Discipline

Exploration of Professionalism, Ethics, and Law

1. Look for examples of unethical public relations. Where did you find them? What was the core ethical dilemma? How did the organization(s) involved explain the situation? What reaction was there toward the situation? What was the outcome?

2. Obtain a copy of The Stockholm Accords from the Global Alliance of Public Relations (GAPR) mentioned in Chapter 1, and review it for what it is and what it sought to achieve. Research the effects and effectiveness of the program over the two years it ran. In 2012 the GAPR launched a follow-up program, The Melbourne Mandate. What evidence do you find that either or both of the programs worked or not to advance the PR profession and professionalism? Why were the programs effective or not?

3. Examine the news for stories about organizations facing investigations by one of the federal regulatory bodies. What was the core legal issue? How has the organization explained it, and how does that explanation compare to the federal agency's explanation? What public relations actions were involved? What was the outcome?

4. Find examples of copyright or trademark infringement, such as Apple Computer and Apple Records or *Vanity Fair* magazine's cover of a pregnant Demi Moore and Paramount Picture's promotion poster for the movie *Naked Gun 33⅓*. Explain the grounds for the infringement, on one hand, and the counterargument that there was no infringement, on the other hand. Which argument prevailed and why?

References

Anderson, J. A., & Englehardt, E. E. (2001). *The organizational self and ethical conduct: Sunlit virtue and shadowed resistance.* Fort Worth, TX: Harcourt College Publishers.

Baker, S., & Martinson, D. L. (2001). The TARES test: Five principles for ethical persuasion. *Journal of Mass Media Ethics, 16*(2/3), 148–175.

Benedict XVI (2009). *Charity in truth.* San Francisco: Ignatius Press.

Boehm, C. (2012). *Moral origins: The evolution of virtue, altruism and shame.* New York: Basic Books/Perseus Books Group.

Brinkmann, J. (2002). Business and marketing ethics as professional ethics. Concepts, approaches and typologies. *Journal of Business Ethics, 41,* 159–177.

Burke, K. (1970). *The rhetoric of religion: Studies in logology.* Berkeley, CA: University of California Press. (Original work published 1961)

Carter, T. B., Franklin, M. A., & Wright, J. B. (1993). *The First Amendment and the fifth estate: Regulation of electronic mass media* (3rd ed.). Westbury, NY: The Foundation Press.

Christians, C. G., Fackler, M. B., Rotzoll, K. B., & McKee, K. B. (2001). *Media ethics: Cases and moral reasoning* (6th ed.). Boston: Allyn & Bacon.

Coombs, W. T., & Holladay, S. J. (2007). *It's not just PR: Public relations in society.* Malden, MA: Blackwell.

Courtright, J. L. (1996). An ethics code postmortem: The National Religious Broadcasters' EFICOM. *Journal of Mass Media Ethics, 11*(4), 223–235.

Curtain, P. A., & Boynton, L. A. (2001). Ethics in public relations: Theory and practice. In R. L. Heath (Ed.), *Handbook of Public Relations* (pp. 411–422). Thousand Oaks, CA: Sage.

Edwards, L., & Hodges, C. E. (Eds.) (2011). *Public relations, society and culture: Theoretical and empirical explorations.* New York: Routledge.

Fitzpatrick, K. R. (n.d.). *Ethical decision-making guide helps resolve ethical dilemmas.* Retrieved May 10, 2010, from http://www.prsa.org/AboutPRSA/Ethics/documents/decisionguide.pdf.

Frankena, W. K. (1973). *Ethics: Foundations of philosophy series* (2nd ed.). Englewood Cliffs, NJ: Prentice-Hall.

Gower, K. K. (2008). *Legal and ethical considerations for public relations* (2nd ed.). Long Grove, IL: Waveland Press.

Gower, K. K. (2012). Public relations law. In C. L. Caywood (Ed.), *The handbook of strategic public relations and integrated marketing communications* (2nd ed., pp. 57–69). New York: McGraw-Hill.

Grunig, J. E., & Hunt, T. (1984). *Managing public relations.* New York: Holt, Rinehart & Winston.

Keane, J. G. (1974). On professionalism in advertising. *Journal of Advertising, 3*(4), 6–12.

L'Etang, J. (2012). Public relations and democracy: Historical reflections and implications. In S. M. Oliver (Ed.), *Handbook of corporate communication and public relations: Pure and applied* (pp. 342–353). New York: Routledge. (Original work published 2004)

Lee, S. T., & Cheng, I-H. (2011). Characteristics and dimensions of ethical leadership in public relations. *Journal of Public Relations Research, 23*(1), 46–74.

Lee, S. T., & Cheng, I-H. (2012). Ethics management in public relations: Practitioner conceptualizations of ethical leadership, knowledge, training and compliance. *Journal of Mass Media Ethics, 27,* 80–96.

Moore, R. L., Maye, C., & Collins, E. L. (2011). *Advertising and public relations law* (2nd ed.). New York: Routledge.

Parkinson, M. G., & Parkinson, L. M. (2006). *Law for advertising, broadcasting, journalism, and public relations: A comprehensive text for students and practitioners.* Mahwah, NJ: Lawrence Erlbaum Associates.

Parkinson, M. G., & Parkinson, L. M. (2008). *Public relations law: A supplemental text.* Mahwah, NJ: Lawrence Erlbaum Associates.

Pieczka, M., & L'Etang, J. (2001). Public relations and the question of professionalism. In R. L. Heath (Ed.), *Handbook of public relations* (pp. 223–235). Thousand Oaks, CA: Sage.

Smudde, P. M. (2005). Blogging, ethics and public relations: A proactive and dialogic approach. *Public Relations Quarterly, 50*(3), 34–38.

Smudde, P. M. (2011). Focus on ethics and public relations practice in a university classroom. *Communication Teacher, 25*(3), 154–158.

Taylor, M. (2010). Public relations in the enactment of civil society. In R. L. Heath (Ed.), *The SAGE handbook of public relations* (pp. 5–15). Thousand Oaks, CA: SAGE Publications.

Zompetti, J. P., Moore, M. A., Smudde, P. M., & Hunt, S. K. (2013). The right to peaceable assembly and social movements: The role of "occupying" space as a way to speak. In N. S. Lind (Ed.), *First Amendment Rights: An Encyclopedia* (Vol. 2, pp. 237–256). Santa Barbara, CA: ABC-CLIO.

Recommended Reading

Bivins, T. (2004). *Mixed media: Moral distinctions in advertising, public relations, and journalism*. Mahwah, NJ: Lawrence Erlbaum Associates.

Fitzpatrick, K., & Bronstein, C. (2006). *Ethics in public relations: Responsible advocacy*. Thousand Oaks, CA: Sage.

Haggerty, J. F. (2003). *In the court of public opinion: Winning your case with public relations*. Hoboken, NJ: John Wiley and Sons.

Moore, R. L., Maye, C., & Collins, E. L. (2011). *Advertising and public relations law* (2nd ed.). New York: Routledge.

Parkinson, M. G., & Parkinson, L. M. (2006). *Law for advertising, broadcasting, journalism, and public relations*. Mahwah, NJ: Lawrence Erlbaum Associates.

Parkinson, M. G., & Parkinson, L. M. (2008). *Public relations law: A supplemental text*. Mahwah, NJ: Lawrence Erlbaum Associates.

Parsons, P. J. (2004). *Ethics in public relations: A guide to best practice*. London: Kogan Page.

Sieb, P., & Fitzpatrick, K. (1995). *Public relations ethics*. Fort Worth, TX: Harcourt Brace College Publishers.

Chapter 4

OPERATIONS TOOLS I:
Plans, Budgets, Time Management, and Billing

No organizational function is an island. For public relations, a strategic approach should not be developed in isolation from other functional areas in an organization, especially if PR's focus is an annual plan for corporate publicity or a concentrated promotional effort, like a product launch. Public relations works among other operating areas of an organization. Marketing, finance, legal, human resources, research and development, sales, and manufacturing could all be affected by and benefit from public relations. These functions may deserve to be included in the PR plan in some way, depending on the business needs and the company's overall strategic plan. For example, marketing's promotional advertising could be timed with editorial placements in publications. Financial performance should be echoed in relevant press releases, company backgrounders, and conversations with influential people in the media or among industry analysts. Legal staff should review PR discourse before it is released and may require management of legal issues. Human resources may require certain employee communications about new benefits plans or other internal programs or policies. Research and development may have created a breakthrough technology that works more simply, cheaply, and effectively than anything available. Sales would need published articles and success stories about the company and its customers. And manufacturing would look to PR to publicize major product or service achievements that affect the company, its customers, and the competition.

These kinds of organizational needs show how deeply public relations can penetrate an organization. Even going a step further, public relations can help corporate leaders reach out to their publics by communicating what they and the organization stand for in the market and society. An overall strategic communications program would integrate PR with executives and other corporate functions to build stronger relationships with an organization's internal and external publics on whom success depends. Through such planned integration, public relations practitioners can anticipate corporate or policy issues that may gain importance and account for them in the formal communication plan.

Top management has high expectations for public relations and wants it to succeed. That success must be on business terms—adding value as a strategically core organizational function. Along with the concepts from the previous chapters, particular "tools" for effective management of a public relations operation, like any organizational unit, are essential. This chapter is the first of two that present and explain selected and fundamental operations tools. In this chapter we will cover strategic plans, finance, time management, and billing. The next chapter will include tools for managing performance and personnel.

Strategic Plans

Plans are to organizations as hymnals are to choirs. Hymnals, ranging from complex pieces like Handel's *Messiah* to grade school performances, show the words and music for a choir of many people who sing various parts—sopranos, altos, tenors, baritones, and basses. Without the hymnals, choir members would not know exactly what to sing and when and how. For an organization, its plan is its hymnal, including the information about what its parts are expected to do, when, and how much. An organizational plan, then, is the one document that presents what everyone in an organization is working toward during a given period of time, usually a calendar or fiscal year.

Planning process

Any organization is comprised of various parts. Figure 4-1 shows how the most basic parts interrelate, from the primary and largest element of the organization itself, to the next level of operating units (i.e., departments or divisions), to project teams, to the smallest and most integral element of individual employees. The bigger an organization, the potentially more numerous the layers, but these four layers work well for our purposes. Along with all operating units in an organization, public relations works *with* management within a single system for what Anthony (1988) calls the processes of strategic planning, management control, and task control. One name for that system is the "corporate performance management" (CPM) system, and it and its processes are owned by management and can involve employees at many levels. (Another term for CPM systems is "business information systems.") Basically, *strategic planning* takes key management initiatives and supports top-down and bottom-up planning processes. This two-way process allows for checks and balances among the various views of what can and must be done among an organization's operating units. Fundamentally, strategic planning involves deciding on an organization's goals and the strategies based on an accurate, complete, and honest situation analysis, then deciding how best to attain them through setting objectives, budgeting, and/or rolling forecasts. (Budgets and forecasts will be treated later in this chapter.) *Management control* supports planning by providing organizational insight, communication, and focus. It involves managers influencing other organizational members to enact the strategies by monitoring plan performance, supporting the analysis of alternatives, and taking corrective action. *Task control* involves making sure specific tasks are carried out efficiently and effectively. It is tactics- or transaction-focused, encompasses the literal results sought in the strategic planning process, and is measured according to the management control process.

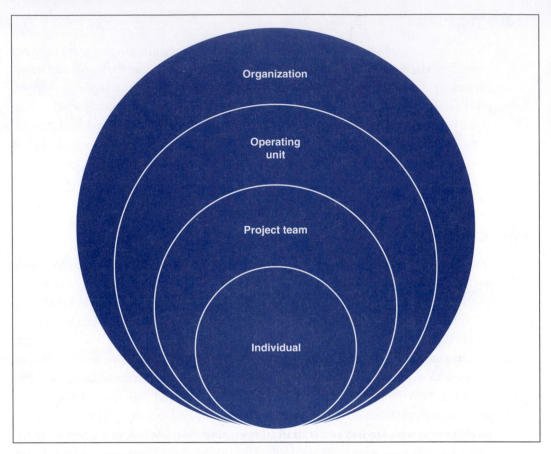

Figure 4-1. BASIC ORGANIZATIONAL PARTS OR LAYERS.

This CPM system for strategic planning, management control, and task control leverages organizational knowledge and insight by blending these processes into a single, synchronous, and ongoing system to better implement strategies, strengthen decision making, and make management at all levels more effective (see Buytendijk, Wood, & Geischecker, 2004; see also Ariyachandra & Frolick, 2008). The system's process is typically engaged annually, and any *ad hoc*, project, or contingency planning would follow a similar path, being in sync with the organization's overall strategic plan and the PR function's strategic operating plan. Indeed, when time is especially of the essence, public relations leaders' strategic thinking is internalized and supported by extensive experience and knowledge of what works and what may not. Strategic thinking in such situations involves a compressed process covering most or all elements of a strategic plan, resulting in efficient and effective management decision-making that is in tune with the organization's bigger strategic picture.

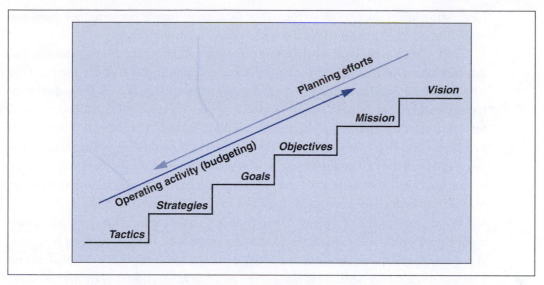

Figure 4-2. STRATEGIC PLANNING PROCESS MODEL.
SOURCE: Smudde (2011)

It is interesting that the starting point for the strategic planning process is really the end point—top management determines what it wants the organization ultimately to be (i.e., the vision and objectives), then it begins the process to figure out how the organization will get there. The strategic planning process, then, is primarily dialogic among leaders and staff in all operating units. As Figure 4-2 shows, developing the strategic plan (i.e., "planning efforts") is a top-down process that begins with top management as it thoroughly analyzes the organization's situation in all respects and then sets the course for the company. Operating activity (including budgeting) is a bottom-up process at the tactical, operational level with employees who have the responsibility, expertise, and experience with day-to-day demands. These people perform a kind of "reality check" on management's strategic course, which can propel the company forward. During the bottom-up process operational units examine management's objectives, decide what is doable and what is not, and allocate resources (i.e., adding, subtracting, or realigning) to ensure success. In turn, management works with operations to fine-tune the plan by aligning needs and wants at all levels. Key assumptions about the organization's current and anticipated future environments are also noted and understood by all parties. Both processes *together* result in a complete view of the business from all perspectives and focused on one vision for the company (also see Drucker, 1994; Mintzberg, 2007; Robert, 1997, 2006). It may take some time to consistently demonstrate the value of public relations before others embrace its value contribution. The planning, budgeting, forecasting, consolidating of performance data, analyzing of performance data, and reporting on results can and must work in public relations' favor.

This whole top-down and bottom-up process can take some time to complete, and it is contingent on an organization's culture and systems. In the end, the result is (1) a single strategic *organizational* plan for the entire organization and (2) individual strategic *operating* plans for each organizational function. Operational plans, budgets, and forecasts must all "roll up" to organizational plan, budget, and forecast. Such an approach ensures that everyone everywhere in the organization is working toward the same ends and they all understand how everyone else will help get there. All sections of the plans are the same, but the content differs because each operational area has its own plan to fulfill the expectations specified in the organizational plan.

What is important to recognize is that an organizational plan specifies how operational units will contribute to the organization's overall success; however, those specifications at the organizational level are not sufficiently detailed to run any given operating unit. That deficiency in an organizational plan means there must be more specific plans at the operational level to provide people with the detail they need to do the work in their parts of the business that will fulfill overall, organizational objectives. In other words, plans for individual projects or programs must directly roll up to the operational plans to which they are aligned, not the overall organizational plan. So there is a hierarchy for plans that is essential to understand because each plan builds upon or, more appropriately, rolls up (and down) to another. Figure 4-3 shows the hierarchy for plans, with the origin being the one organizational plan and a series of subordinate plans needed for an organization's various operational and tactical demands. Certain plans are developed annually while others are developed as needed, and one is generated once. All of them are assessed and updated/revised on a regular basis, depending on contextual factors. It may help to think of the relationship or the fit among these plans into one another like Russian nesting dolls (matryoshka dolls), with the outermost doll being the organizational plan and the innermost doll being the personal/position plan. This conceptualization is consistent with that shown in Figure 4-1 as well.

There is one major caveat: Strategic plans go out of date essentially as soon as they are finalized and approved (see Drucker, 1994). The reason is that the process to develop a plan rests on information about an organization's enacted environment, which is really a snapshot in time. Certain assumptions also were made about the future. This dynamic does not mean planning is a useless exercise—far from it! An organizational plan is needed to ensure everyone knows for what they are working (i.e., the choir must have a hymnal). Operational plans are essential so that people in a particular unit know more precisely what they are doing that will fit into the bigger scope of the organization's plan. Moreover, because things change quickly

1. Organizational	The primary plan with the broadest scope because it concerns the whole organization; it is the foundation for all other plans; produced annually, assessed frequently, and revised when needed
2. Operational	The plan with a specific scope to fulfill organizational objectives through a single unit that is essential to an organization's operation; produced annually, assessed frequently, and revised when needed
3. Project/Program	A plan that targets a particular effort that fulfills one or more objectives in an operational plan; produced as needed ("ad hoc") and assessed during and after implementation
4. Contingency	A plan meticulously developed within an operation's bailiwick to address unexpected or emergency matters (i.e., a kind of unanticipated project) in definitive ways so that those matters can be resolved effectively and efficiently and in tune with the organizational plan and organization's image and reputation; the scope may range from an operation to the whole organization; produced once and assessed and revised at least annually, possibly through drills or simulations
5. Personal/Position	A plan with a scope on an individual to guide her or his performance in a given job or position, potentially including career aims; produced annually, assessed periodically, and revised as needed to accommodate operational changes

Figure 4-3. RELATIONSHIP AND FIT AMONG PLANS.

SOURCE FOR PHOTO: http://community.prometheanplanet.com/cfs-file.ashx/__key/CommunityServer.Blogs.Components.WeblogFiles/00.00.00.01.22/6622.25.jpg inside and outside an organization, all aspects of any strategic plan (at the organizational or operational levels or both) must be flexible enough to accommodate change and still achieve success. Public relations' inherent boundary-spanning capabilities become more potent and important to an organization in this regard.

Plan content

Any plan is meant to be usable, useful, and, most of all, used. Notice that the context so far has been organizational and operational plans, *not* campaign or project plans, which we will address shortly and in the larger organizational context. A strategic plan must contain sufficiently detailed information that enables people at any level in an organization, especially those with managerial/supervisory responsibilities, to direct organizational resources to fulfill specific objectives over a given period of time.

The key parts (but not the only parts) of an organizational plan, as shown in Figure 4-2, are the company's vision, mission, objectives, strategies, and tactics. Other aspects may be required (e.g., situation analysis, critical success factors, key performance indicators, budget, timeline, evaluation scheme), which are presented in Appendix A and will be addressed later on especially for public relations. Here are the key parts of a strategic plan and how they interrelate:

- *Objectives* state the high-level results (**e**ffects) an organization wants to achieve by a certain measurable amount (**g**oal) for a particular public or stakeholder group (**a**udience) over a defined period of time (**d**eadline). (EGAD is a mnemonic way to remember these four essential elements of a well-formed objective.) Note that, depending on an organization's preference, the words "objective" and "goal" may be interchanged, but do not let this terminological problem get in the way. Furthermore, organizations may call a long-term or broad-based objective a "goal" while anything else is an "objective." Again, do not let that stand in your way of understanding what is sought. Objectives must only specify *one* effect that will be directly measured. If an objective states two or more effects are sought (e.g., increasing awareness and sales), the objective must be rewritten into two separate EGAD-based objectives. An objective can be written to encompass any scope, from creating particular outputs (e.g., press releases, meetings with news organizations' editors) to achieving long-term outgrowths (e.g., awareness gains, attitude changes, behavior modifications). The dates for realizing objectives are key to knowing the difference. Additionally, always state a *benchmark* (i.e., the point of comparison from prior experience, secondary research, or other source) for the goal within or after an objective. Maintaining the clarity of what's what within any objective (i.e., EGAD) and its relational parts (i.e., benchmark, strategy[s], and tactic[s]) is essential for proper and accurate measurements of success. Objectives can be written as one of four types:

- *Informational*—concerns a degree of change or impact sought in knowledge, awareness, or understanding (guiding metaphor is the *head*). Example: "Increase employee awareness of new plant safety measures by 60 percent within three months. (Benchmark: 48 percent employee awareness last quarter)"
- *Attitudinal*—concerns a change or impact sought in degree or kind of opinion or emotional buy-in (guiding metaphor is the *heart*). Example: "Promote favorable attitudes toward a new department store among 25 percent of mall shoppers by the end of the grand opening week. (Benchmark: 19.6 percent favorable attitudes in last year's survey)"
- *Behavioral*—concerns a change or impact sought in degree or kind of action taken or not (guiding metaphor is the *hands*). Example: "Stimulate 20 percent higher conference attendance among association members by the opening date of January 15, 2015. (Benchmark: 567 attendees in 2014)"
- *Output*—concerns the creation of one or more things, including discourse (guiding metaphor is *stuff*). Example: "Make five presentations to security analysts each quarter. (Benchmark: none; new practice based on analysts' interests/requests this past year)"

- *Strategies* define the steps toward achieving desired results by identifying categories of activities that apply to one or more objectives. One strategy may help fulfill more than one objective, making it an efficient means for realizing outcomes. For example, strategies can be social media, media relations, events, internal publications, and so on. Notice that embedded in each strategy is a wide range of tactics (see the next bullet item), like Facebook, Twitter, Flickr, Pinterest, and others that are the tactics of social media. Additionally, strategies can be approaches for inspiring cooperation through messages. In this vein strategies include sharing the most salient information, inspiring groups to influence others, leaning on sources' inherent credibility, the force of verbal and nonverbal cues, and choosing channels that pique audience's interests, foster two-way communication, and invite audiences to participate. (See Appendix A, Appendix B, and Chapter 6 for examples and more details.)
- *Tactics* are the very specific forms of discourse you create or activities you will do that (1) fit within the strategy(s) statement(s) and (2) achieve the stated objective(s) associated with them. Vitally important with tactics is

that PR professionals *know* that target publics will, indeed, use them and like them. Sufficient audience research is the key to this knowledge. Because tactics could fit one or more strategies and more than one objective, simply list the same tactic every time it applies to a strategy that relates directly to it. Sample tactics include any mobile phone apps, any social medium, press releases, news conferences, annual reports, websites, trade shows, and any of the other PR discourse types shown in Figure 4-4 (also see Chapter 6 and Appendix B).

All of these parts of a strategic plan must fall within the scope of the company's *mission*, which is a statement about what business the company is in and how it applies resources to get the company closer to realizing its *vision*, which is the ultimate state of being a company wants to reach and stems from a thorough understanding of an organization's state of affairs and capabilities to attain the ultimate state of being. Figure 4-2 shows how these features of strategic planning relate to one another. Appendix A shows a template for a complete strategic plan, including explanations about each section, including these given here. Appendix B shows an example strategic plan, and one important thing to notice in it is the presentation of objectives, strategies, and tactics in the form of a table that associates these three things very directly with one another so they are easily seen and understood.

An organizational plan, again, is the foundation or basis for all other plans shown in Figure 4-3 that an organization may need. Just like everyone in a choir must use a hymnal to sing their parts well and in sync, everyone in an organization must work toward the same objectives. And like a choir, when certain members

Advertisements	Magazines	Press releases
Advertorials	Matte releases	Public Service Announcements
Annual reports	Media advisories	(PSA)
Artirles	Meetings	Satellite media tours (SMT)
Audio news releases	Mobile phone apps	Social media (only specific ones)
Backgrounders	Newsletters	Speeches
Biographical statements	Photo news releases	Tip sheets
Brochures/Pamphlets	Pitch calls	Video news programs
Case studies	Pitch letters	Video news releases
Fact sheets	Podcasts	Weblogs (Blogs)
Flyers	Posters	Websites
Frequently asked questions (FAQ)	Prepared statements	White papers
Interviews	Press conferences	Wikis
Issue reports	Press kits	Written correspondence

Figure 4-4. PUBLIC RELATIONS DISCOURSE GENRES—TACTICS OF PR.

sing while others do not, each part of an organization will work differently to fulfill organizational objectives. For example, an organizational objective (applying the EGAD formula), "to achieve the number-one or number-two position (benchmark of Y) in all the markets it serves by the end of the calendar year," would require the work of people in research and development (R&D), manufacturing, public relations, and sales. But other organizational areas, like finance and accounting, human resources, and legal staff may not have much or any role to play. So, according to the process described for Figure 4-2, an objective in the organizational plan must be assessed for its applicability to any and every operating unit. If an operating unit determines that it has responsibility and accountability for achieving any organizational objectives, that unit must address them in its own operating plan so that it is clear what strategies, tactics, and resources would be applied over time to achieve success. For example, in an operating plan for public relations, one objective that should help the organization establish itself as number one or number two in the markets it serves would be (using the EGAD formula), "to improve customers' perceptions of product quality by X percent (benchmark of Y) by the end of the second quarter in the calendar year."

Notice a pattern developing here: a plan and its associated objectives begs the question, "How?" At the organizational level, the example objective to establish a position as number one or number two in the markets the company serves needs to indicate which operating units would play a role, and that is part of the feedback during the planning process shown by Figure 4-2. At the operating level for PR, the objective to lift customers' perceptions by a quantifiable amount would be addressed by certain strategies (e.g., media relations, customer-interaction campaigns, and advertising) that entail particular tactics (e.g., press conferences and editorial meetings; product trials; and product placements, print and online ads, and Facebook). Figure 4-5 outlines the basic contents of a strategic plan at any level (i.e., organizational to personal), where certain parts may be added or subtracted as needed. In fact, when all these features are presented in writing in a formal plan, they can be formatted in such a way that the information is organized and actionable—even to the point to show which objectives apply to which parts of the budget and vice versa. Appendix B shows one example of such a plan for a small business, which can be scaled up for other and larger organizations.

A key starting point for effective planning is a situation analysis, which would also be accommodated in the visioning part of the process modeled in Figure 4-2, and a simple and powerful approach to it is a SWOT analysis. (Three other methods—gap analysis, force-field analysis, and order restoration—are presented in Chapter 7 and are applied to market analysis.) A SWOT analysis relies on a two-step

- **Executive summary** (very concise summary of the plan's content, focusing on the problem, the solution, and anticipated results; write last)
- **Vision** (concisely say a long-term future state for the organization)
- **Mission** (concisely say why an organization exists and how it does its business)
- **Opportunity/Problem in context** (a.k.a. situation analysis; a concise but thorough description of the state of affairs the organization faces, including analysis of internal and external factors that may affect success)
- **Value proposition** (specify the unique differentiator/idea and the compelling proof points for that differentiation/idea; functions also as the supreme *key message platform* for the organization)
- **Audiences/Stakeholders** (internal and external and why they are vital)
- **Objectives** (big-picture accomplishments sought; must include effect sought, measurable amount of the effect sought [goal], audience targeted, and deadline; should include benchmark for goal)
- **Strategies** (statements that systematize tactics toward one or more objectives and goals; organizational strategies become operational objectives)
- **Tactics** (specific actions to be taken to meet/exceed goals and fulfill objectives)
- **Critical success factors** (things/events that could help or hurt success; why is knowing these things valuable)
- **Key performance indicators** (milestone measurements taken along the way to track progress toward goals; why is knowing these things valuable)
- **Timeline** (overall and by phase; relate to objectives/goals and metrics)
- **Budget and resources** (give data as specifically as possible; explain what's needed and why; return on investment [ROI] and value-added for the change are key)
- **Evaluation method** (*post hoc* measurements and analysis of outputs, outtakes, outcomes, and outgrowths)
- **Appendices** (any additional evidence or documentation specifically needed to support sections of the plan)
- **References** (list of sources used in any of the plan's content)

Figure 4-5. BASIC PLAN PARTS (SEE APPENDIX A).

SOURCE: Smudde & Courtright (2012)

process of (1) brainstorming about the current internal factors that are strengths and weaknesses for the organization and then (2) analyzing those internal factors in terms of known and expected external factors of (a) opportunities to capitalize on strengths, realize opportunities, and minimize weaknesses plus (b) threats of any kind that may hurt the organization to some degree or amount to obstacles that must be overcome. An effective SWOT analysis does not stop at just filling out the strengths, weaknesses, opportunities, and threats. An effective SWOT analysis must examine the data in each of the four parts for their implications (i.e., what they mean to the organization in terms of attributes, like importance, scope, influence, etc.), then it presents possible action items that can address the data in each of the four parts (e.g., doing something specific to capitalize on every stated strength, weakness, opportunity, and threat individually). A four-column, multi-row table, like the one in Appendix B, can be prepared and used most effectively for any organization.

Performance and reporting matters

Throughout the enactment of any plan of any type, organizational leaders and their staffs must monitor the larger economic and social environment for anything that may or will positively or negatively affect the organization's path to success. In a real sense, a strategic plan represents an ideal path to success. Figure 4-6 shows a visual comparison between the ideal path of a strategic plan and the probable, actual path for enacting a plan. The ideal path assumes a reasonably steady state of affairs. But remember that a plan goes out of date as soon as it is approved because it is based on information about the past, present, and future gathered and applied at a particular point in time. And that information about the future is the most tenuous, no matter how well defended it is, because many assumptions also go along with the predictions about the future. As Figure 4-6 shows, in reality many variables can and do change that require one or two or many alterations in course toward the same target for success. Such variables could include changes in regulation, new competitors, mergers and acquisitions, emergency situations, and so on.

Instrumental in an organization's execution of its business and enactment of a strategic plan is its *culture*. This culture is borne of an organization's history and is learned and perpetuated among its members through values, rules, norms, stories, policies, procedures, discourse, symbols, rites, rituals, and so on. Culture, then, is both process and product. In organizations, as Keyton (2011) explains it, culture is characterized by several things. Organizational culture is shared by a defined group of people of any size who all embrace and enact it. It is made up of multiple elements simultaneously, and those elements are artifacts, values, and assumptions. These elements all together combine into a lens through which group members

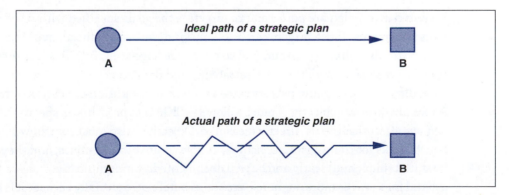

Figure 4-6. PATH COMPARISONS BETWEEN THE IDEAL AND PROBABLE ACTUAL PATHS OF A STRATEGIC PLAN.

view and interact with the world around them. The elements also work together as a system, where one element is not more important to the others but, rather, they inform one another through human action. For a strategic plan, then (see Appendix A), a sufficient understanding and concise documentation of organizational culture can provide critical information and insights about motivations and predictions about why an organization is what it is, does what it does, and may do or not do what it needs to do to be more successful in the ways it wants and needs to. Data sources to learn about and document an organization's culture can be written and unwritten, and they include slogans, philosophies, and value statements; the type of people in an organization; symbols, stories, and heroes; and rituals, rites, and routines (Clampitt, 2010).

From internal culture to local communities to broad markets, the data about operations, competitors, regulations, customers, and many other aspects must be followed to ensure that any plan is still on target, and if it is not, adjustments/revisions to it may be required, including the creation of a whole new plan if absolutely necessary. Information and analysis about critical success factors (CSFs) plays an important role in (1) analyzing past performance and projecting ongoing performance in comparison to the situation analysis and, especially, (2) reporting on performance for better and for worse and recommending courses of action. Indeed, periodic reporting is required, and the schedule for reporting on a plan's performance will be dictated by management's needs for information. We will address reporting matters more in the next chapter. At this point, however, we must look more deeply into the sections of a plan that are perhaps the most focused on performance measurements. (See Appendix A for additional explanation/examples for all parts of a plan.)

Objectives

Required in any plan are performance targets—the goals specified within the objectives statements. Those targets can be of any kind, such as financial, market, knowledge, attitude, behavior, output, and so on. As we have seen, fulfilling any objective is made possible through the stated strategies and their associated tactics. Attaining, exceeding, or missing any performance target is an indication of success or failure. As we already saw, objectives must follow the EGAD approach and specify one *and only one* effect that can be directly measured. Objectives also must somehow state the benchmarks for comparison. Benchmarks give context to objectives, and they must be stated simply and clearly and be well documented. Any organization that has been around for a year or more ought to have some, but if not, especially because it is brand new, benchmarks can be identified by finding out how competitors have performed. This is why the situation analysis is so useful. You also must do some research to find out if any benchmarks can be identified (even though they are not specifically for your organization) through case studies, best practices, news/journal articles, market or industry reports, local/regional/national chambers of commerce, etc. If after all that work you still do not have any benchmarks, you may state that a benchmark is zero (0) because there are no prior data from the client or other similar organizations. *Do not* use this last point as a cop-out for not doing the work!

Key performance indicators

It is never a good idea to wait until after a plan or project is completed to determine whether it was successful or not. Waiting until the end wastes many opportunities to check on progress along the way, just like road signs give you an indication of where you are driving to some destination. You must frequently determine the progress toward realizing objectives. Key performance indicators (KPIs) are important *formative* measurements of performance—they are periodic performance measurements of the objectives that show the degree to which the enactment of a plan is on track or not. KPIs must be divided up reasonably over time so that the ultimate goals, as stated in the objectives, are realized by the end of the timeline. Any KPI must be tied to the respective objective it is measuring and take measurements at predetermined intervals of time leading up to the culmination of the plan (see Appendix A and Appendix B). If possible, KPIs should be shown in comparison to benchmarks for a similar period. All KPIs must also ultimately build up to the final, overall evaluation measurements for the entire plan as stated in the objectives.

Final evaluation

Always remember that the objectives guide all measurements of success, including KPIs and final, overall evaluation. KPIs, as formative measures of performance, build toward holistic or *summative* measures when a strategic plan is completed. All final evaluation measurements must be linked to the stated objectives. Accordingly, the final evaluation approach for a strategic plan must give basic statements about what method would be used to measure each objective. Some key questions to answer when designing your measurement scheme are:

- How will you measure the success of reaching the plan's objectives?
- How have the critical success factors affected the plan's success?
- What have your leading indicators told you?
- Can you create a means for continuous feedback from your target audiences?
- Did the target audiences receive the messages?

- What was the extent of any print and broadcast media coverage?
- How was the organization portrayed in media reports?
- What do people think about the organization now as compared to their opinions before the plan was implemented?
- Did the plan fall within budget and were the resources sufficient?
- What unforeseen circumstances affected the plan's success?

Research methods of quantitative and qualitative designs are essential and at the heart of the KPIs and the final evaluation of a strategic plan. Final measurements for a strategic plan are *summative*—they define overall success/failure for the whole plan—against the objectives and compared to the benchmarks. These final measurements are the culmination of what the KPIs were measuring along the way in a formative way. Use the findings from the final evaluation to help you create future evaluations and communication plans. Finally, you should take the opportunity to note ways to improve things along the way and at the end of the project. Also address how to do things better next time, including alternative methods, discourse, channels, and so on.

Timeline

Time is also an essential performance measure. Any plan needs a timeline, and it should be in the form of a *Gantt chart* (see Figure 4-7) or other visual method, an example of which is shown in Appendix B. A straight list of dates and actions can work well if it is very short, but even then a chart would be much better because its content would be easier to understand because of the visualization of the span of activities over time. In a Gantt chart, such as Figure 4-7, you must show the detail for every tactic under each objective. A strategic plan must be in sync with the organization's fiscal or calendar year. An explanation of the timeline, especially "pressure points" and interrelationships among planned activities, is also absolutely necessary.

Budget

Also required in a plan is a budget, which is a measure of performance based on resource allocations, especially in terms of money. A budget not only shows anticipated income and expenses, it also must include an analysis. Key questions to answer in a budget analysis are:

- What are the assumptions behind the data and resource allocations?
- What do you need to especially point out about the big picture of the budget?

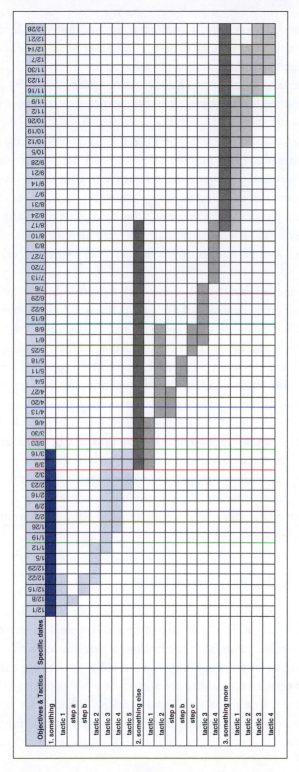

Figure 4-7. GANTT CHART.

- What are important relationships among items in the budget?
- Why is this budget reasonable and accurate as an allocation of resources to implement the plan?
- How will the results from achieving the objectives bring a return on the investment (ROI) of the resources being allocated to this plan?

You must show estimated costs and note the sources/vendors for those costs in your budget spreadsheet. You must also keep records of the estimates you got in case someone wants to see them or has a question. Your budget must be detailed for all the components of each tactic. For example, if you want to produce a brochure, what will be the particular costs for writing, designing, printing (including paper), mailing, and evaluating it? Additionally, you may also want to show budget for time along with each monetary cost. If you do this, make sure it is consistent with your timeline.

Again, budgeting is not only something concerned with money going out and coming in. Budgeting concerns the bigger picture of how resources—the primary resource being money—are allocated across all operational needs to fulfill a strategic plan. Other resources include people, time, facilities, machinery, equipment, and so on. When money is allocated, it is often tied to these other resources (and vice versa), such as when salary and benefits are applied to people, rent and utilities are applied to facilities, and time is applied to the depreciating value of buildings, machinery, and equipment. A PR leader is supremely responsible for all budgeting matters and must make sure all budgets are on track by helping managers understand what is expected and reviewing budgets and actual expenses for accuracy and explanations. More information about budgets will be presented in the next section. These issues now lead us into the realm of basic financial responsibilities for public relations leaders, who are often without a background in finance and accounting.

Finance and Accounting Matters

By now it should be very apparent that mathematics is a critical skill for public relations professionals at least because of measuring performance on financial and nonfinancial grounds. The financial health of a public relations function, just like all operating units in an organization, is usually something that public relations students do not learn unless they are minors or double-majors in some area of business. Indeed, certain aspects related to finance are addressed in the previous section about strategic planning. Although the realm of information about *finance* (i.e., managing an organization's financial resources) and *accounting* (i.e., recording and reporting on financial transactions) is vast, there are certain topics that are perhaps the predominant ones that public relations managers rely on most on a daily basis. To obtain a full appreciation for all the dimensions of finance and accounting, it would be best to take one or more courses in them, including a course in managerial accounting. Short of taking such courses, you may dive deeper into the subjects on your own though books and other sources like those by Schoffner, Shelly, and Cooke (2011), Siciliano (2003), and Droms (1990). In this brief section we will focus on two selected topics: (1) core financial statements and (2) budgets and forecasts. In fact, these particular topics are especially potent when agencies research potential and current clients, and they are critical when corporations research other organizations for partnerships, competitive positions, acquisitions, or other business insights.

The four core financial statements

Any organization must keep track of its financial performance. Accounting is a discipline that is especially focused on that effort. Depending on how an organization is organized, its accounting records must reflect that organization while at the same time upholding Generally Accepted Accounting Principles (GAAP), which are the rules for financial reporting for all organizations. These rules are developed by the accounting profession along with input from the U.S. government. The GAAP rules, then, serve as the framework for producing readable and usable information about any organization's performance and management's effectiveness in running the organization. The accurate and timely recording of financial and other performance data is, therefore, vital to protecting an organization's assets through effective management control and task control. Financial performance data are available to managers and top leaders for "slicing and dicing" in any way possible so they can see how strong or weak any part of the operation is at any time. In fact, a CPM system would allow managers to "drill down" to ever-greater depths of detail in performance data (e.g., projects and budgets) that pertain to the parts of the business for which they are individually responsible.

Standardized reports are used to show an organization's actions in terms of the kinds of financial transactions that account for them. In this way these reports present information at the highest possible level as they cover a whole organization. These reports are prepared on a regular basis (e.g., monthly, quarterly, annually) so that management and stakeholders have the most timely, complete, and accurate information about organizational performance. Those standard reports are called *financial statements*, and they are of four types (Rich, Jones, Heitger, Mowen, & Hansen, 2010):

- *Balance sheet*—reports the assets (i.e., resources) an organization owns and its liabilities (i.e., claims others, including investors/stockholders, have on those assets) at a stated point in time. The data for assets and liabilities must equal each other and, therefore, are said to be "in balance." If they do not, there is a fundamental accounting error somewhere. When reading a balance sheet, notice what the assets and liabilities are as well and how they are accounted for. Different classifications of assets and liabilities can be reported, and a balance sheet indicates how much an organization owns and how much others have a claim on any parts of the organization. Be sure to read the footnotes to line items because they give additional detail.
- *Income statement*—reports how well an organization has performed in terms of revenue, expenses, and income over a given time period. The simplest form of this financial statement (i.e., *single-step* income statement) fundamentally shows whether or not an organization is operating at a profit (i.e., net income) when revenue from all sources exceeds expenses or at a loss (i.e., net loss) when expenses exceed revenues. For *multi-step* income statements, three subtotals are important to note (Rich et al., 2010):
  1. *gross margin (gross profit/loss)*, which is "the difference between net sales and the cost of sales (or cost of goods sold)" (p. 19) and shows the initial profit made from selling a product or providing a service
  2. *income (loss) from operations*, which is "the difference between gross margin and operating expenses" (p. 19) and shows how much an organization spends to sell goods or provides services as well as run the organization
  3. *net income (loss)*, which is "the difference between income from operations and any nonoperating revenues and expenses" (p. 19) and shows the "bottom line" about whether an organization made (or lost) money in its operations

When reading any income statement, look at the subcategories of revenues and expenses and how the data are shown with specific line items that consolidate a lot of data about sources of revenue or expense. Footnotes to line items give additional detail, and you must read them too.

- *Cash flows*—reports on the flow of cash into and out from an organization during a period of time. Line items will show sources of income and outflow. Cash flow indicates an organization's creditworthiness because it is an indication of its ability to pay its bills. This ability to immediately pay debts is also referred to as *liquidity*. When reading a statement of cash flows, look at whether or not the final total is positive or negative and to what degree it is positive or negative for the period of time indicated. The more positive an organization's cash flow, the better. Make sure you read the footnotes to line items because of the additional detail given.

- *Retained earnings*—reports the amount of an organization's income that was kept for the business and how much was distributed to organization owners/investors during a period of time. When reading a retained earnings statement, look at how much income an organization earns but does not distribute to investors in the form of dividends. The amount of income kept for the business indicates how much organizational management plans to invest into the company for future growth. As always, footnotes to line items give additional detail, so be sure to read them.

These four financial statements answer key questions about how well an organization is performing *overall* compared to previous periods of its history, what economic resources an organization has and who has claims on them, and where the organization obtained its cash and where its cash went (Rich et al., 2010). The preparation of financial statements is part of the larger accounting cycle *during* a period of reporting (i.e., analyzing transactions, journalizing transactions, and posting transactions to the general ledger) and *at the end of* a period of reporting (i.e., preparing a trial balance of accounts, adjusting the accounts, preparing financial statements, and closing the accounts) (Rich et al., 2010).

Reading the financial statements is an important skill to develop as a manager because you need to know where in an organization's big picture your operation has its stake and what it contributes (see Berman, Knight, & Case, 2006; Ittelson, 2009). A particularly important section of financial statements that must be read is the "management discussion and analysis," also referred to as MD&A. This section is the official narrative explanation about what the organization experienced and why, including financial data to demonstrate it. Again, the organization's structure will be helpful in finding into what line items in any financial statement public relations and other operating areas fit. Very often public relations work will be covered in the income statement in line items labeled with terms like "promotional activities" or "marketing." Remember that these line items consolidate a lot of data into standard, GAAP categorizations that make the complexity of financial information understandable to people without their having to know the deep details about every operating unit and every project or program they handled. As a leader of a core operation to an organization, you should be able to understand how and where public relations affects revenue and margins. You should also be able to help employees find how their work shows up in these statements and what these statements say about the strength and viability of the organization and the competence of top leaders.

Budgets and forecasts

Much of the deeper detail beneath these financial statements is found in the more basic financial tools of budgets and forecasts, which are typically administered by managers (ranging from operational leaders to project team leaders) with the help of their staff members. Although we addressed budgets earlier in this chapter, there are additional, important matters to cover. *Budgets* are anticipated, periodic patterns for income and expense over a given period for a particular organizational operation to an individual program or project. The lines/rows in a budget spreadsheet are the "accounts" or "cost centers," depending on how an organization wants to refer to them. (See Appendix B for an example.) Budgeting "conservatively" is a preferred approach that calls on managers to be truly realistic about expected income and expenses—to not overpromise and underdeliver.

There are two kinds of budgets: *administrative* and *functional*. The first concerns a whole operational function, like that of public relations, and the second concerns individual projects or programs. Both kinds of budgets are tied to strategic plans commensurate with their level of activity. Administrative budgets usually span a 12-month period (a calendar or fiscal year) and cover planned operational expenses, including wages and salaries, benefits, rent of business facility, telecommunications, postage, printing, and so on. These items are typically based on historical use, which serves as a starting point for expected future expenses. Functional budgets could span any length of time necessary to complete a project or program and make the clearest ties between results and resources allocated to realizing the plan for a given project or program. Key to functional budgets are *direct costs* for necessary material, supplies, and services (i.e., costs from outside companies engaged in the project/program) and indirect costs (i.e., items from the administrative budget and out-of-pocket expenses). Billable hours would be included also and broken out as a separate category in the functional budget for an agency.

A related financial tool to budgets is *forecasts*, which are very short-term views (i.e., days, weeks, months) of anticipated patterns of income and are especially useful in tracking trends. Forecasts have the advantage of being the most flexible compared to budgets because the short span of time is more easily accommodated, but that short time span can also be a disadvantage for forecasts because the horizon for planning and action is always so short. Forecasts are also solely focused on income and not expense, but that focus on income enables managers to identify trends right away. Budgets, however, have an advantage of keeping an eye on the long term and the bigger picture of income *and* expense while also having a flexibility to accommodate changes as needed. Forecasts can be especially useful in public relations to indicate periods of time when an organization may not expect much income and promotional work could be planned in advance of such periods to shore up demand and, thereby, sales. Budgets and forecasts, then, are very potent tools for planning and executing public relations work that should be used in tandem whenever possible.

In either case, budgets and forecasts are kept as confidential information within an organization (i.e., they are not shared publicly). Most important, budgets and forecasts must always be compared to *actuals*, which are the data about real income and expense accounted for at specific times during a reporting period. Comparisons between budgets/forecasts and actuals provide managers with key information about how well plans are being enacted with resources that were allocated and anticipated. Reports about budgets/forecasts versus actuals should be generated and analyzed regularly—in sync with the reporting cycle for the financial statements. Just like the relationship among the various levels of plans, budgets and forecasts must roll up to the successively higher levels of budgets and forecasts. Being "on budget" is good and expected. Being "under budget" could be great, provided there was no loss in expected results and quality. And being "over budget" can be very bad, and there must be compelling and defensible reasons for it.

The budget process

The top leader in an operational area of an organization, such as public relations, is responsible for developing and managing that area's budget—and do so with the help of managers of the various activities in that operation who have direct responsibility for particular parts of the overall PR budget. An organization's finance and accounting (F&A) department orchestrates the entire budgeting and accounting process, providing the framework and rules for creating budgets and forecasts the way the organization needs them. This orchestration is essential because each operational area's budget and forecast must roll up to the organization's total budget, forecast, and other financial statements as needed. F&A, along with top management and the legal staff, is responsible for making sure all financial reporting is in compliance with applicable rules and laws.

Creating a budget or forecast is a relatively straightforward process, and individual organizations have particular procedures and requirements for budgeting and forecasting that must be followed. Generally speaking, when a past budget for the same or similar need of any scale was previously created and is available, it can be used as the basis for determining what income and expenses would be expected under the associated plan to meet that need. If additional money or resources are needed beyond what was used in the prior budget, or if money and resources are needed for new initiatives, a manager must make a formal *budget request* that stipulates (a) what is needed and by when, (b) why it is needed, including the expected valued that will be added, and (c) how much it would cost and through which provider. If there is no prior budget, the process goes on without that documentation. For forecasts, trend data about the past and anticipated future revenue are used along with information about economic and market performance and direction.

The tactical elements of a plan dictate what should be listed as the income and, more likely for public relations, the expenses. Data must be gathered about every aspect of every tactic in the plan that covers costs in terms of time, money, people, equipment, suppliers/vendors, and so on. Include items like postage, mileage, labor, overhead, and 10% for unforeseen expenses. These data then are broken down into categories (i.e., cost centers) based on the objectives they serve in the plan and presented in a spreadsheet with the categories and line-item detail for each income and expense. Appendix B shows an example of a plan-based budget.

Business cycles and budgeting

Organizations experience something called "*business cycles*," which are the increases and decreases in demand for their offerings (i.e., products or services) over a period of time. Figure 4-8 shows a graph of a hypothetical business cycle, where the middle of the year is the period of least sales activity for the organization. The more an organization's business cycle shows great demand, the more an organization stands to gain in revenue. Conversely, the more a business cycle shows reduction in demand, the less an organization will see in revenue and it may even see a loss. One such cycle is based on replacing products after their useful life spans. For very durable products that are used for many years, that cycle can be very long because the products do not need frequent replacement. An example of this is metal stamping machines for car fenders and hoods. Those machines can operate for many years, and only the molds and dies need to be replaced when a car design change is made. Less durable products, like socks, need replacement more frequently. Another cycle is seasonal, which includes industries like agriculture (i.e., the growing season), education (i.e., the academic year), and retail stores (i.e., holiday shopping) that have very predictable periods of great activity.

Because each organization faces its own business cycle, whatever and however long that cycle may be, organizational leaders must know and understand it so they can lead their operations in ways that make the most of the ebbs and flows of business and the revenue that goes with it. In particular, operational leaders, including those in PR, must use knowledge about business cycles to anticipate when during a

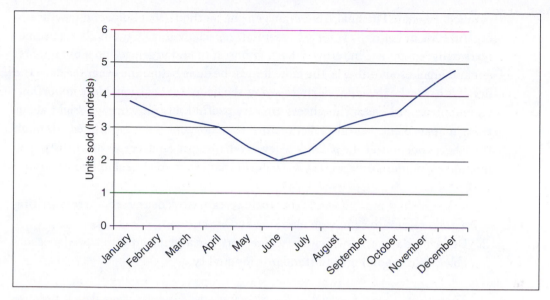

Figure 4-8. BUSINESS CYCLE CURVE FOR SALES ACTIVITY.

year activity and costs associated with it may be best undertaken. Forecasts can be instrumental in this regard. As we will see in Chapter 7, it is possible to plan for the rise and fall of business cycles so that the highs are not so high and, most important, the lows are not so low, which manages revenue flow more evenly over time.

Throughout the process of preparing any financial reports or proposals, be sure to keep all documentation about all aspects of the budget, forecasts, actuals, and other data for future reference and, perhaps, defense in case there are questions or problems with the final budget document. Such documentation would include estimates from outside companies to provide goods or services that would fulfill any stated objective. Other documentation may be in the form of internal reports from other operational areas that are working with or have some bearing on public relations efforts under a given plan. Bottom line: the results of the plan must justify the costs for doing the work.

Time Management

"Time is money" is an old saying that rings true all the time in virtually any business pursuit. Because time is a vital resource among many, it must be effectively managed. The best way to begin thinking about managing time is at the individual level of one's self. How does someone manage his or her time? Is he or she successful? Where can he or she improve? These are important, basic questions that require detailed answers. Personal time-management methods that someone may use to organize his or her daily work are essential, especially if such methods sort someone's daily "to-do list" in terms of both importance and urgency. The more important and urgent something is, the more it must be done before the other tasks on the list. If other tasks are added during the day, the list needs revision. More important, on an operational basis, timesheets are very useful tools for gaining insight about time management. Insight about time management can be gained through timesheets not only at the individual level. When aggregated across an entire public relations operation, timesheets yield valuable data that are useful in two ways:

1. Calculate how much it would cost to do certain work of any scope, from writing a press release to campaign planning and execution.
2. Determine areas of inefficiency where work can and must be improved measurably while upholding high standards for quality.

Timesheets require a level of detail many new PR employees detest because logging time spent on each project seems like true drudgery. Frankly, it is more fun to do the work on a project than to log the details of time and other resources and decisions of that work. However, timesheets are absolutely essential: they document what was done, how much was done and how long it took, for what reasons, and by whom at every level (from intern to chief executive). Timesheets come in many different forms and formats, from sophisticated and secure online systems to spreadsheets or paper logsheets. Fundamental components of timesheets are employee name, client, project name, activity completed, and time used for that activity. The time someone spends on work must be stated specifically and accurately, categorized appropriately (e.g., by client and/or project), and shown clearly to the nearest tenth of an hour (i.e., six minutes is one tenth of an hour). This means that tenths of an hour occur in multiples of six: 6, 12, 18, 24, 30, 36, 42, 48, 54, and 60. Rounding 50 minutes to the nearest tenth of an hour would be 48, or 0.8 of an hour. Note that 15 and 45 minutes can still be listed as 0.25 and 0.75 of an hour, respectively, but may be rounded up to 0.3 or 0.8, respectively. Timesheets must be filled in as someone completes her or his work on any project. Depending on the system formatting, a timesheet may display data-entry lines for the day work was done or for a whole week, including weekends and holidays.

The more someone uses timesheets, the more aware of her or his work habits and efficiency she or he becomes. This result is a very good thing because everyone needs to know how they work and how long it could take to complete any assignment, and having the data helps in making such estimates. From a manager's point of view, data from timesheets are valuable to see how efficient public relations staff members are individually and collectively. Moreover, timesheet data are valuable as the basis on which to make estimates about what it will take to do one kind of job or another and for agencies to bill clients for work completed under contract. Managers, then, must meticulously review each employee's timesheets against the projects to which they are assigned. Timesheets are not just something used in agencies. Corporate PR operations use them to measure productivity but not for billing.

In the end, then, a system for time management that is both simple and powerful for individuals and management is necessary for an effective and efficient PR operation. Time management should and must be a value-added activity for doing public relations work because it is an essential way to document the business of PR professionals that shows contributions from the individual level to the operational level.

Billing

Turning time into money is the realm of billing. Accounting for the other matters about resource allocations used to bring a plan to fruition also is in the realm of billing. Billing, then, is the documentation of all costs that have gone into completing work on another party's behalf. People's salaries and benefits (i.e., compensation), operational expenses for the physical presence and equipment of a PR function, and the expenses incurred for particular programs or projects all are translated into billing statements, also called invoices. Whether at an agency or a corporate PR operation, all work by staff members can be translated into a fair and competitive hourly rate. Hourly rates are much more common for agencies than for corporate organizations, but rates can be useful in determining relative costs for projects and programs that become useful in budgeting corporate PR operations. That rate also depends on external factors that, at a minimum, compare to the rates of other similar operations in the local or regional market. Rates for staff members and leaders are calculated similarly, but the rates are not the same. Agencies typically have a *rate card* that specifically shows what hourly rate is applied to the work its employees do based on their job titles. The difference between the rates of staffers and leaders is based on compensation matters that reflect the greater range of knowledge and experience of leaders over staffers, so the hourly rate for leaders is higher than that for staffers.

Note that the billing process, when viewed as a big picture, begins with estimates. When someone asks a public relations group to "bid" on a job, that means that person wants an estimate for what it will take to do the work he or she specifies. (We will address these specifications, called "requests for proposals," in Chapter 8.) Estimates are not mere guesses but, rather, well-researched and defensible statements about the expected resource allocations that will be needed to complete a job. Those resources include, of course, time, money, and material, including mark-ups (to be addressed shortly). The value of timesheets and solid experience and knowledge now come into play. An estimate, then, includes a statement about the job requested (i.e., a mini-plan) and a breakdown of the amount of time and material needed to complete the job and the costs for personnel and material. Past and potential efficiencies must also be part of the work to develop an estimate.

If the estimate is accepted and a contract for the job is executed, work on the job begins. As the job progresses, all time and material costs are logged and documented (i.e., timesheets, receipts, and progress reports). When an agency purchases material for a job or employs the help of others as a subcontractor in the work for a client, it has an immediate liability to pay for that material and that subcontractor. To cover the cost for those payments before the agency's client pays the bill for the work the agency did, the agency may *mark up* its costs for the material or subcontractor by a percentage that covers the interest for having paid the subcontractor before the client paid the agency. A mark-up of 17.65% on out-of-pocket expenses is common in the public relations business (Croft, 2006, p. 4). Mark-ups are understood and must be reasonable and defensible, and they may be negotiated as a client may ask for an agency to provide services "at cost," which means to not charge a mark-up.

Agency work may be billed in one of three ways, which is defined in the contract between an agency and its client: (1) hourly, (2) project, or (3) retainer. *Hourly billing* is the simple invoicing for the time and material used for completing work for the client. This approach to billing is the most common, and it is considered the most fair because it is a true item-by-item accounting for what was done as it was done. *Project billing* involves invoicing for an entire project once it has been completed. Project billing is based on a client's acceptance of a holistic and comprehensive proposal for completing a wide range of work (e.g., PR campaign or publication project) that includes all costs that will be accounted for in one invoice. *Retainer billing* involves a contractual relationship between a client and an agency that, for the same fee paid monthly or so, covers any and all work, no matter how much or how little work is necessary. This form of billing can be the riskiest for both client and agency because the cycle of business activity may be very high for a period of time but later on very low. Forecasting becomes key in this billing approach. In theory, the retainer approach should balance for both parties over the course of a year, but very close scrutiny to budgets and results is absolutely necessary to make sure one is not losing money and resources. Because retainers are so open-ended in the scope and volume of work that may be done, they can be renegotiated if cycles warrant more or less fees paid for the respective amount of work forecasted. Hourly and project billing are unlikely to be renegotiated because they are contractual obligations. Negotiation of any contract is best handled before signing, as Chapter 3 suggested and Chapter 8 will show.

One or more invoices for the job, depending on the terms of the contract and the duration of the job, show what was done, how much of it, and at what cost.

Applicable taxes must be computed and included as well. Costs are itemized simply but thoroughly so that it is readily apparent how the work relates to the original agreement. A formal invoice is prepared and sent, thereby formally presenting a request for payment for work completed. Invoices, over time, function not only as

EXECUTIVE VIEWPOINT

Strategic Planning in the Big and Little Pictures

Anne Rodriguez, Director of Corporate Communications for WPPI Energy*

The last thing a PR manager wants to hear is, "This is a critical topic for operations (or finance, HR, etc.), but it doesn't concern PR."

At its best, this kind of interaction can be baffling. More often, it's outright disheartening. After all, PR professionals can provide company leaders with important counsel. Our jobs entail gaining cooperation and support from those who can either help or hurt our company's very ability carry out its mission, and when important issues arise, we are uniquely positioned to provide needed insights. But, all our expertise won't help the company with critical issues unless PR is regarded as an essential part of organizational decision-making. In short, we can't help if we're not "at the table."

In nearly 15 years in the field, I have found that my success heavily depends on how PR is valued within the organization. I have also found that the best way to ensure that PR is valued is to demonstrate my understanding of, and PR's ability to help address, business matters not limited to the traditional scope of campaign planning and execution. Doing so depends in large part on many of the topics identified in this chapter: knowledge of the organizational plan, ability to develop PR strategies that support overall business objectives, understanding of the dynamic environment and markets in which the company operates and awareness of the organization's financial context.

When we as PR managers are knowledgeable about the business as a whole, not only do we gain credibility that best positions us to help the organization when challenges arise, but we also ensure that our own department-level plans are well grounded. This is important because, insightful as they may be, our plans will only succeed if we gain the input and buy-in of our counterparts in other business functions, as well as the company's leaders.

When I have seen PR plans fail, internal detractors and lackluster organizational engagement are very often among the culprits. In order for our PR plans to gain necessary internal support, we must seek input from and develop cooperative relationships with various other parts of the organization. We accomplish this by demonstrating understanding of the company's overall objectives and the particular concerns of other business units and departments. I find that doing so—which depends in large part on developing the kinds of organizational knowledge described in this chapter—fosters the mutual regard, trust, and relationships that are essential to our long-term success.

This is particularly true in corporate environments. As a director of communications for my company, I may hire PR agency help when I need creative support, outside perspectives, and specialized expertise. But, for success that is sustainable, I must also build for myself an internal network that reaches far into the rest of my organization. After all, not only would it be very expensive and inefficient to ask an agency to try building those internal connections on my behalf, but the results of doing so would not last beyond the life of that particular project or campaign. Those internal relationships need to be built by those of us who are here doing the day-in, day-out work of the organization for the long term.

Given these conditions, future PR agency professionals should take note: The advice in this chapter applies to you as well. Corporate communicators like me will be more apt to choose an agency if it can demonstrate business savvy about my organization and my industry.

Developing strategic planning expertise is another critical factor for PR's success. The strategic communications planning (SCP) model created by this book's author is one that I have used throughout my career for the development of advocacy campaigns, product launches, and annual department plans. Because my resulting SCPs have been measured, ethical, and grounded in the company's mission, they have been perceived as making valuable contributions to the company's success. In fact, in many cases, the stakeholder insights they offer have helped to shape higher-level organizational plans. In this way, demonstrating strategic planning expertise has also helped me to find my seat at the table.

The applicability of the SCP approach to supporting other departments' corporate objectives is almost limitless. Thanks in large part to this strategic planning orientation my position has evolved over the years. Originally, the scope of my job was focused on writing and producing corporate communications materials. Today, my role includes overseeing the development of those materials, but also providing strategic counsel to senior leaders in my company. I have also used the SCP model to develop legislative advocacy and policy messaging; an area of responsibility that my job has since grown to include.

Finally, in order to make PR a welcome and desired participant in key organizational matters, we must be judicious and flexible about how we engage internal peers and leaders. We may need to modify, shorten, or retitle sections of our SCP to fit audience needs, preferred terminology and interest level. Not only should a plan not be developed in isolation from other functional areas of the company, but to gain long-term support from across the organization, the plan must also be digestible for various internal audiences.

In my particular case, those audiences include the staff team as a whole, my own supervisor and other senior vice presidents, the CEO, the board of directors, and more. If I want their engagement, I must be discerning about how I communicate to each internal stakeholder.

Developing the strategic planning skills and the comprehensive kinds of organizational knowledge outlined in this chapter has taken me a long way toward that goal. I'm confident it will do so for you as well.

* The views expressed here are the author's own.

proof of what was done and how much it cost, but they also function as benchmarks for future planning and budgeting. And when invoices are coupled with the full range of performance reporting about a given program or project, they function as points of comparison that may be used to weigh the merits of the same or competing organizations than may be considered for other jobs in the future.

Public relations involves the measured and ethical use of language and symbols to inspire cooperation between an organization and its publics. A key phrase is "measured and ethical," which directly implies metaphorically a strategic bias to the practice of public relations, not merely or only tactics. It also implies literally the application of methods of measuring performance and success. Strategy and the process of strategic thinking, as covered in this chapter and extended in the next chapter, can be viewed as a systematic, forward-looking approach for a situation that, given certain parameters (e.g., knowledge, experience, research, timing, budget, resources, enacted environment), defines what must be achieved, how achievements will be made, and why the approach can be determined successful or not.

Key Words

Strategic planning	SWOT
Organizational plans	Culture
Operational plans	Performance
Ad hoc plans	Business cycle
Contingency plans	Timesheet
Management control	Budgets (two types)
Task control	Budget request
CPM system	Four core financial statements
Vision	Forecast
Mission	Actuals
Tactics	Bid
Objectives (four types)	Invoice
EGAD	Mark up
Benchmark	ROI
Strategies	Rate card
CSFs	Three billing types
KPIs	

Exploration of Operations Tools I

1. Choose an organization with which you are very familiar. Write a concise situation analysis of it, including a SWOT analysis. Next write two to four objectives (using the EGAD formula and benchmarks) that address that situation. Then develop strategy statements and tactics that will fulfill each objective.

2. Find an annual report online from a prominent public relations agency or a corporation that you admire. Look at its financial statements and identify where in them public relations is probably or definitely included. Explain what you come to understand about PR's role in the overall operation.

3. Track your time for the next four weeks or more. Document your time according to categories of work. Analyze your use of time to complete your work and answer these questions:

    a. In what areas did you spend more time than you thought you would and why?

    b. In what areas did you spend less time than you thought you would and why?

    c. Compared to your past experiences, how does your time management compare?

    d. In what ways do you think you worked efficiently and can use those lessons for other work you do to develop high-quality products?

    e. In what ways do you think you worked inefficiently, and how must you improve your time usage and the quality of your products?

    f. What implications are there for you to better manage yourself and your work during your professional career?

4. Search the Internet for project- or program-based budgets. Examine them for what they contain and how they present the information for the project/program to which they are tied. How are data organized? What line items to you see? What does the budget tell you about the allocation of resources for the project/program?

5. Examine section 3.0 in the strategic plan in Appendix B and devise an invoice for the work specified for one of the objectives. Find an sample invoice on the Internet, use a template in your word processor, or develop one yourself. Compute the time and costs for all aspects of the tasks outlined in your chosen objective, then compute the total costs.

References

Anthony, R. N. (1988). *The management control function*. Boston: Harvard Business School.

Ariyachandra, T. R., & Frolick, M. N. (2008). Critical success factors in business performance management: Striving for success. *Information systems management, 25*(2), 113–120.

Berman, K., Knight, J, & Case, J. (2006). *Financial intelligence: A manager's guide to knowing what the numbers really mean*. Boston: Harvard Business Review Press.

Buytendijk, F., Wood, B., & Geishecker, L. (2004). *Mapping the road to corporate performance management* (Strategic Analysis Report R-22-0731). Stamford, CT: Gartner Inc.

Clampitt, P. G. (2010). *Communicating for managerial effectiveness* (4th ed.). Thousand Oaks, CA: Sage Publications.

Droms, W. G. (1990). *Finance and accounting for non-financial managers* (3rd ed.). Reading, MA: Addison-Wesley.

Drucker, P. F. (1994, Sept/Oct). The theory of the business. *Harvard Business Review, 72*(5), 95–104.

Ittelson, T. R. (2009). *Reading financial statements: A step-by-step guide to understanding and creating financial reports*. Franklin Lakes, NJ: Career Press.

Keyton, J. A. (2011). *Communication and organizational culture: A key to understanding work experiences* (2nd ed.). Thousand Oaks, CA: Sage.

Mintzberg, H. (2007). *Tracking strategies . . . toward a general theory*. New York: Oxford University Press.

Rich, J. S., Jones, J. P., Heitger, D. L., Mowen, M. M., & Hansen, D. R. (2010). *Cornerstones of financial and managerial accounting*. Mason, OH: South-Western Cengage Learning.

Robert, M. (1997). *Strategy pure and simple II: How winning companies dominate their competitors*. Hightstown, NJ: McGraw-Hill.

Robert, M. (2006). *The new strategic thinking: Pure and simple*. New York: McGraw-Hill.

Schoffner, H. G., Shelly, S., & Cooke, R. A. (2011). *The McGraw-Hill 36-hour course: Financer for nonfinancial managers* (2nd ed.). New York: McGraw-Hill.

Siciliano, G. (2003). *Finance for non-financial managers*. New York: McGraw-Hill.

Smudde, P. M. (2011). *Public relations as dramatistic organizing: A case study bridging theory and practice*. Cresskill, NJ: Hampton Press.

Smudde, P. M., & Courtright, J. L. (2012). *Inspiring cooperation and celebrating organizations: Genres, message design and strategy in public relations*. New York: Hampton Press.

Recommended Reading

Austin, E. W., & Pinkleton, B. E. (2006). *Strategic public relations management: Planning and managing effective communication programs* (2nd ed.). Mahwah, NJ: Lawrence Erlbaum Associates.

Beard, M. (2001). *Running a public relations department* (2nd ed.). London: Kogan Page.

Berman, K., Knight, J., & Case, J. (2006). *Financial intelligence: A manager's guide to knowing what the numbers really mean*. Boston: Harvard Business School Press.

Botan, C. (2006). Grand strategy, strategy, and tactics in public relations. In C. H. Botan &

V. Hazleton (Eds.), *Public relations theory II* (pp. 197–218). Mahwah, NJ: Lawrence Erlbaum Associates.

Croft, A. C. (2006). *Managing a public relations firm for growth and profit* (2nd ed.). New York: Best Business Books.

Dozier, D. M., Grunig, L. A., & Grunig, J. E. (1995). *Manager's guide to excellence in public relations and communication management*. Mahwah, NJ: Lawrence Erlbaum Associates.

Ferguson, S. D. (1999). *Communication planning: An integrated approach*. Thousand Oaks, CA: Sage.

Hameroff, E. J. (1998). *The advertising agency business: The complete manual for management and operation* (3rd ed.). Lincolnwood, IL: NTC Business Books.

Lordan, E. J. (2003). *Essentials of public relations management*. Chicago: Burnham.

Mintzberg, H. (2007). *Tracking strategies . . . toward a general theory*. New York: Oxford University Press.

Oliver, S. (2007). *Public relations strategy* (2nd ed.). London: Kogan Page.

Roetzer, P. (2012). *The marketing agency blueprint: The handbook for building hybrid PR, SEO, content, advertising, and web firms*. Hoboken, NJ: John Wiley & Sons.

Chapter 5

OPERATIONS TOOLS II:
Performance Measurement, Performance Reviews, and Human Resources Management

We are all in this together. That is, every operational function in an organization has the responsibility to demonstrate how it has contributed to the welfare of the whole. This demonstration is possible and necessary through the measurement of performance and, thereby, the management of performance through the allocation of resources stipulated in the strategic plan and budget. This chapter addresses generally the larger business perspective public relations managers must know about why and how to measure operational performance. The key topics, then, span the range from the whole public relations operation to the individual public relations professionals who make things happen. This chapter focuses on the important topics of performance measurement, employee performance reviews, and human resource management.

Performance Measurement

A strategic plan includes performance measures in obvious places: objectives, key performance indicators, budget/resource allocations, and evaluation schemes. To determine value contributions, management controls are key, and performance measurements are the ways of tracking how well an organization and its operating units are getting the results needed to achieve objectives and realize the vision. (Chapter 6 will address the topic of value in more depth in relation to managerial decision-making.) Such measurements are based on data that are collected daily and reported on each day, week, month, and quarter—whichever periods are needed. These reports give management the information it needs to run the business, and the reports show employees how their work is paying off (or not). In general, accounting for value must minimally include regular and formal reporting (e.g., expenses, meetings, memos, progress reports) about the management of the public relations function and its constituent pursuits.

This work is part of a corporatewide system for management control, as we saw in Chapter 4. In that system, *performance measurements* are all quantitative and qualitative methods/tools used to evaluate progress toward or against defined objectives. Complementing the measuring of performance is *performance management*, which applies a combination of leadership skills and performance measurement tools to inspire people to attain or surpass objectives. Indeed, a corporate performance management (CPM) system, as we saw in the last chapter, can be a software solution that undertakes the measuring of organizational performance (see Geishecker & Zrimsek, 2002; Micheli & Manzoni, 2009) and provide data to leaders so they may monitor and understand the state and progress of the business in a variety of relevant and timely ways. For public relations, this system would naturally help to fulfill the PRSA's Code of Ethics provision for "enhancing the profession" by being a tool for making the business case for public relations, the role it and its people play, and the value it contributes in dynamic times within and outside an organization. A performance-measurement system, as defined by the American Institute of Certified Public Accountants (AICPA) and Lawrence Maisel (2001) report, is one that "enables an enterprise to plan, measure, and control its performance and helps ensure that sales and marketing initiatives, operating practices, information technology resources, business decision, and people's activities are aligned with business strategies to achieve desired business results and create shareholder value" (p. 12). Simply put, a business measures what it must to make sure it achieves its objectives.

Indeed, for the public relations profession, concerted efforts have been made especially over the last decade to determine increasingly appropriate and accurate ways to account for public relations' value through well-defined methodologies (e.g., Horton, 2006; Paine, Draper & Jeffrey, 2008; Swedish Public Relations Association, 1996; especially see the Institute for Public Relations). The purpose of this section is not to summarize any of those methods, which are amply explained and accessible in sources dedicated to them. This section is solely meant to present the big-picture business philosophy behind performance measurements and present one example of a dominant system used in performance management.

Why *measure* performance?

The point to measuring performance is to make sure an organization and all its departments, employees, processes, teams, etc. work together in the best way possible to achieve the results called for in the strategic plan. The strategic plan, which was addressed in Chapter 4, is a detailed document developed by management that defines the direction of the business for a year or so by describing objectives, goals, and other matters vital to the company achieving success. The working together of all organizational members, systems, and processes means everything is aligned and focused on fulfilling the strategies that will meet or exceed goals to achieve corporate objectives.

From large, multinational organizations to small, local businesses, performance measurements are necessary to keep a company on track. A 1997 study, *Serving the American Public: Best Practices in Performance Measurement*, was undertaken by the U.S. government to document what high-performance public and private organizations do to be so successful and, especially, how they measure their performance (Gore, 1997). The study, whose findings are as relevant today as they were then, featured participants from a large number of organizations in the private and public sectors in the United States, Canada, and the United Kingdom. According to the study, successful performance-measurement systems are characterized by the following aspects:

- *Leadership* is critical in designing and deploying effective performance measurement and management systems, where such executive involvement is active and personal, especially when it comes to communicating expectations and results.

- A *conceptual framework* is needed for any performance-measurement system, and it features ways to think about and apply specified performance measures, like matrix systems, target setting, benchmarking, criteria for the Malcolm Baldridge National Quality Award or the International Standards Organization's (ISO) certification.
- *Effective internal and external communication* are keys to successful performance-measurement system, where it depends on and demands open, honest, and multidirectional communication among all stakeholders.
- *Accountability for results* must be clearly assigned and well understood. Everyone understands what it takes to be successful and where they are responsible for achieving organizational goals.
- Performance-measurement systems must provide *the most relevant, timely, and strategically important information* for decision-makers, not just compile data, so they can accurately assess progress and take action to achieve objectives and goals.
- *Compensation, rewards, and recognition* should be linked to performance measurements, tying financial and nonfinancial incentives directly to performance.
- Performance-measurement systems should *be positive, not punitive*, which means the systems are "learning" systems that help everyone to identify what works and what doesn't so that the best approaches are maintained and the ineffective ones are repaired or replaced.
- *Results and progress* toward program commitments should be openly shared with employees, customers, and other stakeholders so they know, at a high level and without uncompromising sensitive information, where the company is headed, how it will get there, and how it will measure progress.

Any organization must be committed to applying these concepts so that everyone in the company knows where the company is headed and how it is going to get there.

Why *manage* performance?

Measuring the performance of a company, operating units, individuals, processes, programs, products and services, projects, and teams is critical to any organization's success. As the old saying goes, "You can't manage what you don't measure." Proof of the importance of measuring performance and then managing performance comes from a comparison of those companies that did measure their performance to those that did not. According to a study by Schiemann and Lingle (1999),

Measure of Success	Measurement- managed Organizations	Non–measurement-managed Organizations
Perceived as an industry leader over past 3 years	74%	44%
Reported to be financially ranked in the top third of their industry	83%	52%
Three-year return on investment (ROI)	80%	45%
Last major cultural or oprational change judged to be very or moderately successful	97%	55%

Figure 5-1. COMPARISON OF MEASUREMENT-MANAGED AND NON–MEASUREMENT-MANAGED ORGANIZATIONS.

SOURCE: Schiemann & Lingle (1999, p. 10)

companies that did measure their performance and manage their businesses accordingly substantially outperformed all companies that did not. Figure 5-1 breaks down the study's results.

Fundamentally, performance measurements are ways of tracking how well an organization is getting the results it needs to achieve its objectives and realize its vision. Such measurements are based on data that are collected daily and reported on each day, week, month, and quarter—whichever periods are needed. These reports give management the information it needs to run the business (i.e., to manage performance), and the reports show employees how their work is paying off (or not).

It is vitally important at this point to realize that performance measures focus on *both* financial and nonfinancial aspects of the business. If you think about it, financial measures alone only show you where the company has been and only in terms of its revenue, cash and equivalents, and debt and obligations. Financial measures are inherently lagging indicators about what happened in the past, not leading indicators for the future. Nonfinancial measures take into account things beyond finances that add value to the company and cause you to look to the future. Nonfinancial measures, like customer satisfaction, education, brand recognition, image, reputation, community efforts, etc., show key factors driving the business and indicate where a company is headed. The two kinds of measures together, then, make up a complete view of how well the business is doing in realizing its vision and fulfilling its strategic plan.

According to the American Productivity and Quality Center (APQC), "performance measures allow employees to gain a greater sense of accountability, personal ownership, problem solving, and priorities based on stakeholder [e.g. employees, investors, suppliers, customers] needs. Organizations are likely to experience improvements in performance, fairness, objectivity, consistency, response time, and decision making. Performance measures also allow organizations to implement a common language and to be alerted to issues on the horizon" (2002, ¶1). Over the long term, the APQC says, performance measures have critical benefits to an organization. A performance-measurement system "can justify corporate support for capital request, create an enduring focus, and justify capital allocation. Most importantly, performance measures are leading indicators of long-term health and consequently, [*sic*] represent a long-term planning asset" (¶2). We would look for similar benefits at any organization.

A company's own performance-measurement system can live up to these principles and, especially, accrue specific benefits that will help drive success. Some key benefits for a performance-measurement system are in four areas:

1. Financial
   - Develop more accurate forecasts, based on customers in the pipeline, and produce these forecasts more quickly, which gives a clearer picture of demand that must be met.
   - Measure on a market-by-market basis to give a clearer picture of how well sales goals and company objectives are met.
   - Produce sales, financial, and performance reports faster with better data, which makes managing the company's competitive position easier to see overall and by market.
2. Internal business processes
   - Link an organization's mission and strategy, then translate that strategy to operational objectives and measures—turning high-level strategy into action. Everyone works toward the same objectives in ways that pertain to their jobs, which means everyone knows what results are expected and how to achieve them.
   - Provide a link between lead generation and completed sales, which translates into knowledge about organizational performance.
   - Create a foundation for establishing daily, monthly, quarterly, and yearly goals for department, team, and personal performance, which means any measure can be viewed at any time to reveal performance in real time.
   - Make adjustments to or create new measurements as business needs dictate, which means an organization is well prepared to adapt to, measure, and capitalize on market changes.
3. Learning and growth
   - Identify opportunities and problems sooner, perhaps in real time, to meet sales performance goals, take advantage of strengths, and minimize weaknesses sooner.

- Measure aspects of sales that tie back to the corporate strategic plan, which shows how work translates into the overall success of the organization.
- Tie individual performance with team goals to recognize both, while emphasizing team contributions to the organization's growth, all of which means exemplary performance can be more easily identified and rewarded.
- Encourage employees to enroll in education/training opportunities to expand their knowledge related to aspects of the business so they develop professionally, personally, and intellectually in ways that also help the organization grow.

4. Customer focus
   - Track customer relationships and buying behaviors more effectively over time, which means anticipating customers' needs better and, consequently, building the business.
   - Know how customers feel about the organization and its products/services, plus compare the organization to the competition, which means collecting and applying the feedback from customers about organizational performance service for them.
   - Engage in effective communications within target markets to obtain new customers and inspire continued purchases from established customers.

These benefits have been visually organized in a way that puts the company vision and strategy at the center with the four key areas of any business radiating out from it. The visual model is shown in Figure 5-2. In the figure, given the approach to objectives presented in the previous chapter, "targets" would be the goals that would normally be stated in an EGAD-formed objective and associated benchmark. "Measures" are the specific metrics to be taken to measure goals/targets. "Initiatives" are a combination of strategies and tactics, leaning more on the latter, as means to fulfill the objectives.

This way of representing the relationship among the financial, business, learning/growth, and customer perspectives of a business—as they support the organization's vision and strategy—is called a "balanced scorecard" (BSC), and it is arguably the most-used performance measurement approach in the world. The BSC was developed by Robert Kaplan of Harvard Business School and David Norton of the Balanced Scorecard Collaborative (see Kaplan & Norton, 1996). A company's scorecard about its performance is said to be "balanced" when each of the four business perspectives support one another equitably, especially the financial perspective. More specifically, the balance that performance measurements should achieve is possible because they encompass essential dimensions that are financial and nonfinancial, leading and lagging, internal and external, quantitative and qualitative, and short-term and long-term.

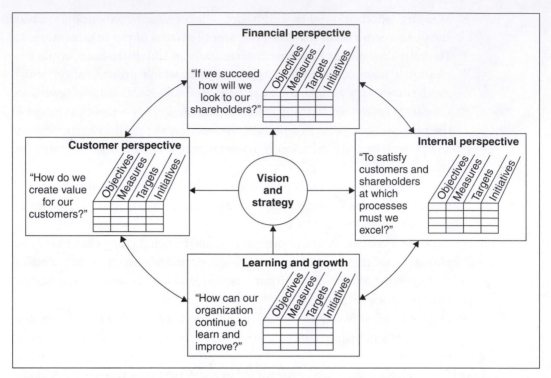

Figure 5-2. BALANCED SCORECARD.

SOURCE: Kaplan (2001)

There is an important distinction to note: the balanced scorecard is not only a system for measuring organizational performance, although it gives us a way to structure relevant measurements in each of the four business perspectives. The balanced scorecard is really a *management* system that helps an organization to clarify its vision and strategy so they can be translated into action by all employees in the work they do. The scorecard also establishes internal and external feedback mechanisms to ensure focus on both business outputs and outcomes through close examination of data from specific performance measurements and other sources. So this model is a useful way for a company to measure and manage performance on financial and nonfinancial dimensions.

All four areas are critical because they each help to manage discreet areas of the business in more effective ways. That is, when taken together, all four perspectives help a company stay focused on where it wants to go, not dwell on what it is been through. As Kaplan and Norton (1996) put it, "The balanced scorecard retains traditional financial measures. But financial measures tell the story of past events, an adequate story for industrial age companies for which investments in long-term capabilities and customer relationships were not critical for success. These financial measures are inadequate, however, for guiding and evaluating the journey that information age companies must make to create future value through investment in customers, suppliers, employees, processes, technology, and innovation" (p. 7).

For the field of public relations, the balanced scorecard is not the only performance measurement framework; however, the BSC does give us a very useful way to capture data relevant to the operational function that rolls up to the organizational performance perspective. In particular, Vos and Schoemaker (2004) have explained a useful way to apply the BSC for PR. Figure 5-3 shows how the parts of their approach fit with the BSC.

In their application of the BSC for PR, Vos and Schoemaker point to the most salient matters of quality in the practice of public relations that intersect with the BSC's four dimensions. The matters of quality are shown in the lefthand column. Each of these quality dimensions, then, is explained in terms of each of the four BSC dimensions. The result is a useful holistic view of how public relations value can be viewed and, most important, accounted for in particular performance measurements in a powerful performance-management system.

PR Quality Dimension	Financial	Internal Business Processes	Learning & Growth	Customers
Clarity	Clear positioning of the organisation	Information to staff is clear	Communication vision is clearly defined	Clear positioning of brands
Environment Orientation	Maintain networks for the organization's reputation	Communication reinforces commitment & supports change management	Communication function is well embedded in the organization	Maintain networks for distribution & sales
Consistency	Coherence with other functions & with other communication domains	Coherence with HR & with other communication domains	Common starting points for communication besides room for organizational units and/or communication domains	Coherence marketing mix, with R&D and with other communication domains
Responsiveness	Monitoring & action based on issue management	Communication contributes to internal views on external changes & communication skills encourage internal responsiveness	Feedback is used for innovation of communication	Monitoring & action based on market research, consumer trends & consumer complaints
Effectiveness & efficiency	Assess corporate image, cost efficient methods	Internal communication audits cost efficient methods	Assess communication quality, time management	Assess brand images, cost efficient methods

Figure 5-3. A BALANCED SCORECARD FOR PUBLIC RELATIONS.

SOURCE: Vos and Schoemaker (2004, pp. 41, 44)

How are performance measurements applied?

There are numerous financial and nonfinancial things a business can measure and report on. The trick is to select only the things that are critical drivers of performance under the strategic plan. So the availability of key information is essential in measuring performance and achieving success. And that key information comes from both internal and external sources that keep tabs on all aspects of the business important to management, employees, suppliers, investors, partners, etc. Most important, cause-and-effect relationships among the financial, customer, business processes, and innovation/learning domains help to determine which things are strategically important to measure and report on.

Effective performance measures, according to the book, *The Strategy Gap* (Coveney, Ganster, Hartlen, & King, 2003, p. 71), should fulfill the following basic conditions:

- Focus on key/strategic business factors
- Be a mix of past, present and future
- Balance the needs of all stakeholders
- Start at the top and flow down to the bottom
- Have targets that are based on research and reality rather than being arbitrary

A company will apply a performance-measurement system based directly on the company's strategic plan. The key parts of that plan are the company's vision, mission, objectives, goals, strategies, and tactics, which were addressed in Chapter 4. Any performance-measurement system that tracks a company's results effectively will reflect the following characteristics, as described in Coveney et al. (2003, pp. 73–74):

- Align top-level strategic objectives and bottom-level initiatives
- Identify opportunities and problems in a timely fashion
- Determine priorities and allocate resources based on those priorities
- Change measurements when the underlying processes and strategies change
- Delineate responsibilities, understand actual performance relative to responsibilities, and reward and recognize accomplishments
- Take action to improve processes and procedures when the data warrant it
- Plan and forecast in a more reliable and timely fashion

At a company level, several important financial and nonfinancial measurements will be taken regularly to manage an organization's business as effectively as possible. It is important for everyone to know that performance expectations are defined on an annual basis and applied periodically. This means that management begins a year with certain expectations, and each department works toward meeting or exceeding those expectations. The assumption is that performance expectations for the year will be met or exceeded as defined in the strategic plan. Only a major circumstance, like a severely faltering economy, a new and aggressive competitor, or unexpected heightened demand for a company's output, would significantly affect the company's ability to achieve its objectives and probably require changes to the strategic plan and each department's work.

The company-level and individual performance measurements will be assembled into management reports that will be run twice a month (biweekly) so everyone can see how well they are doing along the way and not only at the end of the month when it is too late to address matters. Such reporting will present the best view of business performance (e.g., sales actuals and projections) over any period of time.

Monthly performance targets will be established and adjusted up or down so they better reflect customer demand and projected sales. The specific targets for individual performance measurements will be defined together by each person and his or her management, based on projected sales performance and the strategic plan's objectives and goals.

The results of performance measurements, as published in the regular management reports, will help everyone see how well the organization is doing at any time. In this way, each operating unit—and each employee—can make adjustments to take advantage of new situations that come up or anticipate opportunities before they happen to make the most of them. The main idea is that we move closer to realizing the organization's vision and achieving its objectives.

Performance Reviews

When someone joins an organization as a new employee, he or she learns about the many responsibilities and, especially, expectations for his or her position. So at an individual level, what each person does in a company has been distilled to the most important, measurable things that relate directly to the company's strategic plan and the individual activities employees at all levels do. Other key performance measurements can be planned and tracked for particular team members based on their responsibilities, areas of accountability, and performance expectations.

These kinds of links among individual, operational, and organizational performance bring us to the topic of performance reviews. In any job you have ever had and will ever have, your performance in doing what is expected of you is key to determining whether you should continue to be employed and if you may be eligible for any rewards (e.g., pay raise, bonus, promotion, stock options, special recognition award) or for any punishments (e.g., pay cut, demotion, probation, firing). In every case, what is important to recognize is that every organization has its own policies and procedures for conducting performance reviews for employees and others, including volunteers, outside firms, and so on. Indeed, in the big picture, performance reviews are meant to bring each employee and her or his manager's view into alignment over time. This idea is shown in Figure 5-4, which indicates how both internal and external matters of performance feedback have an influence on the process.

When it comes to employee reviews, there are common human resources practices and laws that must be followed. The leader of any operational function must work with the human resources (HR) department to ensure that all policies and procedures for performance reviews are followed. And those reviews require formal, periodic feedback at least once a year and probably at midyear or even quarterly as well. Other reviews would include informal, as-needed feedback while people are doing their work so they know immediately how well they are doing

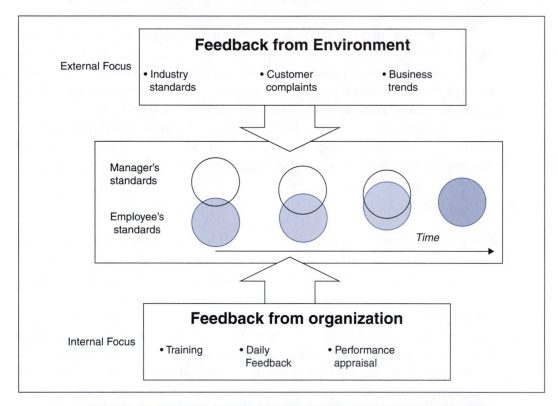

Figure 5-4. BRINGING MANAGER AND EMPLOYEE VIEWS OF PERFORMANCE INTO ALIGNMENT.

SOURCE: Clampitt (2010, p. 155)

compared to expectations. Moreover, performance reviews are opportunities for dialogic communication between individual employees and their leaders, not monologic lectures from the leader to the employee.

Performance reviews depend on four key sources of information between both an employee and her or his leader that facilitate a fair and principled judgment of how well someone has done, is doing, and can better do her or his job (Clampitt, 2010). The first source of performance information is *facts*, which are data about an employee's actual performance. The data concern chiefly the degree to which someone is either on track to or did achieve her or his personal performance objectives—simply put, what was done well, what was not, and what improvements can be made. As we covered in Chapter 1, a potent management approach for this source of information is management by objectives (MBO), which means both an employee and her or his manager set the performance expectations for the employee's job—in tune with the strategic plan—and plot a path to success.

The second source of information is *standards*, which are written (and unwritten) statements about how to judge an employee's performance. These standards encompass general principles and precedents regarding application of them to the facts about one's performance. Everyone working in an organization is expected to know their jobs and expectations. Written standards are the most useful and include broad, organizational statements about employee performance as defined by organizational top leaders and managed by the HR department. A good example is Magna International's "Employee Charter," shown in Figure 5-5. Other written standards are most directly focused on any given employee and are documented in individual job descriptions and departmental plans. Unwritten standards are those that stem from an organization's culture and work environment, including such matters of "collegiality" and "professionalism." Indeed, the interpretation and application of all standards depends on precedents of how past cases of employee performance were judged as satisfactory or not plus whether conduct was tolerated or could be observed as acceptable.

The third source of information concerns *exceptions*. Factors beyond an employee's control (e.g., technology crash, internal reorganization) and factors unique to an employee's life situation (e.g., birth of a child, extended leave of absence because of health matters) can hinder or inhibit her or his ability to fulfill responsibilities and performance objectives. As a matter of fairness to both the employee and the employer, these factors should be taken into consideration and may, over time, become built into the standards when they make sense to account for them any time they apply to an employee's performance.

The fourth and final source of performance information is *judgment*. This source is the reasonable outcome of the previous three, and it rests well within the

Magna International Inc. Employee's Charter

Magna is committed to an operating philosophy which is based on fairness and concern for people. This philosophy is part of Magna's Fair Enterprise culture in which employees and management share in the responsibility to ensure the success of the company. It includes these principles:

JOB SECURITY

Being competitive by making a better product for a better price is the best way to enhance job security. Magna is committed to working together with you to help protect your job security. To assist you, Magna will provide:

- Job Counselling
- Training
- Employee Assistance Programs

A SAFE AND HEALTHFUL WORKPLACE

Magna strives to provide you with a working environment which is safe and healthful.

FAIR TREATMENT

Magna offers equal opportunities based on an individual's qualifications and performance, free from discrimination or favouritism.

COMPETITIVE WAGES AND BENEFITS

Magna will provide you with information which will enable you to compare your total compensation, including total wages and total benefits with those earned by employees of your competitors, as well as with other plants in your community. If your total compensation is found not to be competitive, then your wages will be adjusted.

EMPLOYEE EQUITY AND PROFIT PARTICIPATION

Magna believes that every employee should share in the financial success of the company.

COMMUNICATION AND INFORMATION

Through regular monthly meetings between management and employees and through publications, Magna will provide you with information so that you will know what is going on in your company and within the industry.

THE HOTLINE

Should you have a problem, or feel the above principles are not being met, we encourage you to call the Hotline or use the self-addressed Hotline Envelopes to register your complaints. You do not have to give your name, but if you do, it will be held in strict confidence. Hotline Investigators will answer your call. The Hotline is committed to investigate and resolve all concerns or complaints and must report the outcome to Magna's Global Human Resources Department.

Hotline Number: 1-800-263-1691

EMPLOYEE RELATIONS ADVISORY BOARD

The Employee Relations Advisory Board is a group of people who have proven recognition and credibility relating to humanitarian and social issues. This Board will monitor, advise and ensure that Magna operates within the spirit of the Magna Employee's Charter and the principles of Magna's Corporate Constitution.

MAGNA

a Fair Enterprise corporation

Figure 5-5. MAGNA INTERNATIONAL'S "EMPLOYEE'S CHARTER."

SOURCE: Magna (2013; http://www.magna.com/for-employees/employee's-charter)

jurisdiction of the manager conducting the performance review to make a judgment. The judgment is not only based on the facts, standards, and exceptions the manager has collected and analyzed, but it is also made in response to the employee's perspective about the same matters. In this way, the performance review is a dialog about an employee's performance, with an eye toward continuous improvement in the future. The judgment also recommends rewards or punishments that are in line with organizational policies. Again, performance reviews given in either formal or informal ways must yield genuine and useful feedback whenever appropriate so that individual performance can be corrected or improved. A leader's role, as we saw in Chapter 1, is vital to ensuring success on personal and organizational grounds, and that means all feedback must be actionable not merely abstract.

As a matter of course for managing employee performance, leaders should keep good records about each of their employee's performance. The records can include any information from the four sources explained above. Moreover, leaders can help employees understand themselves and their contributions by using a SWOT analysis that focus on their immediate jobs and their career objectives. Additionally, MBOs can function as a useful and usable way to plot a personal plan based on the SWOT and include milestone checkpoints for progress. A relatively new approach to performance reviews is the "360-degree review," which fundamentally relies on the first three sources of information gathered anonymously from peers, superiors, and underlings (i.e., those who work all around you, like a circle). The information is then aggregated into a single report that an employee's manager shares and discusses with the employee during a formal performance review. These 360-degree reviews are typically done at all levels of an organization but may be especially reserved for people holding formal leadership positions.

Matters of performance at all levels can only be addressed through people doing what is expected of them, including finding ways to do their work better and going beyond expectations. Satisfactory—even great—performance begins with leading and managing the single largest, most expensive, and most important resource any organization has: its people. The next section about human resource management concisely addresses the matters of hiring, firing, managing, and developing communication professionals.

Human Resource Management

As we saw in the previous section, the human resources department is the key to all matters about employees. The *sequence of employment* is an interesting and useful one to concisely capture the "nuts and bolts" of hiring, firing, managing, and developing

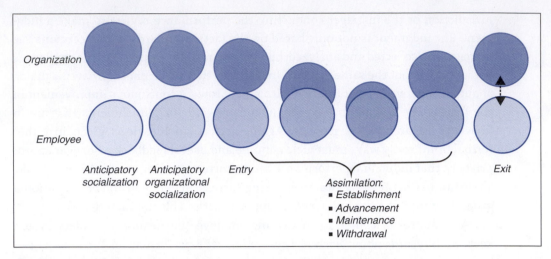

Figure 5-6. SEQUENCE OF STAGES FOR ORGANIZATIONAL EMPLOYMENT.

PR professionals. The sequence is based on a combination of Jablin's (2001) and Baird and Kram's (1983) work. The sequence progresses through five stages: anticipatory socialization, anticipatory organizational socialization, organizational entry, organizational assimilation, and organizational exit. Very important to remember is that the principles of effective leadership and followership from Chapter 1 must be applied instrumentally here. Figure 5-6 shows one way to visualize how it is that someone goes through the sequence from initial interest to exit.

The convergence of the two lines of circles indicates the increasing degree of identification between an employee and an organization. The sequence begins with *anticipatory socialization*, which involves someone making broad career choices based on information gathered from many sources, ranging from personal to mass media, including family, school, peers, part-time jobs, internships, and other experiences. Next, *anticipatory organizational socialization* involves the specific targeting of one or more organizations that participate in the career or industry that was the substance of the prior stage. In this second stage a useful metaphor is that of courtship between an employer and a prospective employee. The key in the courtship is organizational fit or identification. Realistic job previews through the interview process are instrumental in this stage. Figure 5-7 presents something of the reality behind the anticipatory organizational socialization step, at least in terms of the large quantity of applicants for any job and how much an organization must manage the process fairly and efficiently.

Next in the sequence is *organizational entry*, which begins from the moment a job offer is accepted and extends into the first 6 to 18 months on the job, depending on

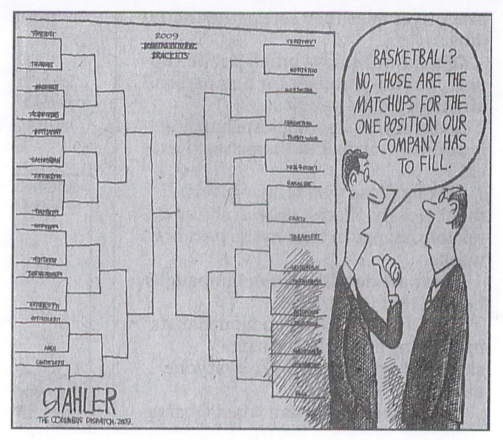

Figure 5-7. HIRING "BRACKETS" FOR A JOB OPENING.

the industry (public relations may be on the shorter side of this range). Instrumental in this stage is the "morale curve," when newly hired employees work through inflated expectations (even after the realistic job previews), culture shock, surprise of the full-time expectations, and ultimately leveling out of expectations due to understanding, acceptance, and routine.

Bridging off from organizational entry is the next stage of *organizational assimilation*, which is the most prolonged stage in the employment sequence. This stage is sometimes referred to as "identification" or "metamorphosis" because there is a quantum change in the employee because the participation between the employee and the employer results in increasingly aligned perspectives. There also is ever-improving fit between the expectations of the employee and her or his manager. In this stage an employee's performance and record of accomplishment should soar, perhaps to also include opportunities to *mentor* new employees who seek the benefits of this kind of professional relationship. In the organizational assimilation stage, four dimensions emerge: (1) *establishment*, which is an employee demonstrating her or his commitment to the organization and vice versa, including any professional-development opportunities (e.g., subject-specific education and experiences through coursework, seminars, and other training); (2) *advancement*, which is an employee's progress to increasing levels of authority, responsibility, and accountability through more exposure to others, challenging work, and other involvement opportunities; (3) *maintenance*, which is an employee's realization that she or he has reached the zenith of her or his career and will likely end her or his career at this level; and (4) *withdrawal*, which includes an employee playing more consultative roles within the organization and her or his operating unit and then, eventually, actively preparing for the final stage of organizational exit. In terms of mentoring, the ideal time to strike up a mentor–mentee relationship between an assimilated employee and a newer employee is in the dimension of maintenance because the other dimensions involve too much self-focus on the world-be mentor.

That final stage in the sequence is *organizational exit*, which concerns employment termination, which can be the result of one of several circumstances—quitting, firing, laying off, dying, or retiring. What is very important to recognize about organizational exit—for those quitting, being laid off, or, especially, retiring—is that exiting employees may hold a special affinity for their former organization. For people who quit on good terms, they can still be interested in keeping abreast of what is going on, primarily through former coworkers who are also personal friends. For those who are laid off, they may harbor ill feelings toward the organization or they may be more accepting. It is paramount that an organization that lays off employees treat them respectfully and helpfully as they forcibly change their career trajectories. For people who die, their coworkers may experience feelings of loss and, perhaps, surprise at their comrade's passing, if the death was caused by an accident or other unexpected calamity. Most important, though, are retirees. These people have spent the bulk of their careers with an organization and have strong emotional and financial ties to it. In many ways, retirees are still insiders, or part of the "family," and they expect good treatment by the organization and its representatives—beyond pension and benefits due to them—in return for the loyal service and important contributions they made during their years of formal employment.

Given this broad view of the employment sequence, we next can focus on particularly salient matters at the core stages that include hiring, firing, and developing employees.

Hiring

The hiring process spans the stages of anticipatory organizational socialization and organizational entry—from the job definition as advertised for the purpose of soliciting applications to the new employee's first day on the job. A critical point to the hiring process is to ensure that you follow the policies and procedures specified by your organization's HR department every step of the way, which must adhere to employment laws. Barring a lengthy narrative, the following outline summarizes the salient matters to conducting a sound hiring process.

- No clones of you! Look for people smarter than you and with skills needed in your group—*adding value.*
- Job definition
  - Obtain or create a definitive job description (used for screening candidates' worthiness)
  - Decide on full-time, part-time, contract, or job sharing, based on personnel needs for the team
  - Define salary target, primarily based on industry comparisons and budget limits
  - Basis for the job definition is the "ideal" candidate for what is needed
- Job posting and channels
  - Usual channels: organization's website, job-search sites, social media, newspapers, professional/industry publications
  - Personal: professional search firms, especially for public relations, marketing, and corporate communication
  - Outsourcing: freelancers, agency, consultants, vendors, temporary employment firm
- Collect and screen submissions—compare each applicant to criteria of job definition and expectations for qualifying, complete applications
- Select and call candidates to interview
  - Carefully listen to and take note of the person and what is going on in the background during the phone conversation
  - Give information about what to prepare/bring, including a basic agenda for a candidate's visit
  - Conduct background checks on and note any peculiarities about prime candidates' credit, social media presence, criminal record, search-engine hits, and other areas (see National Labor Relations Board, n.d.)
- Interview candidates individually (no group interviews)

- Check with HR for legal and organizational parameters for the whole process
- Design and obtain HR's approval for interview questions and basic agenda
- Pay attention to verbal and nonverbal dimensions of candidates
- Probe their thinking, communication, and other things with questions and tests, including writing and personality tests
- Look for personality and enthusiasm fits
- Review and discuss competencies, credentials, and experiences
- Don't cultivate confrontational situations
- Realize interviews primarily reveal how well someone interviews
- Contact references and ask probing questions—within the law
- Additional postinterview tasks for candidate (e.g., tests and problem-solving tasks)?
- Design offer with HR and boss based on:
  - Salary range (operational budget)
  - Candidate's salary history and credentials
  - Competition (if possible)
  - Human Resources Management Association database
  - U.S. Department of Labor statistics on salaries and benefits
- Decide on the candidate with HR and boss
- Offer position, pay, and benefits; engage in negotiation (presume success for both parties); determine starting date
- Give introductions and begin orientation on starting day
- Have workstation and all other things ready

Firing

The firing process is confined to the stage of organizational exit, and it spans activities from initial notification of a problem to formal dismissal. Organizations do not want to be accused of and party to a lawsuit claiming "wrongful dismissal," so it is imperative that the firing process follows the policies and procedures specified by your organization's HR department every step of the way, all of which uphold the law (see Orey, 2007). In short, you have to build a case for trying to help the employee redeem him-/herself and the employee's successfulness in doing so. Again, instead of a lengthy narrative, the following outline summarizes the salient matters to conducting a sound and basic firing process.

- Discuss with HR for procedure and policies
- Document any and all problems and link them to the job definition and performance expectations, even if either or both of them have been revised

- Discuss problems and expectations with employee privately, rationally and earnestly
  - Use the full personnel file and records about the employee
  - The discussion serves as fair warning about the consequences of continued poor performance
- Decide mutually on next steps to solve the performance problems
  - Performance expectations
  - Timeline for completion (usually 90 days)
  - Documentation of performance
- Document and monitor employee's progress on expectations *within the specified timeframe*
- Give feedback promptly (positive and negative)
- If employee still not cutting it, follow firing organization's firing procedures

A special case of firing is *layoffs*. Remember that employees represent the single largest expense to organizations. Layoffs are imposed on many employees at once in multiple areas of an organization in which employment costs are the most effective means for cutting operating costs. Decisions for laying off employees are never taken lightly, and many in management literally lose sleep for days before and after layoff announcements because they care about people. The plan behind layoffs is to reduce the organization's costs and have funds to rebuild the business. In PR agencies, when accounts are lost, entire account teams (leaders and followers) may be laid off because the work they used to do is gone and there may be nowhere in the agency to absorb anyone from the team. In corporations, it is likely that individuals would be laid off in a PR department, and perhaps that department is reorganized with another, like advertising.

A major result of layoffs includes job consolidations, so those who are not laid off will be picking up what those laid off used to do. Great care is taken in deciding in which areas of an organization any layoffs should be made so that losses in productivity and, most important, performance can be minimized with fewer people on hand. Layoffs are not necessarily about people's performance, but that concern can play a role when having to choose whom to lay off and whom to keep. Another result in layoffs is fear and remorse among those who are still employed because they, too, feel badly for their former colleagues and are fretful for the future of the organization. If you are laid off, you would be entitled to certain benefits for having been laid off, such as severance pay and job search help. Chapter 11 covers matters about seeking employment that also apply in a layoff situation.

In the case of layoffs and quitting, organizations may ask these employees leaving the organization to participate in an *exit interview*. Exit interviews are important and nonconfrontational opportunities for an organization to learn what employees think about their organization's strengths, weaknesses, and opportunities for improvement. Exit interviews would be held on an employee's final day of work, led by either the employee's manager or a human resources representative, and use a prepared questionnaire through which information, ideas, and comments are gathered. Exit interviews are not normally conducted with employees who are fired for poor performance, breaking organizational policies, or other relevant grounds for discontinuing employment. For anyone leaving an organization, whether or not they go through an exit interview, any personal identification cards, keys, cell phones, computers, and other company property provided to them to do their jobs will be taken. Immediately after an employee leaves, all points of online and other access the employee had to the organization will be terminated, as will the former employee's pay and benefits.

Developing employees

Developing employees focuses on the organizational assimilation stage of the employment sequence, and the material in Chapter 1 is most applicable. Check with your organization's HR department about any rules and restrictions on professional development for employees. The principal idea in developing employees is to help them become better and better at what they do, how they do it, and who they are while at work. Also in an effort to avoid a lengthy narrative and get to the point, the following outline summarizes the salient matters to conducting a sound employee-development process.

- Help establish a sense of ownership of the business
  - Connect the dots between the organization's objectives and performance and employees' role in them
  - Apply and excel in knowledge, skills, and experiences
  - Involve goal-setting and other appropriate matters
  - Establish ways to measure/document one's performance
- Conduct effective formal and informal performance reviews
- Seek and recommend educational opportunities for employees based on job and/or career objectives
- Entertain suggestions from employees for educational/professional-development opportunities (e.g., degree or certificate programs, classes, conferences, workshops, seminars)
- Have educated/developed employees share/summarize what they learned and how it would be helpful to others and group

EXECUTIVE VIEWPOINT

Measuring Performance with the Science of Public Relations

Frank Ovaitt, President and CEO,

Institute for Public Relations

In any true profession, the practitioner deeply understands the importance of research-based knowledge in guiding the work and measuring the results. In public relations, research is the cornerstone of all communication work because it defines what can be done and, most especially, the grounds for determining effective performance.

There are two topics that I believe are central to the matter of performance measurement and management in public relations: the core elements of the science behind the art of public relations, and essential factors to identifying bad research.

First, there are several core insights about the new thinking that is driving the science of public relations.

- **More attention to the three kinds of research,** as adapted from James E. Grunig, Ph.D. (professor emeritus at the University of Maryland): research *in* the practice of public relations, to guide and evaluate actual PR programs; research *on* the practice of public relations, to better understand what we do and how we do it; and research *for* the practice of public relations—the social science underpinnings for our work.

- **What other disciplines can teach us.** We rarely take time to think about what economics, law, cultural studies, political science, sociology, social psychology, linguistics, and even neuroscience have to say to public relations. That robs us of opportunities to greatly (and quickly) expand our knowledge base and understand what's really going on when we seek to build public relationships and resolve issues.

- **Getting researchers to think more like practitioners, and vice versa.** Too many practitioners seem to equate research to junk-science surveys to get a headline. Too many scholarly researchers seem focused on adding minute points to the academic literature instead of things practitioner actually care about.

I deeply believe that practitioners and academics who really get *the science beneath the art of public relations*™ will hold the real power in this profession as we move into the future.

Beyond these insights, what guidance can be given to practitioners about how to identify bad research? That could be a mission in itself for IPR, but I decided to start by asking our IPR Research Fellows what they would advise. Here is the wisdom that returned to me just for asking.

• Don W. Stacks, Ph.D., Professor of Public Relations, School of Communication, University of Miami: "I'd suggest the following for starters:

1. Watch for rounded numbers. Seldom is research as precise as 25, 75, etc.

2. If a sample is stated as a ratio and the actual frequencies are not given, I'd be very suspicious of it (i.e., 9 out of 10 or 9:1 when you don't know the actual frequencies).

3. See if there is no mention of how reliable the data are (i.e., look for anything beyond simple correlation and suggest that the practitioner at least know the names of several reliability statistics).

4. Don't trust any research that employed a methodology other than experimental if the researcher tries to make causal statements about results.

5. If it isn't well written, then it is probably not well thought out and should be taken with a grain of salt."

• David Michaelson, Ph.D., managing director, Teneo Strategy: "The most important advice I can give about spotting bad research is to assess if the questions are self-serving and biased. This starts with the basic principal of 'garbage in/garbage out.' If the questions are not valid or reliable and are designed to bias results, the research is unreliable from the start. Another way to spot bad research is if the supporting documentation is not available. Can you review the questionnaire? Is the unanalyzed data available? Is the research method clearly described? This gets at the core credibility of the work through transparency. Much of this is discussed in my paper that explores nine specific best practices that will assure quality research. It is available online at http://www.prsa.org/Intelligence/PRJournal/Vol1/."

• Donald K. Wright, Ph.D., Harold Burson Professor and Chair in Public Relations, College of Communication, Boston University: "Methodological approach is a huge problem in both academic and practitioner-generated research. Unfortunately, as PR education grows, universities are hiring faculty who do not necessarily understand research methods. Lately I've seen research that sounds exciting until you get to the methods section and notice the author(s) surveyed their students and/or conducted interviews with 23 people and then have tried to generalize their results to a larger population such as all PR practitioners in the country. This problem is going to get worse before it gets better because potential research subjects are being bombarded with participation requests and some researchers are struggling to find qualified subjects."

• David M. Dozier, Ph.D., Professor and Coordinator, Public Relations Emphasis, School of Journalism and Media Studies, San Diego State University: "This is especially relevant to survey research. Sample size is important but not as important as representativeness of the sample. How were respondents selected? Often, organizations use convenience samples (sometimes called reliance on available subjects) and then mislabel such samples as 'random.' Probability sampling (such as random, stratified random, and systematic sampling) is required to make statistical inferences from samples to populations."

Major corporations and many other organizations of every type already recognize public relations' value by including it as a stand-alone, executive management function. But the vast majority of organizations do not. Public relations professionals must understand their organizations' basic business issues, management theory, performance measurement, and the work of their peers in other organizational functions. The bottom line: public relations' value can only be known and appreciated when it can be clearly demonstrated as directly linked to an organization's business strategy and performance. The operations management tools of this and the preceding chapter subsume many of the salient features of successful public relations management and, most important, show how to connect the dots between the operating function and a larger organization's business. In the next chapter we examine the framework for applying these tools for managerial decision-making.

Key Words

Performance measurement

Performance management

BSC

Performance reviews

Four sources of employee performance
   information

Five stages of the employment sequence

Wrongful dismissal

Layoff

Exit interviews

Employee development

Exploration of Operations Tools II

1. Examine the approaches for measuring PR's value as presented on the Institute for Public Relations' website. What methods do you find? How are matters of performance measurement and performance management addressed? How do these approaches compare to the historically improper methods PR has used in the past, namely advertising value equivalency (AVE) and others?

2. Look for the employee-centered policies of other companies (e.g., Endicott-Johnson and Walden Mills) and analyze how effective they may be to helping to develop a strong, dedicated, and productive workforce.

3. Interview someone who was laid off from a job and ask questions about how the person felt, the reason for the layoff, what the company did to help those laid off, and so on. Analyze what seems to be the best advice for helping employees who are laid off.

4. Interview one or more recent graduates who have begun their PR careers. Ask questions about the hiring process and what it has been like to get used to working full time. Analyze the information gained during the interview and develop a prescription for transitioning effectively into a new career after graduation.

References

American Institute of Certified Public Accountants Inc., & Maisel, L. S. (2001). *Performance measurement practices survey results*. Jersey City, NJ: Author.

American Productivity and Quality Center (2002). *Performance measurement benefits*. Houston, TX: Author. Retrieved July 30, 2002, from the World Wide Web from http://www.apqc.org/pm/pmbenefits.cfm.

Baird, L., & Kram, K. (1983, Spring). Career dynamics: Managing the superior/subordinate relationship. *Organizational Dynamics*, 46–64.

Clampitt, P. G. (2010). *Communicating for managerial effectiveness* (4th ed.). Thousand Oaks, CA: Sage Publications.

Coveney, M., Ganster, D., Hartlen, B., & King, D. (2003). *The strategy gap: Leveraging technology to execute winning strategies*. Hoboken, NJ: John Wiley & Sons.

Geishecker, L., & Zrimsek, B. (2002, July 18). *Use CPM to integrate the enterprise view*. Stamford, CT: Gartner.

Gore, A. (1997). *Serving the American public: Best practices in performance measurement*. Washington, DC: Vice President of the United States. Retrieved June 22, 2002, from http://govinfo.library.unt.edu/npr/library/papers/benchmrk/nprbook.html#strategies.

Horton, J. (2006). *What's it worth? Publicity metrics reconsidered* (revised). Retrieved June 28, 2008, from http://www.online-pr.com/Holding/Publicity_Metrics_Reconsidered___REVISED.pdf.

Jablin, F. (2001). Organizational entry, assimilation, and disengagement/exit. In F. M. Jablin & L. L. Putnam (Eds.), *The new handbook of organizational communication* (pp. 732–818). Thousand Oaks, CA: Sage Publications.

Kaplan, R. S. (2001). Strategic performance measurement and management in nonprofit organizations. *Nonprofit Management and Leadership, 11*(3), 353–370.

Kaplan, R. S., & Norton, D. P. (1996). *The balanced scorecard: Translating strategy into action*. Boston: Harvard Business School Press.

Magna International Inc. (2013). *Employee's* [sic] *charter*. Available online: http://www.magna.com/for-employees/employee's-charter.

Micheli, P., & Manzoni, J-P. (2009). Strategic performance measurement: Benefits, limitations and paradoxes. *Long Range Planning, 43*, 465–476.

National Labor Relations Board (n.d.). *The NLRB and social media*. Available online: http://www.nlrb.gov/node/5078.

Orey, M. (2007, April 23). Fear of firing: How the threat of litigation is making companies skittish about axing problem workers. *BusinessWeek*, 52–62.

Paine, K. D., Draper, P., & Jeffrey, A. (2008). *Using public relations research to drive business results*. Coral Gables, FL: Institute for Public Relations. Retrieved June 24, 2008, from http://www.instituteforpr.org/files/uploads/UsingResearch_DriveBusiness.pdf.

Schiemann, W. A., & Lingle, J. H. (1999). *Bullseye! Hitting your strategic targets through high-impact measurement*. New York: The Free Press.

Swedish Public Relations Association (1996). *Return on communications*. Stockholm: Author.

Vos, M., & Schoemaker, H. (2004). *Accountability of communication management: A balanced scorecard for communication quality*. Utrecht, Netherlands: LEMMA Publishers.

Recommended Reading

Collins, J. (2001). *Good to great: Why some companies make the leap and others don't.* New York: Harper Business.

DeNisi, A. S., & Griffin, R. W. (2008). *Human resource management* (3rd ed.). Boston: Houghton Mifflin.

Davenport, T. H., Harris, J. G., & Morison, R. (2010). *Analytics at work: Smarter decisions, better results.* Boston: Harvard Business School Press.

Eckerson, W. (2011). *Performance dashboards: Measuring, monitoring, and managing your business* (2nd ed.). Hoboken, NJ: John Wiley and Sons.

Epstein, M. J., & Birchard, B. (2000). *Counting what counts: Turning corporate accountability to competitive advantage.* Cambridge, MA: Perseus Books.

Harbour, J. L. (1997). *The basics of performance measurement.* Portland, OR: Productivity Press.

Howard, P. J., & Howard, J. M. (2001). *The owner's manual for personality at work.* Austin, TX: Bard Press.

Kaushik, A. (2010). *Web analytics 2.0: The art of online accountability and science of customer centricity.* Hoboken, NJ: Sybex/Wiley Publishing.

Muller, M. (2009). *The manager's guide to HR: Hiring, firing, performance evaluations, documentation, benefits, and everything else you need to know.* New York: AMACOM.

Pfeffer, J., & Sutton, R. I. (2000). *The knowing-doing gap: How smart companies turn knowledge into action.* Boston: Harvard Business School Press.

Chapter 6

DECISION-MAKING IN TUNE WITH THE CORPORATE STRATEGIC PLAN

Choices define us and our futures. With all the work done to set up the "business" of a public relations operation in any organization, as the previous chapters explained, choices/decisions must be made and defended. Leaders and managers are paid for getting results—the results they said they and their teams could get through the plans they devised and resources they applied. The presumption behind any organizational operation is that it is valued, valuable, and adds value to the whole organization. The strategic plan and the overall operating environment make up the context of what can and must be done to obtain (even exceed) desired results. In turn, these things also are the focus of effective decision-making, which establishes and demonstrates the value contributions the PR function gives to the larger organization. In this chapter we, accordingly, begin with an examination of value and how PR delivers it before we explore the dynamics of managerial decision-making that advance and substantiate that value to internal and external organizational stakeholders. This chapter ends with a brief return to the concept of resource management but strictly in terms of communication media as resource concerns.

Delivering Value

Like the vast majority of professionals in all other fields, public relations people work hard and are proud of their work. Their bosses (and *their* bosses) expect public relations action to add value to the organization. That value is something beyond the planning, execution, and measurement of public relations campaigns and tactics. The concept of value can mean many things and has been the focus of numerous books and articles in the trade press. Very basically, *value* means something has been made better than before or enables something to become better than it was. It is not necessarily tied to strictly financial measures of price, cost, asset worth, and so on. Nonfinancial measures, like reputation and image, can and should be linked to it (see Epstein & Birchard, 2000).

Adding value is the primary concern of all business functions. To do so means, on the one hand, that a functional area's contributions have simultaneously bolstered the organization's mission and moved the business closer to realizing its vision. On the other hand, adding value means pragmatically that a functional area has helped enhance (or at least not hurt, especially in a challenging economy) a company's financial position through its allocation of resources and budget versus actual expenditures. Not that every organizational function has to be cash-positive, because even a function that tends to depend heavily on expenses (like public relations can be) can spur income-making opportunities that drive things like sales, donations, grants, and so on. Public relations has the added benefit of sparking crucial attitude- and behavior-changing opportunities that enhance image, reputation, perception, brand equity, and so on that also affect the financial picture. The link between the two—public relations actions and corporate income/gross receipts—is a tenuous thing to measure directly at best and has been the focus of numerous studies, especially through the Institute for Public Relations.

Delivering value is key to public relations' success. Value is demonstrated through measurements of performance, which are orchestrated through the single system of strategic planning, management-control, and task-control processes addressed in Chapter 4 and Chapter 5. For public relations, value is added constantly, but the traditional measurements for it have been problematic (e.g., advertising value equivalencies, clip counts), but they are at least useful as initial data points to indicate where to further measure campaign initiatives against business objectives (Oates, 2006, p. 12). Most important in this regard are the Barcelona Principles, which were adopted globally by numerous professional communication associations on June 17, 2010, and are a "declaration of standards and practices to guide measurement and evaluation of public relations" (Grupp, 2010, ¶1). Those principles, directly concerned with measuring PR's value, in brief are these:

1. *Importance of goal setting and measurement*—Objectives must be clear, focused, and measurable on things that directly matter to what will define success (or failure) for a given public relations effort of any size and scope.

2. *Measuring the effect on outcomes is preferred to measuring outputs*—The most effective measurements are those things that result in measurable changes in awareness, attitudes, and actions, not merely the production of individual PR discourses.

3. *The effect on business results can and should be measured where possible*—Measurements that tie public relations efforts to business-specific results, such as sales and others, are preferable because they link PR's value to traditional business measures that are part of the organizational strategic plan.

4. *Media measurement requires quantity and quality*—These measurements must focus on the content and the impact of PR efforts on stakeholders in terms of variables like tone, source credibility, medium appropriateness, testimonials from outside spokespeople, sensual prominence (visual or auditory), and degree of positiveness, negativeness, or neutrality/passivity.

5. *Advertising value equivalencies (AVEs) are not the value of public relations*—AVEs never have and never will be proper or effective measures of PR's value because AVEs equate PR efforts with only the cost of media space and not the other dimensions that matter (i.e., awareness/knowledge, attitudes/opinions, and actions/behaviors). Moreover, multipliers of AVEs based on any medium's reported user data (circulation, viewers, listeners, etc.) are also irrelevant and improper because they are merely inflations of the media-space cost calculations based on user data.

6. *Social media can and should be measured*—These measurements are just as vital as traditional media, and all social media measurements must tie to specific, well-wrought objectives. Analysis of social media content should include Web-based analytics, business performance data (e.g., sales, customer relationships), surveys, and other methods.

7. *Transparency and replicability are paramount to sound measurement*—All measurements should be valid (i.e., measure precisely what they are supposed to measure), reliable (i.e., measure that effect accurately every time if and when the method is repeated), and transparent (i.e., easy to identify and understand so that the links between PR and organizational performance are clear).

Spanning across these principles are the integral matters (i.e., "validated metrics") for measurement, namely awareness, knowledge, interest, intent and support, and action. As we saw in Chapter 4 about the construction of proper objectives, the things that inspire people to think with their *heads*, feel in their *hearts*, and act with their *hands* make up a holistic way to determine value, not just any one of these matters alone. Too many campaigns are solely focused on raising awareness but not focused on changing attitudes and/or, especially, changing behavior. In these cases the move from awareness to attitude formation and/or action is assumed, but it must not be. The Barcelona Principles will prove instrumental in ensuring that the matters of the head, heart, and hands are all properly addressed and measured to demonstrate public relations' value.

Of particular importance is Fraser Likely's (2013) framework for reporting usable, useful, and used information about the public relations function to an organization's CEO and other top leaders. His framework is shown in Table 6-1, and it applies Drucker's (1995) five dimensions of information that executives truly need:

- *Foundational information*—concerns basic financial data, from cash flow and liquidity projections to key ratios between certain financial measures, like inventory vs. sales, receivables vs. sales.
- *Productivity information*—concerns how much value is added to the organization over all costs associated with its productivity, relying on benchmarks against best performers in a market or industry.
- *Competence information*—concerns the effectiveness with which an organization can muster its resources for its core business to meet customer demand.
- *Resource-allocation information*—concerns managing organizational performance so that wealth is created through the wise use of capital and people, which focuses on the planning and budgeting process.
- *Environment information*—concerns data about markets; customers (present and potential); stakeholders; technology; industry; local, national, and worldwide economics and politics; global financial markets; and other areas that play primarily in the realm of strategy execution.

Table 6-1. LIKELY'S FRAMEWORK OF PUBLIC RELATIONS DEPARTMENT INFORMATION REPORTING.

EXECUTIVE LEVEL	FOUNDATIONAL INFORMATION	PRODUCTIVITY INFORMATION	COMPETENCE INFORMATION	RESOURCE ALLOCATION INFORMATION	ENVIRONMENTAL INFORMATION
Organization Head/CEO	*Information on historic budget allocation* *Information from benchmarking budget gets allocated to the function (FTEs; salaries; total budget; agency costs; etc.)*	*Information on process efficiencies (tasking; production; delivery; approval)* *Information on legacy program requirements*	*Information on PR/C core competencies vs. non-core competencies* *Information on PR/C team and individual executive performance and organizational relationships and networks* *Information on use of the challenge and coaching functions with senior executives* *Information on corporate result indicators: corporate trust/reputation; stakeholder relations; employee engagement*	*Information on the allocation of resources (capital and people) within the PR/C function (on programs; on campaigns; on channels/media; on product production; etc.)* *Information on the allocation of resources against organizational priorities/objectives* *Information on the benefit-cost ratio for proposed new investments*	*Information on stakeholders and publics (and risks inherent in their positions) for input into the organization's future, intended strategy formulation process* *Information on the state of current strategy execution across the organization and any communicative obstacles* *Information from internal silo boundary spanning about strategy execution discontinuities as input into the organization's emergent strategy formation process*

(Continued)

Table 6-1. (CONTINUED)

EXECUTIVE LEVEL	FOUNDATIONAL INFORMATION	PRODUCTIVITY INFORMATION	COMPETENCE INFORMATION	RESOURCE ALLOCATION INFORMATION	ENVIRONMENTAL INFORMATION
Business Line or Staff Function Head CFO/CMO/CHRO	Information on the previous and proposed spends	Information on legacy program requirements Information on value vs. cost for programs/campaigns Information on in-house vs. outsourcing or contracting out (make vs. buy)	Information on Account Executive and support unit performance Information on innovative performance based on best practice core competency Information on business result indicators for programs/campaigns	Information on the allocation of resources (capital and people) to the business line or staff function (on programs; on campaigns; on channels/media; on product production; etc.) Information on the allocation of resources against business line or staff function priorities/objectives Information on the benefit-cost ratio for proposed new investments	Information on markets/customers, stakeholders and publics for input into business strategies and campaign plans Information on competitor PR/C program and campaign investments, priorities and positioning

These dimensions of information act individually and, especially, together as diagnostic tools to determine the strength and viability of an organization. These dimensions also complement Drucker's (1967/2006) eight practices of effective executives covered in Table 1-2 in Chapter 1. Most important, the information from these five dimensions is valuable to management because it is the basis on which appropriate action can and must be taken. Although Drucker's information dimensions are meant for the broader organization, they, just like an organizational plan, can and must be tailored for operational units, namely public relations. Likely's (2013, pp. 471–473) framework for management information in Table 6-1, then, gives us a way to think about and capture the kind of performance information from inside and outside a PR unit that matters to top organizational leaders and prove PR's value in the larger organizational picture.

In terms of any organization's "business," public relations is part of the *value chain* that brings a finished product, service, or other economic output to a market or target public or customer. Any organizational function exists within a defined value chain of all other functions (see Figure 6-1), and each function—each link in the chain—contributes to the organization's success or failure. The value chain begins with *inputs* of various resources needed to produce an organization's *outputs*. What happens in between is *throughput*, which is the work that all the operational areas of an organization employ to the resources that apply to them to create the outputs required of them. Throughput also involves all of an organization's systems, processes, policies, and procedures that enable the organization to turn inputs into outputs. In this way public relations is as important as research and development, sales, finance and accounting, manufacturing, customer service, human resources, and so on. The value that each function contributes is just different, but it must be significant and, therefore, measured. As long as each organizational function is utilized, each one is expected to add value in specific ways—financial and nonfinancial. Plus, feedback about outputs comes back as inputs, which serves as a means for evaluating performance and making any improvements. Consistent with what we covered in the preceding chapters, organizational functions that contribute significant value are retained and, perhaps, augmented, if it makes strategic sense. Those functions that add little or no value or take away value could well see their resources reallocated or eliminated. The value chain is as strong as its weakest link. A value chain, then, can be made stronger by making links stronger and/or eliminating weak links.

So value is determined by performance measurements, and performance is something that must be managed. As we saw in Chapter 5, performance management combines the rigor of measurement methodologies with the incisiveness of leadership and management practices. Instrumental in performance management

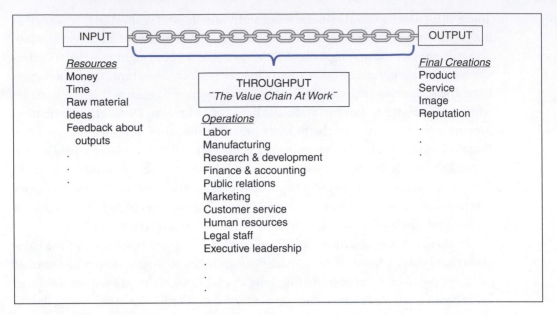

Figure 6-1. VALUE CHAIN.

is the regular reporting of performance measures, and a framework like that shown in Table 6-1 can be valuable in making performance data meaningful and actionable. Those reports ideally should be formal and written so that there is consistency in the presentation of the data and the messages about the data from one period to the next. Performance data, then, are critical points to compare to budgets and forecasts so that adjustments in resource allocations can be made to address swings to the positive or negative. In addition to these performance measures, which are really internally focused because they tie back to the strategic plan, research and analysis about the external world's state and trends of the market, competition, customer base, economy, technology, and other factors can and must be applied. Any problems (definitive or potential, large to small) that are identified must be reported immediately, not covered up or swept aside under the assumption they will go away. All problems must be remedied fast and early, not in "good time" and when they can be gotten around to. An effective decision-making process is key.

Managerial Decision-Making

Given all the information available to organizational members at all levels, there are many pressures to use the best information available to make the best choices possible from one situation to another. These pressures point to the common behavior of judging what is going on for what can and should be done. This behavior is the substance of decision-making, and it has a particular nature for those who lead and manage the operational areas of any organization. Three topics are key in this subject: the centrality of perceptions, the process view of decision-making, and the fact that good leaders can make bad decisions.

Perception is central

Everyone makes thousands of decisions every day, spanning the full range of inconsequential to potentially monumental matters in one's life or other people's lives. People have a powerful cognitive capacity for taking in, making sense of, and acting on immense amounts of data gathered through their senses. But people cannot possibly perceive and process all stimuli. So the human brain has ways to handle any stimuli that matter very efficiently and pretty effectively (but not perfectly) most of the time, resulting in *perceptions* that arise out from a process of sensing, selecting, organizing, and interpreting information so that it all is meaningful, memorable, and retrievable or reusable at another time (DeVito, 2009). Perception is a function of attention: To what do we devote any amount of attention (or not) at any time in any situation, and what do we perceive and what do we miss? The fact that we have certain patterns of perception also plays into the potential for us to experience *deception,* because we think we perceive something that truly is not present or vice versa. Perception can be understood as a five-step process, as shown in Figure 6-2. First, people purposefully *sense and select* which data (e.g., information, experiences, messages, people) they want or need, depending on certain criteria. This step encompasses not only the taking in of data, but also the avoidance of other data because of certain personal criteria for what is interesting, important, urgent, or other reason. This step alone, then, can be pivotal in determining after a decision is implemented why it was good or bad.

When sufficient data are collected about something, people take the second step in the perception process to *organize* things, using "cognitive shortcuts" because people are imperfect—they cannot process absolutely every sensory input. Simply put, cognitive shortcuts allow people to make sense of all the data that bombard them about anything. These shortcuts can also enable deception. They are natural and highly efficient operations of the human brain that virtually instantaneously assess something based on one or more of three kinds of structures. One shortcut structure is *rules*, which sorts data based on proximity (i.e., closeness in space and/or time), similarity (i.e., resemblance to prior experience and present knowledge), and contrast (i.e., differences among things keep them from being grouped together). The second shortcut structure is *schemata* (singular, *schema*), which are mental templates or "cookie cutters" that help sort out patterns in data

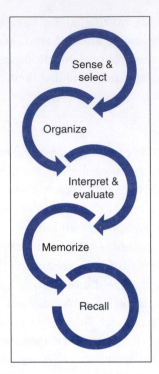

Figure 6-2. PERCEPTION PROCESS.

about, for example, one's self, others, and social roles, based largely on personal experiences. A stereotype is an example of a schema. The last cognitive shortcut structure is *scripts*, which are a kind of schema that outlines a general sequence or basic series of expectations about events, such as a date, a job interview, or a negotiation. Gladwell (2005) explains the very pragmatic dimensions to cognitive shortcuts (although he does not refer to it this way or to the theoretical foundations in cognitive science, namely schema theory; see McVee, Dunsmore, & Gavelek [2005] for a useful summary) as he argues that people engage in the "thin slicing" of experiences to unconsciously and "fast and frugal[ly]" find patterns in situations and behavior based on very small samples ("slices") of all the data that surround an experience.

With the data selected and organized, the next steps of the perception process make the data usable for the future. The third step in the process is *interpret and evaluate*, which is the point where the organized data are given meaning subjectively, based on the cognitive shortcuts themselves and the parameters on which they operate. This step would also be an important one to identify possible deception. The fourth step is *memorize* for later based on certain key factors that stand out so they can be easily retrieved. In this step the cognitive shortcuts help immensely as filters for what goes with what and whether any shortcut needs revision based on new data. The final step in the perception process is *retrieve or recall*, which relies on any cognitive shortcut's ability to be used to make sense of new data. Data that are consistent with cognitive shortcuts are easy to recall, but data that are inconsistent with a cognitive shortcut would be difficult to recall. Moreover, data that are dramatically different from cognitive shortcuts would likely require revision to the applicable shortcut.

Most important about the perception process is one key limitation: its reliance on cognitive shortcuts is, on the one hand, helpful in gaining quick understanding, building memory, and aiding recall, but on the other hand, these same shortcuts—because of their very nature as efficient but not wholly complete structures—can mislead people (i.e., deceptions) or cause recall of impertinent factors if they are not careful to select, organize, interpret, store, and apply truly sufficient data accurately and thoroughly. Trusting your gut is okay to a point, but that gut feeling must also be tested and verified as true or false.

Decision-making as a process

Peter Drucker, as we saw in Chapter 1, provides us with a very usable and useful means (his eight practices shown in Table 1-2) for leveraging our perceptions to effectively manage what is going on in an organization. With ever-increasing knowledge, experience, and foresight, people (the vast majority of the time) become increasingly better at making decisions. That is great news because experience and knowledge, combined with measurable results (successes and failures), contribute to wisdom and efficiency. Often there may be an abundance of information but not everything you want, and a decision still must be—and can be—made and made well in the face of any risks and limitations. Bazerman and Moore (2009) address the decision-making process of organizational leaders. They explain that managerial decision-making is a process that is driven by perceptions and is threatened by a range of biases (personal to organizational) that can undermine effectiveness. Indeed, they explain that decision-making relies on five "bounds" for that process:

- *Bounded rationality*, which subsumes the logical expectations that would result from a decision reached based on an accurately assessed situation
- *Bounded willpower*, which concerns the greater weight given to short-term factors over long-term ones
- *Bounded self-interest*, which tempers one's own interests with concern for the welfare of others
- *Bounded awareness*, which addresses the emphasis of failures over successes and the overlooking of obvious, important, and abundant information

- *Bounded ethicality*, which concerns parameters that drive people to be concerned about and pursue what is considered fair and ethical, especially situations where someone acts in opposition to his or her own principles of fairness and ethics

Because people have an inherent self-interest and a tendency to rely on intuition, they also have, according to Bazerman and Moore (2009), an inability to interpret information without bias, not unfairness. The key to resolving this problem is adopting a more conscious and systematic approach to decision-making that is most appropriate and necessary for sound personal and organizational performance. Gladwell (2005) parallels this point as he proposes that, even though decisions can be made very quickly (i.e., in the blink of an eye) and be as good as decisions made methodically, the limitations of quick decision-making must be recognized because snap judgments, first impressions, and so on can be wrong precisely because of the imperfections of humans. Those imperfections are in line with the explanation of the cognitive shortcuts given above and can be used to determine why a decision was bad. For managerial decision-making, Bazerman and Moore propose a six-step process, a visual of which is given in Figure 6-3.

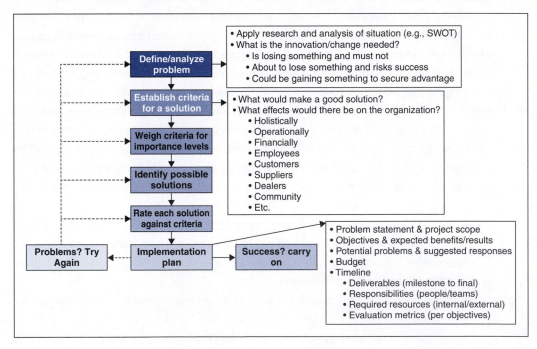

Figure 6-3. DECISION-MAKING PROCESS.

Key to applying the decision-making process in organizations is recognizing the kind of "judgmental heuristic" by which one is operating to reach a decision (Bazerman & Moore, 2009). There are three such heuristics. The first is the *availability heuristic*, which seeks data about frequency, probability, and so on of something based on how much of it is in stored experiences (personally and organizationally). The second is the *representativeness heuristic*, which relies on the presence of data that are consistent with or correspond to previously formed expectations (i.e., schemata). The final one is the *affect heuristic*, which concerns the importance of emotional factors (e.g., personal feelings, extenuating circumstances, environmental conditions) associated with something or someone that can adversely displace other factors needed for sound reasoning about that thing or person.

The objective for effective managerial decision-making is not to make perfectly good decisions all the time. Although that objective is attractive, it is not realistic given human imperfection. Strategies that simplify the assessment of situations (i.e., cognitive shortcuts, thin slices, judgmental heuristics) should be used to produce correct or nearly correct judgments, with the understanding that there are inherent limitations that may well require correction for bias and incompleteness.

Good leaders but bad decisions

There is an important difference between poor outcomes and poor decisions, and good leaders can experience both. In spite of fastidious attention to detail about a situation and expected results, poor outcomes can occur because of the influence of many variables, many of which were likely beyond one's control and/or unforeseen. In contrast, poor decisions are recognized retrospectively as poor, "if the knowledge gained would lead to a different decision if a similar situation arose" (Klein, 1998, p. 271). Indeed, there is a difference between people who see things as black or white ("unequivocal" decision-makers) and people who see shades of gray ("ambivalent" decision-makers). Table 6-2 summarizes the differences based on Wang's (2010) summary of a research study on the subject. Very important, however, as Wang explains, is that influential factors of personality and culture appear to play roles in the two kinds of decision-makers. Additionally, individual characteristics given in the table may not always be present, and one's unequivocality and ambivalence can be determined through psychological testing.

Focused study of leaders making bad decisions by Campbell, Whitehead, and Finkelstein (2009; also see Finkelstein, 2003) reveals decision-making to be a two-part, "hardwired" process. The first part is *pattern recognition* that is similar to schemata. As we saw earlier in this section, the problem is that our brains can fool

Table 6-2. **COMPARING BASIC TRAITS OF TWO DECISION-MAKER TYPES.**

UNEQUIVOCAL DECISION-MAKERS	AMBIVALENT DECISION-MAKERS
• *Speak their minds or make quick decisions*	• *Procrastinate or avoid making decisions*
• *Be more predictable in decision-making*	• *Feel more regret after making decisions*
• *Be less anxious about making wrong choices*	• *Be thoughtful about making the right choice*
• *Have relationship conflicts that are less drawn out*	• *Stay longer in unhappy relationships*
• *Be less likely to consider others' points of view*	• *Appreciate multiple points of view*

us into thinking we understand situations because they somehow fit familiar experiences when they do not. The second part is *emotional tagging*, which involves making associations about paying attention or not and taking action. Aligned with the explanation of perception and decision-making, the problem occurs unconsciously and makes it hard to check the data and logic for good decision-making. Campbell et al. explain that when good leaders make bad decisions, three *red flag conditions* emerge: (1) the presence of inappropriate self-interest, (2) the presence of distorting emotional attachments, and (3) the presence of misleading memories. These red-flag conditions link back to Bazerman and Moore's (2009) recognition of the role of bias in decision-making. Discovering the red flags is key, and Figure 6-4 shows the process for identifying those conditions (Campbell et al., 2009). Beyond identifying the red flag conditions for good leaders on the verge of making bad decisions, Campbell et al. prescribe three safeguards that can and should be made: (1) inject fresh experience or analysis, (2) introduce further debate and challenge, and (3) impose stronger governance.

Add to this view that of *groupthink* (Janis, 1972), which is defined as "a premature striving by group members for unanimous agreement on a course of action," and it "cuts off necessary consideration of the pros and cons of the various decision options" (Ahlfinger & Esser, 2001, p. 32). Groupthink includes "high group cohesiveness, a stressful situation, and a variety of structural or administrative factors such as insulation of the group, promotional leadership, lack of methodical decision-making procedures, and lack of variety among members' values and perspectives" (Ahlfinger & Esser, 2001, p. 32). The presence of groupthink marks fundamentally flawed decision-making, and Figure 6-5 shows the three types of groupthink and

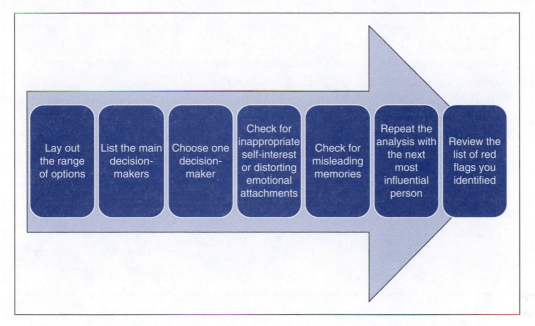

Figure 6-4. PROCESS FOR IDENTIFYING RED FLAGS FOR POOR DECISION-MAKING.

their symptoms, of which Type III is the most scary type. No matter what type, groupthink leads to seven symptoms of defective decision-making (Janis, 1972):

1. Incomplete survey of alternatives
2. Incomplete survey of objectives
3. Failure to examine risks of the preferred choice
4. Failure to reappraise initially rejected alternatives
5. Poor information search
6. Selective bias in processing available information
7. Failure to develop contingency plans

These symptoms actually flow one to the next, and the result is greater likelihood that poor decisions will be made. A good way to protect against groupthink is to take the seven symptoms of defective decision-making and reverse them into their positive forms (e.g., prepare a thorough survey of alternatives, conduct a substantial survey of objectives, examine the risks and benefits of the preferred choice). This approach, especially when joined with an the other approaches for sound decision-making in this section and Drucker's eight practices shown in Chapter 1's Table 1-2, can mitigate against many or all of the problems of ineffective or flawed managerial decision-making.

Type I	Type II	Type III
• Overestimating the group • Illusion of invulnerability • Unquestioned belief that the group's cause is just	• Closed-mindedness • Collective rationalizing away of adverse information • Stereotype enemies as weak or stupid	• Pressures for uniformity • Censorship of misgivings about the group's position • Bolstering illusion of unanimous acceptance of majority • Pressure on dissenting membersto assent • "Mindguards" of external information

Figure 6-5. GROUPTHINK TYPES AND THEIR SYMPTOMS.
SOURCE: Ahlfinger & Esser (2001)

Communication Resource Management

So much of managerial decision-making involves the allocation of resources, and for a public relations function in any organization, agency or nonagency, there are many matters that must be addressed, and personnel matters are among the most vital, as we saw in Chapter 5. Likely's framework for reporting operational performance information can be instrumental in the management of resources. In this final section of this chapter we will address three particular resource management matters for communication because of their special prominence in the profession: the strategic role of tactics, the false dichotomy of controlled and uncontrolled media, and traditional and new media.

Strategic role of tactics

One key to understanding the force of history on people's views of public relations is tactics, as we saw in Chapter 1. After all, publics experience what PR professionals do, not the thinking and the process behind it. Yet public relations as a field has done a poor job of promoting itself. As Budd (2003) finds, "Public relations is too short-sighted, too fragmented . . . to mount any true industry offensive. World class PR demands world class political skills, attributes in short supply" (p. 380).

Remember, too, Budd continues, that public opinion has been long on mistrust toward business, but it can be best overcome by deeds, not words alone. The field, then, still faces a difficult task to better inform the public, inspire a cooperative attitude, and result in supportive actions toward the profession. According to the PRSA's ethics code, practitioners are called to "enhance the profession," which means to do so for anyone—especially those outside the field.

The tactical bias that runs through public relations is especially evident in what it teaches. Chapter 4 argues against a bias toward tactics and argues for a bias toward strategy. But a tendency in industry to seek recipes (i.e., privilege tactics) for effective corporate communications dominates, as professionals are increasingly asked to "do more with less," "work smarter," and adhere to other slogans meant to inspire excellence in work, but, as Deming (1986) tells us, slogans "generate frustration and resentment" (p. 67). Public relations discourse is the sum of the many people's enactments shared, selected, and retained according to organizing recipes during the process through which they make sense of what is going on and what must be done. As Weick (1979) says, recipes are "the means to generate structures that have the characteristics you want. . . . Adapted to organizing, the question becomes: given our need for a sensible enacted environment, how do we produce it?" (pp. 46–47).

This quest for recipes is promulgated through multiple resources. Numerous textbooks and trade books are available about how to write specific forms of public relations discourse. In comparison, far less work has been published about strategy and strategic planning specifically for public relations, but examples like Ferguson (1999), Moffitt (1999), Oliver (2007), and Potter (2006) are available, even though they cover the topic in isolation from the larger organizational picture as this book covers it. Additionally, there is a great variety of "how-to" seminars offered annually by stalwart organizations (e.g., the Public Relations Society of America, the International Association for Business Communication, Regan Communications, Melcrum Publishing, the Word of Mouth Marketing Association), luncheon or dinner meetings in PRSA and IABC chapters that address everything professional communicators might need to enhance their tactical skills, and scholarly and practice-based journal articles that place much emphasis on the tactics of public relations efforts through case examples or lived experiences.

There is immediate satisfaction from tactics—a rush from seeing work come to life. That is why tactics are so attractive and easy to focus on. It also explains why, on the one hand, there is much celebration of especially successful work and, on the other hand, much confusion about why public relations should be involved as a strategic function. *A tactics bias, then, must be meticulously shifted to a strategies bias.* If we think of attention as an economic commodity (Davenport & Beck, 2002), like that of iron ore to steel, silicon to microchips, and so on, the means *and* the ends for getting and maintaining attention are both integral. Tactics are the ends of public relations, but much more important, the means that makes them possible and successful is the intense strategic planning that must be done in advance and enacted effectively, which we saw in Chapter 4. Put in concise terms, "strictly tactical thinking is focused on just 'getting the word out.' But truly effective and successful communications depends on strategic thinking that focuses on the bigger picture, making tactics subservient to larger objectives that tie directly to an organizational mission and vision. . . . Strategy is necessary in the full range of strategic communication efforts, from the simplest announcement to the most complicated crisis" (Courtright & Smudde, 2010, p. 69).

False dichotomy of controlled and uncontrolled media

In the field of public relations there are at least 41 types of discourse that practitioners may use, as shown in Figure 6-6 (Smudde, 2004, 2011; Smudde & Courtright, 2012). Those discourse genres are made all the more publicly usable, useful, and used because of the Internet and organizations' application of it to manage much of their communications in addition to traditional mass media. Which begs the question, "Who has control over any communication effort and the messages?" Courtright and Smudde (2010) demonstrate that sometimes companies have complete control over what, how, and when audiences get any discourse. Other times companies choose to give up that control and rely on the mass media

Advertisements	Magazines	Pressreleases
Advertorials	Matte releases	Pub1ic Service Announcements
Annual reports	Media advisories	(PSA)
Articles	Meetings	Satellite media tours (SMT)
Audio news releases	Mobile phone apps	Social media (only specificones)
Backgrounders	Newsletters	Speeches
Biographical statements	Photo news releases	Tip sheets
Brochures/Pamphlets	Pitch calls	Video news programs
Case studies	Pitch letters	Video news releases
Fact sheets	Podcasts	Weblogs (Blogs)
Flyers	Posters	Websites
Frequently asked questions (FAQ)	Prepared statements	White papers
Interviews	Press conferences	Wikis
Issue reports	Press kits	Written correspondence

Figure 6-6. PUBLIC RELATIONS DISCOURSE GENRES.

to convey messages to audiences. Somewhere in between, however, companies can collaborate with mass media in their strategic communication, which calls into question the traditional (but flawed) dichotomy of controlled and uncontrolled media.

Controlled media involve a company's target audience getting exactly the communication it created for them and in the way it wanted them to get the communication (e.g., mobile phone apps, annual reports, brochures, websites). *Uncontrolled media* involve a company's target audiences not getting exactly what it would like them to get because a third party—the mass media—makes the choices as to what, how, and if any messages would be sent from any discourse a company provided the media (e.g., news releases, press conferences, interviews). For example, when we think of product recalls within the broadest context of all strategic communication efforts, audiences rely largely on uncontrolled media. This reliance makes sense because the best interests of the general public are of the utmost importance. Once we examine other kinds of corporate communication efforts, however, the dichotomy breaks down and becomes a continuum.

Most practitioners know there can be a certain amount of cooperation between them/their companies and media outlets so they both get something of what they want. An easy example is a feature story pitched and ghostwritten for an executive by a communication professional and acquired, edited, and illustrated through an editor at a top trade publication that meets readers' needs while highlighting a company's viewpoint and offerings. Video news releases also exhibit a fair degree of give and take, as companies provide a finished piece and extra footage ("B-roll") that news organizations may use, or they even might add their own footage. Such cocreation of discourse for a company's ultimate audiences results in a middle ground of what Courtright and Smudde (2010) call *semi-controlled/semi-uncontrolled media*, depending on how far toward one end of the continuum one goes with the creation and dissemination of organizational messages.

This continuum (see Figure 6-7), then, becomes much more strategically valuable as practitioners consider what discourse forms may best convey the messages and best fit the occasions they face on behalf of their organizations and audiences. Discourse competence in any or all genres is vital and involves an acute sensibility about the use, benefits, and risks of controlled, uncontrolled, and semi-controlled/semi-uncontrolled media (see Smudde & Courtright, 2012). Being mindful of and implementing an organization's overall strategic plan is the responsibility of all organizational members, especially its leaders and, in particular, its communication professionals.

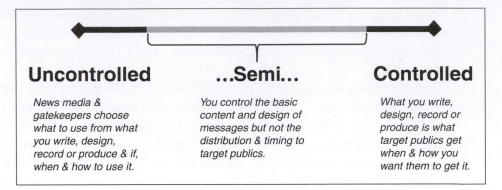

Figure 6-7. CONTINUUM FOR PR TACTICS.

Traditional and "new" media

The developments of movable type printing, telegraph, radio, television, the Internet, and mobile computing have much in common because of the revolutions in communication each caused. The diffusion of technologies is at the heart of these revolutions, and the cries were loud that the existing, "traditional" communication technology would be supplanted by the innovative, "new" technology. A new technology has benefits of its own but also needs to bridge the benefits of the traditional technology. This is why the Internet is made up of "sites," "pages," and other metaphorical references to printed discourse. In fact, the design and usability standards that have developed for the Internet, social media, and mobile technology owe their existence to the rules that govern printed texts and served as the basis for what works and what does not in electronic discourse.

Although the cries about the demise of traditional media are hastily proffered, they are very often greatly exaggerated. The reason is simple: Both traditional and new media have great utility and attraction to many sectors of the population. Only when there is truly little to no use for a technology (such as how the telegraph faded from use after radio and the telephone but is still used as a back-up system) will people cease using a technology. Indeed, Richard Edelman (2012) explains well the scope and, especially, the intersection of the four realms of the "media ecosystem":

1. *Mainstream*—the traditional mass media channels of newspapers, television, radio, and magazines, which are still the largest contributors of revenue to their organizations' revenue
2. *Tra-digital*—the hybrid channels that have arisen from the combination of traditional mass media channels and new, Web-based/digital media, such as newspapers' websites, Huffington Post, and Politico

3. *Social*—the individual online communities built by dedicated companies, such as Facebook, Twitter, Foursquare, and the rest
4. *Owned*—the particular websites, smartphone apps, and content created and maintained for organizations that want them, including the content on organization-specific YouTube channels

Public relations professionals, then, use the full range of traditional media, and many of those media have been adapted to the electronic realm: personal journals (i.e., blogs), news releases (i.e., social news releases), short personal comments (i.e., tweets), and any document that can be turned into a PDF file or hybrid form, like a website, can be an electronic brochure. Additionally, of course, public relations professionals use any social medium to their strategic advantage, provided that they post content that fulfills specific purposes, fits the technological parameters (including data fields) of the medium, and, especially, complements the interests, attitudes, and expectations of users.

One distinction that has been made elsewhere in this book is important to reemphasize: social media do not make up one medium, as is so often mistakenly thought. Social media are comprised of many, separate, Web-based and mobile technologies and digital media channels that facilitate interpersonal interaction, collaboration, and community development among Internet users who create and share their own content. In this way social media are much more idiosyncratic in their facilitation of discourse because of the combination of technological constraints and user/community norms about what is allowed and acceptable content. That content is shared over channels that include blogs, podcasts, wikis, virtual worlds, Internet forums, networking sites, and so on. To this end there are numerous "new" media channels along with traditional media. These media all are forms of PR discourse and, therefore, are matters of tactics that must be chosen in light of a thorough strategic planning process to fulfill specific, measurable objectives.

Social media, like other channels for PR discourse, are tactics that are chosen in light of a thorough strategic planning process (see Chapter 4). In particular, social media and all tactics are resources that require meticulous management, as this chapter shows and, especially, the Executive Viewpoint by Mary Henige explains. Social media make up only one tool for PR that is used for strategic purposes, very similar to how press releases, events, annual reports, and all the rest are used strategically. As Duhé (2007) argues, the complexity of decision-making for public relations leaders is especially intense as publics and stakeholders of all kinds seek ways to interact with organizations. Indeed, Duhé argues that not engaging with publics and stakeholders is far more risky than doing so, especially (although not necessarily exclusively) through digital media, when organizations face situations that need great public/stakeholder support.

What is very important to acknowledge at this point is the paradox of social media's controllability. On one hand, users can employ social media as they wish, which makes that content controlled; but on the other hand other users can respond any way they wish, which makes the use of the initial socially mediated message uncontrolled. For example, while organizations focus on defined publics and stakeholders, there are people who are predisposed to insert themselves into the fray of public opinion. These people are often on the fringes of an organization's known publics and stakeholders, and they do not have the kind of vested interest in an organization as stakeholders do. These people are called *stakeseekers*, and they are "groups that seek to put new issues on the corporate agenda" (Holzer, 2008, p. 51) and, thereby, claim argumentatively to be stakeholders. Stakeseekers include, for example, protest groups and activists for a social movement. They have a great willingness to assert their opinions (and to do so as aggressively) publicly over online communication channels and social media, and they can damage (or bolster) an organization's image, reputation, and brand (Coombs & Holladay, 2012). Making supportive stakeholders out of stakeseekers is the objective, and social media can be one especially potent approach.

Organizations, then, must adopt a strategic approach to using social media as it would for any strategy and related tactics. Breakenridge (2012) prescribes a common-sense approach to taking advantage of social media for PR that can aid critical analysis and decision-making for effective and successful communication that inspires cooperation between an organization and its publics/stakeholders:

1. Monitor social media on a regular basis (sometimes with a dedicated person) for messages on the macro level (i.e., overall outcomes and reputation impact) and on the micro level (i.e., specific programs, buzz/word-of-mouth communication, digital sharing of information, etc.), then share this intelligence with the relevant areas of the organization that need and can act on it.
2. Provide content within a definitive context that will (a) repurpose existing messages in any medium for social media (e.g., turning video news releases into Vimeo sites; revising brochure text for focused Facebook posts), and (b) search for new content ideas that grab publics' attention and entice them to use it (e.g., trending topics; crowdsourcing).

Social media, again, are means to the end of strategic, ethical, and successful communication between organizations and their publics. Integrating social media and any other medium into strategic plans for public relations takes us back to

EXECUTIVE VIEWPOINT

Managerial Decision-Making

Mary Henige, APR, Director of Social Media, Digital Communications, Research and Reputation Strategy, General Motors Corporation

It may seem odd to learn about the importance of effective decision-making in a public relations textbook, but not if we remember that we need to be good business leaders and communicators. If you want to advance throughout your career, you need to learn and demonstrate that you can lead a team, make good decisions, and be accountable for the outcomes of those decisions.

General Motors' first vice president of public relations, Paul Garrett, was one of first PR leaders to teach that PR is a management function. In other words, we are public relations **and** business professionals who ideally report to top leadership. GM President Alfred P. Sloan Jr. hired Garrett in 1931 to help interpret the role of the company to constituents and to advise him and other executives about consumer expectations. Garrett advised GM's top leaders for 25 years until he retired.

Like Garrett, we need to understand the organizations we work for or with in order to be good advisors. As one of my early leaders used to say, "Don't just offer options—make a recommendation—be a counselor." He taught me that even at the earliest stages of our careers we need to give our clients recommendations. It's intimidating when you first begin your career to make a recommendation for fear it won't be the best way or accepted by leadership or your client. So what can you do? Prepare! Effective decision-making is based on research and knowledge of the issue. While you may not be an expert, with careful and thorough research, it's likely you'll know more than enough to make an informed recommendation. It's not always possible to know if you've made the best decision. It takes courage to assert your view, and it's humbling when others don't agree, but get over it. You weren't necessarily wrong, and even if you were, remember that others in the organization likely have greater insight or experience. Learning how to gracefully handle decisions that don't go your way is a sign of maturity.

An example that illustrates why it's important to be counselors, no matter the stage of our careers, occurred when I was 26. In my first significant media relations position, I was responsible for GM's research and development and design areas. This meant that I was the communications advisor to those respective vice presidents and their teams. Design Vice President Chuck Jordan was legendary in automotive design. When I began supporting him he was a year from retirement after working for more than 40 years at General Motors. I had incredible access to him because of the number of interviews he did. One day, after I made a recommendation that he rejected and was feeling dejected he said, "Mary, I like the way that you always tell me what you think, and why. A lot of people here tell me what they *think* I want to hear. I may not always agree with you, but I know when you tell me something it's what you believe I should do so I always take that into consideration."

I can't take credit for being a born decision-maker. I benefited from my PR director's wisdom and coaching as he also was a year from retirement. He taught me, through much trial and error on my part, that we need to bring recommendations to leaders, not just problems, or what did they need us for? He said to think through the pros and cons of various actions, and to strongly make a suggestion, without vacillating. Confidently presenting a course of action and your rationale will demonstrate that you're becoming a strategic thinker.

As the chapter related, decision-making experience is learned over a course of a career. Therefore, the expectation isn't that you'll nail every decision, but that you'll have great support behind your recommendation. At this career stage you don't know what you don't know! Be sure to ask seasoned colleagues for input. There's no prize in making recommendations alone, in fact, your plan will be richer for having talked with others. Additionally, while you want to make informed recommendations, speed is an important factor. Don't wait for a perfect solution, because there aren't any. If the potential outcome of a course of action is neutral to positive, then go— there's an element of risk, so minimize it, because many opportunities are lost because of a slow decision process or teams who look for guaranteed results.

Similarly, don't be order-takers from overbearing clients. Marketers especially like to dictate to public relations professionals what they want done. For example, you may receive a request to create a Facebook page for a client. Many business leaders think creating a social web channel is the answer to everything. It often isn't, and not every channel is right for every brand. Your job is to ask probing questions to learn what it is they want to accomplish by creating a page. Who are they trying to reach? What are their business objectives? What kind of content will they create? How will they manage the community? These are all important questions that the client likely hasn't thought through. Ask for time to do some research and then return with a recommendation of how the client can accomplish his or her objective.

Subsequently, don't doubt your expertise when a client pushes back. Many people fancy themselves public relations experts, but they're not, you are. Effective decision-making is based on research and an understanding of what will or won't work to deliver the results the client is seeking. This isn't a "hunch" game. This is why you need to be thoroughly prepared. You'll be able to explain the research and rationale behind your recommendations. While you may not have thought of everything, at least you'll be able to explain why a client's proposed action may not be the optimal communications solution. Clearly there's a way to present your recommendations, but you were hired to provide counsel, so do so in a respectful and knowledgeable way.

Working at being an effective decision-maker will help you to obtain higher levels of leadership. It also will help you to feel professionally fulfilled, knowing that you have given your clients the best possible communications guidance. Finally, you'll get a reputation from your colleagues, leaders and clients, as someone who carefully considers the options and presents the best solution for consideration. Bottom line, we are hired to deliver results and to add value to our organizations and clients, and if we do this, we'll be sought-after counselors.

Chapter 4 and calls to mind the wisdom of Edward L. Bernays that is vital to decision-making.

Public relations pioneer and "father" of the field Edward L. Bernays is known for his social-scientific approach to his work (see Grunig & Hunt, 1984). Key to his approach to public relations was strategic planning within the context of a big picture—knowing well what had to be done by any means or medium necessary, whether his clients understood or embraced it or not, and doing it well (see Bernays, 1965). Bernays recognized the problems with jumping to tactics, saying in his book, *Public Relations* (1958): "Do not think of tactics in terms of segmental approaches. The problem is not to get articles into a newspaper or obtain radio time or arrange for a motion-picture newsreel; it is, rather, to set in motion a broad activity, the success of which depends on interlocking all phases and elements of the proposed strategy, implemented by tactics that are timed to the moment of maximum effectiveness" (p. 167). Strategic thinking and clear, focused, and rational decision-making that leads to real value contributions is at the heart of any public relations operation. Our next chapter focuses on the work needed to build the business of a public relations operation whether it is an agency or not.

Key Words

Value	*Five bounds for decision-making*
Value chain and its components	*Three judgmental heuristics*
Barcelona Principles	*Two parts to bad decision-making*
Head, heart, and hands	*Groupthink*
Drucker's five information dimensions	*Tactics bias*
Perception process	*Recipes*
Cognitive short cuts	*Media ecosystem*
Deception	*PR tactics continuum*
Decision-making process	*Stakeseekers*

Exploration of Decision-Making

1. How are specific efforts in determining value in the public relations field making a difference in how people perceive PR, especially among organizational and industry leaders? What efforts can you find and summarize that are instrumental in these efforts?

2. Integrate concepts of effective leadership and management with the concepts of effective decision-making. Develop a single prescription for someone to be an excellent leader, manager, and decision-maker in public relations. Why do you think this prescription would work well?

3. Access the digital library of PRSA Silver Anvil Award winners from the most recent year. Choose a few cases that interest you, and explain why in each case jumping to tactics would be foolish and on what grounds success was determined?

4. Which public relations discourse types in Figure 6-6 would you define as controlled, uncontrolled, semi-controlled, or semi-uncontrolled? Why does each discourse type fit the place on the continuum you say it does in Figure 6-7? Give examples.

5. Research the concepts of "paid media," "sponsored media," "crowdsourcing," and "content marketing"; define them, and find at least one example of each. Then explain where and why each example fits on the continuum in Figure 6-7. How different or the same is the use of these media from what PR has done over the years?

References

Ahlfinger, N. R., & Esser, J. K. (2001). Testing the groupthink model: Effects on promotional leadership and conformity predisposition. *Social Behavior and Personality, 29*(1), 31–42.

Bazerman, M. H., & Moore, D. A. (2009). *Judgment in managerial decision-making* (7th ed.). Hoboken, NJ: John Wiley & Sons.

Bernays, E. L. (1965). *Biography of an idea: Memoirs of public relations counsel Edward L. Bernays*. New York: Simon & Schuster.

Bernays, E. L. (2005). *Propaganda*. New York: IG. (Original work published 1928).

Breakenridge, D. (2012). *Social media and public relations: Eight new practices for the PR professional*. Upper Saddle River, NJ: Financial Times Press.

Budd Jr., J. F. (2003). Public relations is the architect of its future: Counsel or courtier? Pros offer opinions. *Public Relations Review, 29*, 375–383.

Campbell, A., Whitehead, J., & Finkelstein, S. (2009, February). Why good leaders make bad decisions. *Harvard Business Review*, 60–66.

Coombs, W. T., & Holladay, S. J. (2012). Internet contagion theory 2.0: How Internet communication channels empower stakeholders. In S. C. Duhé (Ed.), *The new media and public relations* (2nd ed., pp. 21–30). New York: Peter Lang.

Courtright, J. L., & Smudde, P. M. (2010). Recall communications: Discourse genres, symbolic charging, and message design. *International Journal of Strategic Communication, 4*(1), 58–74.

Davenport, T. H., & Beck, J. C. (2002). *The attention economy: Understanding the new currency of business*. Boston: Harvard University Press.

Deming, W. E. (1986). *Out of the crisis*. Cambridge, MA: Massachusetts Institute of Technology Center for Advanced Engineering Study.

DeVito, J. A. (2009). *Human communication: The basic course* (11th ed.). Boston: Pearson Education.

Duhé, S. C. (2007). Public relations and complexity thinking in the age of transparency. In S. C. Duhé (Ed.), *The new media and public relations* (pp. 57–76). New York: Peter Lang.

Drucker, P. F. (1995, January–February). The information executives truly need. *Harvard Business Review*, 54–62.

Edelman, R. (2012). PR and the media cloverleaf: The road to public engagement. In Edelman, R., Holdheim, R., Hass, M., Gomes, P., & Rubel, C., Digital communities: Social media in action. In C. L. Caywood (Ed.), *The handbook of strategic public relations and integrated marketing communication* (2nd ed., pp. 258–261). New York: McGraw-Hill.

Epstein, M. J., & Birchard, B. (2000). *Counting what counts: Turning corporate accountability to competitive advantage*. Cambridge, MA: Perseus.

Ferguson, S. D. (1999). *Communication planning: An integrated approach*. Thousand Oaks, CA: Sage.

Finkelstein, S. (2004). *Why smart executives fail and what you can learn from their mistakes*. New York: Portfolio Trade/Penguin.

Gladwell, M. (2005). *Blink: The power of thinking without thinking*. New York: Back Bay Books.

Grunig, J. E., & Hunt, T. (1984). *Managing public relations*. Fort Worth, TX: Harcourt Brace Jovanovich.

Grupp, R. W. (2010, June 18). *The Barcelona declaration of research principles*. Miami: Institute for Public Relations. Available online: http://www.instituteforpr.org/2010/06/the-barcelona-declaration-of-research-principles/.

Holzer, B. (2008). Turning stakeseekers into stakeholders: A political coalition perspective on the politics of stakeholder influence. *Business & Society*, 47(1), 50–67.

Janis, I. L. (1972). *Victims of groupthink*. Boston: Houghton-Mifflin.

Klein, G. (1998). *Sources of power: How people make decisions*. Cambridge, MA: MIT Press.

Likely, F. (2013, March 6–10). Public relations/communication department CCO reporting: What information do CEOs truly need? In Y. G. Ji & Z. C. Li (Eds.), *16th International Public Relations Research Conference: Exploring the Strategic Use of New Media's Impact on Change Management and Risk in Theory and Practice* (pp. 453–479). Available online: http://iprrc.org/docs/IPRRC_16_Proceedings.pdf.

McVee, M. B., Dunsmore, K., & Gavelek, J. R. (2005). Schema theory revisited. *Review of Educational Research, 75*, 531–566.

Moffitt, M. A. (1999). *Campaign strategies and message design: A practitioner's guide from start to finish*. Westport, CT: Praeger.

Oates, D. B. (2006, Oct.). Measuring the value of public relations: Tying efforts to business goals. *Public Relations Tactics*, 12.

Oliver, S. (2007). *Public relations strategy* (2nd ed.). London: Kogan Page.

Potter, L. R. (2006). Strategic planning: Timeless wisdom still shapes successful communication programs. In T. L. Gillis (Ed.), *The IABC handbook of organizational communication: A guide to internal communication, public relations, marketing, and leadership* (pp. 80–92). San Francisco: Jossey-Bass.

Smudde, P. M. (2004). Implications on the practice and study of Kenneth Burke's idea of a "public relations counsel with a heart." *Communication Quarterly, 52*, 420–432.

Smudde, P. M. (2011). *Public relations as dramatistic organizing: A case study bridging theory and practice*. Cresskill, NJ: Hampton Press.

Smudde, P. M., & Courtright, J. L. (2012). *Inspiring cooperation and celebrating organizations: Genres, message design and strategy in public relations*. New York: Hampton Press.

Wang, S. S. (2010, September 28). Why so many people can't make decisions. *Wall Street Journal*, D1–D2.

Recommended Reading

Argenti, P. A., & Barnes, C. M. (2009). *Digital strategies for powerful corporate communications*. New York: McGraw-Hill.

Breakenridge, D. (2008). *PR 2.0: New media, new tools, new audiences*. Upper Saddle River, NJ: Pearson.

Garten, J. E. (2000). *The mind of the CEO*. New York: Perseus Publishing.

Howard, C. M., & Mathews, W. K. (2013). *On deadline: Managing media relations* (5th ed.). Long Grove, IL: Waveland.

Li, C., & Bernoff, J. (2009). *Marketing in the ground-swell*. Boston: Harvard Business School Press.

Lipman-Blumen, J. (2006). *The allure of toxic leaders: Why we follow destructive bosses and corrupt politicians—and how we can survive them*. New York: Oxford University Press.

Moffitt, M. A. (1999). *Campaign strategies and message design*. Westport, CT: Praeger.

Rice, R. E., & Atkin, C. K. (2013). *Public communication campaigns* (4th ed.). Thousand Oaks, CA: Sage.

Scott, D. M. (2009). *The new rules of marketing and PR: How to use news releases, blogs, podcasting, viral marketing, and online media to reach buyers directly*. Hoboken, NJ: John Wiley & Sons.

Chapter 7

BUSINESS-DEVELOPMENT PRINCIPLES

Organizations do not and cannot just open for business and assume people will be inspired to transact with them. "If you build it, they will come" is an idea that only works in the movies. Public relations is naturally concerned with matters of business development because much of the work PR people do is used by people who are making buying, investing, donating, and other decisions. For this reason, public relations managers must have an idea about what it takes to develop new business from present, past, and potential customers. Indeed, a corporate public relations department must be known for and always produce great work that gets desired or better results for other operating areas of the company. An agency also must be known for and always produce excellent work that gets expected or better-than-expected results for many clients in multiple industries with wide ranges of products and services. In this way, corporate public relations operations and agencies are very similar: They each serve customers—the former is internal, the latter is external, and all are vital to growing the business and value for public relations.

This chapter focuses on three interrelated arenas for business development. First is the arena of promoting the public relations function. PR people are so busy inspiring cooperation between organizations and their publics that they rarely focus on doing the same for their own operations and the profession. And this PR about PR is sorely needed. Second is the arena of market positioning. PR is instrumental in communication that affects people's knowledge, attitudes, and behaviors toward an organization and what it offers. Having an idea about how market positions are determined and how they are central to communication efforts is essential to managing public relations resources. The third and final arena for this chapter is cold, warm, and hot calls. Again, organizations must make a concerted effort to specifically obtain sales that build their businesses. "Sales" concerns transactions between people, and the kinds of "sales" public relations people do (e.g., to sell a story to journalists) are very similar to the sales made by sales representatives. Understanding that there are degrees of calls and ways to strategically engage in sales contacts can help build business—especially public relations business—as greater and greater success is attained.

Promoting the Public Relations Function

Because public relations naturally deals with communication and every human can communicate (of course many are better than others), PR is seen as easy. At the same time it is very interesting to discover how bad organizational leaders can be at writing, public speaking, and interpersonal communication, even though they still "rise through the ranks." Still, when public relations is viewed as easy, it is seen as the organizational mouthpiece and its practitioners merely the vocal chords for what the management brain wants to say. Of course this view is very unfair and unrealistic. It is grounded in the negative stereotypes for the profession that persist and fly in the face of the ethical, strategic, and challenging work of PR professionals that is vital to inspiring cooperation between organizations and their publics. If organizational leaders do not understand what public relations is and what value it offers in business terms, public relations will not be included in the strategic management for the organization. As always, any public relations practitioner has the duty and responsibility to educate people—no matter who they are—about the very real value and power of public relations.

In addition to the added value that public relations offers organizations, as covered in Chapter 6, the exercising of *power* is an important matter for successful public relations management. The notion of power is a tricky one because the concept mixes negative, positive, and neutral meanings. Negative connotations often coincide with the sense and reference of words like "domination" or "oppression." Positive to neutral connotations can often parallel senses and references of words like "control" or "authority" or "influence." But, depending on one's attitude, the negative connotations could be viewed positively and positive connotations viewed negatively. Nevertheless, power is more complicated than positive, negative, or neutral attitudes suggest. Also, power is not a thing to be possessed but, rather, is a direct function of personal relationships. That is, "power is a community-based phenomenon that people confer on each other through their [system of] relationships with one another" (Smudde & Courtright, 2010, p. 184). Organizations are communities of people, all of whom are involved in the *top-down and bottom-up* conferring and, thereby, exercising of power among leaders and followers, executives, and staffers. To this end, power in public relations is not just a matter of one dimension but, instead, a matter of exercising power in three dimensions that coexist and comingle simultaneously. The three dimensions of power for public relations are:

1. *Hierarchical*—Organizations have particular structures, usually defined in charts (see Figure 7-1) that show who relates to whom in terms of rank/title, authority, and sphere of control. Such charts can be larger or smaller (also called "flatter"), depending on an organization's complexity. One alternative organization chart is "circular," as it shows management flow among leaders and followers. Every type of chart depicts a hierarchy, and all are entwined with political issues (for better and for worse) that naturally emerge among people who work together, and those issues play out in the personal relationships people have with one another as they seek to get their work done. So-called "dominant coalitions" are a function of hierarchy and will be addressed shortly.

2. *Rhetorical*—People are unique among other living species in that they are creators, users, and misusers of language and symbols (Burke, 1970, 1989). To this end the effectiveness and effects of human communication are always at play in all human activity. So the ways in which people use language, symbols, knowledge, and discourse make up this dimension of how power is exercised.

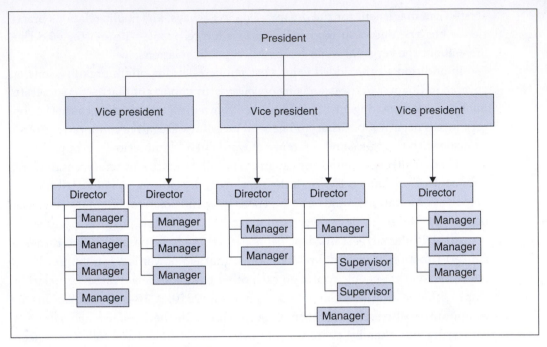

Figure 7-1. ORGANIZATION CHART.

3. *Social*—The combination of individuals and the organization of them in a single, cohesive unit (e.g., business, nonprofit, NGO) is focused on achieving certain shared objectives according to certain rules, practices, traditions, and so on. This dimension subsumes matters of ethics and professionalism, which affect perceptions of the profession because of PR pros' work, attitudes, behaviors, and so on. This interaction among people at the macro and micro levels within a social framework intersects with the two other dimensions.

Power has been problematic for people to understand and use. People tend to think about power in only one of these three ways when they should pay attention to all three simultaneously. Additional factors that cloud people's understanding of power include whether they are approaching it through selfless or selfish motives, which reinforce positive or negative views of power, respectively. Economic, regulatory, cultural, technological, and other factors can also affect the corporate context in which power is exercised and understood. Rather than thinking about power as merely a necessary component of organizational life with which professionals must deal, it can be embraced as something enabling. Smudde and

Courtright (2010, pp. 181–182) present a way to exercise power effectively for public relations professionals, and the approach hinges on five proactive practices:

1. *Coalition building:* At an external level, coalition building involves public relations practitioners working on behalf of one's organization to establish common ground with another person or group on which they can collaborate and achieve mutually beneficial ends. At an internal level, coalition building involves public relations professionals working well with others within their own organizations so that the public relations function is valued and valuable. Central here is recognizing the upward and downward flow plus the micro and macro levels of power that are at play. Especially important, Bowen's (2009) study shows how PR professionals gain membership in an organization's *dominant coalition*, which is comprised of "positions of authority in an organization's structure or hierarchy . . . , including the chief executive officer (CEO), and other C-level executives, such as the Chief Finance Officer, Chief Operations Officer, and Chief Marketing Officer" (p. 419). Bowen's study identifies five routes toward "getting a seat at the table" with the dominant coalition, each route of which is consistent with this book and revolves around answering particular key questions (in order of importance):

   a. *Crisis situation*—How much do I know about crisis management, and am I ready to act decisively when the crisis comes? Answer it primarily by reading about crisis communication theory and cases.

   b. *Ethical dilemma*—Do I feel prepared and knowledgeable enough to counsel and advise on ethical dilemmas? Answer it primarily by reading about ethics plus the building and keeping of trust for organizations.

   c. *Credibility gained over time through correct analyses*—Have I voiced an opinion on important issues and gained credibility for offering correct analyses over time? Answer it primarily by reading about the management of public relations and general business operations and practices.

   d. *Issues ranked highly on mass media's agenda*—Am I prepared to counsel top management on the best ways to manage an issue of high media interest? Answer it primarily by reading about strategic issues management or organizational rhetoric.

   e. *Leadership*—Do I know what characteristics make a great leader, and am I displaying those traits consistently? Answer it primarily by reading about leadership and motivational research.

2. *Strategy development:* Public relations professionals must participate in the process and provide counsel for the organization to manage its strategic plans for

success in its business and operations. It is the province of public relations to act as a seer of future opportunities and threats to an organization's image, business, and legacy and to address them proactively whenever possible. Strategy development, together with the ancillary practices of message design and genre choices, is the unseen element to public relations that publics and stakeholders do not readily recognize.

3. *Message design:* Taking publics' knowledge, attitudes, and actions into account is the essence of effective message design. Through message design, public relations professionals focus on the relationships among their organizations and the publics/stakeholders that they depend on. (See especially Smudde & Courtright [2012 and 2013] for this practice.)

4. *Genre choices:* The actual outputs of public relations professionals' work (i.e., the tactics) must also balance an organization's needs and wants for communication with the publics' needs and wants in communication. In this way, the discourse genres chosen to present any messages must fulfill expectations on multiple levels. (Also see Smudde & Courtright [2012] for this practice.)

5. *Program execution and evaluation:* The final production and dissemination of public relations work to target publics are what most people recognize as public relations but are, in reality, only the result of much hard planning and preparation. Public relations practitioners must also evaluate how well the program worked for both the target publics and the organization through systematic and appropriate measurement methods (see Stacks & Michaelson, 2010). With attention to ethics and professionalism in this and the previous points, public relations may serve as the management of power relations between organizations and publics on whom their success depends.

Promoting the public relations function, then, is naturally a matter of internal selling about the value and power of PR as much as it is an external one. That selling encompasses both the features of public relations (i.e., what it is and can do) and, most important, the benefits of public relations (i.e., the value contributions and power). Competence, integrity, enthusiasm, and savviness are just a few of the characteristics PR professionals must genuinely demonstrate in who they are, what they do, and how they do it at all times. Representing the entire profession is an important responsibility, and it goes hand-in-hand with representing your organization. After all, you are being paid to be an expert communicator and the expert in public relations.

Whether a public relations operation is an internal department or an external agency, relationships matter as much as they do in and for any other operational unit. For public relations, however, the importance is all the more pronounced because relationships are part of its name and its core business for an organization. Public relations for an agency or a nonagency organization still can be viewed as a client-centered operation. To this end, public relations managers and their staffs have the responsibility to look out for the greater good for their clients, whether it is their own organizations or organizations with whom they have contractual agreements to do PR work. Understanding how one's organization/client is positioned in the market is a crucial concern to representing that organization and building business effectively, ethically, and successfully.

Market Positioning

One of the more useful and parsimonious definitions of *positioning* is as follows: It is "what you do to the mind of the prospect" (Ries & Trout, 1976/2001, p. 2). Key to this view is imprinting or affixing a brand or product indelibly in the mind of customers, especially in positive ways at the first experience with it. Positioning is central to an organization being able to create and build its business (for-profit, nonprofit, NGO, or other). Companies seek increased sales from strategic market positions and, if desired, increased investment from investors. Nonprofits seek increased donations, grant funding, material resources, and volunteers/members. Nongovernmental organizations seek increased support for social change, including anything from people, to money, to material.

No matter what kind of organization it is, there are two basic dimensions to market positioning. The first is *brand positioning*, which very basically focuses on the ways in which an organization's brand name is clearly unique from among all the others in a market, especially in terms of value. The second is *product/service positioning*, which basically focuses on direct or indirect comparisons of an organization's product (or service) with those offered in the marketplace, especially in terms of features and, primarily, benefits. Fundamental to both dimensions of market positioning is *differentiation*, which concerns the one thing that makes a brand, product, or service unique from anything else similar to it (Trout & Rivkin, 2000). Differentiation is a natural fit for public relations, and we will explore it further shortly as part of the larger process for determining market positions.

Understanding what positions may exist in a market is important to communicating the right messages in the right ways to the right people. To find a singular way to capture market positioning and the importance of differentiation is not an easy task because of the numerous models and methods available online and in print. Ries and Trout's (1976/2001) main metaphor for positioning is "ladders" of the mind, where each market is defined by its own ladder and brands in each market occupy different rungs, with the leader at the top. Moving up a ladder is harder than moving down. And introducing a new product or service means providing customers with a new ladder. The key to effective positioning is precise language use. More specifically, positioning is largely a function of word choices about one's product or service. As Silbinger (2012) summarizes it, 10 rules for positioning revolve around words:

1. Own a word that uniquely ties to your product/service in customers' minds.
2. Begin positioning with the product's/service's name.
3. Use a unique name for a unique product/service.
4. Own a word by being the first to use it.
5. Stay on message about the product/service every time.
6. Introduce a new brand to respond to a new competitor, and do not dilute the original brand.
7. Create a new market category a leader cannot occupy but a challenger will.
8. Find a niche in customers' minds the leader does not fill but a challenger will.
9. Reposition the competition in a market or undercut the leader's messages.
10. Maintain consistency in the positioning choice for the long term.

For our purposes, Ries and Trout's (1976/2001, 1993) work provides us with a very useful heuristic between their two highly influential volumes about marketing and positioning. The heuristic (see Figure 7-2) is a way to conceptualize the various ways an organization may *position itself and its products/services* in the markets it serves. Ries and Trout also address positioning for followers in a market and how to reposition competitors with your organization's own communication, as Rule 9 above suggests. For our purposes in PR, what is most beneficial about this heuristic is its utility for either brand or product/service positioning. For example, the overall brand of Coke is the leader in the soft drink market, so much so that in parts of the southeastern United States, any soft drink is referred to as a Coke (e.g., orange coke) even though the drink may have its own name (e.g., Orange Crush). Market positions are fluid and take a lot of work to attain and, especially, to maintain. A first mover may be able to create a new market (see Rule 7 above), as Chrysler did with its first minivans, then for a period of time command a market niche (see Rule 8) as other companies begin to break into that new market. In this way, a company may be, as Chrysler has been able to do, a leader for a market niche in which it was the first mover.

To understand an organization's positioning, many questions must be answered that span several categories of needed information. In public relations, you must be able to help position an organization (including its brands, products, and

Leader

- The perceived or recognized leader in a market.
- Examples: Coke, Nike, Google

Challenger

- The perceived next-best option in a market, right behind the dominator.
- Examples: Pepsi, Adidas, Bing

Niche occupier

- A specialty option that targets a narrow band or particular interest in a market.
- Examples: Snapple, L'Oreal ("Because I'm worth it."), Ask.com

First mover

- An organization creates a new market category with a product or service no one else has.
- Examples: Chrysler's minivans, Amazon.com, Zipcar

Repositioner

- An organization chooses to remake itself and, thereby, its place in the market.
  - Examples: Boston Chicken changed to Boston market.
- An organization repositions a competitor and, thereby, redefines its own position.
  - Examples: Wrangler jeans urging customers to check its U-shaped crotch design as more comfortable than jeans made with a V-shaped design.

Figure 7-2. HEURISTIC OF MARKET POSITIONS BASED ON RIES AND TROUT.

services) through effective, strategic communication, whether that organization is the one that employs you or is one that you represent through a contractual arrangement. Again, our focus here is proactive positioning from an organization about itself and its own offerings. For our purposes, seven crucial questions must be answered to establish a firm grasp of an organization's market position so that it can, in turn, be realized through communication and other actions.

1. *What are your organization's differentiators?* An answer to this question relies on three things. First, a *unique selling proposition* (USP) (see Trout & Rivkin, 2000) defines simply the specific benefit that can be had from a product or service that (1) is truly different from all others and (2) can be "diffused" through the marketplace (see Rogers, 2002). Second, *compelling competitive advantages* (CCAs) of a product or service give evidential support for, or proof of, the USP. Third, the *image and reputation* for an organization prevails and even precedes people's ideas about what it is, stands for, and has done. The combination of these three things also produces a highly useful statement that is essential in a strategic plan: the *value proposition*. The value proposition (see Appendix A), in turn, can and should function as the key message

platform because it captures the very essence of an organization (on a macro basis) or an organization's product/service (on a micro basis). The example strategic plan in Appendix B shows an example of how this matter of differentiation is played out and rendered into a value proposition.

2. *What are your organization's strengths and weaknesses?* An answer to this question can be prepared through a SWOT analysis (see Chapter 4) or another environmental scanning method or situation analysis. Three other methods can be valuable. One method, a *gap analysis*, very simply put, seeks data of any kind about why there is a gap between where organization is now (its current state) and where it wants to be (its ideal or future state). Then the analysis of these data determines whether the ideal state is reasonable on applicable grounds/criteria, what is keeping the organization from moving from the current state to the ideal state, if there are alternative states the organization should seek, and how the chosen ideal state could be attained.

Another environmental scanning method is a *force field analysis* shown in Figure 7-3 (Lewin, 1997). Simply explained, this method examines the forces that can enable change for the better (i.e., driving forces) and forces that can inhibit change (i.e., restraining forces). This method is useful when working with social, political, or economic forces because of their broad range of sources and levels of

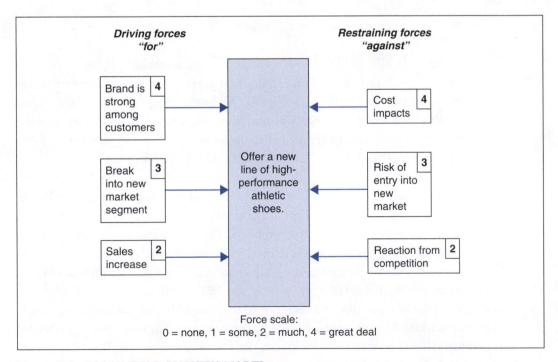

Figure 7-3. FORCE FIELD ANALYSIS MODEL.

strength. Central to a force field analysis is recognizing that not all forces are equal and can counter or balance one another because they have certain *valance*, or strength, which can be rated on a numerical scale (see Figure 7-3). Force field analysis focuses on things that influence people's behaviors, assuming that behavior is influenced by a mix of forces. This form of analysis can also be used to determine critical success factors (see Chapter 4 and Appendix A). The objective, then, is to identify which forces must be increased *and* decreased to obtain the kind and degree of change needed. When forces are in balance (not necessarily a perfect but, possibly, favorable balance), they create homeostasis. By communicating effectively and ethically about these factors, we can alter the balance of forces and affect behavior.

Another model for scanning the environment is the *order restoration model* shown in Figure 7-4 (Smudde, 2011). The model helps us understand the progression of things in context from the way they are now ("order") to the way things need to be ("redemption") through some change that is initiated in such a way that it "pollutes" the order. From there, one understands who or what may have been "guilty" for causing the change (whether internal, external or a mix of both), their

Phase 1: Order	Phase 2: Pollution & Assignment of Guilt	Phase 3: Purification	Phase 4: Redemption
The state of things about and for an organization, what it stands for, and what it offers is stable.	Something from within, without, or both upsets or significantly changes the stability of things, and blame or responsibility must be assigned for it on the public sage.	Efforts to make things right gradually secure the public's approval, where the success of one side over the other becomes increasingly apparent, especially as an organization accepts responsibiliy of it own accord or it saddled with responsibility by others.	• For an organization that secures the public's favor, final vindication of it is given and a new order is created, which would bolster its image and credibility. • For an organization that does not secure the public's favor, it must cope with the new order, which (adversely) affects the organizaion's reputation and credibility.

Figure 7-4. ORDER RESTORATION MODEL FOR ENVIRONMENTAL SCANNING.

level of responsibility for it, and how order can be restored or "redeemed" for the organization and its publics through a process of "purification" that makes things better. In this way, context is as much retrospective as it is prospective about what is going on for an organization (whole or in part). Organizational officers, of which PR pros are a part, can not only make sense of how the order of things changed, but they can also plan to ethically "pollute" the order of things to achieve strategic objectives, like those related to the launch of a unique product into a market or the introduction of a new public policy to remedy a social situation.

3. *How is your organization perceived today?* An answer to this question is contingent on answers to several interrelated matters of perception in the overall market, by current and prospective customers, in the community, by current and potential investors, by industry and market analysts and key publication editors, and by relevant organizations and institutions like professional or trade organizations, research groups, and universities. This information would be valuable as the foundation for what people think about your organization on its own and as it compares to others.

4. *Who are your target customers?* An answer to this question requires the gathering and analysis of valid and reliable data about the details of target customers (people or organizations). Such data may be gathered through primary or secondary research, and it often should reflect customers' demographic makeup (e.g., age, gender, race, education, location) plus their psychographic profile (e.g., attitudes, behavior inclinations, values, lifestyle). This information will be instrumental in realizing the common ground of needs and wants people have based on key factors of their lives as a group.

5. *What are the results of your organization's most recent competition/market analysis?* Answers to this question require reasonably detailed information about the other players in the market(s) in which your organization participates. This point, like the others, works well for for-profit, nonprofit/institutional, NGO, and other types of organization because people need to know who is "out there" and how they "stack up." The salient matters for data collection are identifying any other organizations competing with yours to any degree, things your organization does differently from competitors, unique messages and actions of competitors, recognition for market positions competitors hold, and ways to overcome these and other pressures and perceptions.

6. *How do you want to be positioned in the market?* The answer to this question defines what an organization wants to be. The answer, then, is the conclusion derived from the answers to all the previous questions and results in a final view of what market position the organization will seek to establish along the lines of that shown in Figure 7-2 and, perhaps, in tune with the model in Figure 7-4.

7. *Do you have all the necessary resources to successfully achieve the market position you want?* The answer to this final question could be the one that says, "Go!" or "No

go." A thorough and, most important, honest analysis of an organization's where-withal (e.g., money, people, material, systems) will reveal the degree to which the desired market positioning strategy can be done or not for the duration of time truly necessary to do it right and do it well.

Public relations' role in positioning is a potent one and is "the strategic attempt to stake out and occupy a site of intentional representation in the contested space where meanings are constructed, contested, and reconstructed" (James, 2011, p. 98). Public relations attends to positioning, as James (2011) argues, through the interplay of three factors: an organization's ideal state, the story to support that ideal state, and the particular discourse used to convey that story. Additionally, forces from within and without affect the degree to which positioning can be attained. The challenge is to obtain and maintain customers' attention with a product or service. Organizational messages become important in undergirding an organization's claim to hold any market position. Heath and Heath's (2004) SUCCES model for message design is especially helpful to make messages "sticky" and stay in people's minds. The more of these six characteristics that are used, the better:

- Simplicity: messages are core and compact
- Unexpectedness: messages are surprising and interesting, plus they evoke curiosity
- Concreteness: messages demonstrate human actions and appeal to the senses
- Credibility: messages' ideas have an internal authority and testability
- Emotions: messages appeal to people's feelings, self-interest, needs
- Stories: messages convey real/realistic situations as simulators

Once it is clear what an organization wants to be, based on what it is and from where it has come, communication and other core operations can engage in their work to make it happen. In tune with the strategic plan, market positioning establishes the claim an organization has to do its business for those on whom it is targeting. Instrumental in the work of developing new business is making contacts with all kinds of customers.

Cold, Warm, and Hot Calls

There are basically three *types of customers* you may encounter in sales situations, including those for raising money, signing up volunteers, soliciting material support, and so on. Those three customer types are: (1) those who plan to buy from you, (2) those who would never buy from you, and (3) those in between who need help making up their minds. That third group is the key to increasing sales, because if you do little else, the first group will come to you anyway, and you might as well forget about the second group.

Cold calling is a highly concentrated persuasive activity. Cold calling focuses on Type 3 customers, who have never done business with you or do not even know your business exists. You must use a small amount of words to say a lot in a compelling way to achieve your ultimate goal for any call. Cold calls are instrumental to penetrating the thinking of the people who would benefit from your company's work but have not thought about it. *More than anything, your goal with cold calls is to get a meeting with these potential customers—nothing more.* In a sense, this is the first sale that may lead to the ultimate payoff—a closed deal between your firm and the customer's.

Now before we go further, what does cold calling have to do with public relations management? *The principles and practices given here about contacting customers to build business are precisely the same kinds of things you need to do to promote your clients or your organization.* Such promotion would naturally involve media relations, for example, and you should apply the process for calling journalists and other parties as you might for calling on *Type 1, Type 2, or Type 3 customers.* After all, depending on your relationships (and your clients' or your organization's relationships), calls to journalists, analysts, donors, and so on could be hot, warm, or cold too. So when we refer to "sales" in this section, think about the broad range of things that can be "sold," from products and services to news stories and client expertise.

If you have done any follow-up on news releases, you have an idea about what cold calling is. If you are wary of cold calling, you are not alone. Some people loathe it, yet some love it. In reality most people fall in the middle of these two extremes. Whatever your feelings are about cold calling, remember that all you're really doing is having an impromptu conversation with someone you would like to meet anyway. And you don't spend all day doing it, as you will see later. An important thing to know and remember is that, although cold calling may be nerve-racking to do, it is truly something you can master. *And attitude is everything.* If it helps, think of cold calling as a challenge to take in the competitive arena of sales. You should find it valuable to you personally and professionally as you gain experience, build your network, and grow in success.

This section is meant to (1) help you grow in your comfort in placing cold calls, so you can get closer to having more closed sales and (2) inform you about *how* to do cold calls and *why* what you will do will work for you personally and the company generally. There is much more to this subject, and this section has distilled selected key aspects of it for you to use right away. So this section should serve you well as a kind of tutorial that can get you started. And later on, if you are inclined to learn more, you can seek out resources online, information in print, or training through sales seminars.

Preparation

There is much to do before you make any cold calls. After all, you cannot call just anybody. The "shotgun approach" to cold calling is very ineffective and a grossly inefficient use of your talents and time. You must have a plan and know exactly whom to call and why.

Cold calling differs from what I call "hot" and "warm" calling. *Hot calling* involves talking to Type 1 customers who are already very interested in doing business with you and your company, and they may already have done or are doing business with you and are satisfied or enthusiastic. Hot calls can be thought of as the most "organic" way to build business because you are proposing an existing client take advantage of other products and services. *Warm calling* involves contacting Type 2 customers who may have done business with your company some time ago but haven't recently, and they have favorable feelings about your company and would be willing to work with your firm again. Warm calling also can involve certain Type 3 customers who have never done business with your company but are willing to check out your firm because of good word-of-mouth referrals. Cold calls to Type 3 customers dominate because you are truly prospecting for new business from those you have not served before and would like to. Both hot and warm calls are easier to do than cold calls because of preexisting relationships or favorable preconceived notions about your company. Remember, however, we're talking about cold calling.

No matter whom you call and why, you *must* do a certain amount of research to understand what you want, what your target customers want, who your competition is, and how your work fits into the big picture of your company's business development. Typical products of such research are contact lists of prospective customers who meet most or all of the criteria for a viable customer. (Another similar and familiar list is a media list of journalists to whom you would pitch news.) You may already know much of this, and it is important to document that knowledge so you can make the best use of it at any time. Let's explore each of the dimensions of your preparation.

Know your company

Why is your employer such a great company to hire for advertising and/or public relations? This is a critical, fundamental question you must be able to answer for yourself and, especially, for any customer.

If you think about it, there are several very good reasons for hiring you. All of these reasons are *key messages* that customers should come to know, and your work enables that. So you must be able to talk about these things competently and naturally, and that may mean gathering any necessary backup data to support your claims. (These data will be important for your meetings, described below.) Some specific kinds of information you may need might include:

- Core areas of the business
- Current projects (customers, requirements, challenges, cost [if permitted to give out])
- Most recently completed projects (customers, requirements, challenges, results/successes, cost [if permitted to give out])
- Notable past projects (customers, requirements, challenges, results/successes, cost [if permitted to give out])
- List of customers who'd be willing to be references
- Pricing guidelines (for reference only; do not share with customers or give quotes over the phone—information gained at a meeting will be needed to prepare an accurate quote)
- Any news about the company and its people
- Regulatory pressures
- Website address (give out rarely so people don't use it as an excuse to not meet with you; save for the meeting and give the person a tour of the site)

With this intimate knowledge about your company, you can apply it more accurately to what your target customers want and need.

Know your target customers

Remember the three basic customer types. It is not easy to identify them, but you can and you must. In many ways, you already have an idea of who your target customers are, whether they are predisposed to buy from you or are in need of information about who you are and why they should buy from you. This is where a little research and savvy thinking pay off. *The objective here is to use your research to create a "screen" through which you sift out the best opportunities to schedule meetings with new customers that may turn into sales.*

Knowing your customers will help you focus on their needs and wants when you talk with them at any time. Get to know their businesses. (Know journalists' news organizations inside and out, plus know individual journalists' areas of coverage ["beats"], preferences in being contacted, and needs for developing stories.) Learn all you can about your target customers, because the more knowledgeable you are about them, the more impressive you are as someone who cares enough to learn as much as you can. That is a large component of trust, which is foundational in your relationship.

Most important, the more you know about your target customers, the more you understand what value they are probably looking for and how you and your company can provide them with that value or more. Find out what "pain" target customers (including consumers of journalists' work) have and figure out how you can cure that pain and head off other potential pains that may come along. *It is all about the benefits and value added to the customer's business for the investment in having your company do any project.*

Who are your target customers? You must identify and understand the broad categories of customers important to your company. In each of these categories think about what the ideal customer would be, which amounts to the basic substance of your screen for each category. (See the section "Track Your Progress" for a detailed list of data points that can reflect on your screen as well.) Refine your screens with information about what your target customers need and want by reviewing the projects the company completed over its history, especially over the past couple of years. You will find information about projects' specifications, successes, challenges, etc.

Take note of any current or established customers that show up on your cold-call list (e.g., and make sure they are not among your cold-call targets). Because they are already customers, they really should not be approached like an absolutely new business lead. Do note what business your company is doing with them, because that information may be useful in your calls.

You should also read trade publications that pertain to those customers, so you get a sense of what issues are important, how they talk about them, and what kinds of approaches are employed for any given project. This last item is important because you can stay on top of technology and systems people want to install and know what kinds of approaches may be applied to install them.

Visit target customers' websites, if they have them, and learn all you can. Look for key messages the company wants people to know. Figure out what its strategic direction seems to be. Read any literature on the website that describes the company's performance, operating divisions, markets, etc. Also obtain copies of any printed company literature and analyze them too.

You should also search the Internet and library for news articles about your target customers. You may learn about issues that are helping or hurting the company. You may discover how a particular strategic decision may require new facilities and therefore represent a new business opportunity for you. You may also find out which people you may want to speak to when you call.

Attend conferences or trade shows that your target customers attend. You will be able to sit in on seminars about topics important to them, which will give you vital information about how problems or projects are being addressed. And naturally you will be able to meet many new people and gather leads, set up or have on-site meetings, and follow up on any contacts.

You can use published data about companies in directories like those published by Dun & Bradstreet, local business periodicals, and Gale Research. If a company has stock that's publicly traded, you can look up information on the Internet at the websites for the New York Stock Exchange, NASDAQ, any number of financial news websites (e.g., Yahoo! Finance, TheStreet.com), and the U.S. Securities and Exchange Commission. There are other ways, too, to learn about your target customers, and you've probably used them on other occasions. Use those tools also to your advantage to learn all you can and impress your customers with your knowledge of them, especially during your meetings.

In an important way, the work you do to learn about your customers also serves as a way to identify new business leads—trade shows for example. This area of *lead generation* is part of the research involved in discovering opportunities for cold calls. There is much information available on the Internet, in books, and in articles about effective lead-generation strategies. Although this topic is an important one, it is uniquely separate from the subject of cold calling. If you are interested in understanding it further, seek resources online (search term: "lead generation") that can give you details you need.

Know your competition

What's the difference between what your company can do and any other organization like it? How you answer this question matters greatly, because *what you don't know* becomes at least as important (if not more so) as what you do know. The trick here is to find out what you do not know by researching your competition and add that to what you do know. The good news is that once you do this research, and do it to a reasonable level of detail, you can use the information in myriad ways and only need to update it once or twice a year, depending on market dynamics.

To manage this task for the benefit of each person and the company, apply the simple idea that many hands make light work. Assign each person one competitor to research, then collect all information about all competitors and share it with everyone either in print or electronically by e-mailing the file(s) or accessing the file(s) securely on a company database.

How do you conduct this research? You do it pretty much the same way you did for researching your target customers. Websites are a great place to start. You can also collect and analyze any literature you can from the companies.

What things do you have to know? There are many dimensions to research, but some key ones include:

- Region served
- Markets served
- Services offered
- Pricing and pricing strategies
- Value proposition
- Market positioning
- Awards and other industry recognition
- Quality philosophy
- Customer service
- Customer relationships (direct/indirect; long-term/short-term)
- Showcase customers
- Company mission
- Union work/Relationships
- Employee/Staff expertise
- History/Years in business
- Regulatory environment
- Reputation
- Financial viability/Strength of business
- Aggressiveness in marketing
- Key messages
- Rumors/Hearsay (date them)
- News items (date them with sources)

You may think of other dimensions that should be researched. If you do, add them to your task and share them with others.

The bottom line is: the more complete your research is about your competition, the better you can know what competitive advantages you have over them (or they over you) and the better you can persuade target customers about why your company should do a project instead of anyone else. So you (and your colleagues) must decide to what level of detail you need to go in your research.

In addition, you should discover ways that your company complements the work of other firms, because if a customer has already signed a firm to do work, perhaps there is something it cannot do and you can. Knowing what gaps there may be to fill in a project that's being handled by any other firm can get you additional business by persuading the customer that you can meet that unmet need. (Note: These kinds of issues are best handled at the first meeting you schedule and thereafter.)

Understand the big picture

All this preparation is important because the more you know, the better you can screen out opportunities that, in all likelihood, wouldn't buy from you, and you can focus on those that would. The role of cold calling in the sales process is pretty straightforward. It is the spark that starts the flame of a potentially strong customer relationship. *The equation is simple: no calls = no prospects = no sales = no job.* And you do not want to be solely at the mercy of the market, where you are always waiting for people to call you. If people do not know about you, why would they call? So, think of cold calling's place in the big picture of the sales process in Figure 7-5.

The sales process is broken down into discrete parts. The two most basic are the *calling realm* and the *prospect pipeline*.

The calling realm (which includes hot, warm, and cold calls) is concerned with identifying from the field of all opportunities, which come in many different sizes and kinds, the best ones that are worth pursuing. Having the in-depth knowledge about yourself and your customers, you can accurately assess which opportunities

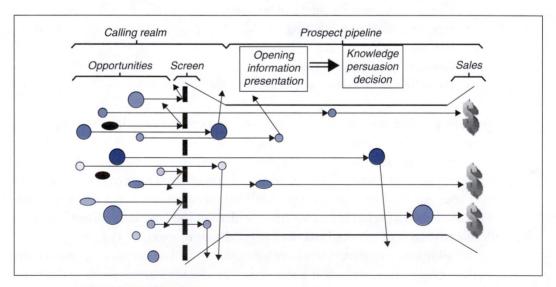

Figure 7-5. THE SALES PIPELINE.

you want to invite into the pipeline through a cold call. That knowledge amounts to a "screen" that you use to sift out the best candidates. Many don't make it through, and some never get a second glance because they don't ever plan to buy from you for any number of reasons. Only a select few get your call, because you believe strongly that these are well worth your time and effort to try to schedule a first meeting.

The second basic part of the sales process model is the prospect pipeline. Notice that any target customer is not called a "prospect" until it fully enters the pipeline because you scheduled a meeting. Until this point, any target customer is merely an "opportunity." It is possible that opportunities will not turn into prospects after your cold call, and that's when they exit the process early. When an opportunity becomes a prospect, there is some length of time between your first meeting and the decision to buy or not, which is represented by the arrows of varying length into the pipeline. Once a prospect decides to buy, it moves on to a closed sale and is considered an established customer. A prospect may, however, decide to not buy, and thereby exit the pipeline; whereas, it may be another opportunity in the future.

In the prospect pipeline you will notice that the sales communication you engage in—the opening, the information you share, the presentation at the first and subsequent meetings—serves the prospect as knowledge, persuasive reasons to buy, and a decision to buy (or not). This communication is instrumental and dynamic throughout the pipeline, and you have primary responsibility for making it work. Remember that you're both establishing and maintaining a relationship, and your language, behavior, and other factors all affect how your customer responds to everything about the deal that's taking shape. And that deal only came into being because you recognized a viable opportunity, made a simple call, and followed through on it.

Complacency is the enemy of sales. When times are good is not the time to relax. What will you do when times are not so good or even downright bad? Placing cold calls is an effective and efficient way to manage market cycles. When business is strong, you're making calls to shore up business when times aren't so good. And when sales are down, you're working just as hard to bring in prospects. Cold calling, then, helps smooth out and control much of the ebb and flow of market cycles. And that is critical for maintaining the business and jobs.

Scripts

Know what you will say before you say it—know it well and be genuine, truthful, friendly, confident, trustworthy, and natural. This principle is key to success in your calls. Believe it or not, the person you call will pick up on what kind of person you are based on how well you present yourself over the phone. Your vocal qualities, from intonation to pronunciation, all affect what impressions someone creates about you—research has shown this repeatedly. Who wants to listen to someone who mechanistically recites a text or sounds like his or her heart is not in it? The caller will not seem worthy of trust, doesn't appear confident, sounds unnatural in his/her speech, and other factors. This kind of call would be offensive to a listener and a waste of time. It would also undermine the caller's credibility. Appendix C gives you sample scripts for you to review and use.

It is important, therefore, to practice, practice, practice. And you may want to practice for a couple of hours and even involve someone to role-play with you so you get it down before you make your first call. Athletes don't go into an event without proper conditioning and preparation, and neither should you.

Fundamentally, your call is an interruption, and anyone you call is not expecting or prepared to talk with you. So you must make sure the person you call understands who you are, what you have to offer, and especially what's in it for him or her. And you must do this simply, directly, yet vividly, with no fancy or gimmicky ploys for attention. Scripts are given in Appendix C that will help you do this.

When is the best time to make any cold call? There's really no right or wrong answer, but there does seem to be some wisdom in the idea that calling earlier in the day, even if you leave a message, you have a better chance of getting through than later on when people are deep in the throes of their work. There also seems to be some wisdom in the idea that you can get results if you call late in the day, after 5:00 p.m. or so (even on Fridays), because people are winding down, major work for the day is done, and they have some time to think more clearly about other things. You need to try times that seem to work best for both you and your target customers. Again, some understanding about your customers can pay off here, too.

The more comfortable and familiar you are with what you want to say, the easier it is for you to have a conversation on the phone with someone you've not yet met. That's why your preparation and scripts are so vital. Add to that the fact that the more calls you make, the more experience you get and the more effective you become. But make sure you truly know your stuff before you even begin.

Remember your goal is to *get a meeting*. (A meeting with a journalist would be included here, too.) Bridge back to this issue gracefully if the person takes you off track. You should answer the person's questions, but not in too much detail, because you want to meet with that person to do that. Examples of how to bridge back to your goal are given in Appendix C in terms of "negative" responses. ("Positive" responses are those that result in a meeting straightaway.)

In case you must answer some specific questions during your calls, based on what you plan to say, have basic information ready. For example, you may need the total number of customers/projects your company's had over time, the names of referenceable clients, and various project examples with relevant summary data about them. Remember that you don't want to give out a lot of detail during the call—give just enough information to maintain interest so that you can schedule a meeting to go into greater depth.

At the meeting

You have done your homework. You have made your calls. You have scheduled some appointments. What will you do at your first meetings? Now is the time for all your preparation to really pay off. And the objective of this first meeting is to get another one or a signed deal, depending on how the prospect wants to proceed. (Play it conservative and shoot for another meeting or even a quote you send.)

Remember that cold calls are, in general, concentrated persuasive endeavors to get a meeting. During your call you made some important claims that you now have the opportunity to prove with evidence. That evidence will come in the form of your presentation, printed material, and any other documentation or oral arguments you make in response to the prospect's questions and statements.

To this end, your presence in person must reaffirm the confidence, enthusiasm, friendliness, and naturalness that you exhibited on the phone. Now you can really bring your research to bear on whatever the prospect says. You should come across as knowledgeable and credible without appearing aloof, pompous, or aggressive. Relax, be yourself, and genuinely reflect interest in the prospect and his/her business.

It is all about the benefits and value added to the prospect's business for the investment in having your company do any project. With this principle in mind, what should you plan to say, and what should you bring? Based on your research, you should prepare an agenda about key points that are of interest to the customer. Those points should relate to the pain that needs curing and the value that your company will add to the prospect's business. It is up to you to organize the points in a logical way that makes sense to the prospect. Leave time for open discussion at the end. It is also up to you to decide what you will say about each item on the agenda.

If you think about what you plan to say in terms of a formal argument, each claim you make requires you to have evidence to back it up and clear reasoning about why that evidence helps you arrive at that claim. This simple pattern suggests that you need to collect only enough printed material and other documentation that you feel will sufficiently back up your claims and are directly relevant to the prospect. (More on that in a minute.) You're doing a certain amount of educated guesswork here, but if you've come to know the prospect well enough through your research, you should be prepared for almost anything. It is, after all, a first meeting, and your objective is to get to the next step: either a meeting to discuss a quote, or another meeting that will result in a request for a quote, or even a signed deal, depending on how the prospect does business.

The basic agenda might be as follows. Note that it begins with a focus on the prospect, which symbolically says your interest in the prospect is primary and that you've done some homework on it.

- Thank you for this meeting
- Review of the prospect and opportunities
- Value that your company can add
- Examples of projects relevant to the prospect
- Proposal for working on one or more of the prospect's opportunities
- *Ask for the business*
- Open discussion and next steps

This agenda sets up a simple persuasive progression: identifying needs, showing how the needs can be met through your company's added value, visualizing that value through real success stories, and proposing a business relationship be started. Also notice that you must formally ask for the business to make it absolutely clear what you're after and how the prospect stands to gain. Remember, your objective is to get to the next step—a closed deal or a new meeting that would lead to a sale.

In your presentation, try to work in the key messages about your company. Also, emphasize the company's reputation for accurate and timely quotes, dedication to safety, and on-time completion record. As a rule of thumb, plan no more than 15 to 20 minutes for one presentation. The whole meeting may last from 30 minutes to an hour. Go with whatever the prospect has time for. And make no mistake: your presentation skills (i.e., your communication skills) must be good. You are not putting on a show, but you are showcasing your company and representing the company. Practice any presentation a few times before you give it. Read up on effective presentations or attend a training session. Again, at this meeting it is important to be yourself, natural, and flexible so that the prospect is comfortable talking with you—*continuing the conversation you started with your cold call.*

In general, some of the best kinds of material to bring to a meeting include printed matter that backs up points you make in your presentation. (At least that means another contact with the prospect.) More specifically, at least bring the following items (use a single binder with the company logo for easy reference and use):

- Letter of introduction from senior executive, president, or CEO
- Current brochure or summary sheet on your company's work

- Individual case studies of the success stories you show
- Biographies on yourself and management
- Full contact information, including website address

If the prospect asks about something that you are not prepared to answer, admit that fact and say that you will send it right away when you get back to your office. Use your follow-up letter (see below) to do two things: thank the prospect for the meeting and highlight the information they asked for that you are sending with the letter. By the way, giving little gifts at a first meeting may be nice, but they really are not deal-makers. Unless it is common practice or you know a prospect really likes to receive trinkets from salespeople (almost as if they are tolls to pay on the highway to a sale), save them as more meaningful tokens of appreciation rather than simple giveaways. Many companies today have rules about gifts, including not allowing employees to accept gifts at all or placing dollar limits on the value of any gifts received. Try to find out these rules for each prospect; if you do not know them, err on the side of caution and do not give gifts.

Follow-up letters

Once your first meeting is done, your work becomes increasingly important, because you have only just begun to establish a relationship with a customer. You must maintain that relationship and ensure that any customer feels he or she matters to you uniquely by following up effectively now and in the future. Follow-ups are generally simple and elegant in character, and they say a lot about how you and your company value any relationship with customers. The best way to show your appreciation for a meeting with any customer and the value that person has to you and your company is to send a letter.

Letter writing has long been an art, tracing back at least to the Renaissance and the art of *belles lettres*. Letters stand as the most powerful and personal way to reach someone after you've met with him or her for the first time. But you don't have to be a gifted writer to prepare and send an effective thank-you letter. You just need to be genuinely appreciative of the customer's consideration and sensitive to what may be the best way to let the person know you listened.

The letters that are most impressive are those that are handwritten. Handwritten notes are much more personal and, therefore, symbolize a higher level of involvement and caring than a typed letter. Realize, though, that this means your notes should not be long-winded. Like your call scripts, you must be both engaging and to-the-point. Thank the person for meeting with you, then address a pivotal issue that came up during the meeting and mention how well your company can respond to it. Think about how to reflect a key message about the company. If you must prepare a long response, with ample detail and attachments, you may want to type a letter anyway. In either case, make sure you use company stationery.

Like any writing, correct grammar and spelling count! You may wish to write a couple of drafts of any letter before you prepare the final version for sending. Have someone proofread your letter, both drafts and final form, to make sure everything is just right. Triple-check the spelling of company names and people's names.

When you mail your letter, use regular mail. Unless time is of the essence, there is no need to overnight your letter—such an act could suggest carelessness and frivolity. However, overnight mail may be best if you have to send information that you didn't have at the meeting.

E-mail may be an appropriate option *only when time is extremely critical and you know the person accepts or prefers e-mail.* Like a typewritten letter on stationery, an e-mail note does not have the same level of personal symbolism that a handwritten note does. You also run the risk of your e-mail being deleted (possibly by a secretary who has access to and screens your contact's e-mail) or, worse, never seen because it was automatically removed by spam-blocking software before it reached your contact's e-mail inbox. You can, however, use this time-critical channel to do the same things you would in a handwritten note. *And remember to not send attached files unless they are completely free of viruses.* So use e-mail sparingly and wisely.

As long as your prospect maintains the relationship, you should follow up with him or her as often as required. At this level phone calls and e-mail are effective channels of communication to check in or report on progress. You must find out what any prospect's preferred channels of communication are, even optimum times for using them.

Track your progress

Record keeping is vital, because you must know how well you're doing in ways that help you become more successful. You should know at least the following things through your cold-calling efforts:

- The total number of cold calls you make over an extended period (e.g., 10 weeks, quarter, half year, year)
- The total number of people spoken to over that period
- The total number of first meetings set up over that period
- The total number of sales visits, including first meetings
- The total number of sales over that period

Based on the data gathered from these dimensions, you can set reasonable and challenging goals. Once you understand how effective you are from these numbers, you can find out what your strengths and weaknesses are and address them. More specifically, you can calculate averages, measure your performance, and set goals as follows:

- The average number of cold calls you must make each day
- The average number of people you must speak to each day to get an appointment
- The ratio of cold calls to first meetings
- The average number of first meetings needed to be scheduled per day or week
- The average number of subsequent sales visits each week
- The ratio of appointments to each sale

There are other statistics you could calculate, like the average number of cold calls you must make each week or the average number of sales visits each week. *The point is that by breaking down the whole data set to meaningful statistics, especially daily or weekly averages, you can see how easy it is for you to manage your calls and overall sales efforts.* This kind of performance measurement is key to knowing how effective and successful you are and where you can improve. As the old saying goes, you can't manage what you don't measure.

This individual level of performance measurement is critical to your success and satisfaction on another level. That is, you want to avoid having peaks and valleys in the sales cycle. You need to make sure there are always opportunities you're turning into prospects in the pipeline. As you saw earlier in this section, if there is ever a time with no prospects in the pipeline, that means no work was done early enough to get them in there. *And no calls = no prospects = no sales.*

New-business leads and sales are vital to building your company's business beyond those customers who would plan to buy anyway, and your cold calls and sales efforts in this success are critical. On a company level, a separate report on performance measurements has been prepared and covers the broader need and implications for ensuring the company is always on track.

The range of data you could track is extensive. You need to select the data that are the most meaningful to you *and* management. The range of data points include the following:

- Company name
- Contact person(s) and title
- Complete contact information for contact person(s)

- Company type (independent, division/subsidiary/operation)
- Company affiliation (individual, franchise)
- Preferred media (by title; traditional and new media)
- Market type (per core business segments)
- Organization affiliation(s) (professional/trade societies)
- Product(s) purchased (project order details, including end date)
- Service(s) purchased (project order details, including end date)
- Date of purchase(s)
- Purchase frequency
- Future purchase plans
- Amount of last purchase (if applicable)
- Amount of all purchases by date
- Promotion or discount used
- Satisfaction score (your company establishes this; score from survey's 5-point scale)
- Loyalty score (your company establishes this; score on a 10-point scale based on total sales revenue, number of purchases over time, probability of future purchases, length of relationship, number of referrals, satisfaction score, testimonials/references)
- Lead source and date (i.e., customer information channels)
- Follow-up service request type
- Willingness to do testimonial
- Third-party source demographics (e.g., Dun & Bradstreet)
- Support sales performance measurements
- Additional important notes that don't fit these categories

It may be impractical to track all these dimensions, and you and management must decide on what data to collect and how to measure and report them. You can create a simple spreadsheet with columns for these dimensions and rows for each cold call you make. You could also use a database program, like ACT! or the similar capability in Microsoft Excel, to manage your cold-call data. Whatever method you use, it must be flexible, easy to use, and powerful enough to make you as effective as possible.

With the volume of data you and others may collect, it is possible that your company may need to implement a dedicated system to handle it all. Such a system is called a "customer relationship management," or CRM, system. Fundamentally, CRM is a management approach used collaboratively across an enterprise to learn more about customers' needs and behaviors, develop stronger relationships with them (especially to retain the "right" customers), and get more new ones.

EXECUTIVE VIEWPOINT

Breaking New Ground for the Business of PR

Ellen Ryan Mardiks, Vice Chairman, Golin

PR people sell for a living. We sell our clients' products to consumers, we sell their stories to media, we sell their cultures to potential employees. And we sell ourselves and our ideas to those clients.

To paraphrase Gordon Gecko from the movie *Wall Street*: selling, for lack of a better word, is good. Too many public relations people think it's bad, or at least a bit unseemly. I feel sorry for those PR people. But I'm happy to compete against them.

This chapter will help you learn how to sell, what to sell, and what it takes to be successful at selling. I have been selling my agency, Golin-Harris, and our ideas to the world's greatest companies and brands for almost 30 years. In that time I've probably done 300 new-business pitches (a scary thought). Here's what I know:

- Clients buy insights, ideas, and people. Sure, they want to know you've been successful before, but what they really want is to know that you'll be successful for them. Prove it.

- I know from experience that it's hard to find a meaningful, true insight—an aha moment. When you do, you will have clients eating out of your hand. Because you will have found a way to solve their problem.

- PR agencies are more the same than different. So you have to be crystal clear on what actually does make you different. And it's probably your insights, ideas, and people! That's what you have to bring to life, in a pitch, in your marketing, on your website. Don't make people guess.

- Simplicity is undervalued. Too often, PR people (agency people, especially, but internal PR departments, too) cram presentations and proposals full of tactics and detail that only clutter the central idea. Why are we afraid to let it stand on its own?

- Clients buy from people they like and trust. Now, how obvious is that point? But it's true.

- Clients believe people who can sell an idea. Become a great presenter. It will serve you well, agency or client side.

- In new business as in life, passion matters. Drama makes an impact. Never be embarrassed to emote in a new business pitch.

- Cold calls almost never work. Almost. We won our first client 58 years ago with a cold call made by our chairman, Al Golin. We are still agency of record for McDonald's, and proud of it.

- The key to that call was that Al knew what he was selling and who he was selling to. He had done his homework. Never "blind call." That doesn't work.

- Relationship building, over time, is the best new business generator of all. This will be proven to you time and time again. And I guarantee you won't spend as much time at as you should.

- Current clients will be your best new business prospects. Many of you won't realize that.

I write these comments from the perspective of an agency lifer. While I've counseled and served many clients throughout my career here, I've never actually been one. But I know that many of these principles hold true no matter what side of the business you're on— agency, in-house, association, not-for-profit.

In-house PR people have to sell too. Every day. A key reason is that they're working for organizations that don't do what they do. Those companies and organizations sell hamburgers, or cars, or financial services, or causes. So in-house PR pros have to sell not only their ideas, but the value of public relations to their colleagues. (Note: I hope those of you who take in-house jobs will never refer to your colleagues as clients. They aren't your clients. That term connotes a service orientation that is inappropriate and inaccurate for in-house public relations professionals.) Even if they don't realize it or wouldn't put it in those terms, they have to be good at selling.

A final thought: If you believe in something, it's easy to sell it. That's ultimately what business development is about. A fundamental, contagious, adrenaline-pumping belief in your agency, your department, your idea.

CRM systems include processes, facilitated by specialized computer software, that help bring together a lot of information about customers, sales, marketing effectiveness, responsiveness, and market trends that affects the many operations of a company, from sales and planning to manufacturing and R&D. When used analytically, a CRM system "applies a variety of data analysis and modeling techniques to discover patterns and trends in customer data. It predicts potential variations so organizations can react to changes before it is too late. Decision makers and front-line employees use these deep insights to understand what their customers want and predict what they will do next" (Phalen, 2001, ¶8). CRM systems can be and should be used to determine how and what media can be targeted to diffuse messages in the most effective ways among target publics.

Final thoughts about calls and business development

Cold calling is a dynamic part of building the business for your company. Your cold calls get meetings where you can showcase our company to qualified customers and start the sales process. To some extent some customers will always come to your business because they know you well or have had a good impression of your business because of its strong reputation. You will likely meet with them too. Even though some customers may never come to your business, you know that there are many customers that need to know your business and what it has to offer—in terms of value, expertise, safety, and responsiveness.

The work you do to make the cold-calling process successful is valuable in many ways, as you've seen. The payoff is in establishing a continuous rhythm of prospects that can become final sales. Managing the business cycle this way means a more dependable flow of future projects, more stable business planning, and greater satisfaction for everyone in your company.

From here the next step is formal responses to specific requests for help in realizing public relations objectives. The next chapter examines RFPs (requests for proposals) and situations for pitching new business to customers of any sort, internal or external.

Key Words

Power	Value proposition
Three dimensions of power	Gap analysis
Organization charts	Force field analysis
Dominant coalition	Order restoration model
Five proactive practices for power	Three types of customers
Positioning	Three types of calls
Two dimensions to positioning	Key messages
Differentiation	Screen
Ladders of the mind	Lead generation
Positioning heuristic	Sales pipeline
USP	CRM system
CCAs	

Exploration of Business Development

1. In what ways can you foresee yourself promoting public relations so that people know better its value and power to society and to individuals? Summarize your approach, including key messages.

2. Examine several organizations (public, private, nonprofit, government, etc.) to determine the level to which public relations is or is not part of their "dominant coalitions." What do you think the place of public relations in organizational hierarchies says about how it is viewed and valued?

3. Use each of the environmental scanning models in this chapter to sketch the state of the business for an organization of which you are a member. What position does that organization possess, what position does it want to possess, and how likely will it get there?

4. Examine the strategic plan in Appendix B to define the market position the company seeks according to Figure 7-2. Use the seven questions to clarify market positioning to help you make the argument for the position that the company seems to target. Also define appropriate methods for the company to build its business with past, present, and potential customers based on your work.

5. Think of one or more news stories from an organization you know well (perhaps your school or a volunteer organization) that would be great to see in the news media. Write a cold-call script (see Appendix C) that you would use to pitch the story to one or more journalists (1) on the phone and (2) by e-mail. Actually seek coverage of your story and track your success along the way and report on that success.

References

Bowen, S. A. (2009). What communication professionals tell us regarding dominant coalition access and gaining membership. *Journal of Applied Communication Research, 37*, 418–443.

Burke, K. (1970). *The rhetoric of religion: Studies in logology*. Berkeley, CA: University of California Press.

Burke, K. (1989). Poem. In H. W. Simons & T. Melia (Eds.), *The Legacy of Kenneth Burke* (p. 263). Madison, WI: University of Wisconsin Press.

James, M. (2011). A provisional conceptual framework for intentional positioning in public relations. *Journal of Public Relations Research, 23*(1), 93–118.

Lewin, K. (1997). *Resolving Social Conflicts and Field Theory in Social Science*. Washington, DC: American Psychological Association.

Phalen, S. (2001, June 15). *Increasing customer value: Harness the power of predictive CRM*. Montgomery Research Inc. Available online: http://mthink.com/article/increasing-customer-value-harness-power-predictive-crm/.

Ries, A., & Trout, J. (1993). *The 22 immutable laws of marketing: Violate them at your own risk*. New York: HarperBusiness.

Ries, A., & Trout, J. (2001). *Positioning: The battle for your mind*. New York: McGraw-Hill. (Original work published 1976).

Rogers, E. M. (2003). *Diffusion of innovations* (5th ed.). New York: Free Press.

Schiffman, S. (1999). *Cold Calling Techniques (That Really Work!)*, (4th ed.). Avon, MA: Adams Media Corp.

Silberger, S. (2012). *The ten day MBA: A step-by-step guide to mastering the skills taught in America's top business schools* (4th ed.). New York: Harper Business.

Smudde, P. M. (2011). *Public relations as dramatistic organizing: A case study bridging theory and practice*. Cresskill, NJ: Hampton Press.

Smudde, P. M., & Courtright, J. L. (2010). Public relations and power. In R. L. Heath (Ed.), *Handbook of public relations* (2nd ed., pp. 177–189). Thousand Oaks, CA: Sage.

Smudde, P. M., & Courtright, J. L. (2012). *Inspiring cooperation and celebrating organizations: Genres, message design and strategy in public relations*. New York: Hampton Press.

Smudde, P. M., & Courtright, J. L. (2013). Form following function: Message design for managing corporate reputations. In C. E. Carroll (Ed.), *Handbook of communication and corporate reputation* (pp. 404–417). San Francisco: Wiley-Blackwell.

Stacks, D., & Michaelson, D. (2010). *A practitioner's guide to public relations research, measurement, and evaluation*. Williston, VT: Business Expert Press.

Trout, J., & Rivkin, S. (2000). *Differentiate or die: Survival in our era of killer competition*. New York: John Wiley & Sons.

Recommended Reading

Cialdini, R. B. (2001). *Influence: Science and practice* (4th ed.). Boston: Allyn & Bacon.

Garten, J. E. (2001). *The mind of the CEO*. New York: Basic Books.

Inside the minds.com (2002). *The art of public relations: Industry visionaries reveal the secrets to successful public relations*. Aspatore Books.

Moore, G. A. (1999). *Crossing the chasm: Marketing and selling high-tech products to mainstream customers*, rev. ed. New York: Harper Business.

Ries, A., & Ries, L. (2009). *War in the boardroom: Why left-brain management and right-brain marketing don't see eye-to-eye—and what to do about it*. New York: Collins Business.

Chapter 8

REQUESTS FOR PROPOSALS AND NEW-BUSINESS PITCHES

If cold, warm, and hot calls are a proactive way to build business for a public relations organization, "requests for proposals" (RFPs) are a reactive way to build business. Calls involve contacting customers, but RFPs are customers specifically inviting expert help. In this way RFPs are tools corporate, nonagency organizations use to solicit the help of qualified external firms. RFPs are not something used within a corporate, nonprofit, NGO, or other organization to obtain help from existing operating units. (The closest thing would be a formal written request for a meeting between one department, say research and development, and another, say public relations, for innovations the organization is creating.) Notice, however, that with a RFP, there are two sides—the inviting organization and the responding organization.

The process for the two to eventually come together is an important one to examine and understand so that it can be managed effectively. It is also the substance of new-business pitches (NBPs) in which both an agency and a potential client engage to determine if there is a good fit between them so that each can help the other meet its needs. This chapter focuses on these two main topics: RFPs and NBPs. Viewing them from both sides of the table—the inviting organization (potential client) and the responding organization (potential agency)—reveals important similarities and differences that play out in the dance that may result in a contractual arrangement for the agency to work for the client.

What Is a RFP?

Requests for proposals are formal documents that specify what an organization needs and wants from external providers/suppliers to solve a particular problem within certain parameters, including time, money, performance objectives, and material. A related but subordinate way to build business is a "request for information" (RFI), which an organization may use to find out more details about an agency's capabilities, client successes, and so on in order to decide if it should be sent a formal request for a proposal. RFPs typically target singular projects, and if a project is large enough, parts of it may be divided into separate RFPs either at the start of the RFP process or as part of the negotiation with eligible providers. The RFP process, simply put, typically proceeds this way:

1. An organization writes and then releases a RFP with a hard deadline for responses (i.e., day, hour, and minute). Any responses submitted late—to the minute—are immediately rejected because it is a reflection of (right or wrong) the responding provider's lack of commitment to timeliness, respect for deadlines, and perception of the project as proposed. Providers must plan on complications in submitting their responses, such as lost or delayed packages during delivery.

2. Providers interested in responding to a RFP must send them to the requesting organization by or before the deadline. The provider must follow the RFP's instructions in every way. RFPs are structured in ways to make comparisons across multiple vendors as directly and as fairly as possible, so the submitted material must be presented in as nearly the same form and format from one agency to the next. Although the ideas can and should be innovative and impactful, save the extra "flash" for the presentation, if invited to give one. The response to a RFP is more about substance than style.

3. Organizational stakeholders in the requesting organization review the responses against the criteria for selection spelled out in the RFP. The result of the reviews is a short list of providers who best fit the criteria.

4. The requesting organization invites the providers on the short list to give individual, private presentations to a small group of selected organizational stakeholders. The providers' presentations focus on themselves and their proposals, going beyond what was stated and, for example, explaining what value they will have added in specific terms during the period of the proposed project. Substance and style merge best here.

5. The requesting organization's stakeholders review the presentations with proposals and rank order them from most preferred to least preferred. Depending on the scope of the RFP, the requesting organization would offer the project to one or more of the responding providers. If, during the negotiation, a provider denies the offer or the offer is rescinded, the requesting organization goes to the next provider in the rankings.

As step one says, the whole process begins when a RFP is needed and must be written. The writing process for a RFP can be lengthy and involve multiple internal parties. For most public relations RFPs, the scope of work would encompass only the PR function and, as needed, involve other organizational units during the course of the project. To write an effective RFP, an organization must know well what problem/opportunity it wants addressed, what objectives must be met, by when, and within what budget. In other words, the problem/opportunity is thoroughly researched and defended in business terms. This analysis defines the nature and scope of the problem/opportunity. Any problem/opportunity will have things that unequivocally must be met ("needs") and other things that would be great to have but are not absolutely necessary ("wants"). The people preparing the RFP must distinguish between needs and wants, with a bias toward making sure the needs are top priorities. Language in the RFP, then, must reflect what is a need and what is a want. Include an attorney during the process to ensure legal protections, like matters of any party defaulting on agreements or cancelling the agreement before it is fulfilled.

During the writing process for the RFP, those responsible for it must have a clear idea about what an ideal provider(s) would be. That ideal would guide statements about the capabilities and expertise requirements a provider must have to be considered and the criteria for selecting the best providers from among those who respond and, ultimately, offering the job to the most-referred provider(s), depending on the scope of the project. Disclosures about the RFP process are included and

- **Background**
  - Organization (offerings, market position target customers & differentiators)
  - Key message platform
  - Need/Situation summary
  - Objectives
- **Scope of Work**
  - Work to be performed
  - Output specifications
  - Contractor's performance expectations
- **Program Management**
  - Management (names, titles & contact information)
  - Schedule (full project, excluding RFP process)
  - Budget & resource stipulations
- **RFP Process & Schedule**
  - RFP invitations
  - Response deadline (date & time)
  - Proposalreviews & shor-list decision
  - Invitation next step (e.g., interview; problem-solution presentation)
  - Final decision
  - Contract negotiation & consummation
- **RFP Evaluation Criteria**
  - Qualifications (firm & team members)
  - Track record (results show successfulness)
  - Quality (proposal's correctioness, accuracy, design/layout, service, etc.)
  - Reasonableness (cost, time, and resource estimates)
- **Proposal Content Requirements**
  - Letter of transmittal
  - Statement of understanding about the scope of work
  - Proposed plan, expacted results & schedule
  - Estimated complete budget
  - Project team & backgrounds of members
  - Capabilities (relevent to RFP & beyond)
  - Business relationship management & daily account management habits
  - Resources needs/access
  - Relevant experiences & references
  - Licensing, bonding & insurance (if applicable)
- **Limitations**
  - Freedom in reviewing and choosing proposals in organization's own best interests
  - Contacting refernces & acquiring any needed information is granted by submitting proposal
  - No representations, warrantees or guarantees are expressed or implied in RFP, including obligations or liabilities between the organization & proposer
- **Confidentiality & Public Records**
  - Safeguard proposals & discussions in confidence under applicable law until final decision or processstermination
  - Applicable law may enable/require sharing of proposals upon request as a matter of "public record"
- **Attachments**

Figure 8-1. BASIC RFP CONTENT OUTLINE SUITABLE FOR PUBLIC RELATIONS.

give specific dates, times, and contact information for those who choose to submit a proposal. Figure 8-1 presents a basic outline of the contents of typical RFPs for public relations work. The content may be expanded or contracted, depending on an organization's requirements. Some RFPs require far more content, such as those for government organizations. So, again, it is very important to know the requirements for RFPs as a writer of them *and* as a responder to them. Note that a RFP is *not* a contract for work but, rather, an invitation for interested and qualified parties to "bid" on the work. Only after a thorough review of providers and their proposals will an offer be tendered to the one that is most preferred and, subsequently, a contract be negotiated and consummated between the parties. Again, legal representation is critical to have during the process, especially during contract negotiation.

From a prospective provider's perspective, a RFP can be relatively simple to very complex, depending on certain requirements from the requesting organization and, if applicable, requirements under the law. Searching the Internet for RFPs can show the wide range of content different organizations use. Figure 8-2 shows an example of the requirements (also called a "scope of work statement") for PR agencies responding to a RFP. Meticulous review of any RFP is essential if an agency thinks it should respond to a RFP. What is said between the lines throughout the RFP is as important as what the lines of the RFP's text say. Realize, too, that second-guessing the requesting organization's desires or motives could be a big mistake. If you have questions about what is said or implied in a RFP, call the contact person and ask appropriate, well-formed questions that get at what you want to know, and do not "beat around the bush" by asking questions that are vague or off-topic from the RFP.

A good, solid, formal submission to a RFP will follow the rules for what prospective providers must provide while also giving a strong case for a provider's expertise, capabilities, and personality. This last aspect of personality is really a matter of "chemistry" between the two parties, and if the prospective provider is called upon to give a presentation about its proposal, then is the time to demonstrate good chemistry. This objective requires detailed research and observation about who the people are at the requesting organization and their organization's

---

PR Agency Requirements:
- Media and industry-analyst relations: open influencers' doors to create and take advantage of opportunities for published articles and reports from publications and analysts.
- Help build top-of-mind awareness about our company among influencers (see Appendix A).
- Secure media placements for editorial coverage in Tier 1 and Tier 2 publications.
- Help keep analysts updated and gain coverage in published reports by Tier 1 and Tier 2 analysts.
- Set up 2 press/analyst tours and follow-up on them.
- Perform other activities as needed to help meet or exceed the PR obectives and goals.
- Speakerss bureau: Find, secure and publicize speaking opportunities for our company's executives (and customers) at appropriate events, including trade shows, conferences, local executive briefings, etc.
- Communications counsel & support: Propose and help implement the more-effective ways to promote our company and to fulfill its external communications goals. Also provide counsel and support for investor relations, internal communications, crisis communications and issues management.
- Fulfill requirements specified in the evaluation criteria given below.

Figure 8-2. SAMPLE REQUIREMENTS ("SCOPE OF WORK") FOR A PR AGENCY.

culture. So an agency's response to a RFP can be as creative as possible, and there are four basic possibilities for response:

- "Yes" (respond to a RFP exactly for what it seeks, no more or no less)
- "Yes and . . ." (respond to a RFP for what it seeks and add more ideas beyond the scope of work)
- "No but . . ." (respond to a RFP to present a vastly different approach to meet the prospective client's needs as defined)
- "No" (respond to a RFP by saying that it simply cannot be addressed for certain business reasons, such as too big, too small, no resources to dedicate to it)

In any case, a reasonably conservative approach to the presentation may be best, as you can loosen up to the degree that works as you learn about the requesting organization's people. Again, know the audience! Some RFPs may be so strict that the requesting organization will only review responses that present exactly what is sought exactly as it wants it. Sometimes multiple meetings or presentations may be required, and if this happens, it is very likely that the requesting organization places an especially high value on chemistry between the two groups that will work together and has a favorable opinion of your group.

Use the evaluation criteria for both needs and wants to ensure that your proposal is as strong as it can be. Figure 8-3 shows an example of criteria for a RFP used to secure the help of a public relations agency. Those who wrote a RFP and will evaluate the submissions to it put themselves partially in the position of the responding organization so that the content would be understandable and usable by prospective providers. By the same token, prospective organizations must put themselves in the position of the requesting organization so that those agencies can best address the knowledge, attitudes, and actions expected of them.

Back on the requesting organization's side of the process, the key question that must be answered compellingly is this: Where is the agency's plan taking the client? The evaluation criteria would be applied fastidiously against the proposal and presentation(s) of the final candidates to answer that question and select the winner to do the work stipulated in the RFP. People in the decision process should evaluate each agency individually and then, later, come together to compare their evaluations and establish a definitive, group-based evaluation.

An effective way to apply the criteria to each response to a RFP is to create a score sheet. List the criteria (needs and wants) like those shown in Figure 8-3 from most important to least important. Assign a numerical value of importance (say 1 to 5, with 5 being the highest) to give the appropriate weight to each criterion. This value for importance helps mitigate the possibility of ties in the final calculation of a provider's final score, if there were no weighting factor for importance. Next

---

Evaluation Criteria ("Needs")

Public reletions agencies that respond to this RFP ill be evaluated on the follwing criteria:

- Core competency in media and analyst relations in high-tech/software sector, especialy for enterprise software and/or ERP (enterprise reresource planning) systems.
- Dernonstrable connections and good relationships with mainstream business writers & publications, plusfinance and IT writers and publications Realtionships with key freelance writers are also important
- Evidence of solid experience and success in investor relations, internal communications, crisis communications, issue management, organizational change communications and other areas.
- Excellent references from strong client list.
- Partnership with client. Evidence of long-term clients that are referenceable.
- Proven track record with moving clients to and maintaing thought-leader status.
- Bias toward proactive measurable measurable work. Measurement, ROI for client.
- A performance measurement program in place for clients and is open to adding client-specific metrics.
- A view of PR/corporate communciations that fits our company.
- Agency location facilitates easy communication with our company in the USA and possibly with UK links to support our UK operation.

Additional Areas of Interest ("Wants")

We are also intersted in knowing details about how you manage the day-to-day business of our account with you. Here are the areas of our relationship that we'd like you to address with clear and concise statements or attachments each of them:

- Reporting visit/calls on program/project status, wins, issues, opportunities, etc.
- Access to agency principals.
- Client & staffturnover
- Relationship structure between the agency and our company.
- Method/approach for daily account activity and overall management.
- Time allowed for account administration.
- Prescribed budget allotment for unforeseen events and project/miscellaneous expenses.
- competitive and market research and analysis capabilities.
- Identifying and scheduling speaking opportunities and related PR
- Biographies of agency principals and those on the our company's account.
- Turnover of clients & agency staff.

Figure 8-3. EXAMPLE OF RFP CRITERIA FOR EVALUATING PROPOSALS.

apply a small scale of values (say 1 to 5, with 5 being the best) to each criterion to determine how well a provider appears to meet a criterion. Then multiply a criterion's value by its importance value to get the final rating for the provider on that criterion. A spreadsheet can be an effective way to format and handle the scoring. The provider with the highest total score across all criteria would be the winner. No completed evaluations would be shared with the prospective provider, as the evaluations are proprietary property of the client. If it is necessary, explaining why a provider did not make the short list can be done by explaining orally the criteria that were and, especially, were not sufficiently met.

One final and important note about the RFP process and any NBP—under U.S. copyright law, summarized in Chapter 3, the material presented in the RFP responses and the NBP presentations is the property of the respective firms and cannot be used by the client. Thus, it is illegal to use the ideas of an agency that bid on your job through your RFP (or other NBP, say if it was shared by e-mail or in an informational meeting like that covered in Chapter 7) that did not win. Such use is also unethical under the codes of ethics for the Public Relations Society of America, International Association for Business Communicators, and other professional organizations focused on communication. If you wish to use one or more of an unsuccessful bidder's ideas, it would be best to negotiate a fee for their use; otherwise, simply file away the unsuccessful proposals because you were not going to go with those firms anyway.

New-Business Pitches from Both Sides of the Table

With the RFP submitted, accepted, and reviewed, a prospective provider waits to find out if it will be called for a presentation. This meeting is a big deal for those on both sides of the table—the requesting organization (client) and the potential provider (agency). Everyone knows what is at stake and what grounds will be used to make all decisions about which firm wins. The three principal factors of the business relationship—*quality* of service and products is high, *service* of the client and account is strong, and *price* for all work to be done is competitive—are scrutinized throughout the process (see Figure 8-4). Indeed, the RFP process seeks information about all three, and meetings and negotiations seek agreement about what will be done, by when, and for how much cost. The written documentation has shown what each side is, but that same material leaves out the personal side of who makes up the organizations. The question on everyone's minds on both sides of the table is: "Who would we be working with?" The meeting is the opportunity to answer that question to a reasonable extent. Then, if the meeting is successful for one agency, it enters contract negotiation with the client.

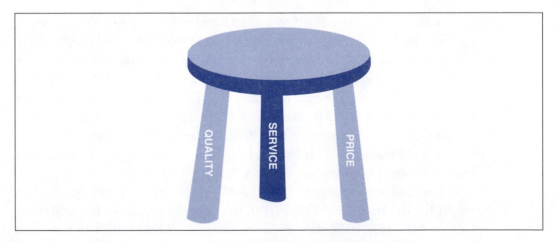

Figure 8-4. THE THREE-LEGGED STOOL OF BUSINESS RELATIONSHIPS.

The meeting

Both parties prepare for the meeting. The substance of the meeting is a new-business pitch, which is the agency making its case interpersonally with the selected internal stakeholders for the client. The client, when inviting the agency for the meeting, would have explained to the agency what the expectations would be for the meeting. If the agency accepted the invitation, it would have to follow the client's instructions to prepare appropriately. For example, a client may give the agency a hypothetical situation to address within the scope of the RFP to see how it responds. That response would reflect many dimensions simultaneously, such as creativity, knowledge of the client, knowledge of the client's market and environmental pressures, problem-solving abilities, resource allocations, client service, communication philosophy, business philosophy and priorities, operations organization, project management capabilities, and so on. Of particular interest to the client would be sensitivity to any organizational-political dynamics, potential roadblocks, and other matters that may bear on the project's success or failure.

Most important, the response as given by agency representatives in a meeting with the client's people highlights the personalities of everyone present. The people in the room may all end up working together in some ways, some more than others. So everyone is being evaluated: Do we like this agency? Do we like this client? However, those from the agency are in much more of a fishbowl for observation because it is they who are seeking the work, and the client has its pick from among those who have submitted proposals. A prospective agency is well advised to get anything clarified in advance that it feels needs clarification, but to do so without being too bothersome and demanding.

Again, the invitation to meet has some ambiguity built in to find out how an agency thinks and can best demonstrate (1) its genuine enthusiasm for the job and (2) its superiority above others to understand what is at stake and to get results. (At this point the great value of the work covered in Chapter 7 pays off.) Those from the agency should have worked well together to prepare the presentation and be the people who would be assigned to the client if the client wins the job. Everyone from the agency team should have something to contribute to the presentation and be ready to answer any questions. Beyond development meetings for the new-business pitch, two or more rehearsals of the pitch should be done as well to make sure bases have been covered from the client's perspective. Experienced veterans would play the role of client representatives as the agency team gives its pitch and takes questions. Any ideas for improvement should be noted and revisions made as a result of these rehearsals.

From the client side of the table, the evaluation criteria in the RFP still rules the day. New-business pitches, then, can be evaluated on those criteria by taking notes on which criteria are addressed well or not. However, a client could choose to develop a new set of criteria that complements the RFP's criteria to evaluate the agency's pitch. In this way the team who developed the RFP and evaluated responses to it may outline how they will know not just a strong presentation but, more important, a strong agency that follows directions, builds upon its proposal, and demonstrates a solid case for its selection as the most-preferred provider—the winner of the RFP process.

Basic matters of public speaking are obvious choices for criteria of agencies' new-business pitches, and those criteria should be included. More specific criteria should be included about the agency team's level of creativity, interpersonal behaviors among agency team members, interpersonal behaviors of the agency members with client people, perceived genuineness in wanting to work on the project and with the client, perceived enthusiasm about working in the agency, clarity in communicating, sense of humor, sense of confidence, and sense of humility, including case examples as evidence of competence and success. The evaluation sheet for the pitches from the finalists can be structured as a kind of score sheet (based on Figure 8-3) with room for notes and comments as a presentation is given. A new score sheet would be used by each client person for each agency pitch. A blank score sheet may be shared with the agency after the meeting, but no completed score sheets or personal notes would be shared, as they are proprietary and the property of the client. If necessary, an oral explanation of the criteria that were and, especially, were not sufficiently met could be given if an agency wants to know why it did not win. For the winner of the job, the next step is negotiating a contract.

The negotiation

During the negotiation process, the nature and scope of the work has been disclosed from the beginning, so there will not be any surprises. The negotiation process proceeds along a line of several steps: planning and preparation (doing the homework to negotiation well), defining ground rules (the who, what, where, and when of the actual negotiations), clarifying and justifying matters (asking and answering questions), bargaining and problem-solving (the give-and-take between parties), and closing and implementing (signing the final agreement and starting work on it) (Robbins & Judge, 2008). Given the client's RFP and additional communication plus what the winning agency presented, however, there may be some alterations because there were some great ideas that may require changes in the nature and scope of work that will, in turn, be transferred to a contract that all parties will sign. Chapter 3 addressed contracts briefly, and involving an attorney at this phase is essential. The content of a contract can vary as much as the work asked for in a RFP can vary. Because of this variance, a basic understanding of key negotiation concepts is important for a public relations leader to have.

Much has been prepared over the years in many media about negotiation and being an effective negotiator, and a PR leader ought to acquire knowledge and skills for good negotiating. For our purposes, there are three concepts that are important to know because of their prominence in the negotiation process: origin of negotiation, situation rules, and process. Greater detail and skillfulness in negotiating can be gained through additional study and, especially, practice.

Origin of negotiation

As long as two or more sides on an issue exist, there is conflict. That conflict may be simple or complex to understand and resolve, if it is resolvable at all. In a RFP process, in spite of there being substantial documentation about what each party thinks, needs, and would like to do, one agreement about what precisely will be done, how, and under what parameters must be reached. Conflict, then, is the source of negotiation, and it can be approached in one of two ways. One way is, "I win, you lose." This is the kind of negotiation that children often use when playing together with the same toys or in the same game. This approach is simple and easy to understand. It reflects a self-centered, take-it-or-leave-it attitude that, depending on the conflict situation and the people involved, may work or may not. If all sides of a conflict have this attitude, a negotiation can break down quickly, and everyone is frustrated.

The other approach to negotiation is: "We win." This kind of negotiation is by its nature more complicated, but it has the benefits of greater engagement among the parties as they come to know each other and their interlocked interests better. Realize that a "we win" approach does not guarantee any agreement may be reached, but it does increase the probability. The reason for the "we win" approach's greater usefulness is that its nature is to emphasize the importance of knowing both one's own and the other party's positions. In the end, a "we win" agreement would give all parties much of what they want but without some of other things they wanted. How such agreements are reached is contingent on fulfilling certain rules for the negotiation.

Situation rules

Within a negotiation the parties involved share a particular situation. In the case of a RFP, that situation of course is bounded by the RFP and other discourse (written and oral) shared by all parties during the process. That situation also encompasses the implied or understood factors in the business environment each party faces that may be known or not by all parties. Having an attorney for your organization involved during the whole negotiation is essential. The parties who will participate in a negotiation need to follow three basic rules to complete the "homework" necessary for an effective and fruitful negotiation. First, define each party's objective for the negotiation. For a RFP process, this rule is relatively easy to follow. The client wants an agency to be and to do specific things within certain limits, including budget, performance expectations, and time. The agency wants the client to provide resources, information, and guidance in usable ways and when needed during the course of the contract, including being paid on time and evaluated fairly for work done.

The second rule is to complete sufficient and accurate research about the other party. The point here is to understand as much as possible the other party's perspectives, interests, and constraints while negotiating. For example, the following questions can be helpful to investigate both the other parties to a negotiation and one's own position for the negotiation:

- How do we/does the other party truly view us and our project?
- What other interests might we/the other party have in entering into an agreement?
- What pressures may we/the other party be facing to enter into any agreement?
- What minimal agreement might we/the other party accept?
- What would keep us/the other party from reaching an agreement?

This rule for research is very similar to conducting a thorough audience analysis before writing an article for a publication or planning a particular communication project. The research does not end after gathering and analyzing data about the other party. The process continues with astute listening to what the other party says and does not say, what the party does or does not do. Listen to and watch what you say, not say, do, and not do as well for the same reasons. All these things convey some meaning and should be considered as relevant as possible.

The third rule is to know the limits for yourself and the other parties. Because of the work you do to fulfill the second rule, you have a sufficient and, presumably, accurate database about what limits likely exist for the whole negotiation. These limits must be understood for your own organization and each party to the negotiation. Additional limits arise in two new categories: assumptions and estimates. For assumptions, the best information available indicates at least the reasons, attitudes, and motives for other parties (and your own organization) to enter into a negotiation. Documenting and understanding them can reveal much about how each party may behave during the negotiation and suggest what they may ask for in the process. The second category of limits is estimates, and it concerns matters about the amounts of financial, material, and temporal resources that may be needed and wanted. Financial resources would encompass the amount paid for the work proposed, including markups for subcontractors, out-of-pocket expenses, and other costs related to completing the work asked for in the RFP. Material resources encompass produced communications, personnel, equipment, facilities, and other things needed to do the work specified. Temporal resources focus on time needed to complete the work plus the length of time produced work should prove valuable during the contract period so that a return on the investment is secured.

Know the BATNAs

The combination of the information and analysis about objectives, rules, and limits among all parties in a negotiation can now result in a singular view of the point at which negotiation may stop. That point is called the "best alternative to a negotiated agreement," or BATNA (Fisher, Ury, & Patton, 1991; Leverich, 2006; Robbins & Judge, 2008; Yemm, 2005). Most people think of the point just before a negotiation stops/fails for a party as "the bottom line," which typically focuses on one dimension and primarily price. One's BATNA is similar to a "bottom line," but it is better because of all the work that goes into arriving at it. A BATNA is "the lowest value acceptable to you for a negotiated agreement" (Robbins & Judge, 2008, p. 500). Value here is the key because it involves price, of course, but it also involves all the things that go into substantiating it. This approach opens up more avenues for creativity in negotiation when one dimension, like price, cannot change but other factors can. So, in addition to having done all the homework in preparation for the negotiation, knowing your own BATNA plus the other party's BATNA will serve everyone well during the negotiation process.

Process-broadening options

If all people did in negotiations was to demand the same thing over and over without consideration of other options, negotiations rarely would be fruitful and all the more confrontational. Instrumental to any negotiation is creativity because many things are at stake and, thereby, open for consideration. In this way negotiation is much more about problem-solving than merely finding a mutually agreeable position. Viewing negotiation in terms of problem-solving naturally invites an attitude of creativity, ingenuity, invention, and innovation. Remember from the negotiation process that what is said or done can be as important as what is not said or done. Add to this the dynamics of interpersonal communication, and the result is many minds working together—with their own best interests at heart, to be sure—to figure out a win-win approach to a problem. So what may not have been said or done in a negotiation may end up being a key to moving the negotiation along, to solving the problem more effectively than if only what was documented was all that could be used. Figure 8-5 summarizes an effective way to broaden options during a negotiation through creative attention to both theory and practice about what is wrong and what could be done.

In this process there is a balance between what is wrong and what could work in theory and what is wrong and what would work in practice. It begins in step one with a clear understanding of the problem and moves through three more steps until ideas that make the most sense and can provide the greatest benefits are realized. Key to the process is defining criteria for an effective solution that would be used to test a proposed solution. The process allows for movement from specific

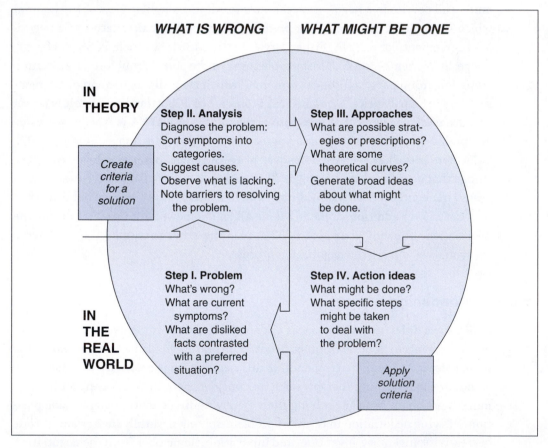

Figure 8-5. PROCESS MODEL FOR INVENTING OPTIONS DURING NEGOTIATION.
SOURCE: Fisher, Ury, & Patton (1991, p. 68)

EXECUTIVE VIEWPOINT

Managing RFPs and NBPs: A Dozen Things to Know and Do

Gary Meyers, Cofounder and Former
President, Morgan & Meyers

I spent 34 years in the agency business; 23 running my own firm. Following are some insights I wish every potential client knew about agencies, our pursuit of new business, and our view of the RFP process.

First, prospective clients should know they are being evaluated, too. Here's a short list of questions we asked ourselves when deciding to pitch a client prospect or to take a pass:

1. Can we do the work well? Are we well positioned and highly qualified? Why pitch an account where we don't have expertise or experience; especially when we're going up against other firms that are a better client match? Why waste the energy? Instead, stay focused on what we do best.

2. Does the client prospect have growth potential beyond the initial engagement? Are there other divisions or product groups our firm can serve in the future? If the initial engagement is for marketing/publicity, is there upside potential for picking up other disciplines such as employee relations, corporate affairs, website management, investor relations, or more? Can the client prospect turn into a long-term "agency of record" account?

3. Does the client prospect want to be an industry leader? Does their business plan reflect an aggressive attitude? Are they properly resourced to achieve their goals?

4. Who will be our counterparts on the client side? Are they experienced pros? Will they be strong and effective advocates for communication within the client organization? Do they understand agencies and are they able to properly represent the agency to the client and the client to the agency? (Will they partner well with the firm's account manager counterparts?)

5. Will the prospective account bring meaningful new experiences and relationships to the firm?

6. Can we make a fair buck on the business? It isn't all about money, but we look for clients who value insights, strategy, creativity, and loyalty. We run away from pure price shoppers who don't appreciate good work and will frustrate every staff member who touches the account.

If the answers to the above questions are satisfactory, then we'll go for it with an unrelenting passion to win.

Now, here is some time- and aggravation-saving advice for any organization sending out RFPs in search of an agency partner:

7. Do your homework. Research and pre-screen the list of agencies and make sure they all show potential. Avoid "cattle calls" with 10 or more agencies invited to pitch. An ideal list includes about 5–6 agencies for RFPs. Then narrow it down to three finalists for oral presentations.

8. Let the agencies know what you're really after. Give them the score card on which they will be evaluated in advance of the RFP response and the presentation.

9. Avoid hidden agendas. For example, if you're looking for a new firm because the former agency was always over budget and missing deadlines, then don't keep that secret. Instead, ask about agency cost-control and traffic systems in the RFP/pitch. Address all concerns head-on.

10. Make sure the decision-makers are on the selection committee from the start. A committee of 4–6 is very workable. But keep everyone on the same page and make sure you have key personnel involved. While it never happened to us, I've heard horror stories from other agency owners who "won the business" in the RFP and pitch, but the company president (who had not been on the selection committee) awarded the account to a golfing buddy's firm or his wife's nephew.

11. Don't be afraid to talk about money. Do it up front. Talk to the agency about rates, billing practices, budget control, and terms. Unresolved financial issues will ruin agency–client trust and ultimately the relationship. Remember, it is in the client's best interest if the agency makes a fair profit. (Our firm has a policy that clients can audit their account's financial records at any time. We stress that point in our RFP responses and pitches.)

12. Realize what you're asking. A RFP that requests agency credentials and case histories is fairly simple to create from preexisting agency files. On the other hand, elaborate proposals that entail speculative (spec) creative can be very time consuming and expensive for the responding agency. The goal of an agency search and the RFP/pitch process should be to identify the firm best suited to serve the client. Ask for enough spec creative to get good insights into how the agency thinks, but don't ask for a full-blown campaign. The RFP/pitch process can take months to complete, especially if the account is large and multiple presentations are involved. New business is costly in both nonbillable agency time and out-of-pocket expenses. It is not uncommon for an agency pitching a large account to invest a significant percentage of the first year's profits in pursuit of the new business. That's especially true if one includes the nonbillable time agencies invest in initial planning and getting "up to speed" during the first year of building the new agency–client relationship.

Taking all of this together, know that agencies view new-business pitches as a competitive sport on a highly professional level. We are motivated. We put together strong pitch teams and deliberately strategize the game plan. Our opponents are the other agencies in the contest. This is serious business. We know that our agency's fortunes rise and fall on how well we play the new business game. Agency leaders look at prospective clients as officials in the game. The client writes the rules and also assumes the role of referee. True agency competitors want and deserve a level playing field.

Press ahead.

ideas to general ones, accepts alternative perspectives from other fields, relies on different arguments with different strengths, and permits changes in the scope of the proposed solution until a final agreement is reached.

In addition to the problem-solving aspects of broadening options there are others. One aspect is time and space. If a negotiation takes a long time to complete, it may be best to rely on distance from the problem by getting away from it for some time. Factors of an organizational or ethnic culture may dictate how negotiations proceed from beginning to end, and those factors must be well understood when working through the three situation rules. Another important aspect is separating people from the problem or opportunity. Although people ultimately will be involved in the implementation of an agreement, all parties in a negotiation must realize the focus is the problem/opportunity, and people involved can be adjusted. With the focus squarely on solving a problem or seizing an opportunity through a rational and fair negotiation, matters like personalities *during a negotiation* have little to nothing to do with reaching an agreement, and their influence on the process is minimized drastically. If those matters arise as problems, they can be addressed separately, but the big picture of success in problem-solving through the negotiation is the key.

Finally, negotiations can achieve one of three possible outcomes. One is a definite yes, and all parties are happy, ready to go, and enter into a legally binding agreement to fulfill particular promises documented in a contract and other supporting discourse. Another outcome is no but with contingencies. This outcome means that there is still hope that an agreement can be reached, provided that certain things are addressed. The last outcome is a flat-out no. In this outcome no one's BATNA was accepted, the negotiation is finished, and it may never be broached again. But maybe not. Perhaps the problem/opportunity can be addressed differently at a different time.

Key Words

RFP	*Requirements*
RFI	*Evaluation criteria*
NBP	*Negotiation*
RFP process	*Conflict*
RFP response possibilities	*Situation rules*
Problem/opportunity	*BATNA*
RFP content	*Options*
Scope of work statement	*Three possible outcomes*
Three legs of business relationship stool	

Exploration of RFPs and New-Business Pitches

1. Find four or more examples of real RFPs for public relations work that have been issued on the Internet. Make sure they come from a variety of organizations—public, private, nonprofit, and so on. What similarities and differences do you see?

2. Choose one of the RFPs you find and put yourself in the position of a PR agency wanting to respond to it. Examine it carefully and identify the things that you believe you know well and the ones you believe you need to know more about. How sure are you of your competence in the things you think you know well? How would you go about learning the things you don't know so that your new-business pitch would be effective?

3. Construct a score sheet for the evaluation criteria in one of the RFP examples you find. What did you experience in creating the score sheet so that it is a usable as possible?

4. For one of the RFPs you found, assume that you won the job over all other potential providers. How would you prepare for the negotiation? Outline the information you would need and the steps you need to go through to get that information and be successful. What do you think your BATNA would be and why? What might the client's BATNA be and why?

References

Fisher, R., Ury, W., & Patton B. (1991). *Getting to yes: Negotiating agreement without giving in* (2nd ed.). New York: Penguin.

Leverich, J. (2006, December 25–31). Negotiate and win. *Enterprise/Salt Lake City, 36*(25), 9.

Robbins, S. P., & Judge, T. A. (2008). Conflict and negotiation. In S. P. Robbins & T. A. Judge, *Organizational behavior* (13th ed., pp. 482–515). Upper Saddle River, NJ: Pearson Education.

Yemm, G. (2005, Winter). Ask for more—you may get more!! *Management Services*, 36–37.

Recommended Reading

Browne, M. N., & Keeley, S. M. (2011). *Asking the right questions with readings: A guide to critical thinking*. Upper Saddle River, NJ: Prentice Hall.

Engel, S. M. (2000). *With good reason: An introduction to informal fallacies*. Boston: Bedford/St. Martin's.

Ries, A., & Ries, L. (2002). *The fall of advertising and the rise of PR*. New York: Harper Collins.

Schultz, D., & Schultz, H. (2004). *IMC: The next generation*. Boston: McGraw-Hill.

TEAM MANAGEMENT

Group work in any profession is not only inevitable, it is a certainty. Even sole practitioners, like freelance writers, graphic artists, and others, must work with and within groups of people on projects. To be sure, much of the work that groups do is done task-by-task by individuals on their own or perhaps in smaller work teams of fellow group members. Nevertheless, the work of each group member, whether done alone or with others, contributes to the overall success (or failure) of the larger group. Individuals contribute through collaboration, for better and for worse. Always remember that teams share in victory and defeat! The whole is truly greater than the sum of its parts, and every part matters. The weakest link in the chain determines the chain's strength.

This chapter is focused on the team side of public relations management. To this end two topics are examined. The first covers the characteristics of highly effective teams, based on long-term and broad-based studies. Principles such as leadership, ethics, strategy, and performance intersect and are extended in this discussion. The second topic examined in this chapter concerns external experts known as freelancers, consultants, and vendors, who may be hired to help a PR team as *ad hoc* team members. The discussion reveals why such experts should be considered, on what grounds they should be hired, why they might be fired, and how the size of external experts' organizations can matter.

Traits of Top-Performing Groups

Much research and advice about effective teams and teamwork abounds on the Internet, in libraries and booksellers, and through seminars, workshops, and other venues. Chapter 1 examined details about effective leadership and management that also apply to teamwork so that teams of any size and sort can be as successful as possible. For our purposes in public relations management, and without going into the rich details about small group dynamics, at least two fundamental questions about teams dominate: (1) What are the traits of effective teams? and (2) On what grounds do effective teams thrive? Two particular long-range and broad-based studies completed by Frank LaFasto and Carl Larson (LaFasto & Larson, 2001; Larson & LaFasto, 1989) answer these questions. In their first study, Larson and LaFasto (1989) identified and studied 32 highly effective teams over a three-year period to discover what the characteristics were that made them so successful. Teams ranged from the crew of a U.S. Navy aircraft carrier to a McDonald's product-development team, from surgical teams to a championship football team. The results of research clearly showed eight common traits of highly effective teams:

- *Clear, elevating goal*—The team has a defined, single reason and purpose for existing, and it both focuses members' work and inspires members to embrace something greater than they are individually and collectively.
- *Results-driven structure*—The team is organized and operates in ways that most effectively and efficiently channels efforts and resources to realize objectives that will yield solid performance and determine ultimate success.
- *Competent team members*—The team is made up of intellectually, emotionally, pragmatically, and interpersonally smart people who know what, how, when, and why to do the right things in the context of the elevating goal—to do what it takes to get the job done.

- *Unified commitment*—The team's members identify with the team, are deeply involved, and are unwavering in their dedication to the team's cause and willingness to expend whatever effort it takes to succeed.
- *Collaborative climate*—The team members establish a work ethic among all members that encourages everyone to work well together and seek input or feedback, test ideas, and confront challenges because more minds are better than one.
- *Standards of excellence*—The team develops and upholds expectations for individual performance, handling responsibilities, and being accountable for outcomes.
- *External support and recognition*—The team enjoys the genuine commitment to and resource allocations for its cause from the larger organization, including the celebration of milestone achievements and reward structures tied to performance.
- *Principled leadership*—The team is led by a someone who places the team's needs before her or his own. The leader is visionary and communicates that vision vividly and in terms that inspire members to embrace it to change things for the better. The leader also enables members to become the best people they can be by unleashing their creativity. Leaders also nurture new leaders.

Each of these traits is made all the more potent when coupled with LaFasto and Larson's (2001) follow-up study. Indeed, this second study is the culmination of their work over a 15-year period that included data gathered from more than 6,000 members and leaders of all kinds of teams in many arenas of human activity, including industry and private and public organizations. Effective team members, according to the researchers, possess two categories of factors: (1) *working knowledge*, which is based on the relevance, depth, and breadth of experience plus acute problem-solving abilities; and (2) *teamwork*, which depends on openness (being candid, honest, inviting), supportiveness (helping others succeed), action orientation (being self-motivated to act and encouraging of others to take action), and personal style (being positive, enthusiastic, confident, fun to work with). The results of this very long-term study showed that the most effective teams thrive on the following five dynamics:

- *Collaborative members*—Team members like and want to work together so that each person and the group achieves success at all levels in all things.
- *Positive relationships among members*—Team members get along well with each other in ways that foster candid communication that strengthens

relationships, enhances productivity, and makes a difference at the micro and macro levels.

- *Productive problem-solving*—The team follows a structured approach to solving problems that is focused, inviting, and communicative so that the physical, mental, and spiritual (i.e., *esprit de corps*) energies expended, although draining, are fulfilling and lead to making the best decisions possible.
- *Leadership that encourages group achievement*—Team leaders consistently define and focus on the elevating goal, ensure a collaborative climate, build confidence, demonstrate technical know-how, set priorities, and manage performance.
- *Organizational environment that truly supports collaboration and teamwork*— The team's work environment enables clarity, confidence, and commitment toward performance expectations, outputs, and ultimate goal achievement through sound management practices, effective operating structure and processes, and effective operating systems geared toward performance standards.

In many ways the cohesiveness of group members is a common thread that runs throughout these insights about effective teams. Indeed, *cohesiveness* is a counterpart to collaboration, which predominates in Larson and LaFasto's work. Cohesiveness, as explained by Hogg (1992), is key in several ways. It attracts members of a group and results in a "feel" for the group. Members look forward to interacting with the group, feel loyalty to the group, and wish to contribute to its projects. Cohesiveness, then, is an important source of motivation and a factor that enlivens discussions with members who come prepared. Cohesiveness emerges from feelings members have for one another, rewards members' experience in interactions with one another, builds value that members attach to the assignments the group undertakes, and cements members' expectations that their work will be supported and rewarded by the organization.

Differences among team members would ultimately affect team management. Very much in tune with the material in Chapter 1, leaders are instrumental in promoting cohesiveness by developing a group identity, building group traditions, stressing the value of teamwork, recognizing good work by members, helping set attainable goals, providing group rewards, keeping psychologically close to members, treating people with respect, and bringing the team back on track if needed. What leaders and their groups do is not done in some willy-nilly fashion but, rather, framed by an appropriate and effective structure.

Group structure

Communication is the glue for effective groups in every way. As Larson and LaFasto's work showed, group structure must facilitate group productivity and, thereby, success. Group structures are created in response to the nature of a group's reason for existing so its task can be handled best and expected results obtained. The structure that a group employs determines individual involvement through communication by virtue of one's place in the structure. In this way group structure and communication structure are essentially one and the same. Two basic communication structures are centralized and decentralized formats (DeVito, 2009). *Centralized* structures put someone, usually the leader, at the center of all group communication. Any and all communication from within or from without must go through the leader. Group members may not communicate with another member except through the leader. There are several advantages of a centralized structure:

- Most efficient when solving simple problems, especially when time is of the essence, taking advantage of strict divisions of labor
- Fewer messages communicated
- Few changes in communication or answers to inquiries
- Central person is the most satisfied and has high morale
- Central person is motivated to be the leader (having keys to information)

At the same time there are two major disadvantages. One is the presence of low morale among group members because they are not involved except when the leader communicates with them. The other disadvantage is that communication interactions among other members are limited. So member dissatisfaction is largely a function of limited information about the big picture and other details of what is going on.

The second communication structure is *decentralized*. This kind of structure is largely democratic and allows for communication among all members equally or with some limited restriction, such as people being permitted only to communicate when their turns come up in a sequence. The advantages to decentralized structures are:

- Solve complex problems with fewer errors, especially when time is not at a premium, taking advantage of open divisions of labor
- High group satisfaction, morale, and motivation

- More opportunities to make friends (talk to everyone)
- More effective generating creative solutions to problems (freely express ideas, etc.)

There are two important disadvantages to decentralized structures. First, the problem-solving process for complex matters is often slow. This disadvantage derives from the second, that having more communication opportunities among all members means more time is needed to entertain, evaluate, and decide on issues.

When people work together in teams using "computer-mediated communication technologies to work interdependently across space, time and organizational boundaries" (Berry, 2011, p. 211), they are operating as a *virtual team*. Virtual teams' members can be across the office as much as across the world. The term "virtual team" is a bit of a misnomer, because the team is real, but it is "virtual" because members meet and work using digital channels of communication, like discussion/chat groups, Google® Docs, GoToMeeting®, Skype®, and others. So they may never meet physically in the same place. Nevertheless, communication structures in virtual teams can be centralized or decentralized, depending on the purpose and constraints they face. Virtual teams share many of the challenges and traits of traditional teams, but the management of teams is all the more demanding because people can do what they need and want to do with much greater independence than teams meeting face-to-face (Berry, 2011). Effective virtual team management, then, relies on stronger-than-usual knowledge and understanding of group dynamics and accountability explained in this chapter so that both task and relationship dimensions are tended to well at all times. Effective leadership also requires savvy use of the team's communication channels because, after all, knowing the audience and her or his perspective is as critical as it is in a face-to-face situation.

Conflict

No matter what structure a group uses, and no matter how well a team may be led and managed, conflict can emerge. *Conflict* occurs when there is a clash between at least two people or parties who perceive each other as negatively affecting something the other cares about (Robbins & Judge, 2008). Viewing conflict as a process makes it manageable, which is a valuable perspective for a team leader. The process, as explained by Robbins and Judge (2008), consists of five stages, shown in Figure 9-1.

In stage 1 certain factors contribute to the emergence of conflict between one person and another. Communication concerns the meaning attached to intentional and unintentional messages of any kind. Structure refers to the multiple variables that exist within the context of the work environment of the people in conflict.

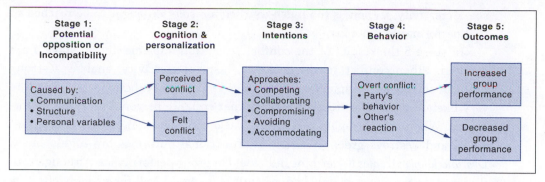

Figure 9-1. CONFLICT PROCESS MODEL.
SOURCE: Robbins & Judge (2008, p. 487)

Personal variables involves personality types and the emotional competence of people involved.

In stage 2 the conditions that gave rise to a possible conflict become real at a perceived level (i.e., when observed) and/or at a felt level (i.e., when emotions are evoked). This stage is the one where conflict is defined and emotions predominate and fuel the conflict process.

Stage 3 concerns the decisions people make to act in certain ways. The decisions are focused on the intentions that one party believes are behind the conflict. Two dimensions of intentions interact: *cooperativeness* (i.e., other focus) and *assertiveness* (i.e., self-focus). Handling a conflict in this stage can be done by identifying certain intentions that appear to be at play:

- *Competing* ("I win, you lose"; low cooperative and high assertive)
- *Collaborating* ("Let's work together"; high assertive and cooperative)
- *Avoiding* ("Ignore it and it will go away"; low cooperative and assertive)
- *Accommodating* ("All right, we'll do it your way"; low assertive and high cooperative)
- *Compromising* ("We all get much of what we wanted"; equally cooperative and assertive)

Stage 4 is the implementation stage for the intention-based solution to the conflict reached in stage 3. Stage 4 involves the statements, actions, and reactions of those in conflict during implementation. The interaction between those in conflict may be *functional* (i.e., controlled behaviors, like discussion, negotiation, and argument) or *dysfunctional* (i.e., destructive behaviors, like threats, walkouts, riots, wars). Note that dysfunction is possible on either level and is counterproductive for group performance. If there is too little conflict, more conflict should be injected to spark creativity; if there is too much conflict, a resolution ought to be reached so that performance is not lost.

In stage 5 the results of the conflict resolution implemented in stage 4 are counted. When conflict sparks curiosity, inspires creativity, enables a strong problem-solving environment, and mitigates groupthink, functional outcomes are very likely. *Functional outcomes* are those that enhance personal or group performance. When conflict spurs discontent, fuels confrontation, dissolves relationships, and destroys group cohesion, dysfunctional outcomes are highly likely. *Dysfunctional outcomes* undermine individual or group performance. Although conflict is often perceived as only bad, when it is managed well for a highly effective team, conflict can be a force for good, especially to drive innovation.

Creativity

Strictly speaking, creativity concerns the creation of something from something else. A potter uses clay to make a vase. An engineer designs a bridge using steel and concrete. A public relations professional produces a campaign using language, symbols, and media. Creativity, then, implies a process of making something. Everyone is creative, and people are creative in ways that others may not be. The challenge for leaders is how best to unleash team members' creativity. Creativity often comes organically, as it does spontaneously when someone is addressing an immediate challenge. But creativity also can be experienced on demand, as it would during "creativity sessions" called by a leader to have team members meet to come up with big ideas for a client. In the public relations profession, people are highly creative and, as we saw in Chapter 1, thrive on leaders who enable them to make the most of their creativity. So a basic understanding of creativity can be valuable for a PR manager.

The study of the process of creativity began "about 400 years ago [when] scientists discovered that our brain, not our heart, was responsible for our intellectual activity" (Green, 1999, p. 26). Over the last century, especially the latter half, many attempts at defining the creativity process have yielded some fairly common characteristics. The incongruity of what is going on with what needs to happen, as is the case in trying to strategize how to rebuild an organization's damaged image, is fertile ground for creativity. Another way to think of it is *cognitive dissonance* (Festinger, 1957), where there is a kind of harmony/consistency/congruity that needs to be established but is not and needs a means to achieve it. Again, creativity is the key—a means to make order out of chaos. In PR or advertising, a creative solution may seek to establish dissonance within a public (e.g., a need in people's lives is not being met when they thought it was), and there is a great way to achieve harmony in their lives (e.g., meet the need with the thing prescribed in targeted messages). Within the context of public relations practice, Figure 9-2 is my model of

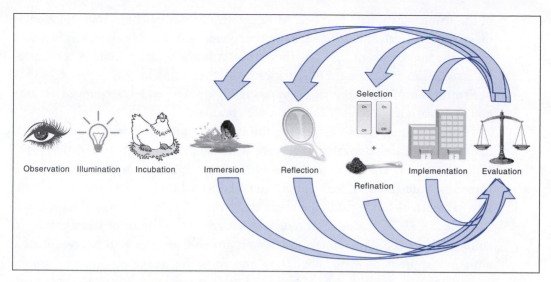

Observation Illumination Incubation Immersion Reflection Selection Refination Implementation Evaluation

Figure 9-2. MODEL OF THE CREATIVITY PROCESS.

the creative process that reflects other attempts of modeling it, complements this chapter's content, and is consistent with the overall approach of this book about public relations management.

The creativity process is both linear and recursive. It is linear in that it proceeds along eight steps because people tend to work one step at a time. The process also is recursive because at later stages in the process someone may go back to and through certain prior steps while still moving the project forward in time toward its completion. This combination of linearity and recursivity accommodates the way the mind works, especially while solving problems. As long as "necessity is the mother of invention"—of creativity—problem-solving is at the heart of creativity.

In Figure 9-2, the creativity process begins with *observation*, which is the identifying of something interesting, perhaps a problem, opportunity, or whatever. Upon that observation, *illumination* occurs, which is the "Aha!" moment of inspiration that the observed thing is seen in a new light. Upon the illumination or idea, *incubation* involves the defining and thinking about the thing/idea and the new take on it for its possibilities, limitations, etc. To make the most of the experience and idea thus far, *immersion* takes place, which is the playing with the idea in various ways, from studying/planning to drafting/prototyping of possible solutions/approaches. Next is *reflection*, which features further thinking and redefining about the thing/idea and possible alternatives and considerations about what could be added or subtracted, augmented or diminished. At this point a two-part step of *selection and refination* focuses on choosing the best thing/idea from among alternatives and refining the chosen thing/idea as much as practicable. With the thing/idea in a workable form, *implementation* involves creating the final version of the thing/idea for its purpose. After the thing/idea has been implemented, it must undergo *evaluation* to determine how good the thing/idea is in any way and make any improvements. During the process it is important to note that the process' steps can fast-forward or -backward to other steps to tend to matters that need attention. A brainstorming session highlights the first few steps quite plainly, and the creativity process builds upon such brainstorming.

From a management perspective, the creativity process should be a gold mine of opportunity and innovation. Everyone has the opportunity to be creative, especially those assigned a task to solve a problem or capitalize on an opportunity. A transformational leader, for example, could best facilitate an environment conducive to creativity among staff members at all times. To spark more and more innovative ideas, a leader could, for example, encourage people to think like a child—to think without the limits amassed through growing up into adulthood—about a situation or problem, especially during brainstorming sessions. Doing so can release ideas that might not be allowed if a more mature, adult attitude prevailed. Critical-analytical thinking would be saved for the later stages in the creativity process. When managing a team for creativity, Florida and Goodnight (2005, p. 126) argue that three principles should be the guide:

1. Help employees do their best work by keeping them intellectually engaged and by removing distractions.
2. Make managers responsible for sparking creativity and eliminate arbitrary distinctions between "suits" (i.e., leaders/managers) and "creatives" (i.e., followers/employees).
3. Engage customers as creative partners so you can deliver superior products.

Key to these principles is the idea that "creative capital is not just a collection of individuals' ideas, but a product of interaction" (p. 126). In other words, the nature, makeup, structure, and processes of highly effective teams enable them to release their creativity in value-added ways. Sutton (2003) researched effective management practices that facilitated innovation and found that unusual approaches to viewing situations can be at least as effective, if not more so, than conventional approaches. To this end, Sutton (p. 97) prescribes a series of ideas to manage creativity in teams facing certain situations; his prescription is shown in Table 9-1.

The idea of "outside-the-box thinking" is a call for creativity that is a widely expressed mantra in organizations and society at large. We must, however, be careful to recognize that we can think outside the box if and only if we know what the box is with which we are dealing in the first place. Not that the original box should constrain our creativity, rather, we must learn from and know what we have—we

Table 9-1. **WEIRD RULES FOR MANAGING CREATIVITY.**

SITUATIONS	CONVENTIONAL IDEAS THAT WORK	WEIRD IDEAS THAT WORK
Decide to do something that will probably . . .	*succeed, then convince yourself and everyone else that success is certain.*	*fail then convince yourself and everyone else that success is certain.*
Reward . . .	*success; punish failure and inaction.*	*success and failure; punish inaction.*
Seek out . . .	*and be attentive to people who will evaluate and endorse the work.*	*ways to avoid, distract, and bore customers, critics, and anyone who just wants to talk about money.*
Think of some . . .	*sound or practical things to do, and plan to do them.*	*ridiculous or impractical things to do, and plan to do them.*
Find some happy people . . .	*and make sure they don't fight.*	*and get them to fight.*
Hire . . .	*"fast learners" (of the organizational code)*	*"slow learners" (of the organizational code)*
Hire . . .	*people who make you feel comfortable, whom you like.*	*people who make you uncomfortable, even those you dislike.*
Hire . . .	*people you (probably) do need.*	*people you (probably) don't need.*
Take our past successes . . .	*and replicate them.*	*and forget them.*
Use job interviews . . .	*to screen candidates and, especially, to recruit new employees.*	*to get new ideas, not to screen candidates.*
Ignore people . . .	*who have never solved the exact problem you face.*	*who have solved the exact problem you face.*
Encourage people . . .	*to pay attention to and obey their bosses and peers.*	*to ignore and defy their bosses and peers.*
Summary	*Efficiency indicates effectiveness in the implementation and use of proven ideas.*	*Creative companies and teams are inefficient (and often annoying) places to work.*

must discern whether or not and to what degree constraints still must be accommodated. This is the realm of effectively managing creativity. Sutton (2003), like Florida and Goodnight (2005), found that creativity needs a management approach that does more amplifying than squelching of innovation. As Sutton put it, "Managing for creativity, I've discovered, means taking most of what we know about management and standing it on its head" (p. 96). An important point in all this is that to do the right thing means having the best environment and people to do it, and sometimes those things need to experience conflict. Creativity, then, is fueled by conflict in many ways (e.g., conventional vs. weird, old vs. new, known vs. unknown, proven vs. untested), which is framed by attitudes about one being thought of as better than another, even though either may achieve desired results. In this context, then, a better term for conflict might be "cognitive dissonance" (Festinger, 1957). The issue, however, is how to achieve even better results. The key is to unleash creativity to view and solve problems in unusual and effective ways. Unleashing creativity can work well when the leadership and management approaches, especially those explained in Chapter 1 as the most effective in the PR profession, genuinely foster innovation for the greater good.

Creativity as it has been addressed thus far has been treated from inside an organization. But it can be fueled from the outside through the hiring of external experts in particular fields.

Freelancers, Consultants, and Vendors

When someone is ill, she or he goes to a medical professional. When someone needs financial advice, he or she goes to a financial advisor. When someone requires legal advice, she or he talks with an attorney. When someone wants personal advice, she or he asks for help from a qualified person, such as a parent or sibling, trusted friend, or priest, for help.

These situations are analogous to those found in organizations. Leaders of operating units in organizations often need or want the help of experts in particular areas—to join their teams on a temporary basis to help with something important. The primary objective in seeking and hiring the help of external experts is to add value to an organization in very specific ways. As you might imagine, an expert's performance in his or her duties will be measured in appropriate ways so that value can be determined definitively, especially if an expert may be used again or, perhaps, recommended to others seeking similar help. Having an outside expert can reap many benefits, especially as there would be a mix of internal knowledge and experience about an organization blended with external knowledge and experience based on multiple organizations' successes (and failures). The RFP process is a useful model for conducting a search for the right external expert to hire, but a full RFP process may not be required because of the typically specialized need for which an external expert may be hired.

In public relations, like other professions, there is a wide range of external experts that practice their crafts—writing, planning, advising about and managing crises, organizing events, producing displays and exhibits, printing, designing communications, coaching executives, and so on. These professionals mesh well with existing PR teams and can be grouped into three commonly used categories of freelancers, consultants, and vendors.

Freelancers

The first category is *freelancers*. "Freelance" is a term that comes from medieval times, when a knight was released by his lord from exclusive allegiance to that lord—the knight was free to use his lance and sword in causes to help defend or fight for other lords, thus the term, "freelance." In today's terms, freelancers are people who, similarly, are free to work for whom they wish with the tools, knowledge, and experience they possess. For the communication field, these experts are independent contractors who very often are sole proprietors (i.e., they work for themselves). Freelancers are highly skilled in specific areas, such as writing, visual design, event planning, photography, and others. Freelancers charge for their work by the hour or by project, providing details about their rates or estimates for projects to clients. Of the two methods of charging for services, hourly rates may be preferred because they are seen as the fairest accounting of the work that was done (Kopelman, Shagas, & Levine, 1995). Other rates, such as word count in the case of writing for periodicals, are common (see Boyd, Clark, Blocksom, & Gilbert, 1997; Brewer, 2013; Yudkin, 1988).

Consultants

The second category of external experts is *consultants*. These experts can be independent (sole proprietors) or incorporated (agencies), and there are numerous books and other resources about effective consulting. Simply put, consultants add value to their clients in many ways, similar to freelancers but with greater access to resources (largely their own) to do their work because they have both the breadth and the depth of knowledge and experience in the communication field. A consultant's value lies in him or her "intervening in a system to stop some destructive human process and to improve the ability of the organization to function" (DeWine, 2001, p. 23). Consultants bring the best of both worlds (internal and external) and can fulfill a number of roles, including provider or technical expert, investigator, advocate, prescriber, teacher or stimulator, change agent, and colleague/collaborator/reflector (Gayeski, 1993, pp. 181–183). The consultation process includes identifying problems or the deeper nature of a problem already identified, conceiving of solutions or actions to take, implementing a solution or action, and following up to ensure successful implementation and addressing areas of added attention (DeWine, 2001, p. 31).

There are many reasons to hire consultants. Obvious ones include strategic reasons; they provide good service, meet deadlines, keep promises, do thorough work, and pay attention to details (e.g., tasks/outputs and billing). Consultants typically have a solid track record of good performance for a variety of clients, and they may charge more for their work than freelancers but be competitive with PR agencies. More specifically, consultants can:

- Provide a second opinion on strategy
- Implement programs
- Fill experience and capability gaps
- Provide overseas resource
- Special situations (e.g., bids and listings)
- Access to contacts
- Research
- Meet workload peaks
- Support subsidiary operations
- Reinforce issues to management (Beard, 2001, p. 129)

On the flip side of the reasons to hire consultants, there may be reasons to fire them. Firing a consultant may be based on, for example, lack of preparation, poor listening, losing touch with a client, using a competitor's product/service, failing to service the account properly, not paying enough attention to client–consultant "chemistry," and poor political savviness within the client's organization (Lukszewski, 2003). Consultants can charge for their work on an hourly, project, or retainer basis.

Vendors

The third category of external experts is *vendors*. These experts are providers of specialized products and services. Examples include printers, videographers, graphic designers, web hosts and programmers, exhibit makers, caterers, promotional items, animal handlers, decorators, etc. Vendors may be hired as subcontractors to agencies, freelancers, or consultants to fulfill work required under a contract with those primary providers. Client approval of a vendor hired by an agency, freelancer, or consultant may or may not be necessary. As a matter of fair disclosure and honesty, it would be best for those primary providers to explain the need and decision to subcontract work to a vendor. Cost, timing, and other issues would need to be defined as proper and appropriate under the contract between a client and its external expert.

Size matters

For all the reasons there may be to hire an external expert of any type, the aspect of size is important to consider. There are advantages and disadvantages to hiring large and small firms. Table 9-2 shows some of the advantages, and Table 9-3 shows some of the disadvantages.

Table 9-2. **ADVANTAGES TO HIRING LARGE AND SMALL FIRMS.**

LARGE FIRMS	SMALL FIRMS
• *Many resources/range of services*	• *Selected resources/range of services*
• *Strong reputation*	• *Focused customer attention*
• *Extensive experience/expertise*	• *Specialized experience/expertise*
• *Industry staying power*	• *Swift response*
• *Huge network*	

Table 9-3. **DISADVANTAGES TO HIRING LARGE AND SMALL FIRMS.**

LARGE FIRMS	SMALL FIRMS
• *Size*	• *Size*
• *Bureaucratic slowness*	• *Specialization and resource limitations*
• *One of many clients*	• *Small network*
• *Billings-driven*	• *Business-building critical (billings-driven)*
• *Not use full range of services*	• *Subcontracting very possible*
• *Cost*	

No matter what size firm an organization hires, learning about the client in all respects will be an issue. The question is, then, how well *and* how fast can external experts learn and then apply that learning competently in work that must be done. It is interesting to notice in comparisons between the pros and cons of large and small firms that size can be both a strength and a weakness for each. On this point size matters not in terms of the scale of a firm's operations but, rather, in terms of other essential dimensions that make up the reasons for hiring a firm of any sort. The three dimensions of quality, service, and price (like three legs of a stool) work together to support a firm's case for being in business and building its business with satisfied (even enthusiastic) clients.

EXECUTIVE VIEWPOINT

Lessons Learned from Watching Communication Teams at Work

Fraser Likely, MA, APR, FCPRS, FAMEC, President and Managing Partner, Likely Communication Strategies

As a management consultant specializing in reviewing and updating a Public Relations/ Communication (PR/C) department's mandate, service offerings, performance, and organization, I have worked closely with Chief Communication Officers (CCO) and their teams when they ask for an expert review and help in improving their operations. This has given me the opportunity to observe firsthand the inner workings of hundreds of PR/C teams.

Whether the PR/C department is in a private, public, or nonprofit sector organization, the department is built on the concept of teams. Teams are the building blocks of the organizational structure. Let me describe three of the typical types of teams found in a PR/C department.

First, the whole department can be considered a team. I have worked with small size departments where the full team has a stand up meeting each morning—to review the day's issues, tasks, and responsibilities. I have observed much larger departments that can only hold once- or twice-yearly off-site meetings with the whole team—the full team both times, but the size of the department determines the type and frequency of these meetings. These all-hands-on-deck meetings have a team-building goal. For the department to be seen as a cohesive team by other departments and internal clients as well as by external stakeholders, it is important that everyone have the same unity of purpose and collective sense of confidence in each other.

Second, one look at a department's organizational chart shows that the department is divided into units. These units might be specialized by the services they provide (e.g., editing, writing, media monitoring, research, measurement, etc.) or by the internal clients they support (e.g., marketing for marketing communications, HR for employee communications, finance for investor relations, etc.) or by the external stakeholders with whom they communicate (e.g., media for media relations, community groups for community relations, governments for government relations/public affairs) or by communication channel they manage (e.g., print publications, websites, Facebook, Twitter, YouTube, etc.).

Each unit is a team, and each team should have a common purpose, an integrated set of plans, a detailed set of procedures and processes, and a coordinated method for measuring the outputs and outcomes of the team. That leads each team to tend to want to operate as an island and to set its own internal "rules." Yet each team is one part in a longer production process that involves most of the other teams in the department, and its inputs and outputs must be integrated with each of the other teams in the department. Therefore, staff members in each unit must balance their allegiance to their unit, with their allegiance to the department as a whole. From experience, I can safely say that this is not easy.

Unit members also need to consider the makeup of the unit team. Is it a team of individual specialists? Or is it a group of generalists? Do employees have the experience and skill sets to move from position to position? Regardless of the size of the team, there will be many times when the team is short-staffed because of a resignation, illness, vacation, maternity leave, or "secondment" (i.e., an employee moves voluntarily from one position to another for only a short period of time specifically to gain additional experience and maximize resource levels in another operation). The inability to backfill empty positions in the short term can undermine the morale of any team. In my experience, this is a real test of the team leader. Can the team remain productive—and happy—in the face of a reduction in the number of warm bodies or in the type of specialist?

Third, the other type of team is the *ad hoc* team. This is a group of employees from across the department (or even from other departments) pulled together into a team and given a specific goal and schedule. Typically, in a PR/C department, these are teams to handle crises, issues, or campaigns. Or they may be long-term planning teams charged with, for example, studying the introduction of social media platforms. Seldom are these teams permanent. Most often the work for the team is above and beyond the work they do in their regular position. The dynamics of an *ad hoc* team is different in that allegiance to the assigned leader is different and work with other specialists from other units does not follow a set of prescribed procedures. I have seen this form of team do tremendous work, but I have also seen others squander an opportunity and slowly die off. Mutual trust and mutual respect are hallmarks of the well-performing ad hoc team. Similarly, there should be less hierarchy and more equality (regardless of anyone's classification level) for an *ad hoc* team to succeed.

These are three examples of "teams" within a PR/C department. Having employees with different backgrounds, experiences, and expertise work together for the common good as a team is vital to the smooth operations of any department. But it is most important in a PR/C department because these departments tend to be on the smaller size in any organization. Teamwork is crucial to getting the most out of the human resources given the department.

Key Words

Eight traits of highly effective teams	*Dysfunctional outcomes*
Two categories of factors of effective teams members	*Creativity*
	Creativity process steps
Five dynamics used by highly effective teams	*Three principles to manage creativity*
Cohesiveness	
Centralized structure	*Weird rules for creativity*
Decentralized structure	*Freelancers*
Virtual team	*Consultants*
Conflict	*Vendors*
Five stages of conflict	*Rate types (three)*
Functional outcomes	*Size pros and cons*

Exploration of Team Management

1. Connect the dots between leadership as covered in Chapter 1 and leadership as it is addressed here for teams. What kind of leader seems most appropriate for highly performing teams and why?

2. Examine the eight traits and the five dynamics of highly effective teams that Larson and LaFasto give us. In what ways do the traits and the dynamics intersect? How do the traits and dynamics favor functional conflict? What are the implications?

3. Find several agencies, consultants, freelancers, and vendors that serve in the public relations field. Examine them to find out their size (i.e., billings/income/revenue, employees, and clients served), areas of specialty, reputation, and special product or service offerings that differentiate them from others. What might be the pros and cons to working with them?

4. What approaches to inspire creativity among a team of public relations professionals do you think would work for the following three situations: (a) the launch of a new product, (b) the managing of a financial scandal, and (c) organizational change? Find actual cases in the news to work from for each of these. Prepare an outline with the proper details about the situations through to the strategies you would use to spark innovative thinking. What results would you expect?

5. Examine a code of ethics and determine in what specific ways freelancers and consultants are covered in it. How would a freelancer and consultant use that ethics code?

References

Beard, M. (2001). *Running a public relations department* (2nd ed.). London: Kogan Page.

Berry, G. R., (2011). Enhancing effectiveness on virtual teams: Understanding why traditional team skills are insufficient. *Journal of Business Communication, 48*(2), 186–206.

Brewer, R. L. (Ed.) (2013). *2014 writer's market*. Fairfield, OH: Writer's Digest Books/F+W Media.

Boyd, A. L., Clark, T., Blocksom, P, & Gilbert, J. (Eds.) (1997). *Making money freelance writing*. Cincinnati, OH: Writer's Digest Books.

DeVito, J. A. (2009). *Human communication: The basic course* (11th ed.). Boston: Pearson Education.

DeWine, S. (2001). *The consultant's craft: Improving organizational communication* (2nd ed.). Boston: Bedford/St. Martin's.

Festinger, L. (1957). *A theory of cognitive dissonance*. Stanford, CA: Stanford University Press.

Florida, R., & Goodnight, J. (2005, July/August). Managing for creativity, *Harvard Business Review,* 124–131.

Gayeski, D. (1993). *Corporate communications management: The renaissance communicator in information-age organizations*. Boston: Focal Press.

Green, A. (1999). *Creativity in public relations*. London: Kogan Page.

Hogg, M. A. (1992). *The social psychology of group cohesiveness: From attraction to social identity*. Upper Saddle River, NJ: Prentice-Hall.

Kopelman, A., Shagas, K., & Levine, J. (1995). *National Writers Union guide to freelance rates and standard practice*. New York: National Writers Union.

LaFasto, F. M. J., & Larson, C. E. (1986). *Teamwork: What must go right/what can go wrong*. Thousand Oaks, CA: Sage.

Larson, C. E., & LaFasto, F. M. J. (2001). *When teams work best: 6,000 team members and leaders tell what it takes to succeed*. Thousand Oaks, CA: Sage.

Lukaszewski, J. (2003, March 19). *Effective consulting: Getting those you advise to listen to and act on your advice*. Presentation at the PRSA Southeastern Wisconsin Professional Development Conference, Milwaukee, WI.

Robbins, S. P., & Judge, T. A. (2008). Conflict and negotiation. In *Organizational behavior* (13th ed., pp. 482–515). Upper Saddle River, NJ: Pearson Education.

Sutton, R. I. (2003, September). The weird rules of creativity. *Harvard Business Review*, 94–103.

Yudkin, M. (1988). *Freelance writing for magazines and newspapers: Breaking in without selling out*. New York: Harper & Row.

Recommended Reading

Adams, J. L. (1986). *Conceptual blockbusting: A guide to better ideas* (3rd ed.). Reading, MA: Addison-Wesley.

Bowen, S. A., Rawlins, B., & Martin, T. (2010). *An overview of the public relations function*. New York: Business Expert Press.

Callen, B. (2010). *Manager's guide to marketing, advertising, and publicity*. New York: McGraw-Hill.

Cooperrider, D. L., & Whitney, D. (2005). *Appreciative inquiry: A positive revolution in change*. San Francisco: Berrett-Koehler Publishers.

Kohr, M. (2012). Creativity: Powering integrated marketing communication ideas. In C. L. Caywood (Ed.), *The handbook of strategic public relations and integrated marketing communication* (2nd ed., pp. 737–750). New York: McGraw-Hill.

CLIENT-CENTERED COMMUNICATION

You are always working for someone. That someone—a "client"—has expectations of you and you of her or him. Mindreading is not a possibility, and even if it were, it might scarcely make sense to another person. Therefore, good communication with your clients is essential. When public relations professionals are employed by a nonagency company, their "clients" are people in other operational units for or with which PR work is being done. When public relations professionals are employed by an agency, consultancy, or vendor, or if PR professionals are freelancers, their clients are the organizations for which they are contractually obligated to complete certain work. When public relations professionals are employed by nonprofits, nongovernmental organizations, or other institutions, their clients are not only the other operating units in their organizations (similar to a company) but also their organizations' constituents, which include donors, benefactors, employees, members, volunteers, community leaders, and others. In every case, clients need and want to know what is going on and why. Also, in every case public relations professionals are serving in the best interests of others, which, as we saw in Chapter 3, has major moral, ethical, and legal responsibilities.

Client-centered communication, very broadly speaking, concerns the reinforcement of gratification about what has been and will be done for a client and its constituents. A related purpose may include reducing buyer remorse in a client who is having second thoughts in the face of a well-laid plan. Obvious dimensions to good communication—openness, honesty, candor, respectfulness, dialog, timeliness, professionalism, accuracy, and so on—are necessarily parts of client-centered communication. So is keeping promises. In this chapter we look at two pivotal topics of client communication: knowing the audience and using certain frameworks for good communication.

Know Your Audience

People have many things going on in their lives that demand their attention. People have varying degrees of control over things that happen or that may happen. And people respond to messages and media differently. Taking just these factors together is enough to suggest how important it is to know what someone needs and wants when communication about something is required. In short, know your audience. This is a maxim that is true of all forms of communication, and it is something we all learned all along in our education, beginning with writing. An effective way to enact this maxim is to apply a "you-attitude," which places the emphasis on the audience through a combination of particular language choices and pertinent themes or topics essential in a communication act (Shelby & Reinsch, 1995).

Remember, too, that you-attitudes go both ways—PR expert to client and vice versa. From the client's point of view, as Croft (2006) explains, the relationship with PR experts requires strategy-based solutions; quick responses with enthusiasm, energy, and creativity; solutions before clients think of them; relentless attention to detail; being part of the client's team; unexpected added value; wise budget management; daring to be different; commitment to client success; expertise the client does not have or cannot afford in-house; objectivity and courage to ask tough questions; good listening; no surprises; making the client a hero; proactive environmental scanning for emerging issues, business opportunities, or threats; exuding a genuine can-do attitude; delivering more than expected results; and thinking innovatively.

From the PR expert's point of view, according to Lukaszewski (2003), the relationship requires information necessary to do the job, methods for enacting planned communications (strategies and tactics), enough time to complete the job, support of the expert to others in the client's organization, problem-solving attitude, courage to raise sticky issues and push the client, and willingness to tell the client when he or she does something puzzling or irritating. Additionally, the client should share responsibility for success or failure fairly equally with the expert, accept responsibility for its ideas and feelings, and share those ideas and feelings with the expert.

In Lukaszewski's (2003) view of client-centered communication, a PR expert (internal and external) must:

- Not overpromise and underdeliver (or vice versa, as either way it looks like something was not thought through correctly)
- Pay attention to one's internal alarm ("gut feelings") because there may be something to it
- Make one's own values and philosophy clear
- Avoid accepting the client's definition of the problem or opportunity
- Look for patterns in what has and what could go on
- State one's own goals and expectations clearly
- Define what will be done and how by both client and expert
- Know the "real client"

Effective listening is vital to working with clients, especially if there are times they resist you and your ideas. Handling client resistance, as Lukaszewski (2003) advises, begins with being able to recognize that it is happening and it has a certain pattern. What is that pattern? The client may use language reflecting that she or he may be avoiding responsibility, flooding you with detail, responding to your questions with one-word answers, attacking you angrily, merely complying with whatever you say without expressing real feelings, changing the subject, maintaining silence, nit-picking at minute details, or asking too early and continuously for a solution. It is important to calmly seek clarification based on the communication behaviors and statements, not any judgments about what may be behind those behaviors and statements. Then continue to listen carefully for verbal and nonverbal, intended and unintended messages. What are they, and what do they indicate? Make sure you remain engaged with the conversation and, especially, support the client's underlying concerns and recognizes any vulnerabilities.

Realize, too, that the way in which something is said matters, and the medium and the message work together. In client (or any) communication, there are pros and cons to any chosen channel (Lengel & Daft, 1988). Theories and research about *media richness* (i.e., the degree to which information can be conveyed over a medium; the more information that helps a task and reduces uncertainty, the richer the medium) and *media synchronicity* (i.e., the degree to which channels enable communication flow and communication combinations across media that pertain to task decision-making) explore and explain how and why it is that communication channels provide varying levels of utility and effectiveness, including in the workplace and among work teams (see Dennis, Fuller & Valacich, 2008; Kahai & Cooper, 2003; Thatcher & Brown, 2010; Turner, Qvarfordt, Biehl, Golovchinsky, & Back, 2003).

People vary in their ability to handle different channels, but more to the point about knowing an audience, people also have preferences in obtaining and sharing information over different media (Gu, Higa, & Moodie, 2011). So communication channels have certain, basic characteristics to consider:

- *Face-to-face*—usually best, richest channel as people are physically in the same place at the same time; much richness of the channel; can gage commitment and engagement; direct feedback; expensive and time-consuming if people must travel to be together; no automatic record
- *Video call (e.g., Skype® or GoToMeeting®)*—mimics face-to-face communication; limits channel richness by technology (e.g., audio quality, video quality, video frame, talking heads, bandwidth, same or compatible technology at both ends); saves on travel expenses; sessions can be recorded; document sharing is possible
- *Telephone*—avoids face-to-face contact; usually not good for complex matters, unless arranged an appointment to call; relies on astute perceptions and handling of paralinguistic features of conversation
- *E-mail, text messages, and voice-mail*—avoids face-to-face contact; poor for complex, personal matters; good for quick matters; texting can wreak of spelling, grammar, and other language problems; e-mail can include attachments to support main messages; provides a record of messages
- *Formal presentations*—focuses attention of group and efficiently conveys an argument in one setting; answers doubts and objections; possible for emerging support to be apparent; may require extra time for people to assess and respond to content
- *Group meetings*—useful for getting status updates and making decisions and assignments; not ideal for conveying information, but good for establishing rationales
- *Memos*—relies on particular organizational rules for their formatting and composition; conciseness is key; provides a written record; can be considered at the convenience of persons addressed; effective writing in all respects is essential
- *Corporate publications*—good as internal records of organizational policies, news, and other purposes; unreliable as to how much they may be read and at what levels in an organization; effective writing and layout in all respects is essential

Across these and other channels of business communication with clients, the important thing to remember is to know in what ways people prefer to be communicated and use them. More ambiguous messages (e.g., those that convey information whose content may be guarded or is still being worked out but is important to say something) require rich media, such as face-to-face channels. Conversely, very plain messages (e.g., those that convey concrete information and data) require lean media, such as publications or memos (see Downs & Adrian, 2004). Convenience in your sending any messages does not necessarily equate to effectiveness in either the client's receiving or knowing message content. To ensure that communication content is strong in any channel, a few simple and useful frameworks offer ways to develop messages.

Frameworks for Client Communication

Client-focused communication may take one of many forms, but the purpose for it very likely will be either informative or persuasive. Informative messages seek to establish a level of knowledge and familiarity with a subject so that it connects with what people already understand and are coming to understand. Informative communication, then, is often educational in nature, as in giving background and details about something. Persuasive messages seek to inspire someone to assent to or "buy into" one's thesis (see Perelman & Olbrechts-Tyteca, 1991). That assent to a thesis or argument is made possible by the combination of, first, the PR expert's text and, second, the client's own knowledge and reasoning—*self-persuasion* (Burks, 1970), which can involve various acts. Self-persuasion can be viewed as a sequence of stages like that of Rogers' (2003) diffusion theory, which is fairly predictable and can feature different communication channels at different times:

- A matter gains one's attention,
- becomes a legitimate concern,
- is tried out,
- is implemented,
- then is evaluated.

As we saw in Chapters 1 and 6, deception is something against which you must be on guard in your own communication and that of others.

Language choice in communication is, of course, vital. One of the most useful frameworks for ensuring effective messages in business communication is the 7 Cs of effective communication (Murphy, Hildebrandt, & Thomas, 1997), and the PRSA endorses a very similar breakdown in its study guide for its accreditation exam for

PR professionals. The 7 Cs (see sidebar) should be used for all client-focused and other professional communication efforts. Capturing and communicating concisely and compellingly what is necessary to make a decision is possible through Lukaszewski's (2003) five-step approach: (1) explain in 40 words why a situation, problem, or opportunity is important to the client; (2) analyze in 60 words the impact or risk with the matter; (3) provide options, costs, and benefits of doing nothing, doing something, doing something more, and doing something else; (4) recommend one of the options for what must be done; and (5) provide a rationale about why that option must be used by differentiating it from among the other options, examining potential unintended consequences, and defending anticipated outcomes. Figure 10-1 shows a worksheet that can be used to capture the relevant information to facilitate the kind of client communication needed.

SITUATION'S IMPORTANCE (IMPACT/RISK): _____
_____

OPTIONS	STRENGTHS	WEAKNESSES	MESSAGES	AUDIENCES
1. Do nothing.				
2. Do something:				
3. Do something more:				
4. Do something else:				

RECOMMENDATION: _____
RATIONALE: _____
TACTICS: _____
_____

EVALUATION:

      OUTPUTS: _____
      OUTTAKES: _____
Projected—| OUTCOMES: _____
      | OUTGROWTHS: _____

NOTES: _____
_____
_____

Figure 10-1. CLIENT COMMUNICATION WORKSHEET.

The Seven Cs of Effective Communication

Completeness

- Provide all necessary information—who, what, where, when, why, how

- Answer all questions asked—stated and implied

- Give something extra, when desirable

Example: Please fax me in return the departures from Singapore to Hong Kong on the 8th. [Your response should give more details about the times of days, airlines flying that route, costs, and departure/arrival times.]

Conciseness

- Eliminate wordy expressions—use one word in place of phrases; one sentence instead of two; read aloud to listen for wordiness

- Include only relevant material—omit trite expressions; ask what information is truly relevant for the reader and your message

- Avoid unnecessary repetition—see if the same word or idea appears too often

Example: Will you ship us sometime, anytime during the month of October would be fine, or even November if you are rushed (November would suit us just as well, in fact a little bit better) 300 of the regular 3- by 5-inch blue felt armbands with white sewn letters in the center?

Thank you in advance for sending these along to use by parcel post, and not express, as express is too expensive.

Revised: Please ship parcel post, before the end of November, 300 regular 3- by 5-inch blue felt armbands with white sewn letters in the center.

Consideration

- Focus on "you" instead of "I" or "we"— see your material from your reader's (listener's) point of view; "you" is generally more desirable than "I" or "we"

- Show audience benefit or interest in the receiver—readers (and listeners) like to know benefits and should be a prominent part of the message

- Emphasize positive, pleasant facts— positive words elicit favorable reactions from readers (and listeners); remember to balance the good and the bad

Example: We don't refund, if the returned item is soiled or unusable.

Revised: We refund when the returned item is clean and resalable.

Concreteness

- Use specific facts and figures—be precise when using factual data

Example:

(1) Eastern Europe is making progress in obtaining investments. [vague, general, indefinite]

(1a) In 1990 investments in Eastern Europe were about $30 million (U.S.). Today that figure has increased 12 percent. [concrete, precise]

- Put action in your verbs—people prefer reading active voice rather than passive voice; use action in verbs rather than in nouns and infinitives

Examples:

    (2) The tests were administered by the professors. [subject receives action]

    (2a) Professors administered the tests. [subject performs action]

    (3) Vice President Smith will give consideration to the report. [action hiding in a "quiet" noun; "deadly" verbs: be, give, have, hold, make, put and take]

    (3a) Vice President Smith will consider the report. [action in the verb]

    (4) The duty of a secretary is to check all incoming mail and to record it. In addition, it is his or her responsibility to keep the assignment book up to date. [action hiding in infinitive]

    (4a) A secretary checks and records all incoming mail and keeps the assignment book up to date. [action in the verbs]

- Choose vivid, image-building words—use these words strategically

Example:

    (5) Some women were stopped in their promotions. [literal, dull]

    (5a) Many women faced the "glass ceiling" in their companies. [more vivid, figurative]

Clarity

- Choose precise, concrete and familiar words—readers (and listeners) prefer words they know; avoid Latin terms when possible

Example: After our perusal of pertinent data, the conclusion is that a lucrative market exists for the subject property.

Revised: The data we studied show that your property is profitable and in high demand.

- Construct effective sentences and paragraphs—(length) use short sentences of 17–20 words; (unity) develop one idea for each sentence; (coherence) arrange words in sentences so idea clearly express your intended meaning and place modifiers close to the words they are modifying

Example: Her report was about managers, broken down by age and gender.

Revised: Her report focused on age and gender of managers.

Revised: Her report about managers focused on age and gender.

Courtesy

- Be sincerely tactful, thoughtful and appreciative—reflect a sincere, genuine you attitude; get someone else's opinion if you have doubts

Example: Clearly, you did not read my latest e-mail.

Revised: Sometimes my wording is not precise. Let me try again.

- Use expressions that show respect—avoid language that may offend your reader; use humor cautiously; ask someone's opinion if you have doubts

Examples: Contrary to your inference . . .
        I'm sure you must realize . . .
        Obviously you overlooked . . .
        We find it difficult to believe that . . .
        Why have you ignored . . .
        You are probably ignorant of the fact that . . .
        You should know . . .
        You surely don't expect . . .

- Choose nondiscriminatory expressions—be aware of gender, race, age, color, creed, sexual preference, and ethnic origins

Examples:

   (1) freshman → first-year student

   (2) manpower → workers; employees; workforce; personnel; people

   (3) Anyone who comes to class will get <u>his/her</u> grade reduced.

 (3a) Anyone who comes late to class will have <u>their</u> grade reduced.

Correctness

- Use the right level of language—formal (unconversational, impersonal, complex style usually for scholarly work, legal documents, governmental assignments); informal (conversational, personal, simpler style typical of business writing); and substandard (colloquial, incorrect/improper words, grammar, etc.)

- Check accuracy of figures, facts and words/names—verify statistical data; double check your totals; avoid guessing at laws that affect you and your reader; have someone read your work; determine if any facts have changed over time

- Maintain acceptable writing mechanics—apply rules of grammar, syntax and usage and discourse conventions for any type of document you prepare

SOURCE: Murphy, Hildebrandt, & Thomas (1997)

This worksheet is a guide for your discussion with a client, not necessarily a document to give to the client. It is something you use to formulate how you (and your team) see a situation and what could be done. Overpreparing is far better than underpreparing! The starting point for using this worksheet is to succinctly define the situation and its importance, including what is at risk or what impact (positive or negative) it will have for the organization. Consistent with Lukaszewski's five-step approach, at least four options must be specified then explored in terms of their strengths, weaknesses, messages that could be conveyed, and audiences who would receive those messages. From this laying out of options, one must be chosen and defended. Importantly, applying the decision-making process in Chapter 6 (see Figure 6-3) would prove especially valuable to recommend one of the four options. That recommended option must also include tactical approaches to make it happen that would fold into a proper strategic plan (see Appendixes A and B). The final formal component of this worksheet is showing initial thoughts about how the recommended option would be evaluated in terms of "the four outs" (Lindenmann, 2006; also see Appendix A):

- *Outputs* (measurements of what tactics were created and how well they were deployed, and the level of exposure for an organization)
- *Outtakes* (measurements of the audience's immediate or short-term responses to communication)

Your feedback is important to us!

Thank you for choosing Bill & Ted's Public Relations. We are committed to providing all our customers with complete customer satisfaction so please complete this brief questionnaire and send it back to us. On behalf of the entire Bill & Ted's Public Relations team, think you for your business!

About You

Your Name_____

Company _____

Street Address _____

City _____ State _____ Zip _____

Phone_____ Fax_____

E-mail _____

Type of Project/Program We Worked on for You

_____Media Relations   _____Product Launch   _____Other:_____

_____Investor Relations   _____Integrated Communications   _____

_____Employee Communications   _____Reputation Management   _____

_____Event Planning   _____Crisis/Issue Management

Notable project details:_____

_____

Personal Service

Was the project estimate accurate?			_____Yes	_____No	_____Not Applicable
Was our account staff helpful?			_____Yes	_____No	_____Not Applicable
Did our project manager address your project's needs promptly?			_____Yes	_____No	

How effective was our account team's communication with you?	Bad	Poor	Good	Very Good	Excellent
	1	2	3	4	5

Comments:_____

_____

Work Quality

Was the project done on budget	_____Yes	_____No
Was the project done on time?	_____Yes	_____No
Were our team members on site with you on time?	_____Yes	_____No
Were our people easy to work with?	_____Yes	_____No

How would you rate the overall quality of our work?	Bad	Poor	Good	Very Good	Excellent
	1	2	3	4	5

Comments:_____

_____

_____

Overall Experience

Overall, based on all aspects of our work on your project, how satisfied are you with us?	Not at All 1	Somewhat Satisfied 2	Satisfied 3	Very Satisfied 4	Completely Satisfied 5
How likely would you want us to work with you again?	Not at All 1	Maybe 2	Possibly 3	Probably 4	Definitely 5

How You Heard About Us

____Referral from someone   ____Website

____Prior project with you   ____News/Magazine article

____Phone call   ____Advertisement

____Literature   ____Other:_____

Marketing Information

Would you be willing to give a testimonial?   ____Yes   ____No

What trade shows do you attend?_____

_____

What trade publications do you read?_____

_____

What news or business publications do you read?_____

_____

Additional Comments

What are our strengths when working with you?_____

_____

_____

_____

How can we do better when working with you?_____

_____

_____

_____

_____

Thank You!

Please mail your completed questionnaire in the enclosed, postage-paid envelope.

Figure 10-2. CUSTOMER SATISFACTION QUESTIONNAIRE.

- *Outcomes* (measurements of the audience's long-term response to communication)
- *Outgrowths* (measurements of the audience's cumulative response to communication as it affects an organization's reputation and image)

Consistent with Chapter 4, audience responses for outtakes, outcomes, and outgrowths are measured against stated objectives over defined periods of time, which would target people's heads (awareness and knowledge), hearts (attitudes and emotions), and hands (actions and behaviors). Additional notes may be added to this form at the bottom as needed to explain or draw attention to anything necessary.

Even after attending to so many matters of effective communication from your client's expectations, there is still every reason to formally measure whether and how effective your communication with the client has been. You may, of course, talk about it and, thereby, obtain personal statements about what has worked and what has not. You may also send an e-mail or memo with the question, "What do you think about how we have communicated with and served you?" But that question is too open-ended and would not be considerate of the client's time and effort to answer it. A better way to obtain the feedback you need that can also serve as documentation of your effectiveness is to prepare and send a brief questionnaire about multiple aspects of customer service (see Croft, 2006). It is important that the questionnaire, an example of which is shown in Figure 10-2, is focused and simple to complete. The content of the questionnaire should touch on the salient matters about the business relationship between the client and the PR expert, including communication.

An important matter for a satisfaction survey is to make sure you get any feedback, so follow up with your client to make sure he or she completes the form and returns it. Once you get the completed form, read it, analyze it, and discuss it with your team. Do a SWOT analysis based on the feedback and other data you have from the client that pertains to your perceptions of its satisfaction with your work. Summarize the findings, prepare some recommendations for improvement, and outline steps to be taken in the short and long terms. Then, finally, discuss this report with the client so that the relationship you share becomes better and stronger.

Unfortunately, on rare occasions, an agency may have a client that is difficult to work with because of any number of factors (e.g., unreasonable, aggressive, in default of paying invoices, etc.). In such a situation, an agency may be better off firing the client. Doing so is possible because, presumably, the contract allows for either party to terminate the business relationship (without financial penalty) at any time for any reason (probably in writing). Similar to firing an employee, the agency will have to at least (1) make a case for why the firing is necessary and (2) propose a means for completing any unfinished work, if any exists, and getting paid for it. Again, like firing an employee, it is best to do it at a face-to-face meeting and to have the required and proper documentation to terminate the business relationship. The client may have a lot of questions and, maybe, feel personally hurt. Focus on the business factors and refrain from using judgmental language. In other words, "take the high road" to firing the client and leave on as amicable grounds as possible. After all, your agency's handling of this situation must be as professional and fair as any other.

Like any relationship between people, communication must be effective. It will not always be perfect, but it must be effective so that people's views of things and expectations are as close as possible from person to person every day. All the principles and practices of good, effective leadership and management in public relations are as important in small matters as they are in big matters. The character of an organization and the character of PR professionals is a supremely valuable asset to protect at all times.

EXECUTIVE VIEWPOINT

Examples of Effective Client Communication

Debra Bethard-Caplick, Principal, Quicksilver Edge Communications

It's ironic that given all the time we spend analyzing the external audiences we need to communicate with, as a profession we fail to consider our clients as one of those audiences, equally if not more important because of the client–agency interaction. In many ways, they are our MOST important audience—without them we have no reason for being.

Everything we do should be client-centered. Even internal communicators have clients: the department heads, employees, our bosses, anyone who needs our services and counsel. It's critical that we communicate clearly with clients or supervisors throughout each stage of the communication process, beginning with the planning and continuing right through the evaluation of results.

Taking clients—whether internal or external—for granted is the fastest way to ruin the relationship. We must invest significant time into understanding what drives our clients, what motivates them and their goals. As a PR agency, at Quicksilver Edge it's our responsibility to manage the client relationship so that we function smoothly as an extension of the client, and that requires a commitment of both time and energy on an ongoing basis. It's not something that magically grows over time.

The same elements that are integral to being an ethical PR professional go into building and maintaining good business relationships: openness, honesty, candor, respectfulness, timeliness, tact, and good judgment. You need to manage expectations on both sides of the relationship: yours and the client's. Both need realistic expectations of what can be achieved, and you need to manage those expectations throughout the process. At a minimum, you both need understand what is involved, what the expected outcomes will be, and how those outcomes will be evaluated. You need to keep the relationship on track by managing clients' expectations of you—as well as of themselves. It's too easy to get carried away by enthusiasm and find yourself with unachievable goals.

Managing the relationship is critical to a successful client–agency relationship. At a minimum, clients expect the agency to understand their business, be strategic in their approach, communicate clearly, and meet deadlines. Agencies have their own expectations for clients, such as access to necessary information and responsiveness. Keep in mind that the client has other issues you know nothing about that can impact your projects. Clients need to communicate key information about these issues to minimize the negative impact on campaigns. Agencies need to know how best to ensure the free flow of crucial information between the two partners.

I once made the mistake of taking a long-term client for granted and slipped into the habit of communicating casually, as if she were a friend (which I considered her to be). What I failed to consider was how my observations in conversation and on my personal blog on the PR mistakes of others would be perceived in the context of the client–agency relationship. She began wondering what I might be saying about the company to others. I never, ever discuss clients with others, but I didn't realize that I had never specifically communicated this policy to clients, because to me, confidentiality is automatic.

No matter how friendly you become with clients, you need to recognize that he or she is still that—a client—and you need to interact accordingly *in settings that are business-related*. I'm not saying you can't become personal friends with a client, or you can't have your friends become clients. But you must have the social awareness of what is and is not appropriate for the business relationship. It's simple sound, *strategic* business good manners that too many new professionals—and many veterans, to tell the truth—fail to grasp, and it can derail their careers. My failure to strategically manage this business relationship taught me to pay just as much attention to managing the client relationship as I do to the relationship I build with the media.

Over the course of my career, two types of people really stick out: those who've made a great impression on me, and those who have done the opposite. Sitting at a networking luncheon, monopolizing the conversation at the table about your clueless boss and how boring your job is may be fun, but it's not professional. I guarantee that every other professional at that table is making a mental note to avoid you in the future. I even have a couple of business cards I've saved with "Do not hire" written on them.

Developing the necessary social skills to build a well-managed relationship between the client and the agency or between yourself and new acquaintances in the professional sphere will ensure that both partners in the relationship will be open and willing to have direct and honest conversations with each other—conversations that are crucial. These people may one day be your client, your mentor, or your boss. You can't achieve an effective relationship when relying on assumptions about the other partner. Client/agency expectations must be discussed in detail and agreed to at the beginning of the relationship in order to be successful. Networking relationships must be professional and strategic. And as the relationship continues, it must continually be managed to ensure that both partners are working together, and not apart. It all boils down to appropriate communication for the audiences you are communicating to—ALL of them.

Key Words

Client

You-attitude

Over-/Underpromising

Over-/Underdelivering

Media synchronicity

Self-persuasion and process

Media richness

Media synchronicity

Channel preferences

Seven Cs of communication

Five steps for recommendations

"The four outs" (outputs, outtakes, outcomes, and outgrowths)

Exploration of Client Communication

1. Using the worksheet in Figure 10-1 and the approach for knowing the client audience, reverse-engineer a case to find out what kind of client-centered communication would have occurred to implement the case. What did you learn about preparing client communication?

2. Explain the ethical and legal dimensions of effective client communication, especially when it concerns the proposing and reporting on projects. Use the PRSA's or IABC's code of ethics to help you prepare your answer.

3. Find at least three examples of public relations discourse produced for three different organizations. Read them and critique them according to the 7 Cs of effective communication. How good is the writing on those grounds? What would you do differently, and how would you do it?

4. Find one or more RFPs online and put yourself in the position of the client and the proposing agency. Where do you think someone could overpromise or underpromise? Why? How would you approach the other party based that there may be a danger of over-/underpromising?

References

Burks, D. M. (1970). Persuasion, self-persuasion, and rhetorical discourse. *Philosophy & Rhetoric, 3*(2), 109–119.

Croft, A. C. (2006). *Managing a public relations firm for growth and profit* (2nd ed.). New York: Best Business Books.

Dennis, A. R., Fuller, R. M., & Valacich, J. S. (2008, September). Media, tasks, and communication processes: A theory of media synchronicity. *Management Information Systems Quarterly, 32*(3), 575–600.

Downs, C. W., & Adrian, A. D. (2004). *Assessing organizational communication: Strategic communication audits.* New York: Guilford Press.

Gu, R., Higa, K., & Moodie, D. R. (2011). A study on communication media selection: Comparing the effectiveness of the media richness, social influence, and media fitness. *Journal of Service Science and Management, 4,* 291–299.

Kahai, S. S., & Cooper, R. B. (2003). Exploring the core concepts of media richness theory: The impact of cue multiplicity and feedback immediacy on decision quality. *Journal of Management Information Systems, 20*(1), 263–299.

Lengel, R. H., & Daft, R. L. (1988). The selection of communication media as an executive skill. *Academy of Management Executive, 2,* 225–232.

Lindenmann, W. K. (2006). *Public relations research for planning and evaluation.* Gainesville, FL: Institute for Public Relations. Available online: http://www.instituteforpr.org/topics/pr-research-for-planning-and-evaluation/.

Lukaszewski, J. (2003, March 19). *Effective consulting: Getting those you advise to listen to and act on your advice.* Presentation at the PRSA Southeastern Wisconsin Professional Development Conference, Milwaukee, WI.

Murphy, H. A., Hildebrandt, H. W., & Thomas, J. P. (1997). *Effective business communication* (7th ed.). Boston: McGraw Hill.

Perelman, C., & Olbrechts-Tyteca, L. (1991). *The new rhetoric: A treatise on argumentation.* Notre Dame, IN: University of Notre Dame Press.

Rogers, E. (2003). *The diffusion of innovations* (5th ed.). New York: Free Press.

Shelby, A. N, & Reinsch, Jr., N. L. (1995). Positive emphasis and you-attitude: An empirical study. *Journal of Business Communication, 32,* 303–328.

Turner, T., Qvarfordt, P., Biehl, J. T., Golovchinsky, G., & Back, M. (2010, August 10–15). Exploring the workplace communication ecology. *CHI '10 Proceedings of the SIGCHI Conference on Human Factors in Computing Systems* (pp. 841–850). New York: Association for Computing Machinery.

Recommended Reading

Beard, M. (2001). *Running a public relations department* (2nd ed.). London: Kogan Page.

Croft, A. C. (2006). *Managing a public relations firm for growth and profit* (2nd ed.). New York: Best Business Books.

Dickinson, D. (2003). *The new account manager.* Chicago: The Copy Shop.

Hameroff, E. J. (1998). *The advertising agency business: The complete manual for management and operation* (3rd ed.). Lincolnwood, IL: NTC Business Books.

Lordan, E. J. (2003). *Essentials of public relations management.* Chicago: Burnham.

Maister, D. H. (1993). *Managing the professional service firm.* New York: Free Press.

Roetzer, P. (2012). *The marketing agency blueprint: The handbook for building hybrid PR, SEO, content, advertising, and web firms.* Hoboken, NJ: John Wiley & Sons.

PERSONAL CAREER-PLANNING STRATEGIES

The focus of this book has been, from the beginning, on the ways of thinking in which public relations leaders engage on a daily basis. This approach has at least two important benefits: (1) it shows you much of what commands management's attention every day, so you can prepare yourself for a leadership position sometime later in your career, and, perhaps most immediately important, (2) it shows you how you will be led and managed as you start in your career, so you can perform better than you would have without this knowledge because you know what your bosses face. This book concludes, then, with this final chapter on ways you can best represent yourself to potential employers and to fellow professionals in the public relations field at the start of and throughout your full-time PR career.

As you think about and plan for your career in public relations, you must remember two simple realities, which this chapter explores. *First, your career is all about you.* The sum of your knowledge, skills, experiences, and personal character make you who you are, and you will fit well in some organizations but not in others. Your quest in your career is really to demonstrate to others that you are competent in all ways that matter. In other words, you will be paid to be one of the best communicators and communication counselors in the organizations for which you work. Always make sure you prove that maxim every day in every way. *The second reality is that only you own your career.* No one else is responsible for your career, although some people may be more influential than others as you make certain choices in life. So much of what you do in your career is choice-driven. As you begin your career in public relations, you have the responsibility to successfully run one of the most important communication campaigns in your life—a campaign about your own value, which will run into your retirement. If you cannot promote yourself well and honestly, why should anyone hire you to promote their organization? Always make sure your campaign about yourself is ethical, accurate, and compelling.

It's All about You

Remember in your childhood being asked, "What do you want to be when you grow up?" Your immediate answer then was likely different than it is now. Probably no one would have answered, "I want to be a PR guy!" But we grow older and wiser, and public relations has become a career of choice and importance for organizations and society. The question itself, however, reveals a profound truth about planning for the future. Indeed, planning for the future requires one to be a bit visionary—to see the possibilities about one's self. But it does not end there. Just like strategic planning for an organization, you should do something similar for yourself. As Figure 11-1 shows, the future you see for yourself can be realized if you figure out the things you need to get there from where you are today. In other words, think backwards—from your ultimate future job to today, and consider the path to get there from here. The path between today and your future is your *career path*. Along that path you will reach certain milestone achievements, such as promotions, new jobs at different organizations (but not necessarily to higher levels of authority), awards, and so on, that all show you are advancing in your career. Setbacks in your career may also happen (e.g., a poorly executed project or bad boss), and over time they will help you grow as a more competent professional and, perhaps, reveal certain opportunities that can evolve into career advances.

Going down that path you have the greatest control of your career. You need to be *diligent*, *flexible*, and *opportunistic* but also *strategic*. Be diligent so you work hard

Figure 11-1. CAREER PATH–PLANNING MODEL.

and do so ethically, enthusiastically, and intelligently, all of which reflect your personal character as a genuinely good professional and good person. Be flexible so you can obtain experiences that make the most of your knowledge, skills, experiences, and interests. Be opportunistic so you can take advantage of circumstances and events that you find for yourself or that arise for you that have promise. Not every opportunity should be followed, however. ("No" is a good thing to say to some opportunities.) So be strategic—no matter what opportunities, diversions, or detours you may take on your career path, remain focused on realizing the vision for yourself and your career. By the way, you may change your path toward your vision, just as you may change a route on a trip so you can see sights you did not originally plan, and still get to your final destination. Alternatively, you may change your vision because of any variety of factors in your life that influence you to make such a change. In this event you embark on a whole new career-life path, and that is okay.

As you embark on your journey down your career-life path, two areas of knowledge are very important. The first is knowledge about yourself, and the second is knowledge about the field.

Know yourself

Socrates professed the maxim, "Know thyself," because, simply put, for one to excel in life, one must first know who one is and in what ways one is moved to action or inaction. In terms of career management, you need to know what drives you to do what you do and to become what you want to become. This drive encompasses all aspects of your life, not just work. After all, as the old saying goes, "No one ever died wishing she or he spent more time at work." Balance between work and the rest of your life matters greatly, and much research and advice has been published over the last two decades to show this point to be true. Companies listed on the 100 Best

Places to Work are ample evidence of the increasing attention to and models for effective *work–life balance* that employers can enact.

Realize, too, that often in life you will work to live, and other times you will live to work. Priorities change, and in the public relations profession, you are frequently needed to work beyond the stereotypical 9 a.m. to 5 p.m. workday, extending into weekends. The reason is simple: organizations need to reach out to or serve constituents at various times and days that suit their schedules, and that means you work on those schedules for your organization. By the same token, organizations recognize that healthy, energetic, and thoughtful employees add the most value when they are fully engaged and enthusiastic because there is concern for them on many levels (see Gebauer & Lowman, 2008; Shaffer, 2000).

So how do you know yourself? The best way is through honest self-reflection. That is, think deeply and candidly about who you are, what is important to you, and what you want to achieve in life. Questions like these are instrumental in self-reflection:

- What are your values (personal and professional)?
- What inspires you to want to work in public relations *and why*?
- How may you best continue to grow in professional expertise?
- How may you best improve as a person for yourself and others?
- How do you prefer to work *and why*?
- What work would you like most to do *and why*?
- Where would you like most to work *and why*?
- What would you like most in an employer *and why*?
- What kinds of people would you like to work with *and why*?
- What dislikes about a job would you want to avoid *and why*?
- What dislikes about an employer would you want to avoid *and why*?
- What dislikes about a work environment would you want to avoid *and why*?

Answers to these and other questions you may have will be valuable to you as you come to know yourself better and, especially, plan for your career as realistically as you can at any time in your life. The "why" parts of the questions are most important because they reveal the reasons for your preferences that, in turn, reflect your values. Values are the foundation of each person and the nexus for understanding who someone is. Check to see if your stated values are consistent with your stated and, especially, unstated values in your answers to the other questions.

Your values are instrumental in how you take advantage of the time you have any day. So be mindful of your commitments on and off the job. Plot out all the regular commitments you have each day of the week, including sleep, church, job, family, friends, and so on. Then examine the open time slots you have to see how balanced your life is. Make adjustments where needed. This work will show you how well you seem to use any day to do what you need to do.

Being always organized and mindful is a matter of self-discipline and essential to being successful in what you do. Projects, commitments, tasks, and so on vary in their levels of importance and urgency. Sort them in a daily to-do list so that you do the most important *and* most urgent ones first, then work your way down to those that are less important and less urgent. Categorize importance using numbers (i.e., 1, 2, 3, where 1 is supremely important). Likewise, determine urgency using letters (i.e., A, B, C, where A is supremely urgent). This way you can classify your responsibilities and get them done within the daily time frame you have.

A modified SWOT analysis can be a very useful way to engage in a self-analysis; Figure 11-2 shows an example of how you can address the salient matters in this process. The form in Figure 11-2 breaks up the SWOT items into two tables so that proper focus can be directed to career-life matters. The first half of the form is for brainstorming about your values, strengths, and weaknesses. These three factors, along with your answers to the questions above, are essential for completing the second half of the form, which concerns how you may act on your values, play to your strengths, and reduce or eliminate your weaknesses. The second half of the form focuses you on what you can do to realize your objectives, especially as you consider opportunities and threats/obstacles within a defined timeframe. Answers to the above questions will be most valuable here. Notice how the first objective is in the distant future and works back to the present. You may set objectives as far out into the future as you wish. This form reflects the career path–planning process shown in Figure 11-1. The work you do for Figure 11-2 is the basis for other work you do for your self-analysis, and it will be refined and revised by additional information, as you will see.

At this point the principles of professionalism and ethics covered in Chapter 3 combine more obviously with who you are. You know well what the public relations field's expectations are, and you can now plot the ways in which you meet or need to meet those expectations. Sources like the Council of Public Relations Firm's (2005) guide on PR careers or *PR Week*'s annual *Career Guide* can be helpful here too. Use this understanding to fine-tune your SWOT analysis from Figure 11-2. As you engage in anticipatory organizational socialization with different employers with which you would like to work, you will discover ways in which your perspectives on work and public relations may (or may not) mesh with those organizations. These points of intersection become grounds on which you can and should make decisions to continue to seek employment with an organization or, if given an offer to work, whether you want to truly work for that organization.

Values (Personal & Professional)	Strengths	Weaknesses

Objectives	Opportunities & Action Steps	Completion Date	Potential Threats (Obstacles)
10 years:			
5 years:			
3 years:			
2 years:			
1 year:			
6 months:			

Figure 11-2. A SWOT SELF-ANALYSIS TOOL.

If you have had one or more internships, they have revealed much to you about the "real world" of working in public relations. But those jobs did not reveal everything because of the nature of your position as an intern and, most important, the limitations organizations can have for involving interns in certain things. For example, full-fledged, full-time employees will be most often invited to participate in pivotal policy or other decisions because that is part of their jobs. As an intern you are not expected to participate in many decisions, but you would likely be involved in developing some aspects of them as management sees fit.

Your first full-time job as a public relations professional, then, plays a new role in your career—as your formal entry into the field. You are more involved in more of the technical aspects of the work of PR pros and called upon more in decisions and actions you were not qualified to do as an intern. Any potential employer may ask you what salary you want, and you must have a good answer. A good answer is one that is based on data about very similar jobs, and you can get that data through credible online sources that use valid and reliable research for the profession and can sort the data on salaries based on zip code and city. Searching the Internet for "salary calculators" can reveal numerous providers you should use to determine what the probable salary would be for the kind of job for which you will interview. Also know that you are eligible for benefits as an employee that you would not get as an intern, including, for example, insurance coverage for health, dental, and life; retirement savings; and perhaps employee stock purchases. You should become familiar with these things so you know what choices you should make based on your personal financial situation. In addition to conducting your own research, seeking the advice of a certified financial planner and/or a human resources/labor attorney can be helpful.

Know the field

Having established who you are and what you have to offer through a self-SWOT, you can go deeper. You should understand how well you fulfill the expected competencies of public relations professionals. You should be familiar with these competency areas because of your study of and, perhaps, internships in public relations. To crystalize the range of competencies into a usable and useful framework for career planning purposes, Sha (2011, pp. 189–190) shows there are 12 categories of work performed by (not practice areas of) public relations professionals:

- *Account/Client Management*—key work activities include "establishing client relationships, coaching and counseling clients, managing expectations, etc."
- *Strategic Planning*—key work activities include "conducting research, setting goals, engaging customers and key stakeholders, developing messages for specific audiences, etc."
- *Public Relations Program Planning*—key work activities include "conducting research, identifying key audiences, producing a detailed PR plan, managing marketing communications, creating measurements of effectiveness, leveraging interactive elements of the campaign, etc."
- *Project Management*—key work activities include "creating and managing the budget, assessing resource allocation needs, planning logistics, managing the team, working with vendors, etc."
- *Media Relations*—key work activities include "identifying audiences, training organizational spokespersons to work with media, pitching stories, writing and distributing press releases in traditional and online ways, monitoring media coverage, coordinating publicity, measuring media engagement efforts, etc."
- *Social Media Relations*—key work activities include "utilizing Web-based social networks, developing social media strategies for communications efforts, producing in-house or client blogs, apprising clients on how to use social media . . . channels for communications efforts, SEO [search engine optimization], blogger relations, etc."

- *Stakeholder Relations*—key work activities include "developing strategies and key messages, arranging tours and conferences, forging strategic partnerships, etc." for defined stakeholder groups.
- *Issues Management*—key work activities include "assessing and developing strategies around long-term and business-impacting issues, writing crisis [and issue] management plans, providing strategic counsel to clients or stakeholders, resolving conflicts, etc."
- *Crisis Management*—key work activities include "executing crisis management plans, coordinating release of information via traditional and social media, understanding the varied and different crisis situations that may erupt, training spokespersons, monitoring and analyzing media coverage of company crises, etc."
- *Internal Relations and Employee Communications*—key work activities include "developing action plans, assessing in-house communication needs, developing and producing in-house publications in print and online, developing Web content, managing organizational change, etc."
- *Special Events, Conferences, and Meetings*—key work activities include "developing themes, promoting products and planning roll-outs, coordinating logistics and external promotions, etc."
- *Community Relations*—key work activities include "sponsoring community events, developing corporate giving plans, communicating with different audiences building alliances, community outreach using social media, etc."

Across these 12 work categories, public relations professionals are expected to possess certain knowledge, skills, and abilities (KSAs) in 10 areas that make up the grounds on which professionals are considered competent or not. The process for a public relations professional to earn the PRSA's Accreditation in Public Relations (APR) is based on these KSAs, which are as follows (Sha, 2011, p. 193) and update an earlier KSA breakdown for the APR credential (Siegel, Appelbaum, & Smith, 2000):

- Research, planning, implementation, and evaluation of PR programs
- PR ethics and legal issues
- Application of communication models and theories to PR work projects
- Incorporation of business literacy skills into PR duties
- Management skills and issues
- Crisis communication management
- Media relations
- Use of information technology and new media channels
- Application of historical knowledge of the field of PR to work projects
- Use of advanced communication skills

You may assess your level of competence in the 12 work categories and the 10 KSAs by rating yourself on a five-point scale, with 5 being the highest level of competence. Figure 11-3 shows a way you may arrange the work categories and KSAs so that you may perform a self-assessment of your level of competence in each area. Understand that a rating of 5 would equate to that of a highly seasoned professional with many years of experience. The analysis of the PR field in Chapter 2 would give you background on how to employ the rating scale. And be honest with yourself! If you have only held a couple of internships and been studying public relations in a PR program, you will likely have many more areas that rate low (say 1 or 2) than other areas, and that is okay. Such ratings show you where you need to focus or, perhaps more to your career path planning, where you would rather focus to realize your career vision. As you go down your career path, you must look for opportunities to acquire the experience, knowledge, skills, and abilities that will make you a better and better PR professional. Use this self-assessment tool periodically in your career to find out how you have grown, and perhaps have your bosses and mentors fill it out for you. Notice also that it is not enough to merely rate yourself, but you must make the ratings meaningful by translating your present level of competence into actionable items for self-improvement in your SWOT analysis. If you want to make this tool more potent, ask a boss or mentor to rate you and discuss your professionalism and competence in PR.

During your journey down your career-life path, you will need to keep track of what you did, when, and how. You will always be in the position of having to prove your value to your current and future employers. Keep track of the *value* you have given every employer in the roles you held, not just the duties you fulfilled in every job. This approach goes beyond a mere list of things you did on typical resumes. You must track your *results* for your work. For example, you may have written press releases, but what were the outcomes in terms of media coverage, knowledge growth, attitude change, or behaviors sought among target publics? Your resume is the primary document you will need to chronicle your work and other relevant experiences and, especially, results during your career. You also must have good, clean examples of the work you produced during your career. These examples go into your portfolio. Creating printed and electronic versions of your resume and portfolio can be very helpful, as you may share your stuff with people in the best ways to meet their needs. Also be ready to prepare cover letters in either printed or electronic form. Appendix D concisely gives you some tips about resumes, cover letters, and beyond for the job search.

Frame your employment record (on paper and in person) like a case study. Show your results as evidence about why you are the best and worth hiring above anyone else because of the high value you provide for companies. At every step of the way, you are advancing an argument that follows this pattern:

Work Categories	Personal Rating					SWOT Relationships
	No/Little Background				*Much Background*	
Account/Client Management	1	2	3	4	5	
Strategic Planning	1	2	3	4	5	
Public Relations Program Planning	1	2	3	4	5	
Project Management	1	2	3	4	5	
Media Relations	1	2	3	4	5	
Social Media Relations	1	2	3	4	5	
Stakeholder Relations	1	2	3	4	5	
Issues Management	1	2	3	4	5	
Crisis Management	1	2	3	4	5	
Internal Relations & Employee Communications	1	2	3	4	5	
Special Events, Conferences, & Meetings	1	2	3	4	5	
Community Relations	1	2	3	4	5	
KSAs						
Research, planning, implementation, and evaluation of PR programs	1	2	3	4	5	
PR ethics and legal issues	1	2	3	4	5	
Application of communication models and theories to PR work projects	1	2	3	4	5	
Incorporation of business literacy skills into PR duties	1	2	3	4	5	
Management skills and issues	1	2	3	4	5	
Crisis communication management	1	2	3	4	5	
Media relations	1	2	3	4	5	
Use of information technology and new media channels	1	2	3	4	5	
Application of historical knowledge of the field of PR to work project	1	2	3	4	5	
Use of advanced communication skills	1	2	3	4	5	

Figure 11-3. SELF-ASSESSMENT TOOL FOR RATING ONE'S COMPETENCE IN PR WORK CATEGORIES AND KSAs.

- *Claim:* I have the "right stuff" for this job and should be interviewed. Ultimately you should hire me.
- *Evidence:* Relevant prior experience, strong results from all work done, appropriate education, awards and other applicable recognition, and strong references.
- *Reasoning:* I fulfill the requirements stated in the job posting and known in field-specific expectations for public relations professionals for this type of job.

This approach is based on Toulmin's (1958) model of argument. Most important, this approach should guide you well throughout your campaign (yes, like a good PR campaign) to obtain not only your first full-time job, but also all other jobs that come your way to advance in your career. The sophistication of your argument will necessarily change over the years as the kinds of jobs and levels of responsibility and authority change/enlarge. In addition to your resume, you should also collect work samples, especially programs (all steps), to show what you have worked on and be able to tell the stories behind the work you did and the overall programs. Throughout your written and oral discourse during your job hunt, focus on the key message platform about your career accomplishments and aspirations—based on your vision and career strategy. (This key message platform is very useful in cover letters and job interviews, too.) Again, Appendix D gives you concise information about the portfolio and other aspects of your job search documentation. In a very real way you are, in tune with the concept of positioning in Chapter 7, establishing and promoting yourself as a brand—"brand YOU" (see Kaputa, 2012). At any time, you are the only person who controls your career trajectory, even in the face of people who may influence your career (for better and for worse). So you must own your career and manage it and yourself well.

Think about your job search like a cold-calling effort. Your overall objective in applying for a job is, of course, to get the job; however, that result will not happen solely from someone seeing your resume and cover letter. So the immediate objective in applying for a job is to get an interview. The immediate objective of an interview is to get a job offer or, at least, another interview. In your cover letter and resume, you must present yourself on paper (or on screen for online applications) as effectively, accurately, and completely as possible, given page-length and other constraints that may be stated in a job posting. In an interview, you must present yourself similarly but now in person. The "tangibles" of a strong background that fits the job is expected, but the "intangibles" of who you are highly scrutinized. From a hiring manager's perspective, she or he will scrutinize you for your attitude, drive, enthusiasm, trainability, fit with the organization's culture, politeness/courteousness, ways of thinking, and ways of expressing yourself. Your manner of communication and personal demeanor with anyone you meet will be noted. The quality of the questions you ask will matter greatly also. To come up with good questions, assume you were hired and ask what would be expected in certain circumstances. Remember, too, that at the same time you are being interviewed, you are interviewing the organization on similar grounds for yourself.

Own Your Career

Only you can truly make the career you want. Other people and circumstances (some of which you control and many you cannot) will have various levels of influence (positive, negative, and neutral) on your career trajectory toward your vision of what you want to be and achieve. You should make or find opportunities for career growth. Keep your eyes and ears open for opportunities to get the experience, knowledge, skills, and abilities you need to grow and succeed. New and different job assignments can do that. Additional education and training in new and different areas can help as well. In all these ways you will meet more people in the public relations profession who may be able and willing to help you. Building your network of people in and connected with the public relations industry can serve you well in developing yourself and moving down your career path as you want to. As you rise into the management ranks, part of your network may eventually include recruiters, especially people who work in executive search firms. These folks can be very helpful in refining your argument for your employability and expertise at higher levels of leadership and in different industries, such as consumer goods, transportation, health and medical, and any other industry.

One particularly valuable component of your network is mentors. As we covered in Chapter 5, mentors are at a unique place in their careers where they enjoy helping up-and-coming professionals to advance in their careers. Mentors can provide the kind of highly valuable insight about professionalism, career management, and organizational idiosyncrasies that few others can. Most important, a trusted mentor can provide you with a level of candor and advice about and for you that can make you a better person and professional. This kind of relationship assumes there is a great deal of mutual respect and openness between mentor and mentee. Such a relationship does not occur immediately and must be cultivated genuinely and honestly between people. Phoniness and selfishness are easy to spot and big turn-offs to would-be mentors. You may find your own mentor or ask for one to be recommended to you. A mentor need not be someone with whom you work but, rather, may be someone who works in another organization and is willing and available to help you at different times. Once you find someone whom you believe is a good mentor for you, genuinely get to know that person and let that person get to know you on personal and professional terms. Meeting for lunch once in a while, chatting after work, asking for advice on a challenging project, working together in a chapter of a professional organization, or going to a conference or seminar together are easy examples of ways to build a mentor–mentee relationship.

Something that you will experience and may want a mentor's advice about is career change. Whether you feel the need to quit a job for another job, have been offered a new job in the same or another organization, are laid off, or have new life pressures that require you to completely rethink your career vision, it is important to recognize when it is time for change. In every case, the intellectual and the emotional sides of career change matter, and one of these—usually the emotions— will appear to rule your thinking. A knee-jerk response is all too often *not* the best response. Instead, take stock of your feelings and your reasons for change. Examine the pros and the cons for change as honestly and as completely as possible. Share your findings, thoughts, and conclusions with a mentor and other important people in your life, especially family and trusted friends or peers.

Career change cautions

Once you have a job, whether you love it and your employer or not (or somewhere in between), there is never anything wrong with looking periodically at the job market for what is going on there. Let's face it: We are curious creatures, and it is somehow comforting to find out that our careers are on the right tracks for us. And if our careers are not on track, we can seek new paths with new employers or other (perhaps entrepreneurial) opportunities.

Remember, though, your employer may not share this enlightened attitude. Your employer made an investment in hiring you and expects you to perform well in every way for the organization. There are many stories of people (and one friend of mine) who lost a job because companies monitor employees' communications. And companies may use that information to dismiss employees for seeking—not necessarily accepting—another job with another employer. The seeking of other jobs includes making phone calls, meeting with people, and sending e-mail. The basic logic is, "You are looking for a job, and that must mean you do not like it here, so you can be on your way right now to do the job searching you seem you would rather like to do." (Looking for jobs within your employer's organization is an exception.)

Is this monitoring of employees' communications legal? Yes. You are working on "company time" with company resources, and your employer has every right to make sure you're doing your job effectively and properly with the resources it gives you to do that job. Your personal privacy is not a company concern when you are "on the clock" and using company resources. You probably signed a contract or other employment agreement that touches on your conduct. And remember that the personnel handbook for your company is loaded with policies you are expected to know and live by.

Because you work for an organization, your behavior "off the clock" also matters to your employer (and your career). People know for whom you work. Just think of Michael Vick and how his direct involvement in dog fighting got him in trouble with his employer, the Philadelphia Eagles and National Football League. His is an extreme case to be sure, but it is illustrative nonetheless. Your conduct outside of the office also should be addressed in the personnel handbook. Even if you do not have an employment contract/agreement, there is ample case law that that could be used to back up your employer's arguments about its decision to dismiss any employee for misconduct on/off the clock (including searching for other jobs) according to company policies and expectations for employees. Your behavior at events that are directly pertinent to your job, such as dinners, award ceremonies, parties, etc., all require you to behave well as a person and, especially, as a professional representing an organization.

If there is no stated policy or expectation about your making contacts for other employment, you could ask someone in HR to clarify this matter. But that approach could be risky because it may suggest that you are already on the hunt, even if you are just curious about the job market. It would be prudent, too, for you to seek advice from seasoned professionals in your local PR industry who also have intimate knowledge about personnel rules and expectations. And remember, the network among PR professionals is wide, and news of job openings and job seekers can travel fast, which can be good or bad, depending on who learns about your ambitions.

It is important to remember that you have the right to seek a better living and career to enable you to have the life you want. Your employer cannot take that away. (A kind of exception is employment with direct competitors, which may be covered in an employment contract/agreement, especially for high-ranking employees. Case law can be applied here too.) But your employer can say that certain activities, such as job searching, are out of bounds when you are on the job. (Again, seeking a new job within your employer is an exception.) Remember that the importance of company policies and expectations presented in the employee handbook is very high.

Based on this knowledge, here are five basic, vital, and ethical steps for you to take to manage your conduct as an employee and a person looking around the corner for your next big gig.

1. Make sure you know, understand, and have on your desk/bookshelf a complete and updated copy of your employer's personnel policies or employee handbook.

2. Review your employment contract/agreement, if you signed one, to relearn what you agreed to. See an attorney if you have questions. (Ideally, you could see an attorney before you sign such a contract/agreement.)

3. Never use your employer's computing system to do any kind of job searching on the Internet or by e-mail. Your employer can still trace your activity—especially your e-mail activity on your noncompany e-mail accounts because you are using your employer's server to access it.

4. Never place phone calls from your desk phone at work to inquire about jobs. And if you have a company-issued cell phone, never take or place calls or text messages about job possibilities. Phone bills show all calls and are a record of your phone activity. Using a company-issued smartphone to do any job searching tasks also can be tracked, so do not do that either.

5. Always do your job searching off company time and off company resources, including your company's wireless network (if equipped). Make phone calls on your personal cell phone off your employer's campus or on your home phone. Access the Internet and your e-mail at home or somewhere else, like the public library or a friend's home. (Lunch time technically does not count either, because your company is legally obliged to allow you that period and, therefore, you are still on company time. But it still may be a useful time for you to use your personal cell phone to make calls away from the office campus.)

Remember that it is important to sustain your employment and be successful at any employer for a "significant and reasonable" amount of time. I say it this way because there is no precise amount of employment time that is standard. But it is important to show future employers that you have staying power, get solid results, and do not skip around from job to job over short periods of time with little or no reason. So before you take any job, make sure any company that offered you a job meets all your criteria for a good, strong, and valuable employer that suits your career vision.

Leaving an employer

If and when you leave any employer for another one, make sure you do not "burn any bridges." Stay on good terms as much as possible because you want your last impressions to be amicable. Be professional and courteous during an exit interview, if you have one (see Chapter 5). Plus you will likely need your previous employer to confirm your employment there, and, if permissible under corporate policy, people there may be willing to be references for you. Always be honest, sensible, and diplomatic with anyone about your experiences and your feelings about pervious and present employers. If you "bad-mouth" any previous employer, people wonder what you will say about your current one.

If you decide to quit a job for any reason, including personal reasons like being a stay-at-home parent or wanting to become a sole practitioner (e.g., freelancer or consultant), you may do so at any time. Organizations generally have an "employment at will" agreement with their employees, which means that either the employer or the employee may terminate employment at any time with sufficient cause and notice. If you are caught in a moral, ethical, or legal dilemma you believe to be problematic, have tried to remedy it, and have been unsuccessful, your only recourse may be to quit. If you have found a new career opportunity at another organization, you should make sure you give your present employer suitable notice of your decision to quit and move to another organization. Joining a competitor may get you moved out of the company the same day (even the same moment) you announce your decision, and you must also be aware of and abide by certain legal obligations you have with your employer that may prohibit you from getting a job at a competitor. If you are laid off, as explained in Chapter 5, you have more freedom to work where you wish, even competitors, because your employer made the decision about your employment, not you. You would also be entitled to certain benefits for having been laid off, such as severance pay and job search help.

Because any of these circumstances (and others) that lead to a career change are possible, you should always make sure your resume and portfolio are up to date. An updated resume and portfolio will serve you well if you take on any work as a sole practitioner so that you can showcase yourself and your expertise. You can examine the job market for fun or for profit—just make sure it is in line with your career vision and *not* in conflict with any employer's policies and expectations.

Final Points

As you look upon yourself for who you are now and who you want to be and what you want to achieve over time, you should realize it is a dynamic process. You are always involved in making sure you are doing the right things in the right ways at the right times for the right reasons for yourself and others. Embedded in this dynamism are two, final topics you must not take for granted: impression management and leisure.

Impression management

First impressions are very important, and they can be difficult to change in people's minds. Remember that how you present yourself in any way—in person, in writing, on the phone, online—all contributes to people's impressions of you. People can spot phony people immediately, so genuine interest, energy, friendliness, curiosity, and so on are vital and expected. Be a Good person doing well in everything you do (see Chapter 3). Be mindful of how you present yourself in any way at any time. As Chapter 5 indicated, hiring decisions include background searches on people who are strong candidates for a job. The Internet (especially Google) has made conducting such searches easy and economical.

From traffic tickets to credit scores and from Facebook pages to Twitter tweets, how you say who you are and how you portray yourself can help you or hurt you. As Conlin (2006) shows most dramatically, "You are what you post." He explains:

> Google is an end run around discrimination laws, inasmuch as employers can find out all manner of information—some of it for a nominal fee—that is legally off limits in interviews: your age, your marital status, the value of your house (along with an aerial photograph of it), the average new worth of your neighborhood, fraternity pranks, stuff you wrote in college, leins, bankruptcies, political affiliations, and the names and ages of your children. (pp. 52–53)

Conlin's report is indeed sobering. Plus, recent studies reported by Johnson (2012) show the increasing frequency with which organizations screen social media before and after employing people. At the very least, as Johnson (2012) reports, organizations should screen job applicants' social media only after getting their permission to do so, should not create fake accounts on social media sites to gain access to users' posts, and should allow applicants to explain or defend problematic information about them on social media sites.

In the bigger picture of this topic, the U.S. National Labor Relations Board (NLRB) has issued three reports (2011, 2012a, 2012b) about multiple cases of employer use of social media in employment matters. The NLRB is focused on protecting employees' rights, whether they are unionized or not. In all cases about social media use, the matters revolve around issues of protected/unprotected speech under the First Amendment. In these reports the NLRB found some employer policies about employees' social media use unlawful but others lawful. In two particular rulings about firing employees for their social media use, the NLRB found the employers' dismissals (one at a car dealership and the other at a nonprofit) unlawful because the employees' use of social media qualified as protected speech (NLRB, n.d.). One important point to take away about social media use is that both employers and employees have rights; however, the evolution of law to protect those rights has been slow to keep up with the frenetic pace of technology advances and people's use of those technologies.

On balance, because of poor impression management of yourself online, given the climate of what is legally permissible, you can put your personal and professional reputation at risk as long as you post words and images that undermine yourself or others, including your employer or client. Remember that the First Amendment does not mean that anything goes, because there are protections for some forms of speech and no protections for others—know the limitations. Plus, just because you can say something does not mean you should say anything. If you frequently post negative messages on social media about anything, you effectively portray yourself as a negative person. Also remember, your friends (and their friends) may be posting stuff about you (accurate or not) without your knowledge and consent, and that may work against you as well. The example of Olympic gold medalist Michael Phelps shows the damage to one's personal reputation that can result from poor choices, after a video of him smoking marijuana ran rampant through social media and the news media covered it. In short, guard your reputation at all times. New tools for monitoring your online image can help.

Although it is understood that you, yourself cannot police and correct all content about you that appears on the Internet (data placed on the Internet is there forever and findable with search technologies), it is understood that you and only you have responsibility for yourself. In tune with the material in Chapter 3, always be the best person you can be anywhere at any time, have fun when you can, and be mindful of the fact that what you say or do reveals who you are and what your values are. The deep self-reflection about yourself through Figure 11-2 can help keep you focused. Know yourself!

Leisure

An important topic that is often overlooked is leisure. The value of leisure is very high, and that is why people look so fondly toward the weekend. But realize, too, that weekends alone are not usually enough. Too often people see that *only* large blocks of time off from work is what is needed to recharge and revitalize. To be sure, any number days off from work does wonders for the mind, heart, and soul. Let us not forget about integrating a bit of leisure during the course of a busy day.

During any day at work you need to relax and release your mind and body from the stresses you have endured, no matter how great or small the stresses have been. Short, frequent breaks that divert your attention to other things, especially restful things, give your mind and body the opportunity to refresh. Truly, how often have you gotten up to get a drink or go to the washroom or take a short walk and been struck by a new idea? It has very probably been a lot more often than you may want or are able to remember. The simple change in focus has released your mind to think differently and freely and, thereby, released a kind of creativity you needed.

As the old saying goes, "Do what you love. Love what you do." Highly effective people in their lives and careers have certain common habits, and Steven Covey (1989, 2004) is well known for explaining those eight habits: be proactive, begin with the end in mind, put first things first, think win/win, seek first to understand then to be understood, synergize, sharpen the saw, and find your voice and inspire

EXECUTIVE VIEWPOINT

Personal Qualities for Career Success in the Digital Age

Bill Heyman, President and CEO of Heyman Associates

As you start to build your communications career in today's digital world, the best way to increase your chance of success is to develop your interpersonal skills. People want to hire, and promote, qualified people they like. Your ability to relate to others in person will help your job prospects and professional growth for years to come. While your technical expertise will get you the interview, your personal qualities will land you the job.

Digital understanding is, of course, still a crucial foundation for your technical skill set. As a professional communicator, you will need to be able to manage the constant volume, velocity, and variety of information in social and digital media. There are many free news aggregator services that let you create a personalized dashboard of information you find important. In addition, you must develop an understanding of how to use social and digital media to impact an institution's bottom line. To become a communications "leader," you will need to connect your communications programs to the overall business strategy of your organization.

What will set you apart from other qualified candidates and your colleagues, however, are interpersonal skills, or "intangible" qualities. These "soft skills" are the unique ways you handle yourself and relate to others that can create a favorable impression on a hiring manager. Intangibles are your people skills, presentation ability, ethical orientation, and sense of courage. Intangibles are what make you, you. You can't fake them and you shouldn't want to try. The goal is not to be perfect; the goal is to be genuine. Real is likable. Connect your job search and career path to your passion; you will feel freer to be yourself. Find environments, industries, companies, and job titles that match your interests. Show your energy and enthusiasm for the position you want. Volunteer within your organization for projects that interest you, regardless of your role. Take on challenging work.

Even though you cannot feign interpersonal skills, you can improve upon your presentation of them. Take a public speaking or business writing course. Read as much as possible to become knowledgeable about and well spoken in current events and other topics of relevance to your career. Expand your perspective by subscribing to publications that are outside of your comfort zone. Take on leadership positions whenever possible. Network all the time, not just when you need a job; you will not only develop your interpersonal skills, you will also make and maintain connections for your own career and help others who may one day return the favor.

You can also hone the presentation of your intangibles as you get ready for an interview. Do your homework. Preparation will enable you to comfortably demonstrate your professionalism, enthusiasm, and likeability. Anticipate the interviewer's questions and practice your answers. The interviewer might ask about your strengths and weaknesses; do a self-assessment before the interview and have examples ready. The interviewer might ask what you know about the company; study the organization's website and look for its mention in the news. The interviewer might ask how you stay current on what is happening in business, politics, and the world at large or what was the last book you read; plan your response. Prepare at least one question for the interviewer to answer in order to show your interest in the job. You might ask why the position is available, what the interviewer likes most about the company, or what a typical day is for your potential role. Do a mock interview with a friend or your school's career center in the exact outfit you plan to wear on the real interview. Also be aware of your body language; poor eye contact or a weak handshake can end an interview before it starts.

Remember that the interview is not over when it's over; intangibles still apply in the moments, days, and possibly weeks after. If you feel strongly about your fit for the position, say so. In a group of equally qualified candidates, the person who receives the offer is often the only one who said, "I want the job." Send personalized, well-written, and prompt thank-you notes to each person who interviewed you. If the potential employer needs more time to interview other candidates and/or make a decision, follow up politely. If the company offers you an entry-level position you want, accept graciously without too much concern over the salary. Get started on your career and prove yourself for promotions in the future. The money will come.

While you focus on your interpersonal skills, remember that your digital brand appears 24 hours a day, seven days a week and can have consequences on your real life/career. Maintain responsible and professional social media accounts. Assume a potential or current employer will see everything you post. I know of one situation in which someone who was about to start a new job tweeted that she was going to like the salary but hate the work; the company rescinded the offer after it saw her post.

In your communications career, qualify yourself with your technical skills, but differentiate yourself with your personality. Become a lifelong learner not only of the ever-changing digital technology but also of the ever-changing you. Constantly improve upon your interpersonal skills to let your passion come through in a genuine, professional, and likable way. For further reading, I recommend Susan Cain's book, *Quiet: The Power of Introverts in a World That Can't Stop Talking*; Jonathan Safran Foer's article, "How Not to Be Alone," in *The New York Times*, June 8, 2013; Malcolm Gladwell's books, *The Tipping Point: How Little Things Can Make a Big Difference* and *Outliers: The Story of Success*; Adam Grant's book, *Give and Take*; and Edie Weiner and Arnold Brown's book, *Future-Think: How to Think Clearly in a Time of Change*, to get started on your career as a successful communicator with excellent intangibles.

others to find theirs. This book about public relations management has addressed these habits in various ways, although not systematically. Of the eight habits, sharpening the saw is especially potent and important to the journey down your career-life path toward a position of leadership and management in public relations.

You need to continuously improve yourself in ways that matter, and that includes taking time to relax, recharge, revitalize, and renew yourself in mind, body, and spirit. Yes, matters of work–life balance are included, but so are matters of education, skills, and motivation to be and to do the best you can plus to be and to do better than you ever have. The better you become as a person and as a professional, the more you help make public relations the valuable and valued organizational function that can truly inspire cooperation between organizations and their publics.

Key Words

Career path	*Portfolio*
Milestones	*Career trajectory*
Personal values	*Mentor*
Career self-analysis	*Mentee*
Competencies	*Employment at will*
Twelve PR work categories	*Benefits*
Ten KSAs for PR	*Leisure*
Cover letter	*Work–life balance*
Resume	

Exploration of Career Planning

1. Look back at Chapter 3 and think about how ethics, law, and professionalism will play out in your career. What things may arise to tempt you from being the good professional and good person you can and should be? What would you do to ensure temptations do not compromise your reputation and character?

2. Look up the most recent list of the 100 Best Places to Work and identify the top 10 things in common that they do to help employees balance their work and personal lives. How might public relations leaders be involved in helping an organization to improve its approach to work–life balance for employees? Remember to think beyond merely communicating about the

existence of or need for work–life balance. How can PR be a force for change for the better in this issue?

3. Use Figures 11-2 and 11-3 plus the explanations around them to complete a self-assessment that can serve you well in your career planning and, especially, your job search. How would you convey your skillfulness as a technician and your basic familiarity with the management side of public relations?

4. Examine your personal network of PR pros, friends, and family. Identify those people who most likely can help you in your career at this stage in your life. In what ways might you expand your network? Who would you like to add to your network, either by name or by experience/expertise in the field?

5. Examine Covey's eight habits of highly effective people in more depth and translate them into eight habits of highly effective public relations professionals. Explain sufficiently what each habit is and how it is characterized by one's knowledge, attitude, behaviors, and results from working well and working hard in public relations. How would these habits work for you in your career planning?

6. Review your social media content on Facebook, YouTube, LinkedIn.com, Twitter, or other channels. Putting yourself in the position of a hiring manager, what do you see about who you are? How would your online presence help or hurt your job search and career? What would you change and why?

References

Council of Public Relations Firms (2005). *Careers in public relations: A guide to opportunities in a dynamic industry*. New York: Author.

Conlin, M. (2006, March 27). You are what you post: Bosses are using Google to peer into places job interviews can't take them. *BusinessWeek*, 52–53.

Covey, S. (1989). *The 7 habits of highly effective people: Powerful lessons in personal change*. New York: Fireside/Simon & Schuster.

Covey, S. (2004). *The 8th habit: From effectiveness to greatness*. New York: Fireside/Simon & Schuster.

Gebauer, J., Lowman, D., & Gordon, J. (2008). *Closing the engagement gap: How great companies unlock employee potential for superior results*. New York: Portfolio/Penguin Group.

Johnson, S. (2012, January 22). Those Facebook posts could cost you a job. *The Pantagraph*, C1, C2.

Kaputa, C. (2012). *You are a brand! In person and online, how smart people brand themselves for business success*. Boston: Nicholas Brealey Publishing.

National Labor Relations Board. (2011). *Employees' Facebook postings about job performance and staffing were protected concerted activity* (Memorandum OM 11–74). Washington, DC: Author.

National Labor Relations Board. (2012a). *Discharge for Facebook comments and for violation of non-disparagement rule was unlawful* (Memorandum OM 12–31). Washington, DC: Author.

National Labor Relations Board. (2012b). *Rules on using social media technology and on communicating confidential information are overbroad* (Memorandum OM 12–59). Washington, DC: Author.

National Labor Relations Board (n.d.). *The NLRB and social media*. Retrieved from http://www.nlrb.gov/node/5078.

Sha, B-L. (2011). 2010 practice analysis: Professional competencies and work categories in public relations today. *Public Relations Review, 37*, pp. 187–196.

Siegel, G., Appelbaum, L., & Smith, V. (2000). *APR practice analysis of the public relations profession: A research project of the Universal Accreditation Board*. New York: Universal Accreditation Board. Available online: http://www.praccreditation.org/Practice%20Analysis.html.

Shaffer, J. C. (2000). *The leadership solution*. New York: McGraw-Hill.

Toulmin, S. E. (1958). *The uses of argument*. New York: Cambridge University Press.

Recommended Reading

Berger, B. K., & Reber, B. H. (2006). *Gaining influence in public relations: The role of resistance in practice*. Mahwah, NJ: Lawrence Erlbaum Associates.

Boldt., L. G. (1996). *How to find the work you love*. New York: Penguin.

Boldt, L. G. (1999). *Zen and the art of making a living*, expanded and updated. New York: Penguin.

Bridges, W. (1994). *JobShift: How to prosper in a workplace without jobs*. Reading, MA: Perseus Books.

Bridges, W. (1997). *Creating you and co.: Learning to think like the CEO of your own career*. Reading, MA: Perseus Books.

Coombs, W. T., & Holladay, S. J. (2013). *It's not just PR: Public relations in society* (2nd ed.). Malden, MA: Blackwell Publishing.

Edwards, L., & Hodges, C. E. M. (2011). *Public relations, society and culture: Theoretical and empirical explorations*. New York: Routledge.

Hansen-Horn, T. L., & Neff, B. D. (Eds.). (2008). *Public relations: From theory to practice*. Boston: Pearson.

Moss, D., & DeSanto, B. (2011). *Public relations: A managerial perspective*. Thousand Oaks, CA: Sage.

Public Relations Society of America. (2013). *PRSA job center*. Available online: http://www.prsa.org/jobcenter/career_resources/.

Tymorek, S. (2010). *Ferguson career launcher: Advertising and public relations*. New York: Checkmark Books.

TEMPLATE FOR STRATEGIC PLANS
WITH DEFINITIONS AND EXAMPLES

This appendix, which largely supplements Chapter 4, is organized to mimic the organization of an actual strategic plan, an example of which can be found in Appendix B. You may use the organization of this appendix for your own strategic plan, making sure you (1) read the explanations and examples in each section and then (2) use those explanations to write your own text that works specifically for your own client's purposes. Also create a nice cover page that names the client and labels the document as a strategic plan for a defined period of time.

Table of Contents

Executive Summary

This section places the entire plan in context and, most important, very concisely summarizes the plan's content by focusing on the problem, the recommended solution, and anticipated results within a specific timeframe. Write it only after the final revisions to the rest of the document are made.

1.0 Organization Background

This section covers necessary information about what an organization is, why it exists, how long it's been in operation, where it operates, and so on.

1.1 Business Definition

This section concisely and concretely states what the business is for your organization. The content in this section essentially states the obvious about what an organization does or offers to customers, and it provides the basic context for the following sections that go into greater detail that are necessary to understanding your organization.

1.2 Vision

Concisely state the long-term, ideal, *future* state for the organization.

1.3 Mission

Concisely state the immediate reason why an organization exists *today* and how it does its business on a daily basis.

1.4 Value Proposition

The analysis of the situation and audiences yields the basis for a statement about the unique value an organization offers to customers. This statement is called a "value proposition," and it is a concise outline about what truly differentiates an organization from any other with which it may compete. The value proposition is key to an organization's market positioning, which would be addressed in section 2.3. A value proposition can be constructed simply as a two-part statement:

1. Theme/Slogan/Thesis—the one, supremely important thing that makes an organization uniquely different and, therefore, valuable for others. This statement asserts why people should rely on an organization or risk failure.

2. Proof points—the handful of individual statements of evidence that directly support why the theme/slogan/thesis is true and compelling. These proof points can include statements of advantages or benefits to people for having experienced the organization in any way through products, services, or other opportunities.

A value proposition functions also as a universal "key message platform" (KMP) for any and all communication an organization may create and share. Individual KMPs would be developed for individual programs and projects, but they must be able to reflect back on the points in the value proposition as a matter of message consistency. The idea is that such a platform helps corporate officials "stay on message" and helps audiences remember the key "takeaways" even if they forget everything else.

- How can the messages best be crafted to establish identification between target audiences and the organization?
- Will the messages work to achieve the plan's objectives?
- Are the messages designed to inform or change attitudes and behaviors?
- Are the organization's expectations realistic?

The key messages should ethically and sufficiently enact the drama about the scene, act, actors involved, means for doing the acts, and reasons for doing them within its situational context. A successful key message platform is one that inspires publics to cooperate with the organization because they identify with the drama the organization enacts in its discourse.

1.5 Organization Structure

This section explains how your organization is organized between upper management and lower-level members. This section should also show how your organization is structured along hierarchal lines by using an organizational chart of some kind. Additionally, the basic job descriptions for management-level positions should be given so that readers know at a glance who does what and for whom in the organization. More detailed information about all positions on the chart may be included in an appendix, such as the section of a bylaws document that defines roles and responsibilities of officers.

1.6 History and Culture

This section summarizes how the organization came into being and what important milestone achievements or events matter to understanding why the organization remains and will remain in operation over the foreseeable future. It also addresses the things that define organizational culture (i.e., beliefs, attitudes, values, and ways of thinking/seeing the world). Note that organizational leaders have responsibility for the maintenance of organizational culture.

2.0 Situation Analysis

What is the state of the business that needs changing? What change is needed? Why? What is the company in danger of losing, what has it already lost, or what could it stand to gain but cannot? Thorough description of the state of the environment the organization faces, internally and/or externally. Can be the substance of the problem-solving process for business cases. Use the steps in that process instead of or in addition to the subsections below. Also address this section's important value to the client and this document.

2.1 Definition and Scope of Situation

This section is simply a narrative that explains in sufficient detail what the situation is that your organization faces and how extensive it is. Any relevant factors about the situation can and should be addressed. This section may need to be lengthy or not, as it depends on many variables that are necessary to document in order to create an effective plan. Depending on the quantity of topics and the depth of content required, this section may need to be organized into subsections to make using the content as easy as possible when referencing particular points about the situation. This section is instrumental in identifying data for the SWOT analysis other approach used in section 2.4.

2.2 Stakeholders Affected

Stakeholders are people on whom an organization's success or failure depends. Publics are people with any amount of reasonable interest but not necessarily a vested interest in the organization. If it helps, think of external and internal publics or audiences that *truly* matter to your client's success/failure, not just anybody. In this section you must explain why each stakeholder matters to the client. Information and analysis here should be considered for the SWOT or other analysis.

2.3 Competition

This section not only lists competitors, which is only half the battle, it also explains how each competitor challenges your organization—which ones are very strong, strong, and weak (or some kind of rating)—and what this all means. Going through this simple analysis reveals great insights about the position your organization has against all others with which it competes.

In this section (or even a separate section), matters about market positioning are crucial to present and analyze in sufficient detail. Building business with present, past, and potential customers is also an important matter, because it concerns how the organization can obtain more market share from competitors, especially by leaning on its value proposition. In all these ways, this section suggests additional material that is important in the SWOT analysis.

2.4 SWOT Analysis (or other environmental scanning method)

This part of this situation analysis section is introspective because it is the place where you candidly, concisely, and concretely present your organization's strengths, weaknesses, opportunities, and threats to success. All the previous work in this and the first section would have revealed what your organization is good at, what your organization must rectify, how your organization can capitalize on its strengths and minimize or eliminate its weaknesses, and what barriers may emerge that are either within or beyond its control that can adversely affect success.

Using a table format, like the one below, is an effective way to document the findings for your SWOT analysis. Working across each row, (1) identify all the strengths, weaknesses, opportunities, and threats you can; (2) define what each item in each SWOT row means to the organization, and (3) identify possible ways to play to a strength, mitigate a weakness, leverage an opportunity, or defuse a threat.

	ITEMS	*IMPLICATIONS*	*POSSIBLE ACTIONS*
STRENGTHS			
WEAKNESSES			
OPPORTUNITIES			
THREATS			

3.0 Plan

This introduction should explain that this section is the culmination of the document, because this section provides the guidance about how to make the organization better. The specific things that the organization must do this fiscal year to get it closer to realizing its vision are specified and defined in this section. Use this paragraph to adequately foreground the substance of the following subsections. (See Appendix B for an efficient way to lay out objectives, strategies, and tactics for easy reading and understanding.)

3.1 Objectives

The SWOT analysis (or other environmental scanning method) is key to the development of this section. The other preceding parts of this document also should give rise to the content of this final section. Objectives for your plan are statements about the big-picture accomplishments sought, which translate into plan's value within the situational context for your organization. Specific objectives are more meaningful than general ones. Objectives guide all measurements of success, including KPIs (section 3.5) and final, overall evaluation (section 3.8). Compare all final measurements to the benchmarks. Proper objectives include only one *effect* that is sought, a *goal* for the measurable amount of that effect, an *audience*, and a *deadline*. Here are some examples:

- Increase customer awareness about UltraExtreme Diapers by 27% by November 1, 2014. (Benchmark: 52% customer awareness in 2013)
- Establish 7% market share growth in the enterprise software segment by December 31, 2015. (Benchmark: 6% market share in 2012)
- Roll out new, more effective production-management system by the end of the third quarter. (Benchmark: previous quarter's and historic trend of system efficiency)

Note in these objectives that the *goal* is included. This approach is much more effective for readability and understanding because all four elements—effect, goal, audience, and deadline (EGAD)—are in a single statement. An alternative approach some organizations use is to separate goals from objectives. If you use this "unified" approach to writing objectives, no separate section about goals is needed.

Also note that in each objective a *benchmark* is given. Because any objective must focus on one and only one effect, a benchmark is essential as a way to provide a point of comparison—to give a clear context about why a goal is meaningful. Without a benchmark, there is no context and, therefore, no way to know if a goal is either reasonable or successful.

Any objective seeking more than one effect (e.g., "Increase awareness and sales of product X by year's end") is ineffective and must be broken into multiple objectives—one for each effect and following the EGAD formula plus a benchmark for each.

3.2 Strategies

Strategies are categories of tactics. Each strategy must be directly linked to the objective(s) it supports. The rationales for strategies must be evident in the SWOT analysis and, possibly, other parts of section 2.0. Strategy statements systematize tactics toward one or more objectives. The strategy section, then, outlines conceptually how the plan's objectives will be achieved by establishing categories for tactical actions. Strategies may be broad or narrow in scope, depending on the objectives and the target audiences. The most effective strategies are usually those that help you achieve more than one objective. Basic categories of ways to secure an effective strategy include several ways to convey messages that inspire cooperation between an organization and its publics (Hendrix & Hayes, 2011):

- *Salient information*—Provide varying levels of information to different target publics depending upon their information needs.
- *Group influence*—Use existing groups to endorse and deliver the message to the target public.
- *Source credibility*—Opinion leaders or influentials; spokespersons; endorsements from members of the target public; third-party implied endorsement of the media.
- *Verbal cues*—Consistent use of key messages, slogans, themes, etc.
- *Nonverbal cues*—Consistent use of logos, signatures, colors, locations, etc.
- *Selective exposure*—Place messages in vehicles/channels that the target public is likely to accept and use. Two basic channel strategies are:
  - *Interactive vs. noninteractive media*—Use media that are interactive with the target public. Or use media that remind the target public of the message, but require no interaction.
  - *Interpersonal vs. mass media*—Engage the target public on an individual, personal level. Rely on the mass media to deliver messages to the target public.
- *Two-way communication*—Design tactics that enable the target public to communicate with the client.
- *Audience participation*—Engage the target public in activities that facilitate delivery of the message.

Writing strategy statements involves beginning with an objective. Then think generally what you would do to fulfill it, and state the general idea of what you'd do based on the types of categories listed above. For example:

- *Objective*: Gain employee understanding of new safety procedures by 30% of employees within 6 months.

- *Strategy 1*: Provide salient information about the new safety procedures for employees in selected internal publications.
- *Strategy 2*: Engage employees on new safety procedures with interpersonal communication.

3.3 Tactics

Tactics concern specifically how you will fulfill each of your strategies (see Chapters 4 and 6). The following three dimensions make up how you will do the work required in the plan. You'll have to describe them either individually or in combination:

- Tactics include the people, discourse types, or technology you'll use, e.g., reporters, face-to-face meetings, or wire service. Tools may be written, spoken, or visual means to facilitate communication between an organization and its audiences.
- Tactics also include actions you want, e.g., get reporters to run a personal finance story about a new corporate bond; write a press release to announce an important corporate achievement, a unique perspective on the business or market, or other appropriate "newsworthy" subject; hold "briefings" between senior management and frontline supervisors about organizational changes.
- Still other tactics include the ways to get done what you need to meet an objective, e.g., make a pitch to reporters that they may interview the CFO for a personal finance story on a new corporate bond; upload an electronic file via the Internet to wire service for distribution; have small-group, face-to-face meetings between senior managers and supervisors as part of an organizational change program.

3.4 Critical Success Factors (CSFs)

CSFs are things/events that could help or hurt success and state why knowing these things is valuable. These CSFs should reflect things you document in the SWOT analysis' "implications" column as they could help or hinder your achieving the goals in the previous section. The whole of the CSFs, then, is more forward-looking, as the SWOT or other approach is mostly backward-looking. To make sure you've considered how your strategic communication will be successful, you must show what things could affect it (positively and negatively) when trying to meet your goals. Those factors can come from several directions (see Appendix B for an efficient way to graphically layout CSFs). For example:

- *Opportunities*—occasions where an organization can capitalize on the situation to garner support and build its image.
- *Barriers*—include but are not limited to ideological, attitudinal, or social opposition to or legal, regulatory, or institutional restrictions on an organization doing what it believes it should to solve the problem in the way it wants.
- *Environment* (*internal and external*)—business issues fuel communications, for example, low profitability undermines company's and its leaders' credibility; product problems and failures damage the company's reputation; third parties are

reluctant to endorse the company; a merger or acquisition diverts attention to organizational changes.

- *Resources*—staff required to fulfill communications objectives is sufficient and supplemented by knowledgeable and experienced outside help to take on intensive special projects when required.

3.5 Key Performance Indicators (KPIs)

KPIs are milestone measurements taken along the way to track progress toward goals. This section, then, presents why knowing these things is valuable. Along the way, you must regularly make sure your plan is on track. You do this by measuring how well things are going in your quest to meet your goals and achieve your objectives. Your leading indicators must be measurable and specific ways you can regularly monitor your progress against the stated objectives. You should check your leading indicators at predetermined intervals (e.g., weekly, monthly, quarterly) so you can make any adjustments. Here are some examples:

- Meet monthly with 10 to15 randomly selected employees and the CEO to discuss company performance and the market, obtain feedback on internal issues, and determine effectiveness of communications
- Make 60 calls a month with key editors about company news and editorial opportunities
- Have 15 or more conversations each quarter with analysts on company progress, key messages, and direction
- Gain 2 or more commitments each month for significant editorial coverage
- Secure 1 to 3 speaking opportunities each month
- Submit 3 or more entries to strategically important award competitions each quarter

3.6 Budget and Resource Allocations

This is an outline and explanation of what will be needed for and what assumptions apply to each aspect of the plan and how much each aspect will cost during the sequence of events. It also summarizes total costs and, if appropriate, makes any comparisons to similar or related programs. Include items like postage, mileage, labor, overhead, and 10% for unforeseen expenses. Identify major supporters and financial resources. In a budget you must give data as specifically as possible, explain what's needed and why, what return on investment (ROI) should be, and the value-added amount for the organization. Bottom line: the benefits of the plan justify the costs for doing the work.

3.7 Timeline (beginning with the proposal's acceptance/approval)

A timetable, either outlined in text or presented in a chart (e.g., Gantt chart), shows the start and finish of all events within the context of the communications plan. The calendar helps to ensure that all events, leading indicators, and milestones are met when planned and relate back to objectives and metrics. Key questions to answer in creating a calendar are:

- Can the program be done in the time allotted?
- Can the results be achieved in the time allotted?
- What contingencies can be made if any time is lost?

3.8 Evaluation Method and Anticipated Results

Now you must measure how effective the plan was in inducing cooperation with target publics. This step typically requires quantitative research methods, like written or phone surveys and content analyses of media coverage, and qualitative research methods, like focus groups and one-on-one interviews. Evaluations are *post hoc* measurements and analysis of outputs (i.e., PR discourse), outtakes (i.e., publics' immediate, short-term responses), outcomes (i.e., publics' responses over a "medium term"), and outgrowths (i.e., publics' lasting responses that indicate cumulative change was established).

All final evaluation measurements must be linked to the objectives given in section 3.1. This section should be more detailed. This section must give *basic* statements about what method would be used to measure *each* objective. The measurements given in this section are summative—they define overall success/failure for the whole plan—against the objectives and compared to the benchmarks. These measurements are the culmination of what the KPIs were measuring along the way. Some key questions to answer when designing your measurement scheme are:

- How will you measure the success of reaching the plan's objectives?
- How have the critical success factors affected the plan's success?
- What have your leading indicators told you?
- Can you create a means for continuous feedback from your target audiences?
- Did the target audiences receive the messages?
- What was the extent of any print and broadcast media coverage?
- How was the organization portrayed in media reports?
- What do people think about the organization now as compared to their opinions before the plan was implemented?
- Did the plan fall within budget and were the resources sufficient?
- What unforeseen circumstances affected the plan's success?

Compile the data, analyze the results, and report on the findings. Also state your conclusions and propose ways to act. Use this report to help you create future evaluations and communication plans. Finally, you should take the opportunity to note ways to improve things along the way and at the end of the project. Your postmortem should address how to do things next time, including alternative methods, discourse, channels, and so on.

Appendices

Appendices are not required, but it is very likely you will have some additional material (e.g., visuals, data, documents) that should be included for easy reference when your plan calls for that extra information. Make sure you refer to each appendix in the order you use them, from the start to the end of your plan. The first appendix you refer to is Appendix A, the second is Appendix B, and so on.

A. Appendix title

B. Appendix title

C. Appendix title

References

If any primary or secondary sources are used to provide evidence in any way in the plan, those sources must be listed separately in this section. Any style (e.g., APA, MLA, Chicago) for documenting sources in the text and in this list will do—make sure they are used consistently and accurately throughout. Material directly from your client does not need source citations, but you should explain/state what client source you used.

Hendrix, J. A., & Hayes, D. C. (2011). *Public Relations Cases* (8th ed.). Belmont, CA: Wadsworth Cengage Learning.

Smudde, P. M. (2011). *Public relations as dramatistic organizing: A case study bridging theory and practice*. Cresskill, NJ: Hampton Press.

EXAMPLE STRATEGIC PLAN

Strategic Plan 2013

Developed for the client by Molly Beil and Lindsey Probst

March 2013

Reproduced with the permission of the authors and the client.

Table of Contents

Executive Summary

Sugar Mama Bakery is a new business in downtown Bloomington seeking to provide gourmet cupcakes and desserts in a friendly atmosphere to the area. The business has great potential to grow both financially and in visibility within the community. Since Sugar Mama Bakery has not been in business for a full year, it is still in a learning process.

The following is a plan to help Sugar Mama Bakery in the last nine months of its first fiscal year (which started January 1, 2013). First, the business will be analyzed to review its underlying values and base operations thus far. Then, the potential for growth will be discussed along with possible problems to Sugar Mama Bakery's success. Several objectives for the business and their budget requirements will be suggested, including:

- A plan to alleviate some responsibilities of the owners by redefining employees' roles and responsibilities in order to increase productivity by 30%
- A streamlined ordering process to increase customer understanding and eliminate confusion of custom cake ordering by 50%

- A plan to seek out five expansion prospects in Uptown Normal to expose the unique specialties that Sugar Mama Bakery offers to the area
- A plan to increase awareness and visibility of Sugar Mama Bakery in the Bloomington–Normal community through five community involvement opportunities

This plan will serve as a guide to carry out the remainder of the year in order to attain these objectives. All employees should know and utilize the plan for it to reach its full capabilities. For the next fiscal year, this plan will serve as a basic guide to develop a new plan for the needs of that year. Compliance with the plan outlined below after its acceptance will bring Sugar Mama Bakery the guidance it seeks to prosper in its early stages.

1.0 Organization Background

This section serves as a basis of knowledge about the core business of Sugar Mama Bakery. It provides the supplementary material necessary to understand the situation analysis in section 2.0 and the plan in section 3.0.

1.1 Business Definition

Sugar Mama Bakery specializes in gourmet cupcakes and desserts, as well as custom cakes. Our bakery offers dine-in seating and individual cupcake selections, carryout desserts, and custom ordering for specialty cakes and cupcake orders.

1.2 Vision

To utilize artists and their variety of abilities in the Bloomington–Normal area by training them and allowing them to create customized desserts at Sugar Mama Bakery.

1.3 Mission

To bring people together in a fun and welcoming atmosphere by making customized gourmet desserts to help celebrate different life events.

1.4 Value Proposition

The value proposition is essential to identifying the factors that make Sugar Mama Bakery stand out from its competition. It includes two parts: (1) a thesis statement describing Sugar Mama Bakery's unique selling proposition and (2) proof points, which support the core idea of the thesis by providing the compelling competitive advantages that Sugar Mama Bakery possesses. The value proposition is as follows:

Thesis: Sugar Mama Bakery provides a welcoming atmosphere by making customized gourmet desserts to help celebrate different life events.

Proof Points:
- The Sugar Mama Bakery facility provides customers with places to sit and converse while enjoying their desserts.
- Sugar Mama Bakery caters to the individual needs and interests of its customers by providing gluten-free and vegan options as well as customized cakes.

- Sugar Mama Bakery sets itself apart from similar organizations in Bloomington–Normal through its use of fondant on custom cake orders.
- Sugar Mama Bakery is civically engaged in the Bloomington–Normal community through its work with nonprofit organizations, fundraisers, and involvement in local schools.

1.5 Organization Structure

Sugar Mama Bakery is a limited liability company (LLC), and the organizational structure consists of 2 members, or owners, and 16 other part-time employees (see chart below). Currently, all part-time employees report to the owners. The owners have specified their responsibilities, and each has a specific purpose in the business. Below are descriptions of the job roles.

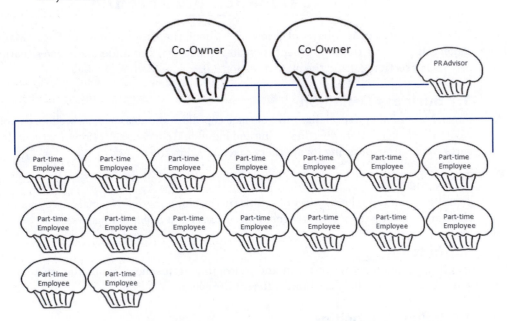

1.5.1. Co-Owner 1 (Krista)

The co-owner is responsible and makes the final decisions for all financial and bookkeeping matters. This position also handles all custom orders made at Sugar Mama Bakery and the communication, consultation, workflow, and decorating needs thereof.

1.5.2. Co-Owner 2 (Susie)

The co-owner is responsible for taking inventory of materials as well as all retail matters. This position also handles all of the baking at Sugar Mama Bakery and trains employees.

1.5.3. PR Adviser

The PR adviser serves as a mentor for the co-owners to assist with social media, advertising, and other promotional needs.

1.5.4. Part-Time Employees

Part-time employees work on a shift basis.

- Shift 1 (Tuesdays to Friday, 5 a.m. to 9 a.m. or bake time)
  - Baker—The first shift needs to open the store and fill the display case with product. This includes getting out the buttercream to soften, turning on the oven, getting out baking supplies, and baking the products.
  - Baker's Assistant—This person helps with preparations for baking products (i.e., wash dishes, line cupcake trays, icing, baking).
- Shift 2 (Tuesdays to Friday, 9 a.m. to 3 p.m.)
  - Baker—This shift bakes the remaining products needed to meet the daily requirement.
  - Baker's Assistant—This person helps with preparations for baking products (i.e., wash dishes, line cupcake trays, icing, baking. This position may float to front of house if needed, after baking).

Sugar Mama Bakery expresses a need to further define each of these roles as addressed in the situation analysis in Section 2.0. With the current structure of Sugar Mama Bakery, the business relies on the presence of the owners. By training a counterpart for each of the owners (i.e., a manager), accountability would be distributed among the employees (see Appendix A for a suggested new organizational chart). The creation of a manager position would involve duties regularly handled by Susie; the employee could stand in during her absence. The format for the new decorator job description would be similar, only geared toward Krista's role. For example, Krista would not have to be the sole decorator (see Appendix B for new job roles and descriptions). This would free her time and reduce the risk of burnout. Krista also has a growing family, whose needs and obligations will grow with them. Krista mentioned that family is a number-one priority for her and Susie. Distributing responsibility would allow both owners to commit to the success of the business, as well as their duties as a mother.

1.6 History and Culture

Krista Gaff realized her knack and passion for decorating baked goods while teaching and growing a family. She showcased these talents on a Facebook page, documenting her new creations and designs. Soon friends and family were asking for custom cakes and cupcakes. Quickly, the Facebook page became a marketplace for unknown customers to order baked goods from Gaff. Demand became high. In January of 2013, she teamed up with business partner Susie Tod and opened Sugar Mama Bakery in downtown Bloomington.

Sugar Mama Bakery believes that food can bring people together. The employees and bakers enjoy being able to provide a sense of togetherness for customers. These employees value this mission and are motivated to produce quality products. The atmosphere in the bakery is fun, gender neutral, welcoming, excited, and full of smiles. Sugar Mama Bakery also values the community and its talents. The small business supports local philanthropic events and local artists.

2.0 Situation Analysis

Sugar Mama faces various pressures from its environment, which makes an analysis of its business situation essential. This section presents details and analysis about Sugar Mama's situation by defining it and its scope, explaining stakeholders affected by its business decisions, explaining the competition, and performing an analysis of Sugar Mama's strengths, weaknesses, opportunities and threats for being a successful business.

2.1 Definition and Scope of Situation

Sugar Mama has been well received by the community, and sales were even higher than anticipated. The business has not had a full year of operation. Productivity and efficiency are areas that need improvement. With only one employee (the owner) able to design the baked goods, production is slow. There is a high threat of not being able to keep up with demand and losing customers to competitors.

Sugar Mama Bakery specializes in gourmet cupcakes and desserts, as well as custom cakes. The bakery offers dine-in seating and individual cupcake selections, carryout desserts, and custom ordering for specialty cakes and cupcake orders. We want to establish Sugar Mama Bakery as the premier location for people in the Bloomington–Normal community to gather together and celebrate life events. Despite the success of the organization since it opened in January, several issues have developed:

- We plan to alleviate some responsibilities of the owners by better defining employees' roles and responsibilities in order to increase productivity.
- The customized ordering process needs to be streamlined in order to increase customer understanding and eliminate confusion.
- We plan to increase the awareness and visibility of Sugar Mama Bakery in the Bloomington–Normal community through community involvement opportunities.
- We plan to expand to an additional location in Uptown Normal to allow more people an opportunity to experience the unique specialties that Sugar Mama Bakery offers.

Implementing strategies to improve these issues will enable Sugar Mama Bakery to become the leading bakery and customized dessert service in the Bloomington–Normal area.

2.2 Stakeholders Affected

Sugar Mama Bakery has many stakeholders on whom the organization's success or failure depends. Owners Krista and Susie are the major source of financial backing for Sugar Mama Bakery. If sales were to decline, the business could fail without support from them. With that, Sugar Mama Bakery depends on its customers to continue to value its products and purchase them. The business also relies on the continued perception of Downtown Bloomington as a trendy, safe, and desirable place to purchase goods and services. If a neighboring business—say Coffee Hound—were to fail, Sugar Mama Bakery's business would be affected. Employees serve as a face of the company to customers. If the employees are improperly trained, motivated, or skilled, the customer will be less satisfied and less likely to be a returning customer.

2.3 Competition

Currently, there are several organizations in the Bloomington–Normal community that Sugar Mama Bakery competes with. The competition is categorized as "very strong," "strong," and "weak." Very strong competition represents a serious threat to Sugar Mama Bakery because those companies offer similar services to the same community. Strong competitors also offer similar products and services but pose less of a threat than very strong competition because Sugar Mama Bakery has superior products. Weak competitors do not pose a great threat to Sugar Mama Bakery because the businesses are not as valued to the customers because of Sugar Mama Bakery's niche in the market and adaptability. However, weak competitors could become strong if not monitored and addressed. The following list presents the three levels of competition:

- Tiers Designer Cakes is an upscale cake shop located in Normal that offers customized cakes for various occasions. Tiers Designer Cakes is a very strong competitor because it offers many of the same products and services as Sugar Mama Bakery and has the potential to draw customers away from our bakery.
- Strong competitors include home-based dessert and bakery businesses because they often operate under the radar and are able to produce their products at lower costs. However, by being a LLC, Sugar Mama Bakery has better control over product safety and sanitation.
- Weak competitors include Janet's Cakes and Catering and Sugar Arts Cakes and Catering. Janet's Cakes and Catering is a bakery and catering service located in Bloomington that specializes in weddings. Sugar Arts Cakes and Catering is located in Normal and offers customized dessert and meal options for special events and parties. These cake and catering businesses pose a weak threat because the focus is on more than just cakes and they often specialize in weddings, which Sugar Mama Bakery does not want to specialize in.

2.4 SWOT Analysis

This analysis of Sugar Mama's strengths, weaknesses, opportunities, and threats (SWOT) reveals categories of advantage, disadvantage, growth, and limitations to its continued operation. Each SWOT item is stated (i.e., "aspect"), defined in terms of what it means to the company (i.e., "implications"), and addressed in terms of what may work to meet that aspect for the company's benefit.

	ASPECTS	*IMPLICATIONS*	*POSSIBLE ACTIONS*
Strengths	*Provide welcoming atmosphere for customers to gather in*	*Strengthens relationship between Sugar Mama Bakery (SMB) and its customers*	*Continue to create an environment that encourages customers to stay and eat their desserts*

	ASPECTS	IMPLICATIONS	POSSIBLE ACTIONS
	Provide customized cakes to help celebrate special occasions	• *Allows customers to have a say in their orders* • *Demonstrates the care and devotion behind each order*	*Streamline the custom cake-ordering process to make it less confusing to customers*
	Cater to customers' specific needs by offering gluten-free and vegan options	*Builds the reputation as a bakery that listens to and cares for its customers*	*Expand menu to include more specialized items*
W*eaknesses*	*Poorly defined roles for employees at all levels*	• *Limits productivity and causes confusion* • *Potential to create a financial burden*	• *Clearly define each employee's role and responsibilities* • *Hold employee meetings on a regular basis*
	Poor utilization of website for custom cake orders and for advertising purposes	*Customers may be hesitant to order custom cakes because of uncertainty*	*List basic options of available product options (batters, icing types) to orientate customers*
	Confusing process for ordering customized cakes	• *Reduces efficiency for making customized cakes* • *Potential to harm positive reputation*	• *Develop a simpler process for customized orders.* • *Train employees in this process to increase the number of orders taken*
O*pportunities*	*Expand the company*	*Creates another place for customers to gather and increases recognition in the area*	*Open a store in Uptown Normal*

	ASPECTS	IMPLICATIONS	POSSIBLE ACTIONS
	Strengthen relationships with local nonprofit organizations and other small businesses	*This may limit time in the bakery, but it will improve corporate social responsibility and add company value*	*Donate baked goods to organizations with members of the target audience in them (mom groups, Girl Scouts, trendy groups)*
	Include local artists in the creation of customized cakes	*This would allow SMB to utilize the community and fulfill its core values*	*Hire an employee or an intern from ISU/IWU in the culinary program*
Threats	*High costs for gourmet desserts and customized cakes*	*Customers may choose to be patrons of the competition*	*Continually advocate the values of community, personalization, and quality to customers through visibility and transparency with the public*
	Other gourmet and customized dessert bakeries in the Bloomington–Normal community that offer similar products	*Customers may choose to be patrons of the competition*	*Continually advocate the values of community, personalization, and quality to customers through visibility and transparency with the public*

3.0 Plan

This section presents a formal and specified plan of action for Sugar Mama Bakery for the remainder of the calendar/fiscal year (April–December, 2013). It is related to the previous two sections. The plan in this section provides Sugar Mama Bakery with the guidance to make the necessary improvements in order to best fulfill its mission and reach its full potential, beginning in 2014. The following subsections include objectives, strategies, and tactics; critical success factors; key performance indicators; budget and resource allocations; an implementation timeline; and the final evaluation method and anticipated results.

3.1 Objectives, Strategies, and Tactics

The following table shows the objectives, strategies, and tactics that make up the central part of this plan as well as the subsequent subsections.

- *Objectives* are the main things the organization needs to accomplish in order to achieve its vision. Each objective includes four parts: (1) a desired effect, (2) a goal, stated as a numerical target, (3) the target audience, and (4) an established target date or deadline. The benchmarks for each goal are presented after each objective.
- *Strategies* are the categories of things Sugar Mama Bakery needs to do to fulfill the objectives.
- *Tactics* are the specific actions that Sugar Mama Bakery will take to accomplish each strategy, which will subsequently fulfill the related objectives.

OBJECTIVES	STRATEGIES	TACTICS
1. *Alleviate some responsibilities of the owners to increase efficiency by 30% by the end of the fiscal year* *(Demand is currently at a level reaching the maximum capacity of supply capabilities for Sugar Mama Bakery. We want to ease the process without increasing sales to levels over supply capabilities.)* *(Benchmark: Record number of custom cakes that Sugar Mama Bakery [SMB] can produce before implementing the new decorator and manager positions [April and June])*	*Empower and train employees to divide the work of the owners* *(see Appendix A for revised organizational chart)* *(see Appendix B for job descriptions)*	*Hire another decorator* • *Position could be filled by current employee or an intern/novice from Illinois State University's culinary program* • *Krista is currently the only decorator on staff; another decorator is needed to increase production* • *May require cutting down the number of part-time employees due to financial restraints* *Create manager position* • *Train two employees as managers to deal with day-to-day operations in absence of the owners* • *This would free time of owners and allow for more efficiency*

OBJECTIVES	STRATEGIES	TACTICS
2. *Increase customer understanding of the customized ordering process by 50% within 2 months to allow for ease of use.* *(Currently, the online custom cake order does not list specific options and is confusing to customers. Krista is the only one who takes custom cake orders.)* *(Benchmark: Record results of comment cards as an overall percentage of satisfaction before updating website and implementing phone order document)*	*Streamline ordering process to eliminate customer confusion*	*List specific flavor, frosting, and decorating options on the website to make it easier for customers to design a custom cake* *(see Appendix C for list of ordering options)*
		Create a checklist-style ordering document that lists specific flavor, frosting, and decorating options to allow more than one employee to take phone orders for custom cakes • *Document would be posted on the SMB website and Facebook page* *(see Appendix D for checklist)*
		Give comment cards to customers who purchase custom orders before and after implementing the above tactics
3. *Owners seek out five opportunities for business expansion during the remaining 9 months of the calendar (and fiscal) year.* *(Benchmark: Survey results of the interest in a new store location. Objective assumes that SMB is currently unaware of new opportunities for expansion; benchmark is 0—with an understanding of potential interest from surveys.)*	*Scan the environment for areas of growth for SMB*	*Poll the Uptown Normal area via a 10-question survey to measure interest in having a location near Normal customers*
		Plan a Grand Opening event for a potential new location

OBJECTIVES	STRATEGIES	TACTICS
4. Owners seek out five opportunities for community involvement during the remaining 9 months of the calendar (and fiscal) year. *(Benchmark: Objective holds that SMB is currently unaware of new opportunities for community involvement; benchmark is 0)*	*Scan the environment for areas of growth for SMB*	*Donate to and sponsor philanthropic events involving key members of SMB's target audience* • *Suggestions of philanthropic opportunities include hosting a decorating class, donating to schools, and sponsoring a fundraiser*

3.2 Critical Success Factors

The following table describes 4 categories of factors that could affect Sugar Mama Bakery positively and negatively when attempting to fulfill its objectives along with the implications related to each category.

- *Opportunities* include occasions where Sugar Mama Bakery can take advantage of the situation to build its image and increase customer support and involvement.
- *Barriers* include, but are not limited to, situational, attitudinal, and environmental opposition to Sugar Mama Bakery.
- *Environment* includes both internal and external factors that influence Sugar Mama Bakery operations.
- *Resources* include the employees and materials required to fulfill business objectives.

OBJECTIVES	OPPORTUNITIES	BARRIERS	ENVIRONMENT	RESOURCES
1. Alleviate some responsibilities of the owners to increase efficiency	*Give part-time employees greater responsibility and an opportunity for growth*	*Limits amount of time each owner spends at Sugar Mama Bakery (SMB)*	*Build relationship between SMB and ISU culinary program*	*Increase productivity and efficiency in the baking/decorating processes*
	Allow owners to be more involved in other areas	*Potentially creates a financial burden on the owners/SMB*	*Strengthen relationship between owners and employees*	*Improve allocation of SMB resources*

2. Increase customer understanding of the customized ordering process to allow for ease of use.	Emphasize the care and devotion behind each order	Hinders the custom cake creation process	Build SMB's reputation as a bakery that listens to and cares for its customers	Improve employee time management
	Allow customers to have more control over their customized orders			Increase employee productivity
			Increase customer willingness to order customized cakes	Increase efficiency of custom cake process
				Improve allocation of bakery resources
3. Owners seek out five opportunities for business expansion	Create another location for customers to gather	Limits time that owners spend at SMB	Build a relationship between SMB and new customers	More employees will be needed for a secondary location
	Increase recognition of SMB in the Bloomington–Normal area		Strengthen relationship between SMB and its current customers	
			Increase recognition of SMB in the Bloomington–Normal area	
4. Owners seek out five opportunities for community involvement	Improve corporate social responsibility	Limits time that owners spend at SMB	Increase recognition of SMB in the Bloomington–Normal area	Provide a use for "leftover" or extra resources
	Fulfill SMB's core values		Provide employees with experience outside of the bakery	More employees will be needed for the events

3.3 Key Performance Indicators (KPIs)

KPIs are intermittent measurements taken by Sugar Mama Bakery to keep the plan on path to success. For each listed objective, specific measurements will be taken by the owners or managerial staff periodically and compared to the benchmark, or level prior to progress.

- Objective 1—Alleviate some responsibilities of the owners to increase efficiency by 30% by the end of the fiscal year.
  - Benchmark—Record the number of custom cakes that Sugar Mama Bakery can produce before implementing the new decorator and manager position (April).
  - KPI—Production of cakes should increase 5% every month over the 6 months after the additional decorator is hired (June).
  - Look at these numbers every month and adjust as necessary.
- Objective 2—Increase customer understanding of the customized ordering process by 50% to allow for ease of use within 2 months.
  - Benchmark—Create short comment cards for customers to fill out as they are purchasing a custom item. Record results as an overall percentage of satisfaction before updating the website and implementing the phone order document.
  - KPI—Give the same comment card to customers after 2 months of the updating the website and implementing the phone order document.
  - Calculate percentage of increase and adjust process if deficient.
- Objective 3—Owners seek out 5 opportunities for expansion during the remaining 9 months of the calendar (fiscal) year.
  - Benchmark—This will be the survey results of the interest in a store location in Uptown Normal. This objective assumes that Sugar Mama Bakery is currently unaware of new opportunities for expansion, so the benchmark is zero, with an understanding of potential interest from surveys.
  - KPI—Seek out at least one new location every other month to reach a total of 5 potential locations.
- Objective 4—Owners seek out 5 opportunities for community involvement during the remaining 9 months of the calendar (fiscal) year.
  - Benchmark—This objective assumes that Sugar Mama Bakery is currently unaware of new opportunities for community involvement, so the benchmark is zero.
  - KPI—Donate to or sponsor one local philanthropic event every other month to reach a total of 5.

3.4 Budget and Resource Allocations

Sugar Mama Bakery is a new business and required several large expenses when it first opened in January of 2013. It is especially important for the organization to have the proper budget and resource allocations in order to implement the plan described in the prior subsections and remain successful. The budget (see Appendix E) lists only those expenses necessary to fulfill the objectives, strategies, and tactics described in section 3.1 because income and sales amounts were unavailable during the planning process for confidentiality reasons.

This budget offers opportunities with Sugar Mama Bakery's best interest in mind. However, other avenues may be taken to reduce costs. For example, the *Pantagraph* is the most widely used newspaper in Bloomington–Normal and should yield the most applicants. If funds are not able to accommodate the price of the job posting, other newspapers in the area offer similar services. The hourly rates and pay increases are estimations based on industry standards that can be adjusted according to the level of skill and experience of the new employees. The costs for the philanthropic events are estimated for 100 attendants at 65% markup. The estimate for each event can be altered to fit the specifics of each event.

It is important to point out that we are not currently budgeting for advertising, although there may be potential to do so in the future. Currently, the resources being allocated allow Sugar Mama Bakery to operate at full capacity. Increasing the level of customer demand has the potential to increase sales to levels above the current supply capabilities. We are instead focusing on our current customers and opportunities before pursuing other opportunities in the future that will increase our expenses.

3.5 Timeline (beginning with the proposal's acceptance/approval)

To ensure the progress of this plan, and thus the success of Sugar Mama, a guideline of when each of the suggested tactics should be implemented is necessary to visualize the entire scope of the plan (see Appendix F for full timeline). Every part, regardless of the objective it falls under, is dependent on whether other items succeed. For example, the comment cards are being implemented after the new hires are made. If the decorator was hired after the cards went out, then the results would be skewed, and they would not simultaneously get feedback regarding the new hire's performance. All efforts to record benchmarks are very important to measuring success during evaluation.

Many tasks occur throughout the remainder of the year. However, June through August will be highly critical. This span includes the implementation of many suggested objectives. However, the tasks are distributed among employees to dilute pressure. December has many tasks since that is the evaluation period. Accommodation in the philanthropic event schedule can be made, but the holiday season is a great opportunity to donate baked goods. The new job implementations will allow normal business to occur while the owners take on these objectives.

3.6 Evaluation Method and Anticipated Results

To determine if this plan was successful, Sugar Mama Bakery will have to evaluate the efforts of this plan. See Section 3.5 for KPIs and benchmarks.

- Objective 1—Alleviate some responsibilities of the owners to increase efficiency by 30% by the end of the fiscal year.
  - If by the end of the year production was able to increase by 5% each month (after the plan begins) or totals 30%, the plan was sucessful.
  - If the plan was not successful, adjust operations for the next fiscal year to reach the increase for next fiscal year.
- Objective 2—Increase customer understanding of the customized ordering process by 50% to allow for ease of use within 2 months.

- Use calculation plan to determine in November if the percentage of satisfaction increase by 50%.
- If if did not increase enough, plan for more adjustments to the ordering process for next fiscal year.
- Objective 3—Owners seek out 5 opportunities for expansion during the remaining 9 months of the calendar (fiscal) year.
  - Evaluation for this requires finding five potential opportunities; if 5 were found, Sugar Mama was successful.
  - If 5 could not be found, an analysis of the necessity to expand is viable and necessary for Sugar Mama in the coming years.
- Objective 4—Owners seek out 5 opportunities for community involvement during the remaining 9 months of the calendar (fiscal) year.
  - Evaluation for this requires finding 5 potential opportunities for philanthropy; if five were found, Sugar Mama was successful.
  - If 5 could not be carried out, adjust the plan to 2 larger events a year.

Success is anticipated for Sugar Mama Bakery with this plan. The objectives provided can easily be carried out by the owners and staff due to the redistribution of responsibilities. If the plan starts to not meet KPIs, adjustments must be made before the end of the plan cycle to remove threat against overall success.

Appendices

A. Revised Organizational Chart

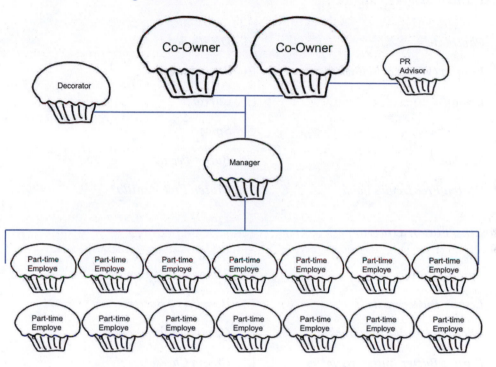

B. Job Descriptions

Decorator—This position will act as a part-time employee but will be tasked with assisting the co-owner with decorating needs. During absences and vacations, this position assumes decorating and ordering responsibilities of co-owner 1 (Krista).

Manager—This position regulates employee behavior, has knowledge of scheduling process, and monitors basic building needs such as light maintenance. Other duties include opening and closing the store, recording inventory, managing cash balance of registers, and staffing. During absences and vacations, this position assumes decorating and ordering responsibilities of co-owner 2 (Susie).

C. Custom Order Options

Cake and Cupcake Flavors

☐ *Chocolate*   ☐ *Devil's Food*

☐ *Vanilla (White or Yellow)*   ☐ *Strawberry*

☐ *Lemon*   ☐ *Carrot*

☐ *Red Velvet*   ☐ *Spice*

☐ *Marble*   ☐ *Butter Pecan*

☐ *Gluten Free Devil's Food**   ☐ *Gluten Free Vanilla**

Frosting Flavor Options

☐ *Vanilla Buttercream*   ☐ *Almond Buttercream*

☐ *Lemon Buttercream*   ☐ *Raspberry Buttercream*

☐ *Chocolate Fudge Buttercream* ☐ *Caramel Buttercream**

☐ *Peanut Butter Buttercream** ☐ *Cream Cheese**

☐ *Caramel Cream Cheese**   ☐ *Strawberry Cream Cheese**

☐ *Raspberry Cream Cheese**

Party Serving Sizes

☐ *6" round: 12*   ☐ *8" round: 20*

☐ *10" round: 28*   ☐ *12" round: 40*

☐ *14" round: 63*   ☐ *16" round: 77*

*Additional Fee

D. Custom Cake Order Checklist

Name: _____

Email Address: _____

Phone Number: _____

Address: _____

City/State: _____

Order Due Date (MM/DD/YY):

Custom orders must be placed and confirmed at least seven days prior to the due date*

Preferred Pickup Time (Hour/Minute/Second):   *AM/PM*

☐ *Delivery*   ☐ *Pickup*

Type of Event (Birthday, Graduation, etc.):

Cake and Cupcake Flavor Options

☐ *Chocolate*

☐ *Devil's Food*

☐ *Gluten Free**

☐ *Vanilla*

☐ *White*

- ☐ *Yellow*
- ☐ *Gluten Free**
- ☐ *Strawberry*
- ☐ *Lemon*
- ☐ *Carrot*
- ☐ *Red Velvet*
- ☐ *Spice*
- ☐ *Marble*
- ☐ *Butter Pecan*

Frosting Flavor Options

- ☐ *Vanilla Buttercream*
- ☐ *Almond Buttercream*
- ☐ *Lemon Buttercream*
- ☐ *Raspberry Buttercream*
- ☐ *Chocolate Fudge Buttercream*
- ☐ *Caramel Buttercream**
- ☐ *Peanut Butter Buttercream**
- ☐ *Cream Cheese**
- ☐ *Caramel Cream Cheese**
- ☐ *Strawberry Cream Cheese**
- ☐ *Raspberry Cream Cheese**

*Additional Fee

Custom Design (theme, colors, decoration details, etc.):

_____

_____

_____

Number of Servings:

- ☐ *6" round: 12*
- ☐ *8" round: 20*
- ☐ *10" round: 28*
- ☐ *12" round: 40*
- ☐ *14" round: 63*
- ☐ *16" round: 77*

Other Questions: _____

_____

_____

_____

E. Budget and Resource Allocation Spreadsheet

SUGAR MAMA BAKERY BUDGE (OVERALL) ~ 2013

ACCT	EXPENSES	HOURS (LABOR)	TOTAL	NOTES
100	Increase efficiency/ productivity	28		HOURS: recording number of custom products old
110	Secondary decorator	15	$7,980.00	Decorator pay: $9.50/hour HOURS: 35 hours per week: includes training **Pay rate and hours are estimates and can be adjusted
120	Manager position	980	$1,470	Pay increase ($1.50/hour): HOURS: 35 hours per week, beginning in April; include training **Pay increase and hours are estimates and can be adjusted
130	Job posting (Pantagraph)	1	$929.80	1 20-Line positing for 7 days in the Pantagraph, Twin City Community News, pantagraph.com, yahoo.com, monster.com (30 days) HOURS: post job description
140	Job posting (ISU website)	1		Student job posting under the job opportunities on the ISU website HOURS: post job description on website
200	Increase customer understanding of custom orders			

ACCT	EXPENSES	HOURS (LABOR)	TOTAL	NOTES
210	*Additional ordering options on website*	*1*		*HOURS: post additional options on Sugar Mama website*
220	*Custom order checklist*	*1*	*$18.00*	*FedEx Kinkos Printing ($0.12 per page HOURS: print checklist*
230	*Comment cards*	*8*	*$3.00*	*FedEx Kinkos Printing ($0.06 per page) HOURS: print cards; give cards to customers*
300	*Seek new expansion opportunities*	*20*		*HOURS: look for and record opportunities for growth*
310	*Survey of Uptown Normal*	*15*	*$12.00*	*FedEx Kinkos Printing ($0.12 per page) HOURS: give survey and record results*
320	*Grand Opening Even*	*15*		*HOURS: Planning for Grand Opening Event **Specifics can be added after a location can be found*
400	*Seek new philanthropic opportunities*			
410	*Community events*	*50*	*$770.00*	*HOURS: planning and labor for event, time spent at event **Prices are estimated for 100 attendants but can be adjusted depending on the event*
	TOTAL		*$10,412.80*	

F. Timeline

2013-2014	JANUARY	FEBRUARY	MARCH	APRIL	MAY	JUNE
				Proposal Accepted		
Objective 1-Efficiency increase	x	x	x	Record number of custom products sold (Krista)		
Tactic 1-Hire Decorator	x	x	x			6-1 Post job in "Pantagraph" (Susie) 6-10 to 5-20 Interviews (Susie) 6-30 Hire new employee/intern (Susie)
Tactic 2-Manager position	x	x	x		Begin to train employee as manager. Start position by 5-20	
Objective 2-Increase customer understanding of custom orders	x	x	x			
Tactic 1-Add ordering options to website	x	x	x			
Tactic 2-Phone ordering document	x	x	x			
Tactic 3-Comment cards						
Objective 3-Seek new growth opportunities	x	x	x	Look for 1 new growth opportunity and record (Krista).		Look for 1 new growth opportunity and record (Krista).
Tactic 1-Survey of Uptown	x	x	x		Survey Uptown, calculate interest level (Employee)	
Tactic 2-Opening Event	x	x	x			
Objective 4-Philantropy	x	x	x			
Tactic 1-Community Events	x	x	x		Be involved in 1 philanthropic event. (Owners)	

JULY	AUGUST	SEPTEMBER	OCTOBER	NOVEMBER	DECEMBER
Record number of custom products sold and calculate for 5%	Record number of custom products sold and calculate for 5%	Record number of custom products sold and calculate for 5%	Record number of custom products sold and calculate for 5%	Record number of custom products sold and calculate	Record number of custom products sold and calculate for 5% increase. Calculate for
Decorator in training (Krista)					Evaluate Employee Performance
					Evaluate Employee Performance
	Add items to website (PR Advisor)				
	Implement list (Manager)				
Begin giving cards to customers (Decorator)	Record results from July (Krista)		Give comment cards to customers (Decorator)	Record, evaluate, and adjust (Krista)	
	Look for 1 new growth opportunity and record (Krista).		Look for 1 new growth opportunity and record (Krista).		Look for 1 new growth opportunity and record (Krista).
					Begin opening campaign preparation
Be involved in 1 philanthropic event. (Owners)		Be involved in 1 philanthropic event. (Owners)		Be involved in 1 philanthropic event. (Owners)	Be involved in 1 philanthropic event. (Owners)

Appendix C

SCRIPTS FOR DIFFERENT TYPES OF CALLS

Customizing Scripts	Cold-calling scripts have been formulated to help you right now, and they are presented below (based on Schiffman, 1999). If the language is not exactly "your style," that is okay. You may customize these scripts for your use, and it may be best to do so for special target customers based on the pitch you want to make to them. The variables that you have to fill in the scripts will also help you to customize your calls. Realize, however, that whatever script you use, it must be as concise and to-the-point as these are. The point: to get a meeting. The directness and specificity in these scripts is there by design, because a no-nonsense approach has been proven to be more effective with customers than any gimmicky approach.
Sample Script with a Positive Response	Here is the core example cold-calling script. It assumes everything works well and you get the response you want. Make sure you fill in the blanks and practice a lot with it before you use it. Again, it is important to recognize the directness of the scripts. For example, you do not (and should never) begin by saying, "How are you?" That is way too vague and a real turnoff. You can get the person's attention best by saying his or her name with your greeting. You will see other aspects of directness in the script. (For a journalist, always ask, "Are you on deadline?" before you go into your pitch.) So here goes:

"Good morning, Mr./Ms. _____. This is <YOUR NAME> from <COMPANY NAME>. We're a <STATE YOUR COMPANY'S CLAIM TO FAME>. The reason I'm calling you today specifically is to set an appointment, so I can stop by and talk with you about our <CONCISELY GIVE SPECIFIC SERVICE(S), EVEN IF IT IS PROJECT SPECIFIC> that will <CONCISELY STATE TANGIBLE BENEFITS/VALUE OF STATED SERVICE(S)>. Mr./Ms. _____, I'm sure that you, like <GIVE SPECIFIC NAME OF AN ACTUAL, REFERENCEABLE CLIENT THAT USED STATED SERVICE>, are interested in <REPHRASE BENEFITS OF STATED SERVICE IN SIMPLE TERMS>."

With an affirmative answer, set an appointment with specific date, time, and location, using the following script:

"That's great Mr./Ms. _____, then we should get together. How's <TIME AND DATE> at your office? . . . Thank you! I'll see you then."

Sample Scripts to Negative Responses

Many cold calls are not as immediately positive as the situation for the core script implies. Turning a negative response to your opening statement (above) into a positive conversation is not necessarily easy, but it truly is doable. The trick is to use the negative response (or the person's question to you, as the case may be) as an opportunity to bridge the conversation back to your goal and make it a positive call.

The following scripts can be used to turn a negative call into a positive one. The scripts do not cover every situation, but you'll get the idea about how to handle others that may come your way. You may find you need to use more than one of these scripts during a call. And you may come up with your own scripts to handle situations not covered here. If you are successful, ask for an appointment at a specific time, date, and location. If you are not successful, finish the call in a genuinely friendly way, which is also given below.

There's one caveat: try not to turn around more than three negative responses in a row. (You do not want to come off as pushy.) Also, realize that all statements in these scripts must be true and potentially verifiable.

SAYS "HAPPY WITH PRESENT PROVIDER"

"I think it is great, Mr./Ms. _____, that you're using <PRESENT PROVIDER> for <STATED SERVICE>. Many other firms like <STATE ACTUAL, REFERENCEABLE CLIENTS> have said the same thing before learning about how we work, especially for <STATED SERVICE>, and how it complements what <PRESENT PROVIDER> is doing. You know, we should get together. How about <TIME AND DATE> at your office?"

<u>SAYS "NOT INTERESTED"</u>

"Well, Mr./Ms. _____, many people, like <STATE ACTUAL, REFERENCEABLE CLIENTS>, had the same reaction you did when I first called—before they had a chance to see how we work and what value our approach to <STATED SERVICE> gives them. Let's get together to explore this. How about <TIME AND DATE> at your office?"

~ OR ~

"I'm just curious, how do you handle <PROBLEM OR STATED SERVICE>? . . . {PERSON RESPONDS}. . . Very interesting. Based on what you've told me, we really should get together, because we've helped other firms on very similar projects. How about <TIME AND DATE> at your office?"

<u>SAYS "I'M THE WRONG PERSON"</u>

"I'm curious, what is it that you do? . . . {PERSON RESPONDS}. . .Then you know what, we absolutely should get together, because <STATE REASON BASED ON RESPONSE>. May we meet <TIME AND DATE> at your office?"

If after all this, the person absolutely is not the right person:

"Oh, with whom should I talk? . . . {PERSON RESPONDS}. . . [Take data and use for next call—see below.]. Thank you!"

Your next call, then, would go like this (there is no need to go through a full explanation, because you're working from a referral):

"Hello, Mr./Ms. _____, I'm <YOUR NAME> from <COMPANY NAME>. We're a <STATE COMPANY'S CLAIM TO FAME>. The reason I'm calling you today specifically is that I just spoke to <NAME OF PREVIOUS PERSON>. He/She suggested that I give you a call to set up an appointment. I wanted to know if <TIME AND DATE> at your office would be okay."

If the referred person asks why you were told to call him/her, you could respond like this:

"I originally called <NAME OF PREVIOUS PERSON> because I had just worked with <NAME OF RELATED COMPANY>. We have an excellent reputation for reliability, customer service, and competitive prices. When I told him that he/she said I should talk with you to set up an appointment. . . . {PERSON RESPONDS} . . . Then we definitely should get together. How about <TIME AND DATE> at your office?"

NOTE: This approach can be used in the event someone refers you to someone else, and this referral amounts to a new-business lead.

	SAYS "I'M TOO BUSY" *"Well, Mr./Ms. _____, the only reason I was calling was to set an appointment. Would <TIME AND DATE> at your office be okay?"* **REQUESTS LITERATURE** *There's more I can show you about the success customers have had in similar projects we worked on for them. Can we just get together? How about <TIME AND DATE> at your office? I'll bring information you can keep.* **THE ANSWER IS STILL NO** *Thank you for your consideration, Mr./Ms. _____. Have a great day.*

Sample Scripts for Messages	When leaving messages, you must say something meaningful in an even shorter text that will elicit a positive response in the form of a returned call. There are a couple of situations in which may need to leave messages (e.g., secretary or voice mail).
	
	LEAVING A MESSAGE (SECRETARY OR VOICE MAIL)
	
	"I'm <YOUR NAME> from <COMPANY NAME>. My phone number is <YOUR PHONE/CELL NUMBER>. I'm calling about <STATE PROJECT OR SERVICE TYPE FROM REFERENCEABLE CUSTOMER>."
	
	    Your response when the person calls back should be:
	
	    "Thanks for calling me back. The reason I called you is that we recently did a project with <REFERENCEABLE CUSTOMER>. The project's success may be of interest to you. . . . {PERSON RESPONDS} . . . Let's get together to discuss your project. How about <TIME AND DATE> at your office?"
	
	LEAVING A MESSAGE BASED ON A REFERRAL
	
	"I'm <YOUR NAME> from <COMPANY NAME>. My phone number is <YOUR PHONE/CELL NUMBER>. Please call me in reference to <STATE REFERRING PERSON'S NAME>."

Your response when the person calls back should be:

"Thanks for calling me back. The reason I called you is that I recently talked with <STATE REFERRING PERSON'S NAME>. He/She recommended that I call you about <STATE TOPIC>. . . . {PERSON RESPONDS} . . . Then we really should meet, because we've worked on similar projects very successfully for other firms. How about <TIME AND DATE> at your office?"

Sample Script for Call Backs	Sometimes when you get through to a person and things seem to be going well, something happens and the person you called asks you to call back so you can finish the conversation. This is a good sign, because the person still has interest and may want to pursue things further with a meeting. You have likely reached this point because you have done well with your pitch so far, and the person you called sees something worthwhile. You now have time to prepare for a "call back" conversation—one that should result in the scheduling of a meeting.

Make sure you get an idea about when to call back, whether it is the same day, next week, in 30 days, in 90 days, or whatever. This way you will know he/she is committed to talking with you again. And if you call a little early, that may be all the better, especially if you are to call back months from now. The person may just need some time to work out something but does not know exactly how much, so you can at least give that person some "space" to do that.

Here's a sample script for such a call. After identifying yourself and reconnecting to the previous conversation, say:

"You know, I was just thinking about you as I <GIVE ACTUAL CIRCUMSTANCE>. I'll be in your area on <DATE>, and I thought we could get together. . . ."

RESUMES, COVER LETTERS, AND BEYOND
By Pete Smudde, Ph.D., APR, & Carol Weber, APR

This appendix summarizes certain key matters about the written and oral discourse required during a job search. It is not meant to cover everything, but to provide you with guidance about foundational principles that govern effective resumes, cover letters, portfolios, and interviews.

Things to Keep in Mind for Your Resume and Cover Letter

- Use quality, cotton-content white or off-white paper for both documents. Buy stationery and envelopes to match. Lay out your content in an easy-to-read design.
- For an electronic version, make sure you use good design principles to visually organize content and verbally make your case about your strong background.
- Proofread! Eliminate misspellings and grammatical errors.
- Font—use standard serif fonts, such as Palatino or Times New Roman, in a readable font size (no smaller than 10 point and no larger than 12 point) throughout. Sans serif fonts, like Arial or Univers, could be used for headings only.
- Margins—have a good text/white-space balance on the page. Use 1/2-inch to 1-inch margins for top, bottom, right, and left.

Resume

Your resume is an information sheet of your credentials. Design it for easy reading and referencing whether in printed form or an electronic file. (See published and online sources for other resume-writing tips.)

- Include name, mailing address, e-mail address, and telephone/cell number(s).
- Career objective or goal—the kind of job you are seeking.

- Write clearly and simply to demonstrate that you are the best one for a job. Include information tailored to the job for which you are applying. Use action verbs to begin statements describing skills and responsibilities.
- Use bullet points to help organize information.
- Write out everything—don't use abbreviations.
- Be brief and to the point, placing the information most important to the employer first.
- Style—highlight important facts and headings by bolding, underlining, indenting, capitalizing, and/or using bullet points.
- Length—a one-page resume is often adequate unless you have extensive experience that is applicable and genuinely needs another page or two.
- Education—degrees earned, majors, minors, special training, GPA (if relevant and impressive), and other significant school experiences; list with dates of accomplishment.
- Experience—list current and former jobs, beginning with the most recent and working backward. Include job title, employer's name, scope of responsibilities, and specific results/accomplishments, showing the value you brought to your employer.
- Honors—special awards, recognitions, and scholarships.
- Activities—service clubs, professional societies, other organizations and interests; include offices held and other leadership provided with accomplishments highlighted.
- References—note "References available upon request" and provide on a separate sheet.

Cover Letter

Your cover letter is your first opportunity to introduce yourself. Your resume is included with your letter. Your main objective in your letter is to argue that you should be interviewed because, as your resume shows, you have strong credentials in all the things that matter.

- Follow one of the typical business letter formats, which can be found in online and printed sources.
- Format usually includes at least three brief paragraphs. The first states the letter's purpose and how you came to know about the position. It may also say why you are interested in the particular job and company. The second paragraph highlights your qualifications and draws the recruiter's attention to particularly impressive results or experience. The third paragraph asks for an interview, suggests times you'll be available, and thanks the person for consideration.
- Always send an original of the letter—do not send a photocopy. Hire a typist if necessary.
- Address the cover letter to a specific person. (Do not send it to "Dear Sir or Madam.") If not specified in an ad, contact the company receptionist or look on the company's website. Get the correct spelling of the person's name, title, and organization.

Portfolio

Prospective employers are frequently interested in looking at samples of a job applicant's work. These are typically collected and presented in a professional portfolio. Professional organizations such as the Public Relations Society of America and the International Association of Business Communicators also require a portfolio presentation as part of their respective accreditation processes. Thus, your professional interests will be well served by developing a portfolio of your actual public relations work and, to the extent possible, the results you've achieved through this work.

Contents: Place a copy of your resume at the beginning of the portfolio. Your professional portfolio should showcase your best work and would include work samples such as news releases, fact sheets, file bios, brief backgrounders, scripts, speeches, feature articles, special-event plans, collateral material, websites or CD-ROMs, and anything else that speaks to your competence and ability as a public relations professional. Work samples may have been executed in class, as part of an internship, or through paid or volunteer public relations work.

Each work sample should be preceded by a reader-friendly, one-page "Statement of Objectives and Results" in which you will:

- Title the work sample.
- Describe the problem or opportunity faced by the client/organization, and explain *why* your sample was needed to address the problem or opportunity.
- Identify the target public(s).
- State an objective for the sample, addressing in one sentence the effect sought, the measurable goal of that effect, the target audience, and the deadline for achieving results.
- Describe how you measured or would measure the success of the sample. If possible, provide documentation of actual results that directly support each objective (e.g., evaluation data, clippings, audience responses, attendance figures, awareness boost, sales increases, etc.).

Packaging: Your portfolio should appear neat and well organized. Work samples should be accessible to the reader. Since you will be continually updating your professional portfolio during your career, a three-ring binder and page protectors generally provide the greatest flexibility. Oversized work samples (e.g., posters) can be reduced to fit in a three-ring binder.

Note, too, that although hardcopy portfolios are preferred, more often they are allowed in electronic form on a memory stick or website—provided that the navigation of the content is easy and perfectly functional. The writing should be completely free of spelling, mechanical, grammatical, and AP style errors. All the elements of a printed portfolio are expected, but creativity and user-friendliness in presentation are also expected.

Interview

Interviews are fraught with uncertainty. There are two basic things you should do to ease your nerves, and you may have already done them.

1. Know the company very well—inside and out. The more you can connect the dots about what, who, why, and how a company is what it is and will be, the better you can demonstrate that knowledge during your interview through your questions and comments. Having such knowledge, then, shows the potential employer that you see the opportunity seriously—so seriously that you've learned a ton on your own because you feel it's that important not just for the interview but for your time as an employee.

2. Know your key message platform. Just as you must for any news interview, you must know what you want others to know and remember about you. Having a key message platform is essential—it is your starting point for all your answers to interviewers' questions and the "stuff" of your proof that you are the person to hire, not anyone else.

The greatest comfort you can have in the uncertainty of an interview is the certainty you have of what you know about a company and yourself. We believe these are the most potent areas for interview preparation. After you start your job, you must "make good" on everything you said during your interview by proving every day that you are the best investment that could have been made in a new employee.

Index